# WITNESS TO
# WORLD
# WAR II

# WITNESS TO WORLD WAR II

## Karen Farrington

**BLITZ EDITIONS**

Published by Blitz Editions
an imprint of Bookmart Ltd
Registered Number 2372865
Trading as Bookmart Ltd
Desford Road
Enderby
Leicester LE9 5AD


ISBN 1 85605 262 1

PICTURE CREDITS
The publisher would like to thank the following organisations for supplying
photographs for use in this book.
Every effort has been made to contact the copyright holders for the pictures.
In some cases they have been untraceable, for which we offer our apologies.

Imperial War Museum; Musee d'Histoire Contemporaine; US Marine Corp;
US Coast Guard; US Library of Congress; US National Archives; US Army
Photo Services; USAF Photo; US Navy Photo Section; Smithsonian Institute; J
Baker Collection; Ford Motor Co; Robert Hunt Library; Bundesarchiv;
Bibliothek fur Zeitgeschichte; Public Records Office of Hong Kong; Kyodo
News Services; Australian High Commission, London; BFI; British Airways;
The Scout Association; The Morning Star via The Marx Memorial Library,
London; Oxfam; Novosti; National Archives of Singapore; Daimler-Benz;
RCA; London Transport Museum; National Museum of Labour History; The
Truman Library; VSEL Vickers; Ufficio Storico Fototeca; National Maritime
Museum; Biggin Hill Archives; Stato Maggiore Aeronautica; RAF Museum;
The Boeing Co. Archives; Renault; Vickers; Los Alamos Scientific Lab; Polish
Underground Movement; Manx Museum; Red Cross Archives; Far East War
Collection/Vic Brown.

THE AUTHOR
Karen Farrington is a writer and former Fleet Street journalist who has
specialised in the study of conflict throughout the 20th Century.
In compiling Witness to World War II she has personally interviewed scores
of veterans from around the world, obtaining a unique insight into the war
through the eyes of the men on the front line. Among her previous books is
'Fated Destiny', an historical pot pourri of the curious, shocking and
mysterious which includes accounts of some of the greatest military
blunders in recent history. Karen Farrington is married with three children
and lives in Exmoor, Devon.

This book was produced by Amazon Publishing Limited
Designed by Wilson Design Associates

Printed in the Czech Republic
51769

# CONTENTS

# WITNESS TO WORLD WAR II

World War II was the most immense conflict mankind has ever known. WITNESS TO WORLD WAR II shows exactly how it took shape, from its beginnings in the confused politics of the 1920s and 1930s to its apocalyptic end in the ruined and shattered cities of Germany and Japan in 1945.

Not only was this the largest conflict ever seen; it was also the most militarily complex, with events at sea and in the air having a defining effect on warfare on land. In order to unravel these complexities, WITNESS TO WORLD WAR II treats war in the skies, on (and under) the oceans and on land separately so that all the details can be fully examined. But the approach is far from being coldly technical: hundreds of separate eyewitness accounts throughout the work illustrate clearly what the war meant to the individuals involved, while the horrors of war – from casual atrocities to the mass-produced death of the concentration camps – are unflinchingly examined.

WITNESS TO WORLD WAR II shows how and why the war was fought and what happened to the ordinary men and women caught up in it. For some it brought out reserves of courage and endurance that they never knew they possessed, but for others it became a terrifying inferno that led mankind to the depths of hell.

# The Soldier's War

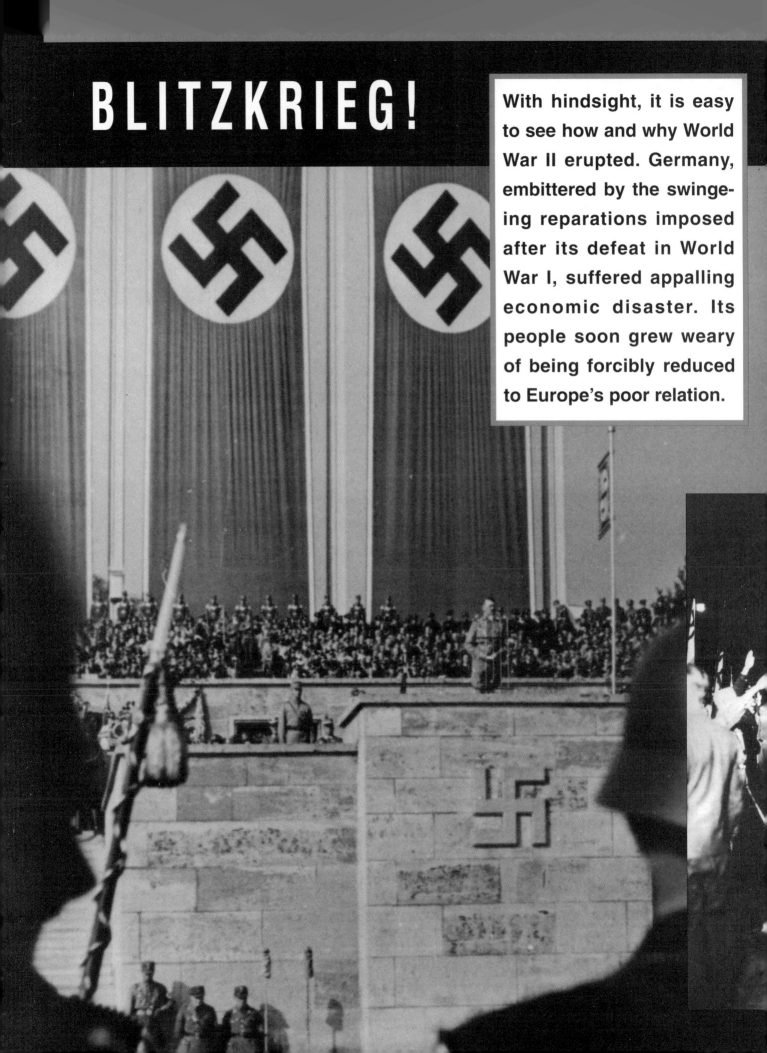

# BLITZKRIEG!

With hindsight, it is easy to see how and why World War II erupted. Germany, embittered by the swingeing reparations imposed after its defeat in World War I, suffered appalling economic disaster. Its people soon grew weary of being forcibly reduced to Europe's poor relation.

The time became ripe for a charismatic leader to sweep into power on the promise of returning Germany to its former glory. Unfortunately for the rest of Europe, those pledges for prosperity at home went hand in hand with an aggressive foreign policy. Nevertheless, Hitler offered the Germans an irresistible chance of stability, vitality and solidarity.

The only difficulty with which to wrestle is just how Britain and France missed the warning signs – and were catapulted into a war in September 1939 for which they were ill-prepared and poorly armed.

Both countries were weary of war, still reeling from the enormous loss of manpower and struggling following a deep world recession to remain on an even keel. At home they were far too preoccupied with domestic problems to heed the warnings of the few who witnessed what was really happening in Hitler's Germany. Violent anti-semitism was put down to the work of a few extremists. Many in power had a sneaking admiration for Hitler who achieved so much by cutting unemployment and building prestigious new 'autobahns'. His admirers conveniently overlooked the fact that Germany had concentration camps, no free press and no free parliament. And few outside the Reich had any idea of the military strength and firepower that the Führer was amassing.

When Hitler marched into the demilitarised Rhineland in 1936, many considered he was only taking back what rightfully belonged to Germany. The annexation of Austria in 1938 was looked upon virtually as an internal matter. Only with Hitler's demands for land from Czechoslovakia later that same year did Britain and France begin to sense the threat.

## Hitler relished the chance to 'free' fellow Germans from 'Polish barbarism'

Their chosen path was appeasement, a negotiated agreement with Hitler designed to end his expansionism. When Hitler marched into Prague in the face of that agreement, Britain and France finally realised the folly of their actions.

All thoughts turned to Danzig, the free city in a Polish-held corridor which split Germany from East Prussia. It had long been a thorn in Hitler's side as he believed it was part of Germany. Hitler relished the chance to 'free' fellow Germans who he claimed were being subjected to Polish barbarism. There was considerably more trepidation in the minds of the Allies.

### ■ CARDBOARD TANKS ■

Much of Germany's rearmament had gone on covertly. Even when war broke out many British people were convinced that their former enemy, hampered by the treaty which ended the previous conflict, had tanks made of cardboard. Indeed, the Germans

*Left:* A Nazi book-burning ceremony. Only works regarded as acceptable to the fascist dictatorship were tolerated.
*Far left:* Hitler addresses a Nazi party rally at Nuremberg in 1938.

did carry out military manoeuvres with cardboard tanks back in the early 1920s before secretly importing and building their own real ones.

Meanwhile, France had the largest army and most impressive air force in the world. Most of its citizens prided themselves on the fact that Germany was unlikely to begin hostilities against such a superior force. As England viewed the Channel as an

## Hitler unleashed a new and frightening brand of warfare called 'Blitzkrieg'

impregnable wall of defence, so France had the much-vaunted Maginot line. It took nine years to construct the frontier defences, brainchild of French minister André Maginot. The network of towers and

## BRITAIN'S FASCIST LEADER

**Oswald Mosley became the creator of the British Union of Fascists in the early 1930s after having been a member of both Conservative and Labour parties and having been linked for a while with the Liberals.**

He had a lively, sharp mind and a clarity of vision. He was even branded the best political thinker of the age. But his frustration at the confines of the accepted political doctrines cast him to the margins where he hit upon the fascism sweeping Europe.

The British, however, were not entranced with uniforms and salutes in the same way as the Germans, Italians or Spanish, among whom fascism flourished. He became a figure of fun, never taken seriously even after the outbreak of war. He was nevertheless jailed in 1940 for four years. Following his release, he was vilified in Britain and finally moved with his wife Diana Mitford and two small sons to France. He continued to exercise his mind around political problems but failed to find a platform for his views. He died in 1980.

tunnels was remarkable enough in itself. Had the Germans attacked it directly, it might have served its purpose well, albeit that it stretched only as far as the Belgian border, and not beyond it.

This war, however, was going to be different to the first international conflict. Static trench warfare, which had claimed so many lives, was now an outdated concept – yet France and

Britain didn't realise it. When Hitler invaded Poland in September 1939, he unleashed a new and frightening brand of warfare into the world – called 'Blitzkrieg'.

First to feel the heat of this 'lightning war', Poland lurched back in helpless horror when the German army crossed it borders at dawn on 1 September 1939. It took only a few hours for the invading force to quell

*Left:* German soldiers survey the results of their fast-moving campaign in Poland.
*Top:* Britain was braced for attack months before it actually came.

*Above:* Germany used its tanks to thrust ahead during the Blitzkrieg it unleashed with great success against Poland, France and the Low Countries.

Polish defences. As the German troops and tanks rolled through the Polish countryside, the country's major cities were being bombed by the Luftwaffe and its ports were shelled by German ships.

Key to the success of Blitzkrieg was the use of tanks in large numbers and innovative style – they were still thought by Britain and France to be valid only as infantry support. The Panzer forces charged ahead independent of the troops, and wreaked havoc among defenders. Bursting through defensive lines, they harried the Poles from the rear, creating confusion and smashing supply lines.

The German air force had learned much aiding Franco during the Spanish Civil War, which ended in May 1939. Now pilots were putting this knowledge to good use and after a month Poland capitulated.

*Above:* **A French cottage is destroyed by advancing German troops, who put French and British defenders to flight.**

Poland's capital Warsaw held out for a few weeks longer than the rest of the country against the Third Reich. Heavy bombardment turned this once-grand city to rubble. As it surrendered, the Germans were triumphant. The hated Treaty of Versailles, which had condemned them to international servitude since 1919, was at last eradicated.

This time Britain and France refused to sit back and watch their ally being dismembered by Hitler. Both declared war on Germany almost immediately – although failed to do anything which would materially assist Poland – and braced themselves for the onslaught. Thankfully, it never came.

Despite the success of the Polish campaign, many German officers were concerned about taking on the might of the French army backed by Britain. Hitler was persuaded to abandon thoughts of an immediate push through the Low Countries into France, in favour of launching a spring campaign.

## ■ REALITY OF WAR ■

The reality of war was slow to strike home in Britain. When the feared air raids and gas attacks failed to materialise, there was an almost euphoric mood as people busied themselves sandbagging homes and putting up blackout screens in windows. The casualties in road traffic accidents caused by the rigorously enforced blackout far exceeded those caused in the war. Phrases full of mock indignation like 'put that light out' and 'don't you know there's a war on' typified the bureaucracy pervading

the country. Joblessness stayed high, war production lamentably low. Reservists were being signed up for army duty surely but slowly, doing drills with bayonets and gas masks – and sometimes wooden 'rifles'.

Nearly 200,000 soldiers in the British Expeditionary Force were sent to France where they dug in on the Belgian border. By now, Germany had mobilised six million men.

Hitler was concerned at the ease with which the British navy had managed to raid a German ship in Norwegian waters. On 9 April 1940 his troops moved into Denmark and Norway in what promised to be another short, sharp campaign.

Denmark was without an army and acquiesced the following day.

Norway, deeply anti-militarist by tradition, nevertheless put up a fight despite the evident popularity with which the Germans were greeted in some quarters. Churchill himself was looking at the possibility of occupying Norway to reap the rewards of its strategic position. The government would do no more than lay mines in Norwegian waters to disrupt a vital German supply line. In fact, the Royal Navy was doing just that when some of the invasion force from Germany sailed up. There was a skirmish in which some damage was inflicted on German ships. That was the only glimmer of optimism in what turned into an otherwise disastrous escapade.

> ## *Churchill himself was looking at the possibility of occupying Norway*

Britain sent landing parties to key points, hoping to steal a march on the Germans. But the small-scale campaign was ill-planned and improvised. The poorly equipped troops had no artillery and no air cover, whereas the Luftwaffe was in control of many Norwegian airstrips and was making full use of them. It wasn't long before the British, and the French forces with them, were forced to withdraw in disarray.

The debacle outraged many people and MPs in Britain, who feared the country was only making a half-hearted attempt at war. On 7 May there was a debate in the House of Commons in which Prime Minister Chamberlain made a statement on

## ◆ BLITZKRIEG IN THE WEST

From 14 May 1940, German Panzer forces bridged the River Meuse and poured into Belgium and northern France, driving all before them. The XIX Panzer Corps under Guderian crossed at Sedan, the XLI Panzer Corps (Reinhardt) at Monthermé, the XV Panzer Corps (Hoth) at Dinant, while Höpner's XVI Panzer Corps swept down from the north east. Within days, German tanks were at the Channel, but then paused. The British attempted a counter-attack at Arras, while the French planned a similar move from the south. These efforts came to little, however, and by the end of May, with German forces once again on the move, the British Expeditionary Force had its back to the sea at Dunkirk, awaiting rescue.

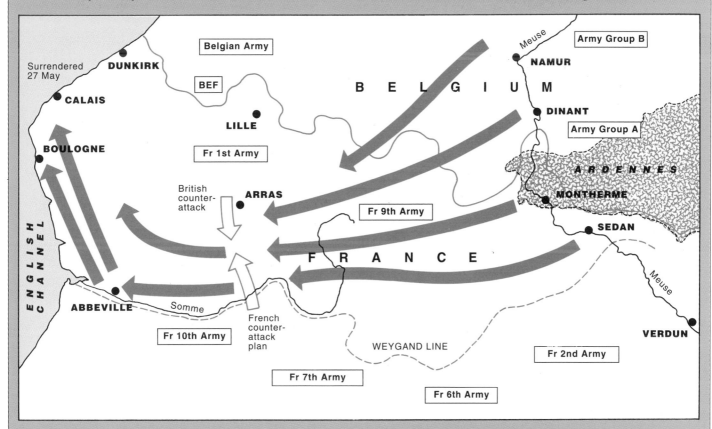

the Norwegian affair. The government won a vote of confidence by only 81 votes, too few for Chamberlain to continue.

## *The spring campaign got underway with a vengeance in western Europe*

He resigned on 10 May, the same day that German troops made their first forays into Holland and Belgium. The spring campaign got underway with a vengeance as the horrors of Hitler's Blitzkrieg came to western Europe.

Airborne troops took the Belgian fortress of Eben Emael, chasing out the petrified defenders. At the same time in Rotterdam, 12 floatplanes landed on the River Maas. Out of each of them came an inflatable dinghy and a clutch of German troops ready to swarm over essential vantage points throughout the city.

### ■ HOLLAND FALLS ■

Also, there came the more orthodox methods of invasion, by Panzer forces over the borders. The French army and the British Expeditionary Force prepared themselves for a surge of German troops coming through northern Belgium. To their huge surprise, however, Panzer divisions had crossed the Ardennes, condemned as impassable by Allied commanders. Amid confusion, a division led by Rommel began a headlong rush west.

Holland capitulated on 14 May. It was another hammer-blow to the morale of the French. Without a dynamic leader – their commander in chief Gamelin was inaudible, indecisive and thought to be suffering

## ◆ EYE WITNESS ◆

**Alf Turner joined a Territorial Army battalion in his home town of Barnstaple, North Devon, when he was 19.**

" In September 1940 we were stationed at Battle. Following Dunkirk it wasn't a case of "if the Germans invade", it was "when the Germans invade". So we had to put a minefield along the beach at Battle.

Not many people knew much about laying minefields. I was with a captain on the beach. We laid about four minefields and were starting on the fifth one. Our driver asked if he could help. The captain allowed him to lay a couple. The driver must have trodden on one and the explosion set lots of the mines off.

The captain and I were lucky to escape. A few days later our brigadier told us it was a vital area and asked us to go back to re-lay the minefield. I told the captain the chances of us coming out alive were only five per cent. Still, we had a job to do.

We re-laid about four and I was leading the way when the captain said he should go first. Soon after he took over he pointed to his right. In the middle of a crater lay the head of the dead driver. The shock must have unbalanced him.

Then the ground seemed to open up and I felt I was going into a great big pit. Yet actually I was being blown upwards. Our new driver was waiting on a shelf some 40 feet above the beach. He saw me go into the air above him and go back down again.

I was cross-eyed, had a perforated ear-drum and an injured arm. Still, I managed to get out of there. I was put under sedation for 24 hours, during which time I jumped out of bed three times. They even asked me to go down to the minefield again. I went – but this time they decided it was too dangerous to tackle again.

I was given a week's leave. The medical officer said if I had had any more, I wouldn't have come back. Going home in the blackout was hard. I had to race across pools of darkness, imagining all the time that parts of a body were coming out at me.

A fellow lance corporal blamed himself for the captain's death. He was a religious man and prayed very hard for me, knowing it was a dangerous job. But he didn't pray for the captain and he felt guilty about that. "

*Above:* Crammed onto the decks of a small steamer, weary troops of the BEF reach a British port.

*Below:* Bewildered soldiers and frightened civilians roam the streets of Dunkirk as the Germans close in.

acutely from the ravages of venereal disease – the French army fell away, their lack of commitment a world away from the fighting spirit they showed so often during World War I.

The British forces found themselves racing back to the French coast, barely keeping a step ahead of the German advance. Despite an attempt to counter-attack at Arras in northern France, it soon became clear the situation was hopeless. Their commander, General Lord Gort, ordered his men to Dunkirk where they would await evacuation.

### ▪ DUNKIRK ▪

Luck was on their side. Hitler ordered his most advanced Panzer divisions to halt, wishing to conserve the cream of his troops for the invasion of Paris. It gave the British valuable time to install a defensive shell around Dunkirk –

albeit fragile – behind which they could stage a daring, dangerous and vital evacuation.

Courageous rearguard campaigners held off the German advance while the Royal Navy sent in ship after ship to remove the stricken forces. By 31 May the news blackout on 'Operation Dynamo', the code name for the operation to save British servicemen, was lifted and scores of small boats set sail for France to give aid to the Royal Navy. Experienced mariners set off alongside weekend sailors to pluck as many men as they could from the beach. It was a tough voyage on small craft but each skipper was imbued with a grim determination.

Before the remaining defenders of Dunkirk surrendered on 4 June, 338,226 men – British, French and Belgian – had been carried back to safety. It was no mean feat, given that the official estimates for the evacuation were 45,000. Disastrously, most of Britain's armoury was left behind. There were too few guns remaining in Britain to arm the country's soldiers.

### ▪ PARIS OCCUPIED ▪

French soldiers, supported in the west by some British fighters, continued a disorderly retreat. Two weeks after Dunkirk, Paris was occupied and region after region continued to fall. When French prime minister Reynaud resigned on 16 June, his successor Marshal Pétain immediately sued for peace.

The final humiliation for France came on 21 June when Hitler had its leaders sign an armistice in the same railway coach where the German surrender was authorised following World War I. Now Britain stood alone against the might of the Third Reich with only 21 miles of English Channel to save it from invasion.

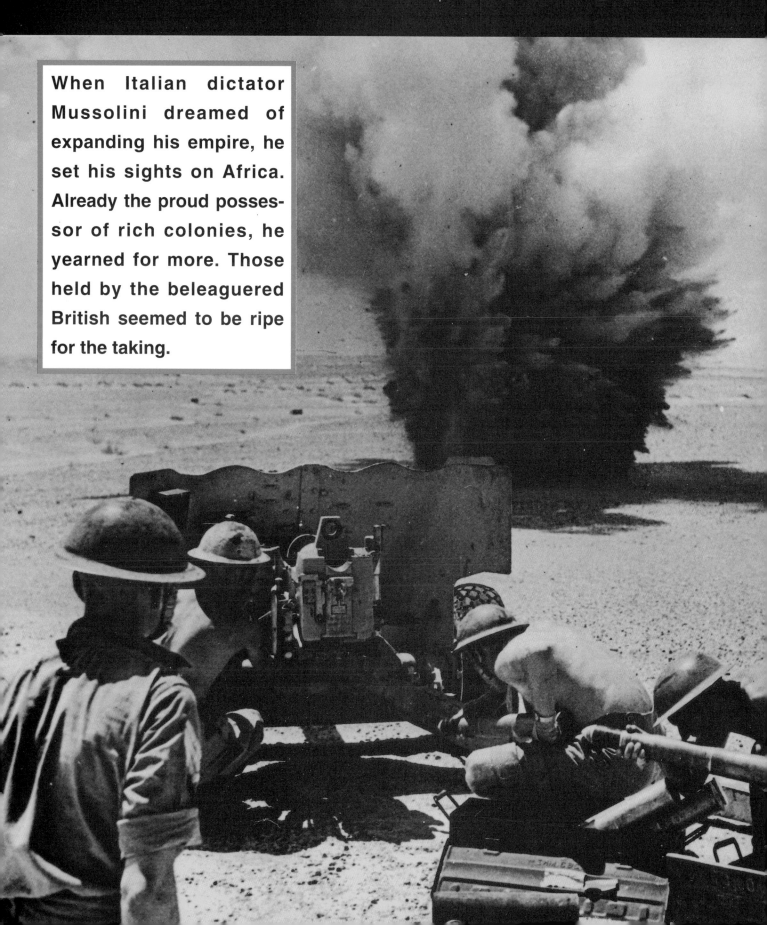

# THE WAR IN AFRICA

When Italian dictator Mussolini dreamed of expanding his empire, he set his sights on Africa. Already the proud possessor of rich colonies, he yearned for more. Those held by the beleaguered British seemed to be ripe for the taking.

who prided himself on getting results. The British found him a surprising and bold adversary after the easy pickings of the Italians. But with the aid of troops from the Dominions, the British were determined to keep their vital foothold in Africa.

### ■ SEE-SAW WAR ■

It was the start of an indecisive see-saw war which lasted for three years and cost thousands of lives. Celebrated triumphs quickly turned to desert dust, as both sides discovered to their cost. British, Australian, New Zealand and South African soldiers got used to digging slit trenches in gritty, rock-hard ground,

*Below:* Thousands of Italian prisoners of war were taken as the British and Commonwealth troops made their initial push across the North African sands.

Germany, which had been stripped of its African possessions at the end of the World War I, had no business on the continent. In any case, Hitler was preoccupied with conquering Russia. If the Axis powers had got their way, Italy would have swept through Africa and the oil-rich Middle East and Persian Gulf, kicked out the British and set up a vast empire while Germany concentrated on changing the face of Europe.

It was not to be. The Italians soon suffered a humiliating defeat at the hands of the British defenders of Egypt and were on the verge of being run into the sea when Hitler intervened. The Führer wanted Allied troops tied up in Africa, while he made progress with his plans elsewhere in the world. And he was mindful that whoever held North Africa had the key to the oil riches of the Middle East, a tempting trump card. He chose to take part in the North African conflict as a potentially profitable diversion.

So, in early 1941, the irrepressible General Erwin Rommel, who had been so successful in western Europe, was dispatched to save the Italians from annihilation, with the aim of securing a new front for the Third Reich. Rommel was a talented leader

much as their predecessors had in World War I. Despite the best efforts of 'Desert Fox' Rommel and his men, it still ended with Mussolini's reputation as a war leader in tatters and dealt a death-blow to his regime.

Italy didn't declare war on Britain and France until June 1940 when Hitler's troops were at the gates of Paris and plans to invade Britain were already a reality.

The Italian strongholds in North Africa were Ethiopia – where Emperor Haile Selassie had been unseated four years previously – and Libya. In August Mussolini sent troops into British Somaliland in East Africa. With vastly superior numbers of troops, the colony fell to him within a fortnight.

Bucked by their success, Italian troops stationed in Libya began to menace Egypt, in British hands.

Without paying heed to superstition, Italian forces crossed the border between the two countries on Friday 13 September and began a five-day advance which ended with them digging into their positions still some considerable distance from their goal.

## ■ OPERATION COMPASS ■

Egyptian ports became collection points for Commonwealth troops. British soldiers were joined by Australians, New Zealanders, Indians and South Africans for a mighty push against the Italians, code-named 'Operation Compass'.

On Monday 9 December British commander in chief General Sir Archibald Wavell signalled the start of the offensive. Before the week was out, 2,000 Italian prisoners were taken at Sidi Barrani. The Australian 6th Division took a further 30,000 prisoners when it overran Bardia on 5 January 1941.

The pattern was set. Sticking to the coast road, the Australians bagged another 27,000 prisoners on taking the strategically important port of Tobruk. Meanwhile, British troops dipped inland to by-pass a large mountain range.

By now the Allies were moving at a pelt across the Libyan region of Cyrenaica, capturing Derna, Beda

# MONTY – DESERT MAGICIAN

**Pride of Britain's armed forces, Bernard Law Montgomery, was born in London in 1887, although his ancestors were from Ulster. When he was two his father Henry was appointed Bishop of Tasmania. The island became his home until he reached his teenage years.**

In later life, he often told how his childhood was an unhappy one. His mother Maud was strict and administered terrible beatings. He resented her greatly throughout his adult life.

After distinguishing himself as a soldier in World War I, it appeared he was married to the army. But to the surprise of all, in 1927 this difficult and irritable character married an artist and mother of two who had been widowed at Gallipoli. Warm and affectionate, they were a happy couple and had a son, David, in 1928.

In 1937, Betty died suddenly in a freak tragedy after being stung on the foot. Monty was desolate and threw himself once more into his profession. In the earliest days of World War II he led a division of the British Expeditionary Force in France.

Following the evacuation at Dunkirk, he was based in Britain until August 1942 when Prime Minister Winston Churchill made him head of the British 8th Army in North Africa. British troops, despite early successes, had been on the run from Rommel's Afrika Korps. It was Monty's job to turn the tide of the conflict – and it was one which he relished.

Just months after taking command of the Desert Rats, he scored a significant victory at the second Battle of El Alamein before chasing the German troops across North Africa into Tunisia where they finally surrendered in May 1943.

His next port of call was Sicily and he successfully led his forces up the foot of fascist Italy before being recalled to London. Before him was the most crucial command of his service life. Promoted to the rank of field-marshal, he was to help lead the Allied invasion of France. In charge of the key offensive was General Dwight D. Eisenhower with whom Monty clashed on many occasions. Later, Monty was criticised for his thoroughness. Accused of being too cautious, he frustrated his colleagues by refusing to commit his men to action until he was satisfied every small detail of the battle plan had been scrutinised and double-checked. However, his policy, which made for steady but slow progress, won the hearts and minds of his men.

Britain's hero soldier led the British and Canadian 21st Army Group across France, Belgium, The Netherlands and northern Germany to eventual victory. After the war he held a series of high-ranking posts, including deputy commander of the North Atlantic Treaty Organisation. He was made a knight of the garter, and was created a viscount in 1946. He died in 1976, aged 88.

Fomm and finally, on 6 February 1941, Benghazi.

It was by any standards a whirlwind campaign. Allied troops travelled across 440 miles in just 60 days and dwarfed the Italian offensive which prompted the action. They were travelling across inhospitable terrain and even attacked Benghazi in a sandstorm. The retreating Italians who threw up token resistance were then caught in a masterful pincer movement by the British and Australian forces.

With Allied action against the Italians in Ethiopia making excellent progress too, Churchill must have revelled in the rout of the Duce. The British prime minister's satisfaction, however, was to be short-lived.

## Churchill must have revelled in the rout of the Duce

Six days after the fall of Benghazi, Rommel arrived in Africa with his keen troops from the 5th Light Division and the 15th Panzer Division. He was welcomed by many resident Arabs who had long resented the British presence in North Africa. Within two weeks Rommel attacked El Agheila, the southernmost tip of the Allied gains.

Despite his lack of experience in desert warfare and a recurring mystery stomach complaint, Rommel was soon making big gains, sending a depleted and weary Western Desert Force back from whence it came. He excelled in warfare on the hoof and preferred a fluid campaign in which

*Above right:* Australians march ashore at Suez in May 1940.

*Right:* The capture of Benghazi was an important first victory.

◆ **EYE WITNESS** ◆

**Bill Jenkins, a sergeant in the Australian infantry throughout the war, explains why so many Australians were keen to fight the Allied corner.**

" At the time we had a population of seven million. We recruited in the first six months of the war over 200,000 volunteers. During the whole of the war, 750,000 people were involved. So percentage-wise I think we did reasonably well for the mother country. The old Australians were very much involved in Empire and considered a trip to England as "going home" even if they were not even born there. World War I was still in our memory, too. We were going off to finish the job that the soldiers then had started. There was the adventurous spirit, the deep feelings of patriotism that ran through many of us. And most Australians love a fight! "

*Left:* Tobruk was a vital port which Rommel fought hard to win. But the besieged Australian forces held fast despite terrible hardships.

he was ever ready to improvise. Unpredictable, incisive and single-minded, Rommel, rarely seen without his goggles, was an inspiration to the men of his Afrika Korps. Contrary to common belief, they were not specially trained for the tropics but underwent only a standard medical. Like their leader, they were professional soldiers who earned the respect of their enemy during the North African campaigns.

### ■ TOBRUK BESIEGED ■

Churchill had risked British, Australian and New Zealand troops from North Africa for the tandem campaign in Greece. It meant Wavell had been unable to crown his glorious advance by taking Tripoli. Now the Allies were paying for this.

By 3 April 1941, Benghazi had fallen once again. Soon Tobruk was under siege. The town was manned by a stoic Australian division integrated with straggling British and Indian troops that had become split from their units in the overwhelming German advance.

Australian commander Major-General Leslie Morshead organised sturdy defences around the town, installing every bit of artillery he could lay his hands on in the fortifications once held by the Italians. The bombardment from Tobruk took its toll on the attacking German and Italian forces. Rommel was by now far from his Tripoli supply base with its crucial stocks of water, food, fuel and ammunition. He needed the port

### ◆ EYE WITNESS ◆

**Arthur Stephenson, of the Royal Artillery, was 21 when he joined up in 1939. He served in Africa and Normandy.**

❝ I've got a lighter at home with a Canadian badge on it. In the desert I was trying to light my pipe. This Canadian came up and went to light it for me.

He was there one minute and gone the next. A shell-burst killed him outright. All that was left was his lighter. He was only three yards away from me and I was completely unscathed. ❞

as an alternative. The Australians, deeply entrenched, held fast. If Rommel made mistakes, it was here when his hand was forced by the gutsy Australians. His efforts to capture Tobruk cost him dearly.

Britain was able to receive new supplies from a Mediterranean convoy which delivered to Alexandria in Egypt. Tobruk was given support from the Royal Navy and the efficient Desert Air Force. Wavell launched a counter-offensive known as 'Operation Battleaxe' to relieve Tobruk overland. His golden touch deserted him, however, and thanks to the wit of his opponent it failed.

*Rommel, who earned his 'Desert Fox' nickname through his cunning, now lured the British forward*

Rommel, who earned his 'Desert Fox' nickname through his cunning, now lured the British forward by feigning retreat. When the armoured units came within range, the superior German anti-tank guns opened fire causing devastation.

It was a costly lesson to the British and one which lost Wavell his job. In his place came General Sir Claude Auchinleck, who arrived to find a stalemate as both sides sought to rearm. He orchestrated 'Operation Crusader' in November, once again with the aim of relieving Tobruk. During the eight months they spent holed up in the port, the Australians had not been idle. They delivered some severe blows to Rommel from their fortress, targeting tanks in particular. Now Auchinleck found a corridor for Allied forces to link up by December. Once again, however, victory hung in the balance.

Both sides benefited from aerial support. The Luftwaffe had easy access to North Africa from its bases in southern Italy while the RAF Desert Air Force proved crucial to the success of Allied troops on the ground. Rommel had recharged his men and was looking for revenge. He beat Auchinleck to a counter-attack which he made as early as January 1942 and forced the Allies back once more. There followed a fierce exchange in May at Gazala in which the bold Rommel led a charge through enemy minefields and lines. Auchinleck was squeezed out of Libya, back into Egypt. The retreat was compounded when Tobruk was surrendered in June by the South African garrison then holding it, after

only a week under seige, and 25,000 prisoners were taken. Now Rommel was promoted to the rank of field-marshal by a delighted Hitler. Without pausing to celebrate, he pressed ahead with his campaign.

---

**From decoded inter-cepted messages from Rommel, Churchill believed the German commander was in dire need of assistance**

---

Churchill was devastated by the Allied armies' swift reversal of fortunes. From decoded intercepted messages from Rommel to Berlin, he believed the enigmatic German commander was in dire need of assistance and on the verge of capitulation. Churchill failed to understand that

this sob story was a device used by Rommel to win more supplies and men – which were rarely forthcoming.

Rommel's men were, however, weary. Auchinleck's air and artillery bombardment as they advanced towards El Alamein had the desired effect and stopped them in their tracks. A brigade from the 9th Australian Division broke out of El Alamein and swept forward. But the efforts of the Australians and the 8th Army failed to do much more than dent the Afrika Korps.

Now it was Auchinleck's turn to feel the wrath of the British prime minister. While defending El Alamein in Egypt, he was replaced by General Bernard Montgomery.

Although painstakingly calculating and methodical, Montgomery had

*Below:* **Sir Claude Auchinleck served in Norway and India before succeeding Wavell in North Africa. But his failure to hold Rommel cost him his job.**

the same fire for victory inside him that drove his rival Rommel. With an injection of powerful Sherman tanks from America, Monty regrouped his British, Australian and New Zealand forces after fending off an unsuccessful stab at the defensive lines by the overstretched Germans in September and prepared his battle plan.

Monty preferred a confrontation rather than the more fashionable lightning manoeuvres perfected by the Germans. It was his aim to destroy as much of the enemy army and artillery as possible. In his words, it would be a 'dog-fight' and by his standards it was an almost reckless campaign in its intensity.

## *Arguably still medically unfit for command, Rommel found himself overwhelmed*

The second Battle of El Alamein began on 23 October, the day Rommel returned to his post after a spell of sick leave in Germany to relieve his replacement who had suffered a heart attack. Arguably still medically unfit for command, Rommel found himself overwhelmed by the reinforced Allied army which for the first time now substantially outnumbered his own. He soon discovered that, even if he had wanted to, he was unable to adhere to Hitler's orders not to retreat.

Allied firepower rained down on the Afrika Korps. In fact, there was some disarray in Allied lines and the thrust forward was belated. But finally a bold brigade of Australians drove north, at immense cost in terms of personnel.

Montgomery regrouped and came forward again in 'Operation Super-

## ◆ EYE WITNESS ◆

**Stanislaw Lachoda was an 18-year-old signalman in the 2nd Battalion of the Polish Carpathian Brigade, a volunteer group made up of Poles who had escaped Nazi and Soviet occupation. In August 1941 the brigade was taken from Alexandria to Tobruk by the Royal Navy to replace Australian troops at Tobruk.**

'Soon after 'Operation Crusader' got underway, I was seconded with two other signalmen for an operation to mislead and disorientate the enemy in the western sector.

Well armed with Brens, Tommy guns and a plethora of hand grenades, attacking squads wearing desert boots and overalls silently crept behind the Italian positions and, on a given signal, let everything go at the enemy.

It was only when the mission was accomplished that the Italians recovered from the shock of being fired on from the rear and it was then their turn to lay a heavy barrage of machine-gun and artillery fire on us retreating along the narrow wadi towards the safety of our own positions. Despite the failure of communication due to the destruction of our radio's antenna, our own artillery laid protective fire for us at the right time when we were clear of the enemy's positions.

In situations as fluid as desert mirages, those who dared and took risks were the gainers and the timid ones got what they deserved.

By 8 December neither side scored a resounding victory despite heavy human and material losses but there appeared signs that the battle-weary Afrika Korps was contemplating disengagement. Our own patrols confirmed that the western sector based on the hill Ras El Medauar was still held by Italians. It was our next target.

The attack on the southern slope of the hill was spearheaded by 2nd company to which I was attached as one of the signal patrol. Our job was to provide telephone links with the battalion HQ. We moved silently step by step through the treacherous minefields, along a cleared narrow lane marked by white tape.

There was chaotic fire from Italian Breda guns as well as flares as we edged along. The last obstacle, a thick concertina of barbed wire, was dealt with and a final jump into noisy heaps of empty tin cans covering the slope led us into an elaborate system of concrete pill-boxes and bunkers. Most of the Italians surrendered after token resistance, the stubborn ones were dragged out from murky and smelly hideouts. Before sunrise the white and red Polish flag was hoisted up. The capture of Ras El Medauar was celebrated with fireworks, using up a huge stock of captured flares.'

charge', with New Zealand and British infantry going into the jaws of battle under cover of artillery fire. Rommel, who had been ordered not to retreat, replied in kind. But while the British had healthy supplies of arms and men, Rommel was far from his base. The creeping successes of Allied troops forced his hand.

## ■ ROMMEL ON THE RUN ■

Rommel's army fled back along the coast road, the scene of so many retreating marches, with Monty's 8th Army and the 2nd New Zealand Division led by the courageous and skilled General Freyberg at its heels. The Desert Air Force inflicted terrible damage. Monty refrained from attempting to outflank his enemy,

guessing that British troops would not carry out this by-now familiar German tactic so ably. He favoured a set-piece move against Rommel and his confidence in old-fashioned text-book battlecraft paid dividends. There was another factor for him to consider, too. In November combined Anglo-American forces began landing in North Africa in the territory of Vichy France. These were the 'Torch' landings, the first slice of action seen by many American soldiers and British reserves.

While Vichy rulers were implaca-bly opposed to Britain, their attitude towards the Americans was ambiva-lent. The local Vichy commander was persuaded to switch sides from Germany to the Allies in November 1942 after some skirmishes in which the Allies easily managed to gain the upper hand. This left the path clear for the fresh forces to take on the cornered German Afrika Korps.

Hitler in turn provided reinforce-ments at last, bolstering the defences of Vichy-held Tunisia where Rommel headed from Libya. He was not ready to seize an opportunity for a counter-attack. His troops were short on supplies and still in the minority. Despite the excellent defensive position offered by the mountainous borders of Tunisia, he realised the situation was hopeless.

## ■ AXIS SURRENDER ■

Rommel was recalled in March 1943. His men continued the fight until May when Tunis fell. The surrender of the Axis forces in North Africa came on 13 May, with the capture of 275,000 soldiers. It was a relief to the Allied army, which had by now known the very worst of desert warfare. Montgomery was hailed a national hero, and Rommel, although the loser, was in turn hailed a military master.

*Left:* A pensive Monty displays his famed taste for unconventional battledress.

*Below:* American troops stride ashore unopposed during the 'Torch' landings, November 1942. They soon met fierce German defenders.

# BARBAROSSA – TARGET RUSSIA

Hitler has become infamous in history for his hatred of Jews. Yet he also singled out the Russians as a worthless, reviled race: he called them 'sub-humans'. It became his avowed aim to see the people in chains and Communism eradicated once and for all.

**B**efore the war between Hitler's Germany and Stalin's USSR began, the German Führer laid down the ground rules to his generals. In essence, there were none:

'The war against Russia will be such that it cannot be conducted in a knightly fashion. The struggle is one of ideologies and racial differences and will have to be conducted with unprecedented, unmerciful and unrelenting harshness. The commissars are the bearers of ideologies directly opposed to National Socialism. Therefore the commissars will be liquidated. German soldiers guilty of breaking international law . . . will be excused. Russia has not partici-

pated in the Hague Convention and therefore has no rights under it.'

These words set the tone for a brutal and bloody conflict, far exceeding the ruthlessness shown so far by invading Nazi forces in western Europe.

Hitler's first problem, however, was how to bring the Russian Bear to battle at all. For months during 1939 the USSR's tyrant leader Stalin had been courted by Britain and France, both anxious to get Soviet support for the forthcoming hostilities with Germany. Hitler's disparaging views of Russia were well known, not least among the

*Above right:* 'Barbarossa' unleashed the fury of Germany's erstwhile ally. *Below:* Hitler and Soviet foreign minister Molotov (left) reach an uneasy peace, 1939.

*Left:* Joseph Stalin. Hitler feared and detested Communism and all other left-wing ideologies. Stalin's regime in the USSR embodied all that Nazism opposed.

Soviet people themselves. In the circumstances, it seemed Stalin was a natural ally of Britain and France.

### ■ FRAGILE PACT ■

Suddenly, however, the carefully wrought diplomacy collapsed like a house of cards. Out of the blue came the Berlin-Moscow Non-Aggression Pact, signed at the Kremlin by Ribbentrop, for Hitler, and Molotov, for Stalin, in August 1939. Hitler found himself the closest ally of his hated adversary. Stalin guessed it would at least buy him time before his country became involved in a war it neither wanted nor could afford.

*'The war against Russia... cannot be conducted in a knightly fashion'*

And the reason behind the gleam in Stalin's eyes at the signing of the pact was revealed just a month later. Two weeks after German forces marched into Poland, Russian forces invaded from the east. The two countries proceeded to partition the helpless Poland as they pleased. If Stalin was concerned that he was dancing with the Devil, he comforted himself that Britain and France

using superior tactics and winning some impressive victories. It wasn't until March 1940 that the war was finally over with the surrender of little Finland, time enough for the Finns to have inflicted humiliation on their giant neighbour, which lost an estimated one million fighting men. Hitler noted the failings and flailings of the Red Army with more than a passing interest.

commanders during a devastating purge of the army which began in 1937. It happened after whispers of a military uprising against him. Whether the threat was imagined or real, no one can say. What is certain is that Stalin wreaked a terrible

*Below:* **General Heinz Guderian, architect of Blitzkreig in the west, keeping up morale in Russia in 1941.**

would tie up sufficient numbers of German troops on the Western front to make the opening of a second front an act of idiocy by Hitler.

In November, encouraged by his easy success, Stalin engineered a war with Finland. When the Finns flatly refused to hand over disputed territory, the Red Army marched in, anticipating another quick victory.

Six weeks later their hopes had been dashed. The vastly outnumbered Finns put up a fierce fight,

Stalin was livid with the poor performance of his army. But there

---

### Stalin wreaked a terrible revenge to defend his lordly position

---

was no one to blame but himself for the debacle – as he had ordered the deaths of many of his leading

revenge to defend his lordly position.

By the end of 1938 three out of every five of the Red Army's marshals were dead as well as 13 out of 15 army commanders. More than a quarter of the army's brigadiers and more than half of the divisional commanders had been executed, too. There was also bloodletting among the politicos involved with defence. Those that remained were untalented and uninspiring. They hampered the progress of the fighting force with

outdated ideas, which included the abandonment of automatic weapons and the halting of the comprehensive tank programme in favour of horse-drawn artillery. So the army was left woefully lacking in experience, for which it paid a terrible penalty.

Nevertheless it was still the largest army in the world, although Hitler had other considerations than this in preparing his battle plan.

### ■ GREEK DIVERSION ■

By 1941 he was convinced he could overwhelm the Soviet Union and kill off Communism there for good. But he was compelled to delay the invasion due to the German involvement in Greece, an unexpected diversion which cost the Reich valuable men and time.

It was a late spring that year, too, leaving roads clogged with mud and rivers swollen by the slow thaw. Germany needed the best possible weather to make a clean, quick strike into the heart of its foe.

By the beginning of June, all the indications were that Hitler was ready to pounce. As many as 76

different warnings came to Stalin to that effect. Churchill gleaned top secret information from his Ultra decodes, telling of the proposed invasion. Spies stationed around the Axis world delivered similar warnings. One German soldier, a closet Communist, even escaped across the border to warn Stalin of the impending attack.

Still the inscrutable leader refused to believe Hitler would wage war on him. He remained primarily concerned about his frontier with Japan, the growing menace in the east. Even the rapid and unexpected fall of France failed to persuade him that Russia would be next on the German Führer's hit list.

Stubbornly, Stalin dismissed the international warnings sent to Moscow as scandalous rumour-mongering and barred his top army commanders from mounting defences along the border, for fear of provoking Hitler. He even had the runaway German soldier shot.

His policy of appeasement designed to keep Russia out of the war stretched as far as sending train loads of oil, grain and metals to the Third Reich even while its troops were congregating on the borders.

On 22 June he was forced to think differently. 'Operation Barbarossa' got underway with 165 divisions

*Left:* The summer offensive against Russia progressed rapidly at first, until the German invaders ran out of good weather.

*Below:* A Red Army observer on the lookout for enemy aircraft in Moscow, 1941. The Soviets were ill-prepared for a German attack.

## THE GREAT DEBATE

**By 1940, America was caught up in 'The Great Debate', about whether or not it should enter the war.**

The largest body of isolationists campaigning to keep America out of the conflict was the America First Committee, centred in the Mid-West where anti-British and pro-German sentiments were strongest. Fascists united with Communists and radical Irish Americans in wanting to keep America neutral. In opposition was the Committee to Defend America by Aiding the Allies, founded in May 1940.

Among those contributing to the debate was Colonel Charles A. Lindbergh, who in 1927 became the first aviator to cross the Atlantic non-stop, and whose two-year-old son was kidnapped and murdered in 1932. He had visited Nazi Germany, inspected the Luftwaffe and declared the force was invincible.

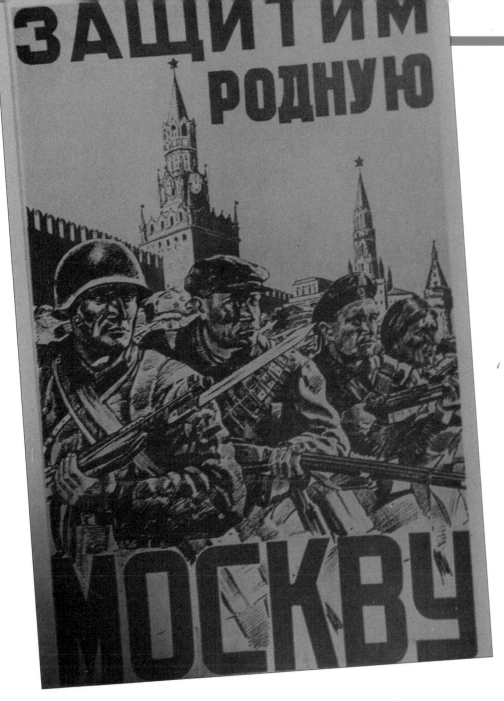

**ЗАЩИТИМ РОДНУЮ МОСКВУ**

major military disasters of the entire conflict when he refused to allow his men to retreat.

Hundreds of planes in the sizeable Red Air Force were immediately knocked out. All was going according to plan for Germany. It seemed like the army would be at the gates of Moscow in six weeks as forecast by the enthusiastic Hitler.

Yet within a month the Soviets began fighting back. Their resolve began stiffening, their exploits became harder to contain. In fact, the Russian soldier proved a formidable enemy in combat because he was prepared to

trundling into Russia in a three-pronged attack. The 2,500,000 Germans in the invasion force were not alone. Lining up with them were divisions of Romanians, Hungarians, Italians and Finns. There was even a Spanish unit involved. Before the attack was launched there was no formal declaration of war.

At first it was the by-now familiar story of Blitzkrieg. Panzer divisions ploughed through the Russian countryside heading for Kiev, Leningrad and Moscow. Occasionally the dirt-track roads were difficult to pass and local communications poor. Yet nothing stopped the

*Above:* **Farm workers and factory hands were called on to defend their country alongside Russia's soldiers, as the German onslaught swept in from the west.**

motorised units for long. In their wake the infantry marched at a pelt, straining to keep up with the successful advance and mopping up resistance along the way.

They picked up thousands of prisoners, many caught by the rear sweep of the advance unit which snared them in a bag. Stalin, who believed that being on the offensive was the only answer to Germany's aggression, engineered some of the

fight to the death. His willingness to make the ultimate sacrifice became particularly apparent as the war progressed. The Germans treated their Soviet prisoners with callous contempt. They were given fewer rations than other Allied prisoners of war and there was a catalogue of cruelty and atrocities. During the war, a staggering 3,300,000 Soviet prisoners of war died in German custody.

### ■ DEATH SQUADS ■

When the Russians got to hear of the treatment being meted out to their comrades they fought harder than ever. There was also increased incentive to fight to the last, as they knew that imprisonment would be worse than death. Equally, anything construed as cowardice by the soldiers and failure by their commanding officers led to execution by death squads of their fellow countrymen.

At the end of July Hitler made a controversial decision which perhaps cost him the war in Russia. Concerned at the rapid pace of the Panzers compared with the slow-moving infantry, he ordered a change in tack which had the advance units of his campaign veering off in another direction. The effect of this was to give the big cities valuable time to defend themselves.

His leaders in the field were mystified and outraged. In particular, General Heinz Guderian, who stood only 220 miles from Moscow, sought to disentangle himself from the order.

---

*When the surge forward began again, the first winter chill began to creep into the air*

---

*Above:* **In 1941, before winter set in, Third Reich forces were entrenched in battles on the outskirts of Moscow, shaking the foundations of the Kremlin itself.**

But despite some initial hesitation, Hitler was convinced he was right. It caused a flurry of resignations from his senior commanders, who knew instinctively that the time was right to press forward for Moscow. With the shelter the city offered to an army, the icy arctic winter might just be tolerable. Without it, the German hierarchy – who could only guess at the ravages such a winter would hold – gave an involuntary shiver.

When the surge forward began again, the first winter chill began to creep into the air.

By September, Riga, Minsk, Smolensk and Kiev had fallen. A record 665,000 soldiers were taken prisoner when Kiev collapsed, the

23

*Left:* German soldiers quickly began to realise the perils of fighting in a Russian winter when thick snow disabled much of their machinery.

'immersion-foot'. The condition occurred when wet feet were not dried out for days or weeks on end. Numbed and uncomfortable, the infected feet frequently turned purple and, in severe cases, the nerve endings died and gangrene set in. Trenchfoot was to plague the Italian, American and British armies later in the war as they battled in Europe.

The Russian roads, pitted and broken at the best of times, now turned into mires of mud. The German Panzers were literally bogged down and progressed at a painfully slow pace. Mechanical failures began to haunt each division as its desperate soldiers fought to keep the wheels turning.

most ever taken during a single wartime operation. (Stalin ignored the advice of one of his most seasoned officers to evacuate the area before it was too late.) Leningrad, like Sevastopol in the Crimea, was under siege. Western Russia was pock-marked with destruction. Stalin had ordered a 'scorched earth' policy among his men which meant retreating armies torched everything in their wake to both hinder the enemy and deprive them of possible supplies.

The residents of Moscow and Leningrad had not wasted their unexpected breathing space that summer. An army of women, old men and children spent their every waking hour digging in. Between them they provided the key spots with miles of earthworks, anti-tank ditches, barbed-wire walls and pill-boxes.

### ■ TRENCHFOOT ■

During their labours, their spirits must have lifted with the first deluge of autumn. The Germans, now wearying, depleted in numbers and burdened by casualties, looked up to the same endless grey skies with despair. The spring and autumn rains brought about cases of 'trenchfoot' – the vile affliction the Americans call

> **An army of women, old men and children spent their every waking hour digging in**

## HITLER'S LONELY LOVER

**Eva Braun spent 12 years as mistress to the hypnotic German Führer and no more than a few hours as his wife.**

Braun probably began her bizarre relationship with Hitler as early as 1931. Yet he refused to accord her the public recognition she desired despite his apparent regard for her.

Much of their relationship was spent apart, with the sporty, attractive Braun, born in 1910, waiting for Hitler to finish his state commitments before squeezing in some time with her. Hitler's chauffeur described her afterwards as 'the unhappiest woman in Germany. She spent most of her life waiting for Hitler.'

Even after her sister married General Fegelein, a member of Himmler's staff, she was unable to persuade Hitler to formalise their relationship. She attempted suicide twice, in 1932 and 1935, on account of Hitler's involvement with other women.

On 15 April 1945 Eva Braun arrived in Berlin to join Hitler for what were clearly his final days. In the early hours of 29 April they were wed. The following afternoon they were dead, Hitler having shot himself and Braun having taken poison. Her body, clad in a dark dress, was placed in a shell hole at the rear of the Berlin bunker and set ablaze alongside that of her husband.

The frosts of October came as a relief to the Germans. At least the ground was hard enough to support the tank tracks, and the stride towards Moscow quickened.

Haunted by the fate of the French emperor Napoleon back in 1812, who also made mighty advances into Russia only to be crippled by the winter freeze, Hitler declared that Moscow was to be taken.

### ■ OPERATION TYPHOON ■

The final thrust of 'Operation Typhoon' brought German troops tantalisingly close to their goal. Some reports insist the leading units penetrated a suburb of the capital and saw sunlight glinting on the roof of the Kremlin itself. Even now they were able to take 660,000 more Russian prisoners. But their progress was slowed and finally halted.

By now 200,000 members of the Germany army had been killed. The

*Below:* It wasn't just the weather that was bitter. Fighting between Russia and Germany on the Eastern front was some of the bloodiest of the entire conflict.

surviving German soldiers were no longer fresh and energetic. Five months of fighting had taken its toll even among those who were not injured. The resistance they found among the defenders of Moscow was fierce, the military machinery they relied on for spearheading their attack was failing. And now the relentless winter had set in, bringing with it snow storms and temperatures of minus 20 degrees Celsius.

German soldiers were inadequately clothed for the biting cold. The greatcoats they wore were scarcely thick enough to protect them from the bitter winds. In a feeble attempt to insulate themselves, they tore up paper and stuffed it inside their clothes. For snow camouflage they used bed sheets which again offered precious little warmth. Now frostbite was the worst enemy, claiming many more victims among the demoralised Germans than the fighting itself.

Vehicle oil froze unless it was kept warmed, so the Germans were unable to move at all. The fine German horses used to pull artillery and supplies perished by the thousand.

Hitler had ordered 'no retreat', perhaps realising that any movement forward or backwards posed a danger to his troops. It would be three years before the supplies of winter clothing to German troops from the Reich were adequate.

The Soviet army, meanwhile, was well used to the weather. Sheepskins and furs were standard issue. Great-

> *Now frostbite was the worst enemy, claiming many more victims than the fighting*

est among their assets were heavy-duty felt boots soon supplied in bulk by America where they were made to Russian specification. Russians knew how to care for their animals in the coldest weather; indeed, their ponies were bred hardy and tough. A squad of crack Siberian troops was being called in, experts at winter warfare and at home on a pair of skis. The fate of Moscow hung in the balance.

# JAPAN'S LIGHTNING WAR

With the success of Pearl Harbor under their belts, the Japanese were eager to capitalise on the supreme advantage of surprise. Defending British, Australian and American forces were caught off-guard throughout South East Asia and the Pacific as Japan began a 'Blitzkrieg' of its own.

Key targets were Hong Kong, the Philippines, Malaya, Singapore, Burma, Thailand, the Dutch East Indies and the stepping stone islands of Wake and Guam. Each offered the new Japanese empire mineral or agricultural wealth that was badly needed, or was a necessary land-base to protect precious cargoes.

Hong Kong was the first of the British domains to fall. Only 400 miles from Japanese air bases in Formosa (now Taiwan), it was vulnerable from the outset. The defence of Hong Kong and other prestigious British outposts had suffered thanks to the war effort in other parts of the world. During 1939 and 1940, troops, ships and aircraft were sent to trouble-spots like North Africa and the Mediterranean at the expense of the far-flung colonies, which appeared to be in no imminent danger.

By August 1940, Churchill accepted the view held by service chiefs that Hong Kong was practically indefensible and that the garrison on the island could be better used elsewhere. Japanese intentions were far from clear at this point. However, perhaps with growing indications that Japan was possibly hostile, no one acted further on the recommendation. In fact, the following year the Hong Kong garrison was strengthened by the addition of two Canadian battalions. In the event, they only added to the huge numbers of prisoners taken during those early Japanese exploits.

An initial strike made by the Japanese on 8 December proved to be devastating. The Allied troops were driven back to Hong Kong city within a matter of days. For a week, the Japanese were held at bay across the water barrier. Under the cover of darkness on 18 December, the inevitable Japanese landings on Hong Kong island began. Following Churchill's declared policy, resistance was slight. A wedge was driven between the defending forces. On Christmas Day one arm surrendered. Their comrades gave up the fight a day later. For the loss of 3,000 dead and wounded the Japanese had captured Hong Kong, together with its force of nearly 12,000 men.

The Philippines were to have suffered their first Japanese air bombardment on 8 December. Although not an American possession, they were reliant on US support before becoming independent. In fact, morning fog grounded the aircraft based in Formosa, delaying take-off.

The Americans, meanwhile, were debating whether or not to carry out a bombing mission in Formosa. The indecision proved fatal. In the early afternoon, when the US B-17s were finally being prepared for a sortie, the overdue Japanese aircraft finally

> *For the loss of 3,000 dead and wounded the Japanese had captured Hong Kong*

arrived. With the American planes presented on an airfield, the Japanese pilots did their destructive worst. A number of the planes intended to protect the Philippines were wrecked.

*Left:* Victorious Japanese troops enter Rangoon after quickly annihilating opposition troops in Burma. The Burmese people gave them an indifferent welcome.

*Above:* Dejected British soldiers file through the streets of Singapore after the disastrous fall of the colony to the Emperor's forces.

## RATIONS

Rations were boosted – and cut – for Britons on the home front throughout the war. Here is a typical weekly allowance per person.

8oz sugar, 3oz cheese
3oz cooking fat, 4oz bacon or ham
2oz jam, 2oz sweets, 2oz tea or coffee
1 egg, 3 pints milk, 1lb meat

Bread, fish and sausages, although not rationed, were scarce. Although there was no restriction on fruit and vegetables, many were impossible to get. Lemons, bananas, onions and even pepper were rarely, if ever, seen during the war years in Britain.
   Inventive housewives made chocolate truffle cake from potatoes, and banana pudding from parsnips.

*Right:* General-Marshal Homma makes an assisted landing on Luzon in the Philippines on 24 December 1941, ousting defending American troops.

The Japanese 14th Army quickly captured off-islands and made landings on Luzon, the largest Philippine island, as early as 10 December. There were continuing probes until the main landings, which took place on 22 December.

Coastal defences, comprising poorly trained and fearful Filipinos soon crumbled. A core of American troops was kept in the capital, Manila, by commander General MacArthur until it became clear that the defence of the island was an impossibility. He then ordered a withdrawal into the Bataan Peninsula in the hope the 31,000 troops could mount an adequate defence.

The Americans did manage to repel a number of raids. Then both sides became severely weakened through rampant malaria. Morale sank further in the American ranks when it became clear there was little or no effort being made to evacuate them. When the Japanese offensive began again on 3 April it took only six days to force a surrender.

There remained almost 15,000 Americans on the nearby island of Corregidor. The fight for this scrap of

### Coastal defences, comprising poorly trained and fearful Filipinos, soon crumbled

an island was to be fierce. The Japanese carried out daily artillery bombardments across the straits from Luzon as well as waves of air attacks. When much of the American artillery had been knocked out, the Japanese mounted an invasion with 2,000 troops. More than half were lost in the battle that ensued during the night of 5 May. But despite their losses, the Japanese managed to land some tanks, enough to crush the remaining resistance.

A surrender bid by American General Wainwright was hampered by guerrilla action adopted by the Americans. By 9 June, however, all resistance was crushed.

The loss to the Americans had been considerable; likewise to the native forces. A combined total of 95,000 were taken captive by the Japanese. Yet the defenders had held out for six months with no outside assistance, a significant achievement given the domino fall of islands in the rest of the area.

On paper, it appeared the British defenders of Malaya and neighbouring Singapore were more than a match for the invaders. There were about 100,000 Allied troops taking on just 30,000 incoming Japanese. In Britain there was confidence that Singapore particularly was a fortress with stout defences. It was unthinkable that the stronghold would be overrun. As so often happens during wars, the unthinkable happened – at speed.

The defeat of the British and Allied forces at the hands of the Japanese was a shocking one for which few at home were prepared. Yet there were shortcomings in the defences of the countries invaded which allowed the enthusiastic Japanese to run rampant.

Despite the signs of militarism evident in Japan, the British government remained convinced this small country would not take on the combined might of America, Britain and Russia. After the war, Churchill admitted he among others had underestimated the threat posed by Japan, particularly in its air power.

The Allies had no tanks with which to blast the enemy while the Japanese rolled over the inhospitable terrain with something in the order of 300. And while the Allies possessed more than twice the amount of artillery, much of it was in Singapore facing seawards to repel a southerly invasion. The Japanese flooded in from the opposite direction.

### ■ OPPRESSIVE HEAT ■

As for aircraft, the Allies had only a sixth of the number of aircraft that the Japanese had at their disposal. In a war which proved air might was imperative, the British were left seriously underequipped.

Moreover, Japanese troops were trained for jungle warfare and the dense vegetation and steamy atmosphere did not daunt them. The British and Australians were quickly wearied by the oppressive heat.

In command of the Japanese was General Tomoyuki Yamashita, a

devoted servant of Emperor Hirohito and a military marvel. Among his troops, he was known as 'the tiger'. The Allies, meanwhile, were under General Arthur Percival, held with such low regard by his men that he was called 'the rabbit'.

On the day that the prize British capital ships Prince of Wales and Repulse were sent to the bottom of the sea, Japanese forces marched into Malaya. With waves of air cover, they were quickly able to force the British down the Malay Peninsula in a rolling retreat. The highly organised invaders cut quickly through any defences they encountered. About 4,000 British troops and their equipment were stranded in central Malaya when Japanese tanks broke through their lines and seized a road

*Below:* Seasoned jungle warriors, the **Japanese troops found far less difficulty operating in the tropics than their beleaguered enemies did.**

# WAVELL VICTORIOUS

When British and Commonwealth troops under the command of General Sir Archibald Wavell drove Italian troops into a spectacular retreat early in 1941, there was rejoicing at home at the first glimpse of meaningful victory. The *News Chronicle* wrote:

'It is still too early for any complete estimate of General Wavell's happy and glorious achievement; but from what we already know two factors stand out and demand the most generous praise: the perfect co-ordination of land, sea and air forces and the superb Staff work that preceded the attack and made the co-ordination possible.'

*Somewhat prematurely, it ended:*
'Rapidly the Axis is becoming a meaningless phrase: an axis requires two ends, and, if it is to function, each end must perform an equal task. Otherwise the whole thing crumbles away. One day that will happen, and General Wavell, by his care and genius, has brought that day nearer than two months ago we dared hope.'

bridge, curtailing their withdrawal. The capital, Kuala Lumpur, was abandoned by the Allies on 11 January and still the retreat continued to gather pace.

### ■ MALAYA FALLS ■

It took the Japanese just 54 days to overcome the resistance in Malaya. Their casualties amounted to around 4,600, compared with the loss of 25,000 Allied troops, many of whom were now prisoners of war. Thousands of Indians recruited to fight for the Empire already had doubts about the wisdom of risking their lives for the country which oppressed their own. Now many took the opportunity to join brigades organised by the Japanese and were fighting against former comrades.

Fleeing British and Australian forces made a dash for Singapore and blew up the bridge connecting the island with Malaya as they went. Japanese forces mustered threateningly on the other side.

Singapore was bombed on the day the war with Japan began. The casualties were mostly among the civilian population yet it forcefully illustrated the intentions of the Japanese. Perhaps for the first time, Churchill realised the folly of leaving the island of Singapore so woefully lacking in defences.

In January 1942, he declared: 'Not only must the defence of Singapore Island be maintained by every means but the whole island must be fought for until every single unit and every single strongpoint has been separately destroyed. Finally, the city of Singapore must be converted into

a citadel and defended to the death. No surrender can be contemplated.' On 8 February the Japanese troops put his words to the test by swarming across the Johore Strait which had so far barred them from the island. Some used small boats and dinghies. Others simply swam across. The Australian defenders in the region might have been expected to use the spotlights especially installed to light up their targets and blast the invaders out of the water.

Yet the order to switch on the lights never came. The soldiers were

## *The soldiers were left firing at darkened objects in the night*

left firing at darkened objects in the night. Not only that, the troops were soon ordered to fall back rather than to counter-attack. It was a symptom of the faulty lines of communication that dogged the short campaign by the Allies to keep Singapore. The standard of leadership among the

*Right:* A Japanese artillery detachment making its way through the jungle in late 1941 during the Singapore campaign. They found little standing in their way.

*Above:* **US soldiers surrender to Japanese troops. Ahead of them is a gruelling march to a harsh prison camp.**

Allies was also continually poor, with tactical blunders being made time and again. Ill-thought-out orders to withdraw from strongly held positions around the coast gave the Japanese an open door. All of this did nothing to buck the spirits of the beleaguered Allied soldiers wondering why they were left without the benefit of air cover.

## ■ SINGAPORE SHAME ■

Nor did the sight of thick black smoke rising over Singapore city do much to improve their state of mind. It plumed from oil tanks set alight by the British themselves in the harbour area to keep them from falling into Japanese hands. From it came a pungent black rain which fell across a wide area. A flurry of activity by Japan's supporters in Singapore added to the chaos and confusion in the city.

Food stocks were running low and the water supply was under threat by the time street battles commenced. Percival realised that to proceed with the fight was futile. A package air-dropped to his headquarters in a

cascade of red and white ribbons invited him to surrender. It bore the following sinister sentence from Yamashita: 'If you continue resistance, it will be diffcult to bear with patience, from a humanitarian point of view.'

He chose to ignore Churchill's orders to fight to the bitter end. Percival marched to meet the triumphant Yamashita with a Union Jack and a white flag, held aloft side-by-side. The close proximity of the national flag and the symbol of surrender did nothing to endear him to the establishment at home. His signature ended the British domination of Singapore at a conference held in the Ford factory on Bukit Timah hill. Some 80,000 British, Indian and Australian troops were snared, forced to face four years of gruelling captivity under the harsh Japanese regime. With the loss of Singapore came the

bitter realisation that Britain's proud boast of being able to defend its colonies no matter where they were in the world was now a sham.

Afterwards, it was described as 'the greatest military disaster in [British] history'. For years Percival was an outcast, held personally responsible for the loss of a glittering prize. While his leadership was certainly flawed, he was only one of many Allied commanders who found themselves bowled over by the Japanese steamroller.

The extent of the Singapore debacle was only revealed fully after the war when Yamashita revealed he considered himself on the brink of losing the vital campaign: 'My attack

*Right:* Japanese soldiers soon adapted in the jungle, making use of local elephants to forge a path through dense vegetation. The Allied defenders could not match the invaders proficiency in jungle warfare.
*Below:* General Tomoyuki Yamashita, one of Japan's most successful military leaders, pulled off a dramatic coup when he captured Singapore.

on Singapore was a bluff. I had 30,000 men and was outnumbered more than three to one. I knew that if I had been made to fight longer for Singapore I would have been beaten. That was why the surrender had to be immediate. I was extremely frightened that the British would discover our numerical weakness and lack of supplies and force me into disastrous street fighting. But they never did. My bluff worked.'

December 1941 also saw the invasion of Burma. It was inadequately protected, with Malaya and Singapore seen as having greater requirement for military resources.

Once again, Japan had by far the most effective air force. It was to be another story of inglorious retreat, this time over 1,000 miles into India.

The Burmese capital Rangoon was being bombed by Christmas. The British forces were once again forced back under the onslaught of the 35,000 invading Japanese troops, who proved themselves faster and more adept in jungle warfare. On 6 March 1942 the order came to evacuate Rangoon.

## ■ MONSOON SEASON ■

After both sides had reinforced, the British, assisted now by Chinese forces, defended a 150-mile line south of Mandalay. The Japanese merely sidestepped the line and enveloped the troops manning it. By now it was April and the British troops not only had to consider the advance of the enemy but also the onset of the monsoon season, due in May, which would turn the roads vital for retreat into mires. Burmese soldiers, always unhappy about the colonial control of their country, were deserting in droves to join the

new national army that was fighting with the Japanese invaders.

British rearguard forces held up the Japanese advance before making the final dash for safety themselves. The tanks of the 7th Armoured Brigade made repeated counter-attacks to delay the enemy campaign.

*Burmese soldiers, always unhappy about the colonial control of their country, were deserting in droves to join the new national army*

A week before the monsoon season began, the majority of the British forces fell back exhausted and relieved behind the Indian frontier. They had lost much of their equipment and had suffered three times the number of casualties that the Japanese had incurred. But given their circumstances, it was a miracle that any succeeded in escaping at all.

## ◆ EYE WITNESS ◆

**Hugh Trebble, a local newspaper journalist, joined the Civil Air Guard before the war when it offered the chance to learn to fly for one penny per minute. In 1940 he was recruited into the Royal Air Force, in which he was a clerk.**

❝I was posted overseas in June 1941 and got to Singapore by August. From there I went to RAF Butterworth, overlooking Penang Island in north west Malaya. One of our first instructions when we got to Butterworth was that between 2pm and 4pm you were either in bed or out of barracks. It was impossible to raise a British officer during that time on the peninsula.

There was a lot of personnel in Malaya and Singapore but no equipment. At Butterworth we were still flying old-fashioned Bristol Blenheims. I never saw any combat aircraft the entire time I was there. Our junior officers were principally Australian.

After the Japanese invaded down the east coast we were pulled back to Kuala Lumpur to a base called Sungeibesi. A few weeks later General Wavell flew in to assess the situation. As soon as his Hudson took off we blew it [the base] up. We retreated via a rubber plantation down to Singapore.

There, we were put in a camp at RAF Seletar. There were hundreds of us that couldn't be gainfully employed. The last flight of so-called bombers that set off from there was made up of obsolete Vickers Wildebeest, twin-engined bi-planes. They took off but they never landed. They were destroyed before they could put down.

There was a desperate atmosphere in Singapore, even more so after the battleships *Prince of Wales* and *Repulse* were sunk. When they left port it was with a total absence of air cover and destroyer cover. They should never have been sent out in the first place.

In Singapore there were fixed guns facing over the sea – when the Japanese came overland. They didn't need fifth columnists in the city to help them. Japanese soldiers easily overpowered anything we had.

Some Allied soldiers got off troop ships and were taken prisoner virtually straightaway. They never fired a shot in anger. They had nothing to do any fighting with anyway.

On 13 January 1942 I was among many who were evacuated from Kepple Harbour on the *Empire Star*, a Blue Funnel ship, heading for Java. Clearly, we were sent to Singapore for propaganda purposes – nothing else.❞

British and American forces were put under a single command, known as ABDA, led by Britain's General Archibald Wavell.

Although the Dutch resistance was soon annihilated, the Australians proved a more formidable foe. Yet there was little they could do to protect the scores of tiny islands from Japanese occupation.

After the disastrous Battle of the Java Sea, which the Allies lost in February 1942, the Japanese could count the Dutch East Indies as their own.

### ■ EYES ON CEYLON ■

Other casualties in the Japanese lightning war were Guam, Wake Island and the Gilbert Islands, which fell before the end of 1941. In the spring of 1942, the Bismarck Archipelago, the Solomon Islands and north eastern New Guinea all succumbed to Japanese forces.

Britain now feared attack from the Japanese navy in the Indian Ocean, where Ceylon was a prime target. Strategically, it was crucial to the British. On 5 April 1942 the British braced themselves for attack following an air strike by more than 1,000

> *Britain now feared attack from the Japanese navy in the Indian Ocean, where Ceylon was a prime target*

planes at Colombo, the capital of Ceylon. Two British cruisers were sunk and the port was badly damaged. The distances were too great for an invasion to be sustainable, however, and the Japanese knew it. They withdrew behind the lines of their expanded empire and concentrated on defence.

The Dutch East Indies came under attack in December 1941, too. This arc of wealthy islands, at its easterly point just 300 miles from the coast of Australia, was rich in oil and thus an important target for the oil-starved Japanese. In a bid to halt the Japanese, the defending Dutch, Australian,

# THE EASTERN FRONT

Winter weather had brought the German advance in Russia to a standstill. Yet Stalin knew that freezing temperatures and snow flurries alone would not be enough to defeat the might of the Third Reich's army.

He was neither a gifted tactician nor a seasoned campaigner, unlike his enemy Hitler. In personal command of his army, Stalin was isolated at the top. The blunders he made as the barbarous campaign against his country got underway cost millions of lives. He would soon learn by bitter experience about how to run a war.

He enjoyed a certain degree of good luck and, in time, he used it well. To his advantage, he had a seemingly inexhaustible supply of men.

After Pearl Harbor, Stalin realised Japan was too embroiled with its actions against America to now threaten Russia. So the men tied up with defending its eastern rear were at last free to man the German front. In addition, there were countless thousands of reservists, recruited from all over the Soviet Union, to replace fallen comrades.

It was this perpetual sacrifice of men above all other factors that

## D-Day could not have gone ahead without the Russian front diverting German resources

changed the course of the war. If Stalin had found his people with less resolve and more ready to capitulate, Hitler might have won on the Eastern front. And a victory there would have ensured him triumph in the west. D-Day, the single most decisive action of the entire war, could not have gone ahead without the Russian front diverting so many German resources.

Somehow this massive country survived its appalling casualty rate. It

prompted the frustrated German chief of staff Halder to comment: 'We estimated that we should contend with 180 Russian divisions; we have already counted 360.'

Wherever possible, the Soviet Union's heavy industry was moved nut by nut and bolt by bolt to the east

*Above:* The half-frozen mud is littered with the bodies of dead Russian soldiers. Total Soviet losses, military and civilian, in the war may have exceeded 20 million.

*Left:* Resignation is etched on the face of a German soldier on the Eastern front, more than two years after 'Barbarossa'.

**Above:** A smouldering tank is stopped in its tracks during the campaign, its crew almost certainly dead inside.

of the country to prevent it being swallowed up in the German advance – from here productivity was now stepped up. While the Germans suffered from privation, with inadequate supplies being ferried along overstretched lines beginning in occupied Poland and beyond, the Russian forces had their needs seen to swiftly and without hindrance along railway tracks still running into Moscow despite the conflict.

Key among the Russian supplies was the new T-34 tank, heavily armoured, fast and tough. It was equal if not superior to the tanks being driven by the Germans. By 1943 Russian industry was able to produce twice as many tanks as its German counterpart.

### ■ MARSHAL ZHUKOV ■

Russia also received fresh stocks from the Allies. Perhaps the most significant of these was a mammoth consignment of trucks from America. It enabled Stalin to move men around his huge country at increased speed. He had a fine commander in the field in Georgi Zhukov, whose military genius shone out from the floundering incompetents left at the top of what remained of the Red Army.

## When they arrived they would face a quick court martial before being shot

**Below:** Marshal Zhukov (left) pores over a battle plan as high-ranking Russians grapple with modern warfare techniques.

Zhukov joined the Tsar's army as a conscript at the outbreak of World War I, aged 18, winning two medals before the Bolshevik revolution. By 1919 he was in the Red Army and a Communist Party member. A personal rapport with Stalin saved him during the military purge of 1937. He remained one of the few generals able to speak his mind to the Soviet dictator, although on at least one occasion he was demoted as a result of doing so.

### ■ RETREAT AND DIG ■

Not all the other Russian generals were so lucky. After war broke out, Stalin habitually telephoned commanders who had been compelled to pull back their armies and summoned them to Moscow. When they arrived they would face a quick court martial before being shot for dereliction of duty. Stalin was the only leader of World War II who continued with the outdated notion of shooting generals for failure in the field.

That was not the only old-fashioned element of warfare evident in Russia. Russian generals were forced on the offensive by Stalin no matter what the odds, as it was the

## RICKY

**In the treacherous task of clearing minefields, the British invasion force used specially trained dogs. When the dog sat down it was clear to his handler that a mine had been sniffed out.**

Welsh sheepdog Ricky was clearing a canal bank in Holland when a mine blew up just three feet away from him. Ricky was wounded in the face while the blast killed the section commander. Regardless of his injuries, Ricky returned to his duties and found several more mines before retiring for treatment.

His courage won him the Dickin Medal, created by the People's Dispensary for Sick Animals, to recognise the courage of animals in the front line. Inscribed on it are the words 'For gallantry, we also serve'. Ribbons attached to the disc are green, brown and blue to represent sea, land and sky.

only way he knew of achieving victory. Devoid of any inspiration until the arrival of Zhukov and his protégés, they would send waves of men 'over the top' to hurl themselves at the Germans, much as soldiers did during the trench warfare of 1914-18. The unfortunate troops were cut down in waves.

It took Stalin at least a year to realise that his strategies were fatally flawed. When he began lending an ear to the new breed of generals, he finally realised that technique was everything in modern warfare. It was then that Russia began to turn the tables on its foe.

### ▪ MOSCOW REPRIEVED ▪

After an inconclusive Russian counter-offensive out of Moscow in December 1941, both sides suspended operations until May 1942 to give themselves valuable time to recoup men and hardware. Moscow was at least saved from occupation but its people still suffered the deprivations of war.

While Stalin was convinced Moscow remained the Third Reich's prime target, Hitler had other ideas. The need for more resources for his spiralling war effort became more pressing. He eyed the Soviet oilfields in the Caucasus greedily, knowing that success in capturing such prized

*Below:* **Prepared for invasion. Moscow was lined with anti-tank devices to halt Hitler's progress in the capital.**

assets would not only buoy Germany but would deprive Stalin of precious fuel resources as well.

Code-named 'Operation Blue', Hitler's drive east began at the beginning of May. In characteristic style, the thrust was dynamic and 170,000 Russians were taken prisoner in the first week. Two Russian counter-attacks ended in disarray. The first German objective, to take the tank-making town of Kharkov, was achieved by the end of June.

But frustration followed victory as the Germans lost the initiative when they became involved in a battle for the city of Voronezh. Russian fighters, released from the order to stay their ground by Stalin, could finally strike and then melt away, causing the maximum damage and nuisance to the Germans.

It delayed the German stab towards Stalingrad, the gateway to the Caucasus, which Hitler had earmarked as his own.

In October the German 6th Army finally reached Stalingrad and launched a bloody offensive with the aid of endless strikes by the Luftwaffe. Russian defenders of the city adopted the tactics of guerrilla warfare, going underground to snipe at the oncoming Germans.

## ■ OPERATION URANUS ■

Even as the winter set in, German commander Paulus braced himself and his men for a final effort, during November 1942. Although the killing went on, he achieved little.

But now the Russians were to bring into play some of the devastating tactics they had learned the hard way, at the hands of the invading Germans. Paulus found his flanks surrounded by a mighty Russian force ready to put a noose around the weakened 6th Army. This was Stalin's 'Operation Uranus', devised

between himself, Zhukov and Chief of General Staff Vasilevsky.

When he heard about the disaster, Hitler was furious. He pledged supplies would be dropped by the Luftwaffe to the beleaguered Paulus

and organised a relief column. But he refused to give Paulus the lifeline he needed for himself and his men – the order to break out of the encirclement or retreat.

## ■ GERMANS BESIEGED ■

At Stalingrad the outlook for the Germans was bleak. Only a fraction of the food and medical supplies needed were being flown in. Injury or sickness accounted for as much as one fifth of the 100,000-strong force.

The Russian commanders were confident enough to offer Paulus an opportunity to surrender as early as 8 January 1943. Paulus knew the Führer would be maddened so he stood fast.

*Left:* German pilots notched up some stunning successes on the Eastern front despite facing grim flying conditions.

*Above:* **Stalingrad proved a vital turning point for Germany in the war. Flouting Hitler's wishes, Third Reich troops surrendered to the Russians following a gruelling and costly winter battle.**

Another heavy bombardment rained down on Stalingrad a few days later, leaving the depleted fighting force even more demoralised and desperate. In a last-minute frantic gesture, Hitler promoted Paulus to the rank of field-marshal. Paulus knew well enough the politics behind the honour. No German field-marshal had ever surrendered. The message was clear, fight to the death.

In the misery of snow and ice, Paulus must have glanced around at some of the bodies of the thousands of German soldiers who died in those hellish weeks and wondered why.

Now Paulus found the courage to be the first field-marshal to wave a white flag. At the close of January his headquarters was overrun and he surrendered to the elated Russians. He went on to join a turncoat regiment of Germans who, following

capture, fought for the Russians. For the victors there was the prize of 110,000 prisoners. For the defeated, it was unmitigated disaster.

Germans were on the run elsewhere in Russia as well, chased by an increasingly confident Red Army who were at their best in winter. It was far from the end of the war at the Eastern front. But it was the beginning of the end for Germany even if Hitler remained blind to the fact for months to come.

## Now Paulus found the courage to be the first field-marshal to wave a white flag

The subsequent drive by the Russian army between January and March was fruitless. Crack German commander Field-Marshal Erich von Manstein staged a determined recovery. This small consolation did little

for Hitler's morale. He was broken by the Stalingrad debacle, losing his self-confidence and intuition.

Fighting continued in explosive spats until the scene was set for a major confrontation at Kursk. Hitler allowed the planned offensive, 'Operation Citadel', to be delayed time and again while his commanders struggled to get sufficient numbers of tanks in position.

It was 5 July before the battle commenced. By 12 July there were some 2,700 German tanks and 1,800 German aircraft ranged against almost 4,000 Soviet tanks. It was the largest head-on tank battle in history, an epic test of firepower which would leave both sides battered and worn. Tank after tank went up in flames, its crew having little chance of escaping the inferno. At the end of the day there were 300 German tanks smouldering. Still more Russian tanks were burnt out but the German advance had been halted. It spelled defeat once more for the Reich. And the dramatic loss of so many tanks would take Germany many more weeks to recover than it would Russia, leaving their armoured divisions sorely lacking in firepower and mobility.

Now it was for Hitler to contemplate withdrawal. It was alien to his nature to pull out of territory fought over and won two years before. But the Red Army was flexing its muscles and was already chasing the German army out of the Crimea and the Baltic lands. The plan favoured by commanders like Manstein, to pull back to a single defensive line, soon

*Below:* **The tank battle at Kursk was an epic trial of strength. In the end it was the Russians who triumphed.**

## DIEPPE

**Twenty-one years after the disastrous raid at Dieppe which cost the lives of hundreds of Canadian servicemen, an investigation was launched to probe whether an advertisement for soap flakes gave the enemy vital advance information.**

The commando raid at Dieppe in August 1942 involved 5,000 Canadians, 1,000 British, 50 American Rangers and some Free French fighters. Only half returned. The rest were killed or captured after being pinned down on the beach by the Germans. A week before it took place English newspapers carried an advertisement for Sylvan soap flakes under the title 'Beach Coat from Dieppe'. The copy afterwards read: 'How could you have known when you bought it that sunny day before the war that such a flippant little coat would be so useful about the house in war-time?'

There was speculation that in the advertisement was hidden the message 'Beach Combined Operations at Dieppe'. The woman pictured carried secateurs. Were they in fact wire cutters? Scotland Yard and MI5 swooped on the advertising agency Graham and Gillies and on the manufacturers of the soap flakes. They were persuaded it was a horrible coincidence. But no one knows whether the Germans had read the advertisement and seen secret codes where none in fact existed.

became the only option. If only there had been enough materials and men to build the defences envisaged by Hitler, perhaps the gains he made would have been preserved at least for a while. But the Germans were unable to dig in along the 2,000-mile front and provide an effective defence. Their greatest protection to date, the ineffectiveness of the Red Army, was no longer relevant. Hitler's dream to take Russia had

turned into the same nightmare that afflicted Napoleon 150 years before.

By January 1944 the Red Army was at last able to lift the siege of Leningrad. The city had been encircled since November 1941, suffering months of artillery bombardment. When liberation came after 900 days, only one third of the original population of three million were left alive.

Just as the winter of 1941-42 caused devastation among the

invaders, so it brought misery and despondency to the hemmed-in people of Leningrad.

Rationing was down to just nine ounces of bread per day for working people and half that amount for those too young or too old to be employed. Cats, dogs, even rats, were eaten in a bid to stave off starvation. In front of the desperate people lay the no-man's land of defences against the Germans. Behind them lay frozen Lake Ladoga, over which there was a narrow trail into free Russia.

*When liberation came after 900 days, only one third of the original population of three million were left alive*

Minimal supplies found their way across the trail at first and even the smallest relief attempts were harried by German aircraft. By the spring, the residents had learned a harsh lesson. Every available inch of land was cultivated and there were fresh

*Above:* **The sight of Russian tanks lying uselessly by the roadside provide a grim spectacle for passing troops.**
*Right:* **Many German soldiers died as they vainly struggled to repair vehicles frozen in the snow.**

vegetables available throughout the rest of their imprisonment. Electricity was also rationed, the sewers were brim full and even clean water was in short supply.

When the saviour army lifted the blockade, they were greeted with a weary relief by the Leningraders.

Between March and April the Red Army reclaimed 165 miles of territory. Their greatest push was yet to come, however, in the form of 'Operation Bagration', which began in June, just as Hitler came under acute pressure from the D-Day landings in Normandy. Before it began, the partisans working for the Russians behind German lines set to work by setting off a series of disabling explosions.

The operation was characterised by now-familiar tactics employed by the Red Army. A burst of artillery fire to 'soften up' the enemy followed

by the rapid advance of the infantry. Thousands of German soldiers were taken prisoner as Minsk fell once again to the Russians. Their humiliation was to walk down the silent streets of Moscow on their way to prison camps, watched through the narrowed, loathing eyes of the city residents. Now the German forces in the east were stretched to breaking point. Stubbornly, Hitler refused to let his troops pull back even when

they had been overrun. The Führer's behaviour only offered more to the Russians by way of enemy casualties and prisoners.

By August, the Russian troops were on the Polish border. They had been forced to contend with more than three times the number of troops facing the Allies in Normandy and had proved themselves equal to the task. For the first time, the war was to be carried into Reich territory.

# A FORGOTTEN ARMY

**Just like the British fighters in Burma and the American soldiers assisting the Chinese, the troops who fought to regain Italy believed themselves to be 'a forgotten army'.**

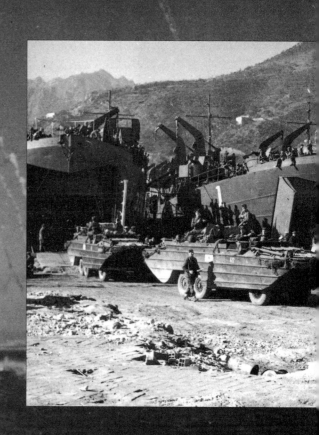

Theirs was a protracted campaign remembered mostly for its mud, miscalculation and unexpectedly high casualty rate. Churchill had described the Italian peninsula as 'the soft underbelly' of the Third Reich. Fierce German resistance proved his judgement to be wildly awry.

After nearly a year of strenuous fighting, the Allies took Rome on 4 June 1944. The trumpeted D-Day operations which began the following night swallowed the limelight. Forces who felt they had lost the recognition they deserved joked wryly thereafter about themselves being 'D-Day dodgers in sunny Italy'.

The opportunity to open a second front in Europe occurred when the fighting in North Africa was brought to a victorious close in 1943. For months, the Americans had been pushing for a campaign on the continent. Their chosen siting was northern France. But Churchill and his commanders felt it was premature, preferring instead to squeeze the Germans from the south.

By July 1943, the invasion of Sicily, code-named 'Operation Husky', was prepared. Montgomery was to lead his weary but able 8th Army in one assault while General Patton, heading the US 7th Army, came via a different route. The aim was to trap the defending German forces in a pincer movement.

During the course of the invasion, Italy swapped sides in the war, having overthrown the dictator

## Little did they know that the resolve of the Germans was harder than ever

Mussolini. Despite the chaos that this caused among the Germans, a staggering 40,000 were able to slip through the British and American trap and escape to the mainland.

Nevertheless, Sicily was in Allied possession by 17 August. An armistice was signed on 3 September as the 8th Army crossed the Straits of Messina to land in Calabria, in 'Operation Baytown'. The effect of the revelation of the Italian volte face on the troops poised to continue with the invasion of the mainland was disastrous. There were cheers and celebrations before the operation had even begun. The men believed south-

*Above:* Weary from a foot-slog in Sicily, US soldiers prop themselves up at the foot of an Italian memorial to the soldiers of World War I.

ern Italy was theirs for the taking. Little did they know the resolve of the German defenders to stop them was harder than ever, and they were mentally ill-prepared for the brutal fighting which awaited them.

### ■ SALERNO LANDINGS ■

On 9 September the next phase of the invasion began. A total of 165,000 British and American servicemen spilled out of 500 ships in a large-scale amphibious landing. The landings at Salerno, code-named 'Operation Avalanche', were scheduled by US commander General Mark Clark to last three days. He had supreme confidence in the ability of the troops to secure a quick victory. Within just 72 hours he expected Naples to have fallen, giving the Allies a crucial harbour

*Far left:* The sky is decorated by a fireball, following a German dive-bomber attack on an American cargo ship during the invasion of Sicily.
*Left, inset:* Allied DUKW amphibious vehicles, nicknamed 'ducks', are loaded aboard a landing ship at Salerno harbour in preparation for the next phase of the invasion of Italy.

facility. In fact, it took 21 days of gruelling battle. An attack staged at Taranto designed to divert the Germans failed. Crack German troops held the British and Americans at Salerno until reinforcements had been brought forward.

The fastidious and highly critical Montgomery, who expressed doubts about the planning of the campaign

**Above: Allied artillery in action against targets in Italy. The gunners, from 97 Heavy AA Regiment, Royal Artillery, feel the heat.**

from the outset, encountered tough resistance as he and his men tried to fight their way up the toe of Italy to rendezvous with the rest of the invasion force. He was horrified to find the German positions had been reinforced. Clark's and Montgomery's troops finally made the planned link up on 16 September. In those weeks 25,000 soldiers and civilians died.

Although a first vital and substantial foothold in Italy had been carved out, the fighting didn't get any easier. The terrain of rocky peaks and steep escarpments favoured defensive positions, all of which were held by the Germans. Time and again, the Allied soldiers found themselves fatally exposed.

By 15 November the campaign was brought to a halt, hampered as it was by winter weather. Relations between the British and American commanders were equally chilly.

The next tactic to bring about a breakthrough took the form of the Allied landings at Anzio in January 1944. In 'Operation Shingle', the beachheads were quickly secured, yet the Allies had difficulty spearheading an advance. Indeed, they only narrowly missed being driven back into the sea by a determined German counter-offensive. Soon Anzio was under seige. Conflicts there were bitter. The Allies were desperately seeking routes to push forward.

By now the Allied reinforcements consisted of British, American, French, Canadian, New Zealand, South African, Greek and Brazilian troops. Even the Japanese were playing their part. The Nisei-Ameri-cans, Japanese settlers in America who had been reviled at home after Pearl Harbor, made several vital strikes on behalf of the Allies.

## ■ MONTE CASSINO ■

The road to Rome was marked by the architectural treasure of Monte Cassino, a sacred Christian site founded in 529 by Saint Benedict. It was filled with cultural riches gathered through the centuries, kept lovingly in archives by the monks who lived and worked at the abbey.

Perched high on a mountainous ridge, Monte Cassino looked down into the town of Cassino and away across the plains. Monastery and town were connected by a funicular railway which climbed the sheer rocky face of the peak with ease.

Cassino was in the hands of the Germans in January 1944, a major strength in its defences known as 'the Gustav line'. It became the target of Allied plane attacks but even a heavy

*The Americans then took one of the most contro-versial decisions of the conflict – to bomb the delightful monastery*

pounding failed to eradicate the defenders. Soon, it became clear the Germans were using the abbey as a defensive stronghold, unassailable at the mountain top.

The Americans then took one of the most controversial decisions of the conflict – to bomb the delightful monastery which was consequently smashed to smithereens.

Little was achieved. Still Allied forces were left clinging to the mountainside, scrambling forward a few yards whenever they could. It

*Right:* The German forces in Italy finally surrendered to the Allies on 2 May 1945.

wasn't until May that the Allies by-passed the hazard, leaving the ruins of the abbey to fall to the Polish army in the rear. With heavy casualties, the Polish, assisted by a British contingent, took 1,500 prisoners – men of the German 4th Parachute Regiment.

To capture Monte Cassino, the Allies used 27 divisions with 1,900 tanks, together with 4,000 aircraft. Casualties on both sides were appalling, with some 105,000 Allied soldiers killed or wounded alongside 80,000 Germans.

### ■ FALL OF ROME ■

Although Rome fell soon afterwards and the incoming troops received a tumultuous welcome from its citizens, it was not the end of fighting in Italy. Still Germany threw men and ammunition at the advancing Allies. Pockets of resistance around Rimini and Bologna held the advance until the winter months, when by necessity it all but ground to a halt. Allied troops were forced to dig in during the inclement weather, experiencing the same dreadful conditions that faced their forebears in the trenches of World War I.

As late as 9 April 1945, the Allies were compelled to begin another offensive. It wasn't until 2 May that a surrender was negotiated with the weary and disillusioned Germans.

*Right:* The fierce battle at Monte Cassino left the monastery a shattered wreck.

### Casualties were appalling, with some 105,000 Allied soldiers killed or wounded

### ◆ EYE WITNESS ◆

Lieutenant-Colonel Alex Borrie was in a New Zealand brigade involved in the battle for Italy and later wrote *Escapades around Cassino*. In his diary dated 18 March 1944, he wrote:

" Our C Company moved past Castle Hill to attack Cassino. Their main objectives were 'Hotel des Roses' and 'Hotel Continental'. They were to retreat to a cave above part of the Monastery Road at 6pm. I was sent up the hill with a team of soldiers carrying food and medical supplies. The 4th Indian Division was beyond our Company on Hangman's Hill. Passing from Castle Hill to the road, the Germans put up many flares. We felt most conspicuous but the experienced soldiers said: "Stand still!" No shots were fired. At 9.10pm we reached the cave spot on time. I called out "Any Kiwis here?"

"Ssh, quiet, we just arrived ten minutes ago. There are Germans everywhere." On the way down, supplies had been dropped by parachute. Someone once said to me: "Parachutes make wonderful underpants." I tore off plenty but back at the R.A.P. it was red thick cotton – useless. "

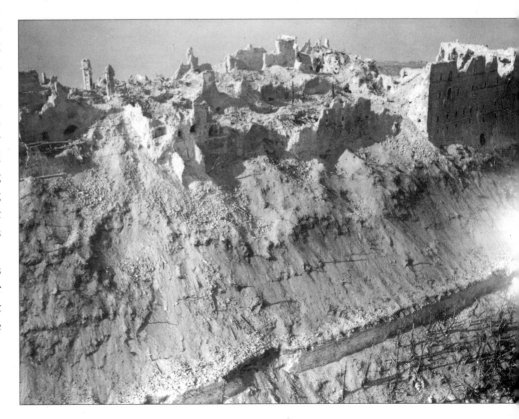

# OVERLORD!

It was the day that Europe had been waiting for, when Allied soldiers would tread again on French soil. In the event, many had to step over the bodies of fallen comrades lying lifeless in the Normandy surf before their feet touched Nazi-occupied France.

The Americans had been pressing for an assault on occupied Europe virtually since their entry into the war. Cautious British commanders, stung by heavy losses during the trial foray onto the French coastline at Dieppe two years previously, at last thought the time was right to begin the liberation of the continent. A defeat could have been a death-blow to Britain's war effort, leaving her without an army. The commanders were finally convinced that victory was likely to be theirs.

The Germans, too, had been waiting with trepidation for the day that their enemies would try to get a foothold once more in Europe and had fortified the French coastline accordingly. Construction on the lines of tunnels, guns and bunkers to protect Hitler's Europe stretching 3,000 miles from Holland to the south of France began in September 1941 and got underway in earnest when Rommel took charge of the huge task in 1943.

German intelligence was good yet they still had no idea when and how the invasion would come. Norway, the Balkans and Calais were all strong possiblities. The imminence of the invasion, however, was beyond doubt in anyone's mind.

Hitler hoped it would be Disaster-Day for the Allies, with the German defenders casting the invaders back into the sea. He guessed rightly that the outcome of the attack would decide the war. Fulfilling everybody's expectations, the invasion came in early June. 'Operation Overlord' was the culmination of more than a year's

*Left:* **When Utah beach was secured, troops and supplies flooded ashore from the scores of ships in the Channel.**

*Right:* **Dwight Eisenhower sent a 'good luck' message to all those who took part in 'Operation Overlord', the Allied invasion of occupied France.**

work. It was an elaborate plan involving thousands of soldiers, sailors and airmen. The troops who would be scrambling up the foreign shores and overwhelming the German opposition could only guess at what fate held in store for them when they set sail across the Channel for France.

The shortest route from Britain would, of course, have been from Dover to Calais, where German and British troops could already spy each other on clear days. For this reason, German defences were tight on that section of the French coast in readiness for an Allied invasion.

Despite the advantage of the brief crossing, the beaches around Calais posed too great a threat to the

## Further west, they found the answer – the long, golden beaches of Normandy

troops. Allied commanders had to look elsewhere. Further west, they found the answer to their conundrum – the long, golden beaches of Normandy. Here the German defences were comparatively thin.

Before 'Operation Overlord' got underway, there were key factors to consider which would help the Allies win the battle – and triumph in the

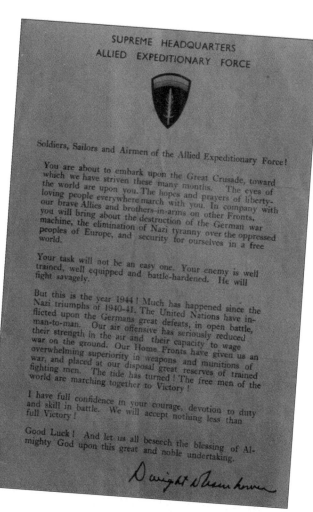

SUPREME HEADQUARTERS ALLIED EXPEDITIONARY FORCE

Soldiers, Sailors and Airmen of the Allied Expeditionary Force!

You are about to embark upon the Great Crusade, toward which we have striven these many months. The eyes of the world are upon you. The hopes and prayers of liberty-loving people everywhere march with you. In company with our brave Allies and brothers-in-arms on other Fronts, you will bring about the destruction of the German war machine, the elimination of Nazi tyranny over the oppressed peoples of Europe, and security for ourselves in a free world.

Your task will not be an easy one. Your enemy is well trained, well equipped and battle-hardened. He will fight savagely.

But this is the year 1944! Much has happened since the Nazi triumphs of 1940-41. The United Nations have inflicted upon the Germans great defeats, in open battle, man-to-man. Our air offensive has seriously reduced their strength in the air and their capacity to wage war on the ground. Our Home Fronts have given us an overwhelming superiority in weapons and munitions of war, and placed at our disposal great reserves of trained fighting men. The tide has turned! The free men of the world are marching together to Victory!

I have full confidence in your courage, devotion to duty and skill in battle. We will accept nothing less than full Victory!

Good Luck! And let us all beseech the blessing of Almighty God upon this great and noble undertaking.

*Dwight D Eisenhower*

war. First was the training of the men involved. Although amphibious landings had already been tried and tested during the war, nothing of the same magnitude had ever been attempted. British, American and Canadian soldiers were posted around Britain for rehearsals.

Coastal resorts like Woolacombe, Gosport, Westward Ho!, Salcombe, Studland Bay and Slapton Sands played host to hundreds of soldiers sent to practise beach landings in an environment similar to that which they would encounter in France.

Slapton became a scene of disaster when live ammunition killed some of the soldiers taking part. Then, on 28 April 1944, mass devastation was wreaked when German E-boats slunk into a convoy in training off the coast, sinking two landing craft and killing 749 soldiers and sailors.

# ◆ 'OPERATION OVERLORD'

During the night of 5/6 June 1944, the armada carrying 21st Army Group – the 'Operation Overlord' strike force – approached the coast of Normandy. The assault was to be concentrated on five beaches: the two in the west (code-named 'Utah' and 'Omaha') were the responsibility of the Americans under Bradley; the three in the east ('Gold', 'Juno' and 'Sword') were the target of the British under Dempsey. The army group was under the overall command of Montgomery. Early in the morning of the 6th, the reconquest of continental Europe began as the first Allied forces hit the beaches and struggled to establish beachheads. German resistance was tough, but the liberation was underway.

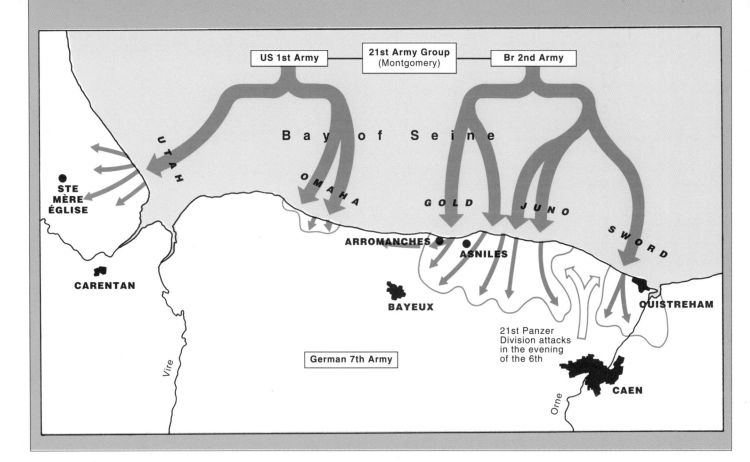

Support for the soldiers and sailors promised to be greater than anything known before. Construction firms all over the United Kingdom set to work on a top secret engineering project, each company manufacturing a different component for a giant concrete jigsaw. Few of the workers involved could guess that they were building massive harbours called 'Mulberries', to be towed across to France for docking purposes by 150 tugs. Now the invading forces didn't have to capture a ready-built harbour, always a costly exercise in terms of human lives. Tanks, trucks, big guns and supplies would roll along the Mulberries with ease.

## ■ PLUTO ■

A pipeline under the ocean (code-named 'Pluto'), made from steel or sometimes steel and lead, was installed to bring essential fuel quickly from Britain to France; it was laid on the sea bed by slow-moving tugs. After the war, it was salvaged to provide plumbing for 50,000 houses.

Reconnaissance was meticulously detailed. Air force pilots flying Spitfires stripped of ammunition to make them as speedy as possible photographed as much of the coastline as they could. In addition, an appeal for holiday photographs and postcards of the region reaped thousands of pictures of the area. Further aided by maps provided by the French Resistance, cartographers began to build up a three-dimensional impression of the targeted Normandy beaches.

Midget submarines went on dangerous nightly missions to the Normandy coast. Their occupants braved the water and the German patrols to bring back soil and sand samples and up-to-date information on the position of German defences.

Last but not least the British authorities embarked on a highly detailed decoy campaign to fool the Germans, who were equally involved in reconnaissance.

Along the Kent coast, some 150 miles from the British heart of 'Overlord', there was an impressive collection of armour and shipping being prepared. Only on close inspection was it revealed that the tanks were rubber and the ships were made from plywood. Lines of tents were empty apart from army cookers puffing smoke through the chimneys to make them appear authentic. The oil depots, planes and jetties that

## Only on close inspection was it revealed that the tanks were rubber

mushroomed in the area were also shams, designed to convince the Germans that the Allied thrust would be launched against Calais.

'Operation Fortitude', as it was code-named, was vital to the success of the invasion. The Allied forces could still be driven back into the sea if the might of the Third Reich descended on them within the first few days of the assault. With a variety of bogus intelligence messages, the commanders behind 'Fortitude' managed to convince the Germans that the invasion in Normandy was only a diversion and that the real attack was coming at Calais. Given that information, the Germans refused to move their forces from Calais, thereby saving the Allies from an onslaught.

## ◆ EYE WITNESS ◆

**William Ryan, of the US 16th Infantry Regiment, was in the first wave to land at Omaha beach. At 18, it was his first action. He went on to serve 30 years in the army and is a veteran of the Korean and Vietnam wars.**

We loaded up the transports at Portland, Weymouth, about 2 June. We were supposed to attack on 5 June. They cancelled it due to weather. We were on the ship all those days.

Everyone was sea-sick. At about 2am on 6 June we loaded on to small 36ft LCVPs, we were 12 miles out. They wanted to surprise the enemy. The seas were six or eight feet high. By now most of the men were so sick they didn't care whether they lived or died. They were too sick to be scared. Even coxswain was sick. I ran the boat for five miles until he started to feel better.

My company was assigned six boats. We lost two boats almost immediately – they were swamped with heavy waves. Heading for the beach the coxswain lost his bearings. When he realised we were off course he had to try again.

The guys from the next sector blew over into our beach – their boats filled the beach so we couldn't get in. We had to circle around like sitting ducks. When we finally started into the beach we lost all four boats with the fire from the German 88s.

I was blown over the side and knocked unconscious. I was told later that two of the men in the boat with me dragged me through the water and propped me up against an embankment. Otherwise I would have drowned.

At first there were five or six wounded with me. Then there were hundreds. I laid on the beach in that same position from about 8am until 10pm when they evacuated us. I had concussion in addition to shell fragments in my head, shoulder and leg. All this time I was going in and out of consciousness, looking down on Omaha beach. It was just a madhouse.

Troops were pinned down by the gun emplacements. Eventually a US Navy destroyer came in as close to the beach as possible without running aground and started firing at all the German emplacements. In a little while two or three other destroyers started shelling as well. In my opinion, that is what saved Omaha beach from defeat.

I heard afterwards the skipper on the ship was ordered to go back to a safe position. Apparently he said he wasn't leaving while US soldiers were pinned down on the beach. He could have been court martialled for what he did. But he should have got a medal.

I didn't have anything to eat all day. In the afternoon a US soldier came over the hill with a couple of bottles of French red wine which he gave to us. You are never going to beat Americans in war. They are crazy.

*Right:* D-Day would not have succeeded had the Allies not had mastery of the skies. A B-26 Marauder returns home after carrying out a bombing mission unchallenged over Normandy.

A double stood in for Monty and made a public departure for Algiers – when the real Montgomery was safely ensconced in 'Overlord' headquarters, which was Southwick House, Portsmouth.

The initial landings were to be made by 156,000 men, mostly Britons, Americans and Canadians. With them was an impressive turnout from occupied Europe. The line-up included an armoured division from France, a Belgian brigade, a Dutch brigade, a Polish division, as well as multi-national seaborne forces. In the skies, the main air forces were joined by squadrons from Norway, Czecho-slovakia, France, Poland, Australia and New Zealand.

More men and equipment were held in reserve for future operations in Europe. It took an armada to ferry the men for the first action across the Channel. By late May, 359 warships, 1,000 minesweepers and associated vessels, 4,000 landing craft, 805

*Above:* A US ship returns to a British port loaded with 'Overlord' casualties, while in France the action continues.

> **Local people became used to the sight of tanks and trucks lining the streets, as major military traffic jams built up**

merchantmen, 59 blockships and 300 other small craft were at the ready.

Overhead, more than 11,000 aircraft were assembled. Some would be towing gliders to be released over France. Each of these carried some 30 troops, tasked with tackling inland enemy positions, including vital landmarks which would halt a German advance, like Pegasus Bridge. The seas and the skies belonged to the Allies. Montgomery had promised his men that the invasion would not go ahead until that umbrella of protection was firmly in place.

Anyone living on the south coast of England could have had no doubt that an invasion was poised to go ahead. Local people became used to the sight of tanks and trucks lining the streets, as major military traffic jams built up on the main roads to Portsmouth. Now there were 1,500,000 American troops alone massed on British shores. Then, one morning, they were gone.

Beginning on 2 June, the hordes of men and machinery bound for Normandy boarded their ships. The weather had been unseasonably poor. High winds and rain had lashed southern Britain, putting the entire operation at risk. It had to be postponed once from 5 June. General Dwight Eisenhower, supreme Allied commander, considered a further postponement in the face of the driving winds and rains which could wreak havoc with a seaborne landing force. The next date in June when the tides and the light were compatible was not for almost another two weeks. Some commanders favoured waiting. Others, like Montgomery, believed the strike should go ahead. It would, after all, be impossible to keep aboard ship those men already embarked. Each soldier and marine had already been interned in a camp for at least three weeks and was primed and ready for action. Any postponement could only have led to a deterioration in their mental and physical fitness. Anyway, the risk of them talking once they got ashore – and giving the game away – was too great.

Eisenhower smoked and read Westerns while he pondered the dilemma. Finally he made his decision. Heartened by predictions of a break in the weather, he signalled the go-ahead for 6 June, with the words 'OK, let's go'.

### ■ IKE SPEAKS ■

Eisenhower, fondly known as 'Ike', gave this message to the departing men of the Allied Expeditionary Force: 'You are about to embark upon the Great Crusade, toward which we have striven these many months. The eyes of the world are upon you. The hopes and prayers of liberty-loving people everywhere march with you. In company with our brave Allies and brothers-in-arms on other Fronts, you will bring about the destruction of the German war machine, the elimination of Nazi tyranny over the oppressed peoples of Europe and security for ourselves in a free world.

'Your task will not be an easy one. Your enemy is well trained, well equipped and battle-hardened. He will fight savagely.

'But this is the year 1944! Much has happened since the Nazi triumphs of 1940-41. The United Nations have inflicted upon the Germans great defeats, in open battle, man-to-man...The tide has turned! The free men of the world are marching together to Victory.'

The only message to reach the expectant public that day was a short, sharp statement, reading: 'Under the command of General Eisenhower, Allied naval forces, supported by strong air forces, began landing Allied armies this morning on the northern coast of France.'

As the soldiers and sailors bobbed in darkness on a choppy sea, they were nervous, tense, euphoric and excitable. Some were sea-sick, some prayed, many fought an overwhelming feeling of doom. Still more found enough spirit to tell jokes. The huge size of the armada involved in 'Operation Neptune', which got them across the Channel, only served to inflate their confidence.

The troops heard the drone of aircraft overhead – a big boost to their morale. Not only were the planes going to bombard enemy positions along the coast in preparation for the landings. Some were carrying paratroopers who, in the first leg of 'Overlord', were being

### ◆ EYE WITNESS ◆

**Henry 'Marty' Martin, from Chicopee, Massachusetts, USA, witnessed the tragedy of 'Operation Tiger' at Slapton Sands while training for D-Day.**

❝ When the German E-boats attacked we just thought it was just part of the exercise. I was right in that exercise and I didn't find out for another 43 years that 749 men had drowned. These guys were wearing their life jackets around their waists when they should have been up around their armpits. With 30-35lb packs on their backs they were just tipped upside down in the water and couldn't right themselves.

I can understand why the government kept it secret at the time because the news would have been a terrible blow to morale. I only question why it took so long for the facts to come out. ❞

*Right:* **Allied soldiers pause to inspect a French memorial to those who died in the carnage of World War I, before continuing with the liberation of western Europe.**

dropped at 2am into east and west flanks of the landings.

When they approached the beach, they saw what appeared to be men walking on water. These were crew members of the midget submarines used to guide in the flotillas of landing craft. Men lashed themselves to the masts of their tiny submarines, which floated low in the water to signal to the captains of much larger vessels.

### ■ H-HOUR, D-DAY ■

Just a few hours later, naval big guns were joining the aircraft in the pounding of enemy positions. Before 6am, the first men were ashore, putting months of rigorous training to the test.

British and Canadian troops were destined for the easterly beaches between Arromanches and Ouistreham. The three beaches earmarked for landings were code-named Gold, Juno and Sword.

In the west, the Americans tackled beaches Utah and Omaha, stretching between Les Dunes de Varreville and Colleville. On each of the beaches there were barbed-wire hazards, anti-tank stumps entrenched in the sand and other menaces. First to come off the boats were the commandos who were to knock out the pill-boxes, and the sappers, charged with clearing a safe path up the beach.

The operation surprised the Germans, who at first believed the landings to be a diversionary tactic. Rommel, in charge of defending the Atlantic Wall, was so unprepared for the Allied arrival that he was in Germany celebrating his wife's 50th birthday when the landings occurred. After Rommel heard of the invasion

at 10.15am, he began a frantic drive back from Germany to his post. 'If I was commanding the Allied forces right now, I could win the war in fourteen days,' he confided to a colleague on his staff.

After the war, Rommel's son Manfred recalled how his father had told Hitler many times that the invasion battle could not be won. Hitler refused to listen. 'All my father could do was to pull the front further and further back and, until he was wounded, carry out his duty.'

When he was told of the early-morning events of 6 June, Hitler ordered his troops to clean up the beachheads before nightfall. He knew the only way to save his extended

## The Führer refused to release two Panzer divisions from the east of France

empire was to throw the Allies back into the sea. But convinced it was a false alarm, the Führer refused to release two Panzer divisions from the east of France to counter the Allied attack until 3.40pm.

Troops on Sword, Juno and Gold made solid progress in spite of

casualties, although many soldiers landed without their guns and ammunition, which were lost in the water. They had to wait in huddles until the beach was taken before resuming their war. Blasting in their ears was the non-stop sound of the naval guns. On Utah beach, the German defences found it impossible to keep the swarms of Americans at bay. It was speedily taken with fewer than 200 lives lost.

### ■ HELL OF OMAHA ■

Unfortunately, on Omaha the poor weather combined with strong currents and fierce resistance to make the landings a hellish nightmare. Here the failure of the air forces to knock out large artillery was keenly felt. There was also the unexpected presence of a German division posted to Normandy on defensive exercises.

More than 2,000 men lost their lives. They were drowned when they were swept away by a changing tide with heavy equipment strapped to their backs. Some died when they trod on mines. Others perished from artillery, machine-gun, mortar and rifle fire from beach pill-boxes and from positions on cliffs above the beach. Wounded men strewn on the beach were in danger of being run over by tanks. There was little shelter and no escape.

George Ross, from Glasgow, was called up in 1939 when he was 19 years old. He recalls how as sergeant major of 101 Company, 5th Beach Group, he landed on Sword beach in the early hours of D-Day.

'We didn't know what we were going to come up against. The crossing was rough. Our craft was led by a chief petty officer. He had been at sea 25 years and never been sea-sick. But he was sick as a dog that morning.

Coming ashore, the first thing we noticed was a camouflaged pill-box. We got underneath the slits and launched a grenade attack. Our job was to establish a route where our tanks could come through. I honestly cannot say I was nervous. I was anxious but I had been warned about what to expect during six months of lectures beforehand.

There were bodies in the water of both British and Germans. One of the officers told us afterwards how, when he was walking up the beach, he felt he was walking on cushions. It was bodies of dead soldiers he was walking on.'

Lieutenant-General Omar Bradley considered a withdrawal. It would have been disastrous for the invasion, offering an opening for the Germans to attack both British and American flanks. Yet hardy US Rangers finally scaled the coastal heights to tackle the problem guns and alleviate the problems on the beach.

### ■ LONGEST DAY ■

Some of the men on the beaches were battle-hardened veterans. There was, however, a large contingent of raw soldiers, particularly among the Americans. They were pitched into the most intense, violent battleground, and forced to pick their way among the dead and dying amid the roar of big guns overhead and the sensation of small-arms fire whizzing past their ears. The air was filled with the pungent smell of flesh, blood and cordite.

Particularly on Omaha but also true of the other beaches, the first wave of men forced to fight their way ashore were cut down. Preparing to take to the beaches, the second wave witnessed the carnage then ran past the bodies of their comrades, hoping they didn't meet the same miserable fate.

Alongside panic there was determination – each flash of cowardice displayed by frightened, confused men was matched ten times by instances of heroism and stoicism. Minor troubles and petty differences lay forgotten. Each man was focused only on surviving for the next minute, the next hour and into the following day.

Ahead of them lay the task of capturing German-held towns, some of which fell more quickly than others. Russians who had been forced into German uniforms after being captured on the Eastern front were eager to lay down their arms. French

*Below:* **A Sherman tank, affectionately nicknamed 'Betty', goes ashore to fight the battle of Normandy.**

people rushed out to greet the liberating Allies, offering drinks, flowers and greetings. A few French residents near the beaches braved the conflict to aid the wounded and dying.

Tales of outstanding courage filled the newspapers for months and years afterwards. One commando corporal led his men up the beach past enemy pill-boxes, bellowing encouragement. He fell only when he had passed the pill-boxes – he had received more than 50 wounds.

The defending Germans were mostly in chaos. One senior commander reported in panic that American gliders were landing Volkswagen cars in Normandy which were driven by American troops in German uniforms. Arguably, the day was as much lost by the confusion and indecision that paralysed many Germans as won by the heroic efforts of the Allied troops.

By the end of 'the longest day', 10,000 Allied soldiers had fallen. The figure was a third of that estimated by Allied command. But there was no turning back. The Allies had achieved the Normandy landings. Nothing and nobody was going to force them out of France again.

# TANKS COME OF AGE

The tank came of age during World War II and proved to be a battle winner – or loser. The first tanks had been designed by Sir Ernest Swinton and saw action in the Somme offensive of World War I in 1916. Caterpillar tracks enabled them to cross treacherous terrain where no other vehicle could go. They were equipped with one or more guns, the crew sitting behind armour plating and firing off salvos at the enemy.

Now German general Heinz Guderian used the outbreak of World War II to put his own theories about the use of tanks to the test. Tanks should not be pinned down to flanking foot soldiers, he argued. Their purpose was to break out against the enemy, putting a speed into land-based warfare which it had never known before.

With that in mind, he formed his highly efficient Panzer divisions. The tanks were fast but lacked adequate protective armour. Nevertheless, they were an integral part of 'Blitzkrieg', the lightning war, a tactic with which Hitler easily won Poland, France, Holland and Belgium.

The technique took Britain and France by surprise. Although France had an enormous number of tanks at its disposal, 2,475 to be exact, their effectiveness was muted because of the old-fashioned way in which they were deployed. Instead of combining the firepower as Guderian did, each tank was evenly spaced down a long defensive line. In time Allied

## When a tank 'brewed up', the escape hatches were wholly inadequate, or blocked

commanders mimicked Guderian to get the best out of their tanks. Used individually, they were easy targets.

If tankmen in World War I were better protected than their colleagues in the infantry, the same could not be said of their counterparts 20 years on. In fact, there were few infantrymen who would willingly change places with tankmen. For while tanks

stole a march on the enemy in the the killing fields of Flanders, technology had now caught up. Now there was a wide range of anti-armour artillery designed to knock tanks out. Men inside a stricken tank had little or no chance of escape.

And for the first three years of the war, German tanks and anti-tank weapons were appreciably better than their British counterparts. For example, the Mark II Matilda was known for its weak steering clutches, the Valentine offered only limited vision to its commander, the Crusader was mechanically unreliable. It took only an armour-piercing shell from one of the new breed of anti-tank guns used by the Germans to finish them.

That's when infantrymen remained heartily glad they had the job they did. For when a tank caught fire, or 'brewed up', the tiny escape hatches on the tanks were wholly inadequate and, in any case, were often blocked. Sometimes there was a matter of seconds before fire took a hold and

*Above:* **Tank crews during World War I were rightly delighted with the new hardware, which provided them with ample protection. But in World War II, a variety of anti-armour weapons existed to make life hell for the tankman.**
*Far left:* **The men of an armoured division running through the smoke-filled streets of the German town of Wernberg.**

the tank's ammunition began to explode. Sometimes there was not. Nicknames for tanks during the war included 'steel coffins', 'tommy cookers' and 'Ronson burners', because, like the products of the same name, they would always 'light first time'.

### ■ BLACKENED DOLLS ■

One witness gruesomely detailed the effects on the men trapped inside: 'Little blackened dolls about two feet high have been found in tanks. Once these were men.'

As the war progressed, the Germans learned about the shortcomings of their tanks, which were

*Left:* Matilda tanks were favoured by the British military but they failed to match the firepower of German Tigers, pictured below.

A later generation of Allied tanks, including Shermans and Churchills, began to overcome some – but not all – of the difficulties. Yet no design, no matter how superior, could compensate for the problems thrown up by the terrain the tanks were working in. Every theatre of war offered its pitfalls to tanks. In Europe the rain

lacking in firepower and suffered from flimsy armour. Their most painful lesson came on the Eastern front when their troops encountered the fearsome T-34 tanks of the Russian armoured divisions.

Accordingly they introduced the Panther, in July 1943, and the Tiger, in September 1942, which were battle winners thanks to the enormous range of their guns, quite outstripping the British models, which were unable to get close enough to counter-attack effectively.

### ■ THE DEADLY 88 ■

By the time the British developed the six-pounder gun, the Germans had in their armoury the heavier 75mm weapon. As the Americans caught up, with their own 75mm gun, the Germans leaped ahead again, fitting the deadly 88mm guns, which were originally designed as anti-aircraft guns but wreaked havoc when mounted on the Tiger tank.

As an illustration of the immense advantage kept in hand by the Germans in terms of tank technology, a single Tiger tank operating in Normandy knocked out 25 British tanks, 28 armoured vehicles and killed an additional 80 infantrymen.

It seemed as if the British had learned nothing from their experiences in the desert a full two years earlier. The poor state of British and American

## *The poor state of Allied tank technology was little short of a scandal*

tank technology was little short of a scandal. It left Allied tank crews disheartened and reluctant, a malaise which never affected the Germans.

made the earth unacceptably boggy; in North Africa the desert dust clogged engines and sharp stones tore the tracks; in Asia, where there were few tanks, the humidity affected the engineering. In nine days of fighting in Germany in 1945 the 9th Royal Tank Regiment and the 147th Regiment suffered 85 tank casualties – and only 17 were due to enemy action. No less than 36 succumbed to mechanical problems while 32 got stuck in the mud. Nevertheless, while tanks did much to speed the progress of Germans into France, they also helped to chase those same invaders out of France. This time the innovators were the British. A series of modified tanks were used to breach the beaches at Normandy. Witnesses reported that some German soldiers threw down their guns and ran at the sight of this bizarre new breed.

Behind them was Major-General Sir Percival Hobart. Like his brother-

> A series of modified tanks were used to breach the beaches at Normandy

in-law Montgomery, Hobart was outspoken and did not suffer fools gladly. His forthright manner won him few friends at the War Office and by 1940 he was retired. It was only the personal intervention of Churchill which installed Hobart back in the fight against Hitler.

### ■ HOBART'S FUNNIES ■

Mindful that Allied troops would encounter all manner of defences during the landings, his priority was to install tough armour to protect the troops. Then he looked at ways of tackling an amphibious landing, crossing a minefield, blasting a well-fortified pill-box and travelling with heavy vehicles across boggy ground.

To get hefty tanks ashore from landing craft, he came up with the Duplex Drive, an amphibious tank with propellers and a canvas skirt to protect it from the water. When the tank made it to the shore, the canvas was lowered.

An adaptation of the Churchill tank helped to combat the threat of minefields. On the front he installed a large rotating drum hung with heavyweight chains, turned by power from the engines. This 'Crab' would

# ROMMEL – DESERT FOX

**Erwin Rommel, courageous soldier and gifted leader of men, became known as the Desert Fox thanks to his cunning in North Africa.**

The son of a teacher, Rommel joined the army from his home town of Württemberg as an officer cadet and proved his early promise during World War I. Between the wars he taught at Germany's military academies and authored a book about infantry strategies which was published in 1937.

When war broke out, Colonel Rommel was put in charge of the troops guarding Hitler. Frustrated with his behind-the-lines role, he seized the opportunity early in 1940 to command the 7th Panzer Division which he took into action in France before it was occupied, striking as far north as the Channel coast.

A year later he was put in charge of the German troops sent by Hitler to bail out the beleaguered Italians in North Africa. He shone in his new role, despite his misgivings about his wavering Italian allies. His impressive early victories won him the rank of field-marshal.

He was held in high esteem by his men for his initiative and bravery. In an example of his charismatic leadership, he once leapt from a car to address a division of men: 'There is an English Armoured Brigade getting ready to attack you from the north and in the south there is an English mixed force which is advancing. Take care that you are finished with the first before the second arrives!'

Yet he was all but ready to pull out his exhausted men when Hitler ordered a strike on Cairo in Egypt. Once again, he found remarkable success until his supply lines became hopelessly overstretched as he ventured further into British-held territory. Weakened by lack of essentials and wearied by months of fighting, he was finally defeated and pursued out of Africa.

In 1944 Rommel was ordered by Hitler to secure the French coastline against Allied invasion. Even though he was already convinced the war was unwinnable, he tackled the unenviable task with a deep professional pride. Yet he received little practical support from the Führer despite his warnings that all would be lost if the enemy penetrated the insubstantial coastal defences.

Although at heart he was non-political, Rommel was recruited by plotters who wanted Hitler replaced. The popular and realistic Rommel was their chosen leader. It is unlikely, however, that he knew about plans to assassinate the Führer for he was deeply opposed to killing for political ends.

In any event, an attack by British bombers put Rommel in hospital with serious injuries when the abortive coup took place. Hitler himself was reluctant to expose Rommel as part of the plot against him. He knew only too well that he was vulnerable to the grass-roots affection won by Rommel. So he dispatched two generals to see his reluctant adversary to offer a deal. Rommel and his family would escape the shame of public exposure if he would take poison and eliminate himself as a threat to Hitler. On 14 October 1944 Rommel did as his leader asked and was buried with full military honours.

*Right:* **Rommel (left) confers with a subordinate during the desert campaign.**

explode the hidden mines without causing damage to the tank or its crew and could beat a path up a beach for soldiers to follow.

Another anti-mine device was the 'Plough', a harrow attached to a tank which would uproot mines before

## When SS troops captured the crew of a Crocodile, they would shoot them

they could do any damage. The 'Ark', a tank with four long beams at each corner, became a bridge to span small ravines and enable troops and armoured cars to cross.

Providing a roadway for troops and vehicles through soft ground became the job of the 'Bobbin' tank. It had a large, rolled, heavy-duty canvas roadway attached to its front. As the tank trundled along, it unfurled the roadway for following traffic. But

perhaps the most fearsome of his designs was the 'Crocodile', another modified Churchill tank, this time designed to throw a scorching flame for 120 yards. Attached behind was its own fuel depot on wheels. Its effect on the enemy was instant. So feared was this flame-thrower that when SS troops captured the crew of a Crocodile, they would shoot them straightaway. Inappropriately, the stable of inventions was called 'Hobart's Funnies' – although they offered little to the enemy to smile about.

### ■ RIFLES AND GUNS ■

These were not the only technological advances that assisted the Allies. In just four years, the advances in gun capabilities had been enormous. When the war started, the Allied stock of rifles dated mostly from the previous world war or before. Bolt-action guns like this were slow and cumbersome to carry and use.

Now rifles were smaller and lighter than ever before and fired faster too. Rates of fire were up in

machine guns as well. The British Bren could now dispense an astonishing 500 rounds a minute, the same as the US Browning. New mortars were light enough for infantrymen to carry with them into battle.

But just as these assisted the battle in one respect, they were a hindrance in another. The pack of equipment loaded onto the back of the infantryman was heavier than ever. Soldiers had to rely on good, old-fashioned mules in some cases to transport the guns to the top of high, hostile escarpments in rugged terrain.

Even then the pre-prepared defences installed by the enemy were strong enough to resist the firepower of such weapons. Only bombs would have a sufficiently devastating effect and that called for air support.

*Left:* Versatile Jeeps were put through their paces in Normandy during the autumn of 1944. Medics even used these rugged, four-wheel-drive vehicles to transport the wounded.

*Left:* Allied soldiers in Burma used newer, more powerful weapons to get the better of their enemy.

advantage over their Japanese enemy through the regular supplies dropped in by aircraft. In Europe and Africa, improving methods of amphibious landings allowed the trucks which were being turned out by the thousand in America to reach the battle fronts and replenish the men.

### ■ WILLYS JEEP ■

Transport had to be reliable and tough to be of any use. In 1940, the Jeep made its debut, its name derived from the full name first given it – general purpose (i.e. 'GP') vehicle. First constructed by the Willys Overland Company, this legendary creation had speed and agility and was an instant hit with the army. It could tackle even the roughest terrain and was useful for transporting troops, small arms and other light loads. It further helped to make horses redundant on the battlefield.

Given the firepower, the men made use of it, expending thousands of rounds of ammunition a day. The prospect of ammunition shortage, not to mention shortage of fuel for tanks and food for men, was a daunting one. As all armies discovered during World War II, a fighting force was only as good as its supply line.

In Burma the Chindits had an

---

## ◆ EYE WITNESS ◆

**Sydney Hartley suffered a badly injured leg when he was in the third of three tanks sent forward to pinpoint the whereabouts of the enemy during a battle in the Tunisian campaign. It was later amputated just above the knee. He was 28 years old.**

❝ I knew the dangers of crossing open ground on enemy territory but I clearly remember thinking that, with a bit of luck, we might again just get out of this unscathed with us being the last tank in a line of three.

After about 150 yards I heard the voice of the squadron leader come through my headphones. "Third troop, halt. Turn right and engage the enemy tanks." As we turned we realised we had run into a trap. Just coming into their final positions were two German tanks or self-propelled guns. We were all taken by surprise.

I knew this was the moment of truth, life or death. I quickly estimated the range, our big 75mm gun was loaded, I put the sights on the target and fired. It was impossible to follow the tracer bullet because the sun was lying just behind the target. Then it didn't matter as I saw the German tank's gun flash and a split second afterwards our world exploded. Everything suddenly went black and I felt what seemed like a red-hot poker against my right leg.

Flames were rising and I knew I had to get out quickly. I tried to

pull myself out of the turret but at waist high I realised something was holding me back, because I was still wearing my headphones. Then I made a superhuman effort and flung myself the eight-foot drop to the ground. I knew something was terribly wrong with me. I heard this soul-destroying scream – it could have been any one of us. I dragged myself away. Looking at my right leg, the shock was more mental than physical. The armour-piercing shot had taken away half of my calf and broken up the calf bone. The foot was dangling from what flesh remained.

I took out a large field-dressing from my pocket and made a tourniquet. It looked like the driver and co-driver hadn't made it out of the tank. The next tank in line was burning although the crew got out safely. Mortar bombs were dropping all around. The troop corporal carried me to the rest of the men which was excruciatingly painful. I had morphine tablets but felt faint from blood loss. I didn't know which was most painful, my leg or the burns on my hands and face. The top skin of my hands peeled back like roller blinds. I had a very bumpy ride on a Bren-gun carrier back to the echelon alongside an injured German soldier and his friend.

I was laid out on a stretcher, looking up at the sky, when I saw a Messerschmitt 109 come into view. It appeared to be heading straight for me. He started machine-gunning us. It was the first of three aircraft attacks before I was put in the ambulance and driven away. ❞

# THE PACIFIC

Sweeping Japanese gains left the Allies with their work cut out, yet there was a grim resolve among them to push the invaders back. The rocky road to triumph over the extended empire of the Rising Sun began in New Guinea.

Japanese plans to take the unoccupied sector of New Guinea with a seaborne invasion were dashed following the Battle of the Coral Sea in May 1942. But they had not given up hope of seizing the island. Another offensive was planned, this time overland.

On 21 July 1942 an advance party of 2,000 Japanese soldiers landed at Buna, Papua, without a shot being fired. Their aim was to take Port Moresby, still in Allied hands. Ahead of them was a choice of two jungle tracks across the 1,200ft Owen Stanley mountains – hostile and steamy terrain. They chose the most accessible or least impassable.

Defensive forces on New Guinea at the time comprised some scattered Australian brigades backed up by a limited number of indigenous New Guinea riflemen.

The Japanese forces seized the interior in little more than a week, scaling the rocky heights of the mountain range. Racing against time, the Australians rushed through reinforcements. By 12 August Lieutenant-General F. Rowell, in command at Port Moresby, decided he had enough troops at his disposal to send an expedition into the mountains.

### ■ PORT MORESBY ■

Another Japanese force, numbering about 11,500, was landed, enabling a significant thrust to take place against the Australians. The prospects looked bleak for the Allies as the Australians fell back and back. The Australian commandos were swallowed up in the Japanese advances.

But by now the Japanese were encountering some difficulties of

their own. Allied aircraft were making a fine job of disrupting the already treacherous lines of supply. It meant soldiers fighting in the most torrid conditions were left without adequate food and medical supplies.

In addition, the spectre of dysentry and other debilitating diseases loomed. Troops were weakened and finally killed by highly infectious

## *Troops were weakened by highly infectious wasting diseases in jungle conditions*

wasting diseases which medics were unable to counter in jungle conditions. By September their advance had run out of steam. They were brought to a halt just 32 miles from Port Moresby.

The Australians had little time to even draw breath. More Japanese troops had landed at Milne Bay, to the east, with orders to occupy the all-important airfield there. About 2,000 Japanese soldiers fought

*Above:* Japanese marines begin their march on New Guinea, confident of yet another victory.
*Left:* One of the Emperor's vessels lies wrecked off Guadalcanal, which became a graveyard for ships.

fiercely to reach the edge of the airstrip. Then the tide of battle turned against them. The Japanese had thought the Australian presence there was depleted. In fact there were nearly two brigades of men, two fighter squadrons and plenty of established artillery.

In a counter-attack at the end of August by the 18th Australian Brigade, the Japanese were chased back to the sea. Finally, on 6 September, the remnants of the landing force were withdrawn.

Now the focus was back on the Japanese holed up in the mountain range. Australian troops reinforced by Americans forged up the Kokoda trail, the same route the invading Japanese had followed but in the opposite direction. A parallel force hoping to outflank the enemy embarked up the Kapa Kapa trail, even more remote and difficult.

Ahead of them lay the Japanese, securely dug into three defensive positions at the peak of the Kokoda trail. On 16 October the first Japanese post was taken by an Australian brigade. Yet the supreme effort in the face of determined opposition sapped what little strength the Australian soldiers had left.

Without the help of their Melanesian porters, who carried their equipment and sometimes the men themselves, they would not have got as far as they did. Try as they might, they could not budge the invaders from the other two dug-outs. Casualties mounted from sniper fire, with the Japanese apparently secure in their fox-holes.

The Australians were equally vulnerable to disease. The main cause of dysentry in New Guinea was polluted water. Springs were fouled by natives and the fighting men themselves, who were often too far away from their latrines to use them.

## ■ JAPANESE ROUT ■

It took fresh troops, who relieved the exhausted Australians, to add impetus to the assault. After intense fighting in swampy insect-ridden undergrowth the Japanese were finally routed. All the while, the Australian and American troops were benefiting from supplies dropped by air in the jungle. While some consignments went astray, the Allies were undoubtedly better off than their Japanese counterparts, who were still reliant on supplies coming in by sea and being passed up country. Australian troops found the bodies of their foe were emaciated and diseased. There were even signs of cannibalism as no doubt starving soldiers had resorted to eating human flesh to stay alive.

Every mile of the jungle between the heights of the mountains and the coastal plains was bitterly contested by the two sides. The stop-start campaign was at its most deadly when the Japanese were cornered in well-built defences, with their backs to the sea. Both prongs of the Allied forces joined up but there was stalemate as the Japanese sat tight in their well-dug positions.

Even the arrival of new Allied troops to wage the battle brought piecemeal results. For every fighting soldier, the conditions were nothing short of appalling. Climate and disease combined to make life barely tolerable. Allied troops were forced to pick off Japanese men and guns one by one as

---

## ◆ EYE WITNESS ◆

**Bob Cartwright, from Wimbledon, south west London, was a lance corporal in the Royal Army Medical Corps who saw action in North Africa before being posted to the Far East. He served as a Chindit in the 44th Recce Regiment on the force's second foray.**

'There were 400 men in every column. The men from the medical corps like me travelled either at the front or the back. Conditions were ruddy awful.

The recce men had to tackle unmapped mountains with gradients of one in one. They were so steep that men had to crawl on their hands and knees. Even the mules fell by the wayside. They plunged down ravines and couldn't get out.

On my back was a 60lb first aid bag. For six weeks we were living on bully beef and biscuits and on any rice we could scrounge from local Burmese people, which wasn't much. Then US 'K' rations were air-dropped to us. In one of the daily meals there was usually a bar of chocolate. We used to melt it on to the rice to make a pudding.

We were on our way to Kohima to relieve the siege there when we were ambushed in a teak forest. The leaves of teak trees are very big and crisp. We had to wait until it rained before we could get out without the Japanese hearing our every footstep.

We had to take malaria and salt tablets. If you weren't wet from perspiration you were wet with the rain. Men suffered from malaria, tick bites and ulcers. I don't know anyone who didn't lose weight.

Everyone thought the world of Orde Wingate, the man behind the Chindits, even though he wasn't liked by the big shots in India. All they did was criticise him.

He had eyes that looked right through you and a really magnetic personality. I met him on two occasions. He inspired the troops.

We marched 600 miles through the jungle. I was out there about six months before they flew us out.

The men were in excellent spirits. I don't think I heard anybody moan about what we were doing. It was only the weather that bothered us.

There must be many unmarked and unknown graves in Burma.'

---

*Right:* US soldiers take a well-deserved rest after action on New Guinea.
*Below:* Behind a screen of palms, the tanks of the US Marines rumble towards the Japanese front lines on Guadalcanal.

the doomed and diminishing force refused to capitulate. It wasn't until 3 January 1943 that the last of the Japanese resistance was ended. It had taken six months and cost an estimated 5,700 Australian, 2,800 American and 12,000 Japanese casualties.

As Australians and Americans fought to free Papua New Guinea, so US Marines were battling to liberate Guadalcanal, an island in the Solomons crucial in importance because of its airfield, Henderson Field. The conditions were equally squalid. Frequent rain squalls in the sauna heat made it a perfect breeding ground for mosquitoes. Malaria was rife among soldiers already weakened by the humidity. Nevertheless, both sides were doggedly determined that Guadalcanal should be theirs. Documents from Japan's high command captured later revealed the immense importance they attached to the island. 'Success or failure in recapturing Guadalcanal is the fork in the road which leads to victory for them or us.'

### ■ GUADALCANAL ■

On 7 August 1942 11,000 Marines were landed on Guadalcanal, surprisingly, without opposition. It would take a long time before Japan's soldiers on the island were eradicated, however. Japanese forces on neighbouring islands gave a more rousing reception to landing parties. On Tulagi, there was a hectic battle. At the end of it, the Marines were victorious. Tulagi was theirs. In total 108 US Marines had died while the Japanese force of an estimated 1,500 was wiped out.

## Frequent rain squalls in the sauna heat made it a perfect breeding ground for mosquitoes

Like the Australians and the British, the American forces fighting the Japanese in the Pacific discovered that jungle warfare was a battle of nerves. The vegetation was host to scores of unusual animals making weird and terrifying noises. Sounds of birds, lizards and insects echoed through the night, each one sounding like an approaching sniper. And sometimes it was indeed the enemy, creeping stealthily in the dark before moving in for a kill. It was vital for guns to remain quiet unless there was an attack, since a burst of fire pinpointed a soldier's position for the enemy.

The Japanese, throughout the Pacific and South East Asia, displayed a mastery of cunning jungle warfare tactics. They knew a grenade thrown from somewhere in the night would result in havoc in an Allied camp. Startled and confused, the Allied soldiers would fire wildly and draw their knives, often injuring their comrades in the subsequent chaos. Meanwhile, the Japanese melted back into the darkness.

There were reports of Japanese soldiers leaping suddenly into Allied foxholes brandishing knives – then equally quickly jumping out again.

*Below:* **A tense moment as US soldiers, with guns at the ready, probe a jungle hideout in search of Japanese snipers.**

The Allied soldiers were left tussling among themselves in panic with weapons drawn.

In the darkness, a voice might sound: 'Please, Johnny, help me.' It was tempting for the soldiers to rise up and respond to a call for help. If

## The Japanese displayed a mastery of cunning jungle warfare tactics

they did so, it would spell their doom. Here was yet another technique used by the Japanese to get the enemy to reveal itself.

The US occupation of Guadalcanal sparked some vital sea battles. But the first land-based reprisals from the Japanese came on 18 August when 1,000 Japanese troops were landed

on Guadalcanal. All were killed and their commander Colonel Ichiki committed suicide.

Aircraft from the US carriers patrolling in the region deterred further large-scale landings although there were numerous small-scale attacks mounted by Japanese units, all successfully repulsed. Japanese commanders had grossly underestimated the number of American troops stationed on Guadalcanal. The American garrison, now numbering 19,000, was able to prevent wholesale Japanese landings with naval and air support even though the empire gathered 20,000 men from around the region for an October offensive.

The Americans were, however, handicapped by the frequent attacks on Henderson Field made by battleships and aircraft, as well as by the nuisance raids led by the Japanese who had successfully landed on

Guadalcanal. It wasn't until the three-day Battle of Guadalcanal at sea that the hard-pressed American defenders enjoyed some respite.

It was then that the Japanese navy decided to pull back from Guadalcanal and defend a different line. Senior navy commanders recognised the increasing strength of the Americans reduced the chances of taking Guadalcanal to virtually nil.

### ■ CHINDITS ■

The army was keen to continue the campaign, confident that the 30,000 troops it now had on the island would eventually overcome. But, without naval co-operation, there was no way of transporting further reinforcements to the island, or supplies to its troops.

Here was a chance at last for the Marines to withdraw for some recuperation after four months of jungle warfare. Their replacements finally totalled about 50,000 men, fit enough to drive the remaining Japanese forces from the island with relative ease. By February 1943, all had been evacuated by sea.

In Burma, the Japanese were still holding their own, having chased the British and Australian forces back to India. Yet the British were not left

playing with an empty hand. They had one card left, which may not have been a winner but certainly kept them in the game. This was the first ever deployment of Long Range Penetration Groups, later known as the Chindits.

Behind the Chindits was Orde Wingate, an unorthodox soldier with broad experience of organising guerrilla operations. His men from the 77th Indian Brigade derived their name from the mythical Burmese temple guardian, the chinthe, half lion and half eagle.

Earlier in the war, Wingate had attempted suicide by stabbing himself

*Above:* B-25 Mitchell medium bombers of the US 5th Air Force deliver destruction to a Japanese airstrip on New Guinea in March 1944.

in the neck while suffering from malaria and depression. He was saved and a year later brought his charismatic brand of leadership to an enthusiastic bunch of men.

### ■ INTO BURMA ■

Their aim was to operate behind enemy lines, causing disruption and damage wherever possible. That meant they had to be skilled jungle fighters with the qualities of the chameleon, able to fade away into the thickly forested landscape as quickly as possible. Those in demand for the first Chindit expedition in February 1943 were men who were masters of demolition skills and also able radio operators. The radio operators were vital to the success of the mission as they were responsible for contacting base and requesting supplies. These were dropped by air, giving the Chindits an essential advantage of endurance.

Together with elephants, mules and buffaloes, two groups compris-

---

## ◆ EYE WITNESS ◆

**Bill Jenkins joined the Australian armed forces in 1939 when he was 18 years old and served until 1945, seeing action on the infamous Kokoda trail in New Guinea.**

❝ We had just come back from the Middle East. I had three days' leave after two and a half years at war when I was recalled and put on a boat headed for New Guinea. Things were getting pretty desperate. The Japanese were in rowing distance of Australia itself. The pitifully small forces there to meet them were militiamen or home guard members who were decimated. We joined them and gradually drove the Japanese back over the Owen Stanley range of mountains. Sickness was terrible, with scrub typhoid, malaria and malnutrition claiming many lives. It was difficult for the planes to spot us and drop supplies. My brigade began with about 2,500 men. Less than 200 were evacuated at the close of the campaign. I returned weighing less than seven stones instead of 12 stones. ❞

ing 3,200 men set off into occupied Burma, each ready to sub-divide into columns to achieve its aim. So well supplied were the men in the beginning that they even carried spare pairs of false teeth – as a man who could not eat, could not fight. They set off with the poetic words of Orde Wingate ringing in their ears:

## ■ WINGATE'S WORDS ■

'It is always a minority that occupies the front line. It is a still smaller minority that accepts with a good heart tasks like this that we have chosen to carry out. We need not, therefore, as we go forward into conflict, suspect ourselves of selfish or interested motives. We have all had the opportunity of withdrawing and we are here because we have chosen to be here; that is, we have chosen to bear the burden and heat of the day. Men who make this choice are above the average in courage. We need therefore have no fear for the staunchness and guts of our comrades.

'Our motive may be taken to be the desire to serve our day and gener-

# ◆ EYE WITNESS ◆

**Alf Turner was a member of the 6th Battalion, The Devonshire Regiment, when he was posted to the Far East in 1943.**

Our sergeant major told us it was the best draft of all and that we wouldn't do anything for six months. That was a load of tripe.

After arriving at a reinforcement camp we were sent up to Bhopal to do a month's jungle training. Then we set off for Burma.

All you can see around you in the jungle are trees. If somebody fires, you don't know which way it is coming from. Being a country boy, I found it a bit easier than the Londoners out there who weren't used to night-time noises and wildlife.

The Japanese soldiers would shout out in the night: "Tommy, where are you?" And they would beat bamboo sticks to unnerve us. They tried to get us to give away our positions.

After one attack an apparently wounded Japanese soldier was calling: "Tommy, help me, help me." One of our officers who couldn't stick it any more went out to him. We told him not to go. When he got near, the soldier jumped up and threw a grenade at him. The officer lost his leg.

The Japanese put grenades under dead bodies in the hope you would turn them over.

Near the Irrawaddy river we came across a village where all the men had been beheaded by the Japanese and all the women were hung up by their hands and disembowelled. They were cruel fighters.

We took very few prisoners. Those who were wounded would rip their bandages off after being treated. They wanted to die in battle.

We belonged to the 20th Indian Division and I was a technical sergeant in charge of transport. I had to use sticky tape to repair tyres. We came across some Japanese supplies and used those to keep the trucks going.

There were giant ant hills. In the monsoon season they would collapse and you could find yourself knee deep in earth with ants crawling all over your legs. Then there were the leeches. The only way to get them off was with a lighted cigarette butt. We also had snakes slithering over our legs, jungle sores and prickly heat.

In France and Germany the troops had fleets of invasion craft. When they liberated towns, the people came out to cheer them. In Burma we had a few 'ducks' but mostly we had to make our own rafts to see us across the rivers. And we were never welcomed by the people. They didn't seem to care if it was us or the Japanese.

*Left:* **British troops of the 14th Army advance cautiously on the mud huts in the newly taken prize of Meiktila in Burma, March 1945.**

ation in the way that seems nearest to our hand. The battle is not always to the strong nor the race to the swift. Victory in war cannot be counted upon but what can be counted upon is that we shall go forward determined to do what we can to bring this war to the end which we believe best for our friends and comrades in arms, without boastfulness or forgetting our duty, resolved to do the right so far as we can see the right.'

Wingate's bold and unexpected plan took the Japanese by surprise. When the forces crossing the main

Irrawaddy and Chindwin rivers were spotted, commanders believed these were small groups on reconnaissance who would be easily dispatched. Only when major railway bridges were blown up did the Japanese suspect an orchestrated attack against them. At that stage, two

tion began to fall apart. When food ran short, they ate their mules. But then they had no transport.

### ■ BAREFOOT TO INDIA

Four months later, some 2,200 men returned to India, hungry, physically frail and many with bare feet, veter-

ans of a remarkable physical trial and fully conversant with both jungle and guerrilla tactics. True, they had proved little more than a mild hindrance to the Japanese. Yet important principles of warfare had been tried and tested by them, including that of air-dropping supplies. The

divisions were sent to flush the British out of the jungle.

By now, the Chindits were dispersed into smaller, isolated groups, some faring better than others. That the Japanese were now aware of their presence made life increasingly difficult for the jungle warriors, who became trapped in the dense vegetation while their enemies had the run of the roads and tracks. Inevitably, the tightly planned opera-

*Above:* Gurkha troops march past giant statues of chinthe – after which the Chindits were named – having liberated a key Burmese city.

## That the Japanese were now aware of their presence made life increasingly difficult

soldiers rarely visited local villages for food and drink, where they might have been captured.

The Chindits were a difficult enemy for the Japanese to pin down, moving as they did under cover of darkness. So concerned were the Japanese army by the exploits of the Chindits that they revised their defensive policies in upper Burma, which not only tied up forces but ultimately laid them open to defeat.

# REICH IN RUINS

By the end of 1943, the Germans were on the run from Stalin's forces. The Battle of the Atlantic had ended in their defeat and U-boats were being systematically blown out of the water. Germany itself was suffering a barrage of bombing campaigns, Italy had changed sides and, to many in the Nazi hierarchy, it seemed the war was already lost.

The following year brought little by way of relief. The long-awaited landings of thousands of Allied soldiers finally occurred in Normandy in June. When German soldiers were unable to defend the beaches, it was clear the destination for the Allies was nothing short of the German Fatherland itself.

During their first few weeks on French soil, the Allied armies encountered some strong resistance, particularly centred at Caen. Here was a professional SS division and a green German unit culled from the Hitler youth. Although some fighters were as young as 16, they were fired with enthusiasm and proved to be formidable opponents.

The British forces failed to capitalise on their surprise attack to gain their D-Day objectives and paid the penalty for their short delay while regrouping, as the Germans dug in with a vengeance. It took two major pushes, code-named 'Epsom' and 'Goodwood', to oust the few

hundred Germans in residence, costing hundreds of Allied lives.

Countless numbers of French civilians died, mostly in the enormous air raids launched by the Allies which reduced the historic town of Caen to rubble. Fires raged in Caen for 11 days after the main bombing attack. Estimates put the number of French dead as high as 10,000. Still the German resistance held fast. The net effect of the air raids was simply to provide new hazards, like blocked roads, for the Allied ground forces.

### ■ TANK BATTLES ■

There were bitter tank battles between the newly landed British and Canadian forces and the Panzer units which rushed to the area from eastern France and Poland. Supplies began to falter when a gale blew up in the Channel on 19 June, wrecking the Mulberry harbours, onto which the Allies were unloading.

Churchill and the American leaders were filled with angry frustration. There was talk of sacking Montgomery for his failure to move forward. But while German reserves

were embroiled in the battle, other Allied divisions were given a free hand elsewhere on the coast.

The Americans were making more headway. Having captured the Cherbourg peninsula, troops broke out to make a sweep through central Normandy. US troops discovered too the horrors of fighting in the Normandy bocages. This was the ancient hedgerow and field system covering the countryside providing havens for German snipers and hazards for Allied tanks and infantrymen.

## *Churchill and the American leaders were filled with angry frustration*

The German reinforcements, which had at last made their way to Normandy, created more firmly held pockets of resistance, which were tough to shift. Falaise, Metz and a number of other towns formed serious blockages in the arteries of the Allied invasion.

Soldiers who on D-Day had never fired a shot in anger or seen a dead body were within a matter of weeks brutalised by the harshness of conflict. If they were fearful, they hid their feelings. Many were overwhelmed with elation when they killed an enemy soldier. As one US Ranger explained: 'It was not joy that I had killed him but that he hadn't killed me.'

**Far left:** French inhabitants and US soldiers rejoice after Cherbourg is won from the Germans.
**Left:** German soldiers surrender to the US military near Toulon, in southern France, following the invasion of the south of the country in August 1944.

By 15 August 1944 the Germans found southern France was also at risk. 'Operation Dragoon' got underway 10 weeks after D-Day, with the forces of the US 7th Army making landings between Toulon and Cannes and meeting only mild opposition.

## *The advance through France was known as the 'Champagne Campaign'*

Among the soldiers to land at the beaches south of St Tropez was a 20-year-old Audie Murphy, later to be a Hollywood hearthrob, who single-handedly wiped out an enemy machine-gun nest.

The US forces drove up France, keen to link up with their comrades swinging down from the north. Such was the ease of the advance, and the joy of their reception by the French, it became known as the 'Champagne Campaign'. Paris was liberated by Free French forces on 25 August.

### ■ ARNHEM ■

By September, Montgomery and American general Omar Bradley had thrust through Belgium and Luxembourg. The fighting remained gruelling with British paratroops experiencing horrific losses when they tried to take Arnhem, Holland, at the end of September.

Finally, the successes of the Allies began to take their toll. The front line forces were running out of ammunition and other supplies while enemy soldiers were making stronger

*Right:* **Although General de Gaulle was never popular among Allied war leaders, he won the undying adoration of his people for his uncompromising views.**

## ◆ EYE WITNESS ◆

**Rudolf Valentin was among the German soldiers who fought at Monte Cassino, and revealed some of his experiences to New Zealand author Alex Borrie. He saw some tough fighting as the Germans tried to recapture Hangman's Hill.**

'Our situation was not an enviable one. Whoever came out of cover during the day became a sure victim for the Indian sharp-shooter. The Gurkhas on Hangman's Hill were in a similar position. They also had to make themselves scarce during the day otherwise they drew German fire.

The set of circumstances meant that almost all attacks were switched to night-time. Just after the onset of darkness, we had to repel the first attack and two others followed. With the beginning of the new day, we had to creep into holes again which we enlarged with the spikes of our jack-knives. We had to survive the armed attacks in these holes.

In the evening the murderous close-combat began again. During this one often had to let the enemy advance until only metres away before one was able to recognise him by the shape of his helmet. In addition to this, hunger and especially thirst were also becoming factors.

At dawn on 19 March the 1st/FJR 4 [a German paratroop unit] came out to us with about 120 men from the monastery with the order to capture Rocca Janula again. After approximately 10 minutes of machine-gun fire and shelling our comrades overwhelmed the Rajputanis at the lower hair-pin curve and stormed the walls.

A terrible hand-to-hand combat flared up there. The Germans were attempting to scale the walls. They succeeded in blasting a hole in the wall. But the enemy from the Essex Battalion fought with the same determination and beat off the attack causing heavy casualties. Courage and the willingness to make sacrifices did not help at all. The castle could no longer be captured. This attack cost the lives of half the comrades, the rest had to retreat.

But the English and the Indians also suffered such heavy casualties that they had to abandon their intentions to capture the monastery in this way. On this day a ceasefire lasting several hours was agreed upon in order to recover the dead and wounded. It was at this point that we exchanged cigarettes with the enemy and helped each other out with bandages. The English even lent us stretchers to transport our wounded to the monastery. At the same time the Gurkhas took their wounded through our positions. A short time later the men who helped each other out in such a comradely fashion were once again the bitterest of enemies. What madness!'

*Right:* German soldiers came uncomfortably close to succeeding in their objective of reaching the Belgian port of Antwerp during the Battle of the Bulge.

stands than before. Waiting for relief, the Allied initiative ground to a halt in December 1944 before going on to make headway in Germany.

The infantrymen were heartily relieved. It had been a long, arduous haul which cost many lives. Combat exhaustion as well as other maladies were striking the servicemen who had survived the fighting. Seemingly ceaseless rain and acres of mud weighed their spirits down.

## ■ SLOW ADVANCE ■

Many soldiers were weary of the inch-by-inch advance they had experienced in some of the fiercest battles waged on the Western front, which resembled the trench warfare known by their fathers two decades earlier. A rash of self-inflicted wounds began bringing waves of soldiers to the sick bays. Anyone who was suspected of having deliberately injured himself was instantly court martialled.

Their commanders, meanwhile, were frustrated in their desire to push relentlessly onwards. Hitler seized the

---

### *The fury of the American and British air forces was brought to bear on the Germans*

---

opportunity to strike back. Choosing the same route which had served him so well some four years earlier, he proposed a surprise attack through the Ardennes with the intention of driving a wedge between the Allied forces and capturing Antwerp, the

Belgian port through which vital Allied supplies were being brought.

Luck was with the Germans as the bold offensive got underway on 16 December. Low cloud was keeping the Anglo-American reconnaissance aircraft on the ground. The Allied commanders had no idea of what was coming until it arrived.

Field-Marshal von Rundstedt commanded the German forces, comprising ten armoured divisions and 14 other divisions. However, only the 6th SS Panzer Army was up to full strength and adequately equipped. When the weather cleared, the fury of the American and British air forces was brought to bear on the Germans. Fighting raged on over Christmas and into the New Year, with the Allies gradually gaining the upper hand. The Battle of the Bulge, as it was called, was over by 23 January when the Allies took St Vith, the last remaining German stronghold. Another, less substantial German thrust into northern Alsace which began on 1 January 1945 was also quickly suppressed.

The cost of the two German assaults was high. Both had weakened the German defences elsewhere, a fact that didn't go unnnoticed by Allied commander General Patton. At last the fortified Siegfried line, built to protect Germany, was in danger.

February saw a further big offensive in north west Europe from the Allies. In a series of pushes the Allied armies managed to link up to form a formidable front line.

## ■ REMAGEN ■

They were bucked when a sharp-eyed US sergeant spotted a railway bridge left intact by the retreating Germans, spanning the Rhine at Remagen. The Germans had viewed the Rhine in much the same way as the English saw the Channel, a vital line of defence which would be hard to penetrate. Now troops forged along the bridge while further up- and downstream their comrades made less comfortable crossings on swiftly assembled pontoons. The defences of the Fatherland had been breached.

## ◆ EYE WITNESS ◆

**LeRoy Stein, from Michigan, USA, was 24 when he joined up and was a member of the 87th Division in Patton's 3rd Army in the battle for Normandy.**

'It was very frightening. I was in a mine platoon which was shaky work. We laid mines and booby traps and would take them up if they had no more use. Each one was supposed to be removed. A permanent record was supposed to be kept on the whereabouts of these explosives. But they were not properly taken up. There are still people being killed by them today.'

Airborne troops landed on a large scale helped capture stalwart German towns. By early May, key regions including the Ruhr, Hamburg, Bavaria and Austria were in the hands of the Allies. Yet the battles had been grim. The German defences were cleverly conceived and included mines and booby traps.

Frequently, the morale of troops was low. In addition to seeing bloody action and burying their friends, the infantry had to endure apparently endless hours of foot-slogging. Their rations were pitiful, consisting mostly of tinned spam, corned beef and soya sausages. Despite the strong camaraderie of men forced to suffer unspeakable hardships, there were numerous instances of insubordination and desertion in the field.

Meanwhile, Russian troops had been pouring into Germany from the east, their target Berlin. Even the most hopeful of German commanders must have realised the end was near when a tidal wave of Russian

*Right:* US army engineers attempt to put rails across the bridge at Remagen. Four hours after the picture was taken, the bridge collapsed into the Rhine.

troops overran the Silesian industrial basin in January. Albert Speer, head of war production, wrote a memo to Hitler, beginning with the words: 'The war is lost.' Speer realised that Germany could not sustain its industry or defence when the region which produced 60 per cent of its coal had been snatched from it. But Hitler refused to listen.

### ■ RED FLAG RISES ■

Russian generals Zhukov and Konev encircled Berlin by 25 April and began another relentless advance towards the very heart of the Reich. Fierce street fighting raged as loyal Nazis battled to stop the Russians closing in on their beloved Führer. Loyal members of the Hitler Youth aged 12 to 14 joined in. Despite their efforts, a Red Flag was raised over the Reichstag on 2 May 1945.

As for Hitler, he finally summoned his long-time mistress Eva Braun to be at his side in the middle of April, realising that his days were numbered.

His 56th birthday on 20 April was marked by more catastrophes in the field. Nazis including Goebbels, Göring, Himmler, Ribbentrop and Bormann joined him for the muted celebrations. They urged him to flee

south but Hitler refused to leave Berlin. In fact, he rarely left the 18-room bunker beneath Berlin's Chancellery that had become his home. With him were the commanders who had remained close to him, and his most valued aides.

He slept for no more than three hours at a time, partly as a result of the pounding of the incessant air raids. Incredibly, Hitler still talked of inflicting defeat on the Allies. The next day he ordered a last-ditch stand

> *Albert Speer, head of war production, wrote a memo to Hitler beginning with the words: 'The war is lost'*

against the Russians, bellowing that every last man should be thrown in. The counter-offensive never had a chance to get off the ground.

When Hitler finally realised there was no hope, he erupted in a volcanic fury, accusing all his closest commanders of cowardice and treachery. For the first time he spoke of killing himself. Still, he refused to abandon

*Above:* Soldiers of the US 9th Army flush out German soldiers in a battle-scarred town over Germany's western border. Meanwhile Russian troops bore down on Berlin from the east.

the war effort, a stand which cost the lives of countless German soldiers left fighting against atrocious odds around Germany.

Inside the bunker the nervous exhaustion and psychological tension among its occupants reached new heights. Although he was sometimes calm, Hitler exploded in rage when he heard that his hitherto faithful lieutenants Göring and Himmler were both making advances to the Allies for peace.

On 27 April, Hitler carried out a macabre rehearsal of his suicide and the deaths of the faithful still at his side. However, it wasn't until 29 April that he dictated his will to his secretary. There was no expression of remorse for the misery and death he had caused worldwide, only the same tired tirade against those he held responsible for his misfortunes: 'More than thirty years have now passed since in 1914 I made my modest contribution as a volunteer in the First World War which was forced upon the Reich. In these three decades I have been actuated solely by love and loyalty to my people . . .

'It is untrue that I, or anyone else in Germany, wanted the war in 1939. It was desired and instigated solely by those international statesmen who were either of Jewish descent or who worked for Jewish interests.'

The last paragraph in Hitler's will read: 'Above all I charge the leaders of the nation and those under them to scrupulous observance of the laws of race and to merciless opposition to the universal poisoner of all peoples, international Jewry.'

## ■ HITLER'S END ■

In the early hours of the same day, Hitler married Eva Braun and had a champagne celebration with Bormann, Goebbels, his secretaries and his cook. Within hours he heard of the death of Mussolini, shot with his mistress Clara Petacci and then hung by the ankles in a square in the centre of Milan.

On the afternoon of 30 April, with the Russians just a street away, Hitler said his final farewells, retired to a sitting room with his wife and shot himself. Eva chose to end her life by taking poison.

The instructions he left for the disposal of his body were carried out, with his remains being burned by petrol fire in the yard of the bunker. With Hitler turned to ashes, his successor as Führer, Grand Admiral

◆ **EYE WITNESS** ◆

A diary recovered from a German soldier killed in the Allied push from Normandy contained these words.

❝ It's Sunday. My God, today is Sunday. With dawn the edge of our forest received a barrage. The earth trembles. The concussion takes our breath. Two wounded are brought to my hole, one with both hands shot off. I am considering whether to cut off the rest of the arm. I'll leave it on. How brave these two are. I hope to God that all this is not in vain. To our left, machine guns begin to chatter ...

In broad waves you can see him across the field. Tanks all around him are firing wildly. Now the American artillery ceases and the tank guns are firing like mad. I can't stick my head out of the hole – finally, here are three German assault guns. With a few shots, we can see several tanks burning once again. The infantry take cover and the attack slows down. It's stopped. It's unbelievable that with this handful of men we hold out against such attacks. ❞

Karl Dönitz, commander in chief of the German navy, tried to negotiate a peace settlement, but the Allies were unimpressed. They wanted nothing short of an unconditional surrender. And so, as pockets of German resistance capitulated around the former Reich, the surrender was finally signed on 7 May 1945.

# BLACK SANDS OF IWO JIMA

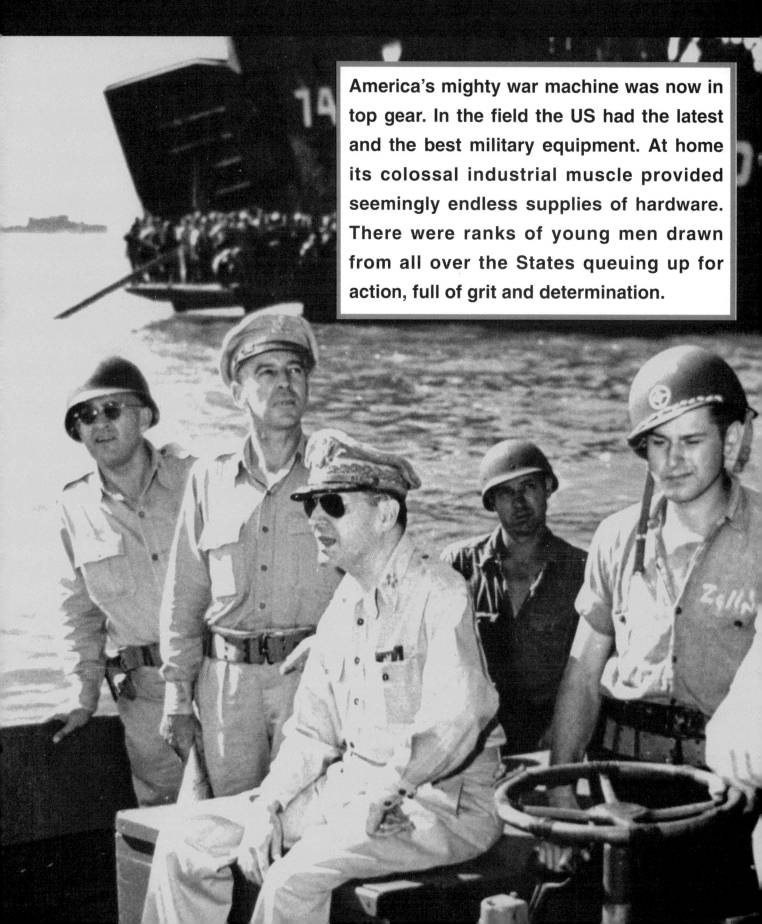

America's mighty war machine was now in top gear. In the field the US had the latest and the best military equipment. At home its colossal industrial muscle provided seemingly endless supplies of hardware. There were ranks of young men drawn from all over the States queuing up for action, full of grit and determination.

In opposition, an over-extended Japan was war-weary. The country's battle losses in ships and planes far outstripped the number of replacements being produced on the home islands. Japan itself was being starved of the materials it desperately needed by the naval blockade imposed by America. Its industry was targeted for devastating air raids. Long-term jungle fighting had taken its toll among the surviving troops, despite their rigorous training.

Yet still the Japanese soldiers were threatening and tenacious. Against all odds, they were determined to hold back the American advance. In-bred in the Emperor's men was an oriental code of honour which dictated that they must fight to the death. In most cases, this is just what they did, costing many Allied lives. The hallmark of the Pacific campaign was prolonged savage fighting and huge loss of life.

*Right:* Admiral William Halsey, commander of the 3rd Fleet, sits deep in thought on the bridge of the USS *New Jersey* en route for the Philippines.

were a selection of Japanese strongholds on New Guinea still to be beaten.

Meanwhile, Admiral Halsey, of the South Pacific sector, already had the Russell Islands, Vella Lavella and Bougainville in the Solomon Islands under his belt.

Both MacArthur and Halsey recognised the value of leap-frogging many Japanese-held islands and outposts, picking for attack mainly those that were inadequately defended. The rest were left to 'wither on the vine', increasingly isolated from Japanese lines of communication.

### ■ TARAWA ■

Now nine crucial atolls under Japanese control, collectively known as the Marshall Islands, had to be taken. A taste of the fierce fighting to come occurred on one of them, Tarawa, defended by 5,000 Japanese. When a similar number of US Marines landed

on the island on 21 November 1943 they found themselves pinned down on the open beach. Before night had fallen, 500 of the Americans were dead and a further 1,000 wounded. Japanese gun positions were only silenced when their entire crew was killed. Only an additional landing of

## *The hallmark of the Pacific campaign was prolonged savage fighting and huge loss of life*

With a victory established in New Guinea by the start of 1943, Allied commander of the South West Pacific General Douglas MacArthur was already pondering his route to the Philippines, a campaign dear to his heart. Before he could take it, there

*Left:* General MacArthur remained determined to push the Japanese out of the Pacific. *Right:* An island beach devastated by gunfire becomes a depot for US troops.

troops won victory for the Americans. In all 1,000 Marines died along with virtually all the Japanese.

The Americans learned a valuable lesson. When it came to taking another atoll in the group, Kwajalein, there were no landings until a heavy bombardment neutralised much of the defence.

## Fleas, flies, lice and mosquitoes were liable to be carrying appalling disease

Although the American campaign was fast, there was immense hardship for the troops brought about by the conditions. Fleas, flies, lice and mosquitoes plagued them. More than just pests, they were liable to be carrying appalling disease. It wasn't until 1944 that DDT sprays were introduced to combat the insect swarms.

Once an island was taken, it became a top priority to bury the dead on both sides. For the corpses attracted not only flies but also rats, which came in droves.

### ■ MARIANAS ■

Truk, a key naval outpost for the Japanese navy, came under fire on 18 February 1944 in a raid orchestrated by Vice-Admiral Marc Mitscher. There were 30 separate strikes at the base which destroyed 275 aircraft and 39 ships.

Next stop was Saipan in the Mariana Islands, a fearsome task given that 32,000 Japanese soldiers were garrisoned there. Nevertheless, it was a dual disaster for the Japanese. For soon after the American landings on 15 June came the Battle of the Philippine Sea, in which their Fleet Naval Air Arm was decimated.

## ◆ EYE WITNESS ◆

**Ito Masashi spent 16 years in hiding in the jungle of Guam after it was overrun. He describes his reason for not surrendering in his book *The Emperor's Last Soldiers*.**

❛ By the start of October the only sound we heard was the shell fire so far off that it sounded like distant thunder. But the fighting continued. The enemy no doubt considered it simply mopping up but for us it was a full-scale and bloody battle.

We had eaten what little there was of our portable battle rations of dried bread and now we lived on what berries and fruits we could find. We kept up a vain defiance with nothing left to help us but our grenades. But now the vital will to fight was absent. Our commanders sent messages advising us to end the senseless resistance, to give up our arms and pack it in. But somehow we didn't. We were afraid to.

Afraid that our useless rifles and guns – marked with the noble crest of the Imperial Chrysanthemum – might fall into enemy hands, we buried them deep in the ground. And we prepared, quite resignedly, for death as the only possible outcome. For us soldiers of Japan, the only thing left to our way of thinking was to deck out our last moment as nobly and bravely as we could.

By now there was no supply base for us to go back to and we didn't know whether there still existed any company or battalion headquarters where we could have got orders. So we formed sad and sorry little squads, hardly alive, now hiding ourselves away in the jungle, now moving aimlessly along the paths and lanes. We had been reduced to the status of a ragged band of stragglers. Even during this period however there were a number of incidents when we tangled with Australian troops backed by tanks or fell foul of a line of pickets. Fortunately, we always managed to get in our grenades and escape. But on every occasion the number of our already small band would dwindle by the odd one or two. ❜

And by July the defenders of Saipan were running short of ammunition. They chose to kill themselves by the score, along with the 22,000 civilians who had been living on the island since before the war, when it was a Japanese dominion. American troops looked on helplessly as women and children joined their menfolk in plunging from

high cliffs to be dashed on the rocks below rather than face the ultimate shame of surrender. Saipan was under US control by 9 July.

The islands of Tinian and Guam were the next to go. Then the Palau group of islands. Although it didn't take nearly as long to achieve victory here as it had done on Saipan, the fighting was every bit as ferocious. It frequently included suicidal rushes at secure American positions by shrieking Japanese soldiers, who were duly mowed down in their masses. With fighters refusing to surrender in even the most hopeless of battles, the Americans were forced to use armoured flame-throwers to clear well-protected pockets of resistance.

By October 1944 the Americans were ready to redeem the Philippines. The island of Leyte was their chosen point for invasion, poorly defended by just 16,000 men. While a memorable victory was quickly carved out for the Americans at sea,

the land-based struggle for supremacy lasted longer, with the Japanese counter-attacking in December. The losses on both sides were heavy. The Americans mourned 15,500 fighters, while the Japanese suffered the body-blow of 70,000 deaths. Yet once Leyte was won for the Americans, the rest of the Philippines fell to them with gratifying ease.

## At Iwo Jima the US Marines were cut down in droves by the defenders

Now it was time to approach the Japanese home islands. Choosing to by-pass several strongholds, including Formosa, the Americans decided to take the Ryuku Islands, less than 400 miles from Japan itself. A stepping-stone island between the

*Above:* **US Marines hold their weapons aloft as they wade ashore on the stepping-stone island of Tinian, unsure about what awaits them beyond the beach.**

Philippines and the Ryukus was deemed necessary as a rendezvous for American planes. Iwo Jima in the Bonin Islands was selected for invasion in February, while an operation to capture Okinawa, the largest of the Ryuku Islands, was timetabled for April.

At Iwo Jima the US Marines were cut down in droves as they tried to penetrate the complex defensive system constructed by the defenders. Bombardment by battleship prior to the landings had not obliterated the defences as hoped. In fact, the Japanese were so deeply entrenched it had made little noticeable difference.

Amphibious landing transports were beached and blown up and the Marines found themselves without an iota of cover on their route up the

## 'FRIENDLY FIRE'

**'Friendly fire' took its toll during World War II, particularly during the Normandy campaign.**

Bombers had failed to dislodge German gun emplacements before D-Day. This should have acted as a warning against so-called precision bombing. Yet American heavy bombers were called on in July 1944 to target the German lines. Instead, the bombs fell on US troops, killing 25 and wounding 131. The next day, the same mistake was made again, only this time 111 American servicemen were killed and 490 were wounded. Among the dead was US Lieutenant-General Lesley McNair, the highest-ranking Allied officer to be killed in the Normandy campaign.

Three weeks later, 'friendly fire' claimed more Allied victims from above. This time 77 Canadians and 72 Polish soldiers died. 'Friendly fire' incidents occurred through poor weather conditions, imprecise briefings, lack of training and sometimes through nervous fingers being on the trigger.

beach. There was also little opportunity to remove the wounded from the firing line.

Japanese commander Lieutenant-General Kuribayashi's order to his men was acidly clear: 'No man must die until he has killed ten of the enemy.' He added that each of his men must think of his defence position as his graveyard. It was widely considered to be the worst landing the Marines experienced in the war. Iwo Jima finally fell into American hands on 16 March after they had used bulldozers to bury defenders in their bunkers. The tally

*Below:* **Pinned down by mortar fire, Marines of the 5th Division inch their way up the slopes of Mount Suribachi, determined to seize Iwo jima.**

of dead among the Americans amounted to 6,821 but yet again there was a far more devastating number for Japan as virtually all the 21,000 troops were killed.

On 1 April the landings by the Marines on Okinawa, as part of 'Operation Iceberg', were in stark contrast to the blood-bathed beaches of Iwo Jima. An estimated 50,000 Americans got ashore barely hearing a shot and for the following five days there was hardly a skirmish. It was a deliberate lull engineered by the Japanese before they unleashed a storm of incredible violence.

The Japanese had drawn up a defence plan code-named 'Ten-Ichigo', which involved thousands of 'kamikaze' missions. The Japanese commanders

were even prepared to sacrifice their prized battleship Yamato in a suicidal attack. On 6 April the ship left its base with sufficient fuel for a one-way journey to Okinawa. Its aim was to wreak havoc there among the landing forces.

### ■ KAMIKAZE ■

However, soon picked up on radar, the great warship came under fire from 280 US aircraft until she was finally crippled and sunk on 7 April with her 2,300 crew still aboard.

Meanwhile, swarms of kamikazes were setting about the US Navy as it cruised off Okinawa. On the first day, three destroyers, two ammunition ships and an LST (Landing Ship Tank) were destroyed. It temporarily halted the drive forward, through lack of ammunition. On the next day a battleship, a carrier and two destroyers were hit. Of the 16 destroyers sent forward to give early warning of kamikaze raids, 14 were sunk before the end of the campaign even though they were of minimal strategic value. The story goes that one destroyer's crew erected a poster complete with arrow bearing the words: 'To Jap Suiciders.

*Right:* On Okinawa, advancing Americans were forced to use fire power to oust tough Japanese resistance.

*Right:* On Okinawa, advancing Americans were forced to use fire power to oust tough Japanese resistance.

Carriers are that way.' And still kamikaze fliers descended on the fleet.

During the battle to secure Okinawa, which raged between April and August, there were an estimated 2,000 kamikaze raids carried out by both army and navy aircraft as well as about 5,000 conventional sorties. In total 20 ships were sunk by kamikazes, often under a barrage of attacks by suicide pilots, against six sunk by other aircraft manoeuvres. Kamikaze planes notched up a further 217 strikes against ships.

Yet inevitably the Japanese resources were wilting under the strain. After two months of sustained kamikaze raids, there were few aircraft left for such missions.

On land the fighting was equally horrific. In one of the early battles, to win the off-island of Ie Shima and its landing strip, more than 4,700 of the 5,000 Japanese defenders died in battle. Towards the end of the eight-day confrontation, local women,

some with babies strapped to their backs, draped demolition charges around their necks and rushed at American positions.

It took until the last days of June to eradicate the last of the Japanese land-based resistance on Okinawa. Total American losses amounted to almost 7,000 men as well as numerous ships and 763 planes. Unusually, the Americans found themselves taking prisoners, some 7,400 in all. Many of these were too sick or severely wounded to kill themselves.

Meanwhile, 110,000 died in battle, with all the senior officers committing ritual suicide in their offices, and there was carnage among the population. The Japanese stood the loss of 7,800 aircraft.

> *After two months of sustained kamikaze raids, there were few aircraft left*

The hostilites in South East Asia were just as gruesome for the troops involved. Following the Chindit offensive into Burma and a second, unsuccessful, attempt by the British to re-enter Burma at Arakan, the Japanese commander in Burma, General Renya Mutaguchi, decided that going on the attack against the British in India was probably the best form of defence.

On 6 March 1944 the 'U-Go' offensive opened, with three Japanese divisions setting off for Kohima and

*Left:* Billowing smoke marks the path of a kamikaze plane which caused devastation on the USS *Bunker Hill*, hit off Okinawa on 11 May 1945.

Imphal, high in the Assam hills. For the first time in the conflict, British troops stood firm against Japanese aggression in defence of India.

### ■ KOHIMA ■

Both Kohima and Imphal were under siege by the first week in April. There followed some of the harshest fighting of the war.

Japanese soldiers were in the majority but the Commonwealth troops were in no mood to be routed this time. The bitterest of the fighting was at Kohima. Japanese soldiers had killed everything in their path until they reached the tennis court of what was once the Deputy Commissioner's bungalow. They dug in on one side while the defenders were holed up just 20 yards away.

Grenades and mortar bombs rained down on the Commonwealth forces, taking a toll on the troops. However, they repelled the frequent Japanese charges with surprising ease. Each one was accompanied by the traditional 'banzai' cry and screaming. The Allies were able to

open fire and cut them down. There was little opportunity for the Allies to collect their dead. Bodies lay rotting on the ground, emitting a terrible stench. Sometimes they were buried where they had fallen, in shallow, inadequate graves, with arms or knees left exposed. A cloud heavy with the pungent smell of burning flesh hung over the Allied position as the Japanese cremated fallen comrades.

## Both sides were racked with tiredness and riddled with disease

Both sides were racked with tiredness and riddled with disease. Any minor abrasion could quickly become life-threatening through septicaemia and gangrene. After 16 days of gruelling fighting the defending regiments were relieved by the 1st Royal Berkshire Regiment.

They left behind 1,419 dead, among them 19-year-old Lance

*Above:* After a siege by the Japanese, the British 14th Army was finally able to open the Imphal-Kohima road.

Corporal John Harman – born and bred on the tranquil island of Lundy – a strapping soldier who ran up to a Japanese machine gun, shot the crew and hoisted it up on to his shoulders to bring it back behind his own lines.

Further, he stormed a bakery held by the Japanese, set it on fire and came back to his dug-out with a wounded Japanese soldier under each arm. It was as he was returning from one of these astonishing feats that he was fatally wounded. He was awarded the Victoria Cross posthumously for his incredible efforts.

Airlifts by the American air force and RAF continued to aid the defenders of Kohima and Imphal. The Japanese soldiers had pitiful rations by comparison. It was a staggering 80 days before the Japanese were compelled to withdraw, with just a quarter of the original force left on their feet. Over half the casualties were claimed by sickness.

# War at Sea

# WEAPONS AT SEA

For years naval warfare had remained largely unchanged. It was a case of tactics combining with firepower to achieve the victories sought after by the seafaring nations.

**B**ritain excelled at the art of the sea battle and was proud of her navy traditions. By 1939, however, the rules of the game had changed and, unfortunately, nobody informed the major players.

No longer was it enough to have impressively large ships capable of blasting the enemy vessels out of the water. In fact, capital ships were a positive disadvantage as they were large targets which could only move slowly to evade enemy fire. It meant Germany's Bismarck and Tirpitz ships and Japan's Yamato were obsolete when they originally rolled down the slipway in time to see action during World War II. The great hopes that they carried with them were badly misplaced.

The power lay with aircraft and a navy was only as good as its fleet air arm. Britain didn't have a fleet air arm at all as it had been incorporated into the Royal Air Force. Many British naval chiefs refused to believe the age of the big ships had drawn to a close. It took the death of the battleship Prince of Wales and battle cruiser Repulse off the coast of Malaya in December 1941 at the hands of Japan's skilful fliers to convince them of the fact.

Now ships would stay out of reach of enemy guns and send in versatile

## *The power lay with aircraft and a navy was only as good as its fleet air arm*

and effective planes to wreak havoc with opposition navies. As the range of the aircraft increased through the war, the big ships could stay hundreds of miles away from the hub of the fighting.

Britain was, however, better placed regarding the advent of navy planes than Germany. At least the British could call on seven aircraft carriers, including the Ark Royal and Illustrious during the conflict. Hitler, in contrast, had only one aircraft carrier in his navy, Graf Zeppelin, which was never completed.

### ■ ARMOUR PLATING ■

The importance of air battles at sea in turn made the bodily defences of each ship key to its survival. Each navy discovered to its cost that only the thickest armour plating was impervious to bombs dropped by

*Left:* Mangled wreckage after the surprise Japanese strike at Pearl Harbor, revealing the scale of damage inflicted.
*Below: Illustrious* was one of Britain's few aircraft carriers at the outbreak of war.

planes. Those ships which crumpled easily under fire from above were the first casualties of the conflict.

At the start of the war, Britain had the largest navy in the world – 12 battleships, three battle cruisers, 15 heavy and 45 light cruisers, 184 destroyers, 58 submarines and 27 motor torpedo boats. The navy was probably in better shape than the army or the air force but still unprepared for war. At least there was a construction programme that would considerably improve the size of the navy. The largest British ship was Hood, sunk by Bismarck in 1941.

*Left:* **Human torpedoes, nicknamed 'pigs', were launched from this tiny hatch on the Italian tanker *Olterra*.**

## *The largest of the British ships was* Hood*, sunk by* Bismarck *in 1941*

Italy had a sizeable navy consisting of six modern battleships, 19 cruisers, 132 destroyers and torpedo boats and 107 submarines.

In Japan's navy when it entered the war in 1941 the number of aircraft carriers outnumbered the number of battleships by 11 to ten. This accounts for Japan's success on the high seas in the opening months of the war. Also lining up under the emblem of the rising sun were 23 cruisers, 129 destroyers, 67 submarines and 13 gunboats.

Much of the American strength in the area was decimated by the attack on Pearl Harbor. For months US shipyards laboured to repair the damage wrought by the Japanese planes and refloated many of the sunken vessels. America only had

On the other hand, the German navy was the least favoured branch of Hitler's armed forces. He promised his Admiral Erich Raeder plenty of time to prepare for war in Europe. The conflict arrived about five years too early, as far as Raeder was concerned.

He had two battleships, Scharnhorst and Gneisenau, in readiness as well as three pocket battleships. In addition there were seven cruisers, 21 destroyers and 12 torpedo boats in the fleet. His strengths lay in U-boats, of which he had 159 and planned many more. He also made good use of auxiliary cruisers or armed raiders, as they were better known. Merchant ships in their appearance and war ships in their weaponry, they launched bandit attacks on shipping throughout the world.

three operational aircraft carriers in the Pacific, 24 cruisers, nine battleships, 80 destroyers and 56 submarines. The hidden weapon that America possessed was its ability to produce sufficient replacements and reinforcements for its navy throughout the war.

Submarines also came of age during World War II, although only Germany and America fully grasped the potential offered by this sleek, sinister vessel.

The German U-boats could very well have changed the entire course of World War II if only there had

its proper name, radio detection and ranging. Pioneering scientist Sir Robert Watson-Watt developed the system during the twenties and thirties and personally oversaw its use for the benefit of all the British military following the outbreak of World War II.

---

*Astonishing advances made in code-breaking offered plenty of new chances to the fleet*

---

attack. The first was an Explosive Motor Boat with a one-man crew. The bows of the boat were packed with explosives which would fire on impact. It wasn't a suicide vehicle. The courageous pilot escaped by throwing himself backwards with a float before the EMB made contact with its target.

Also among their gadgets was a torpedo submarine measuring about 22 ft which was driven by a two-man crew sitting astride the strange weapon. Cast into the water by full-sized submarines, the men wearing diving suits guided this timed missile

been enough of them during the crucial early years. Hitler saw too late the massive opportunity he had passed up by reining in resources due to his navy.

American submarines executed a brilliant strategic move against Japan, destroying the vast majority of its merchant shipping and isolating the four home islands from outside trade, effectively starving the people and industry of vital goods. Any other country which did not have the shame and dishonour of surrender woven deeply into its culture would have surrendered on the strength of the submarine stranglehold alone.

The Allies possessed one ace which helped them considerably in their war at sea. It was radar or, to give it

Radar detects distant objects by sending out a microwave pulse beam. The reflection of the beam indicates the position of the object.

Its advantage to the Allies at sea was soon apparent. They would get fair warning of approaching enemy ships and planes. Bad weather was no longer the cloak to vision it once had been. Action under cover of darkness would now achieve more accurate results.

### ■ CODE-BREAKING ■

Also at sea, the astonishing advances made in code-breaking offered many new chances to the fleet who were forewarned about enemy movements.

The Italians came up with some ingenious waterborne methods of

***Above:*** It took courage and endurance to man the Italian torpedoes which wreaked havoc in the Mediterranean.

towards its target and attached it to the underside of a ship's hull before making an escape.

The British, too, had their midget submarines. These were based on an early submarine design, it was 51ft long, eight and a half feet wide and ten feet high. Inside there was just enough space for four crew members, a commander, a lieutenant to operate the engine, a navigator and an engineer. The capabilities of the midget submarines were most impressive. They could dive to a depth of 300ft and boasted a speed of four knots.

# GRAF SPEE

When war was declared, the British people expected an instant torrent of bombs to fall from a sky blackened by enemy aircraft. The wail of the air raid siren sent people scurrying for shelter clutching their gas masks in fear of being enveloped in a cloud of poisonous chemicals.

It didn't happen and soon the opening stages of the war were labelled 'the Phoney war' or even 'the Bore War'. The sceptics at home who believed the war would be over once Hitler had his way in Poland had to wait nearly a year to see action over Britain. But at sea it was an entirely different story.

A lone U-boat set the tenor of the sea-farers conflict when the liner Athenia sailing out of Glasgow was sunk off Ireland the day after hostilities were officially opened. U-boat captain Fritz-Julius Lemp believed he had an auxiliary cruiser or troopship in his sights. In all, 112 lives were lost including 28 Americans. There was shock at such an atrocity, even in Germany, and it prompted fresh orders to the U-boat commanders, to target only freighters and Navy ships. It was only a matter of months before the tighter rules which governed the U-boats were disregarded once more, however.

> ## More than 800 sailors died when a U-boat slid into Scapa Flow and destroyed a battleship

The brutal attack on Athenia sparked an Allied blockade of Germany in which ships were stopped and searched at the rate of 100 a week. Although the Royal Navy did capture some German ships this way, it caused acrimony between Britain and other neutral countries who resented the intrusive action.

By the end of September 1939, 20 Allied ships had been floored by U-boats, including HMS Courageous,

lost in the Atlantic with 515 men. Even neutral boats heading to Britain bearing vital supplies were not safe from the prowling German submarines. Already the spectre of life without the benefit of essential sea-borne trading links was looming in Britain.

### ■ MAGNETIC MINES ■

Britain's mariners fared little better in October. More than 800 sailors died when a U-boat slid into Scapa Flow, the anchorage of the British Fleet 10 miles off the north coast of Scotland, which was thought to be a safe haven, and destroyed a large British battleship. Under the command of Captain Gunther Prien, the submarine manoeuvred through a narrow, unguarded channel leading into the

harbour area and dealt a deadly blow to the Royal Oak. Claims that the battleship's armour could withstand a torpedo attack proved to be nothing more than a pipe dream. Just 396 members of the 1200-strong crew survived.

Shipping not only had to contend with the phantom U-boats. Germany was laying hundreds of mines, with devastating effect. The Reich had pioneered a deadly magnetic mine which could be dropped by air on to the sea bed, to later rise and attach itself to any passing ship, with deadly consequences. It was far superior to the mines being laid by Britain, designed to defend its shipping.

Fortunately, one of the mystery mines was jettisoned in error on land. Thanks to one courageous naval officer who tackled the explosive, its secret of success became known. The antidote was 'de-gaussing', with an electric cable fitted to ships which neutralised magnetism. The plague of the magnetic mine at least to British ships was quickly overcome.

**Above:** After the Battle of the River Plate the *Graf Spee* limped into Montevideo for repairs. However, it could not escape its predators for long.
**Left:** U-boat Captain Gunther Prien was hailed a hero in his homeland for penetrating Scapa Flow.

Above the waves were the determined ships of the Reich's navy equally adept at picking off British vessels. Among them was the pocket battleship Admiral Graf Spee. By agreement before the war, the Germans were only supposed to build ships up to a certain size. These were tagged pocket battleships, larger than cruisers but smaller and less effective than battleships.

The Graf Spee slipped out of port just before war was declared, sidestepped the ensuing Royal Navy blockade and headed for the South Atlantic. It was then the pride of the German navy with its high speed and thick protective plating. In the first three months of the war, it had notched up nine British ships, including the liner, Doric Star.

Canny British commander HMS Exeter, and two light cruisers, Ajax and Achilles, one from Britain and one from New Zealand.

## ■ CRUISERS DAMAGED ■

Graf Spee's captain, Hans Langsdorff, reckoned he could outgun the opposition, believing the heavy cruiser was accompanied only by destroyers. He opened fire, inflicting serious damage on the Exeter and the Ajax. The reply from the British ships crippled his own. With smoke pouring from the German ship, there was a chase led by the Graf Spee which was heading for the safety of Montevideo in Uruguay.

Although Uruguay was a neutral country, it was inclined to support the Allies. In international law, the Graf Spee was only entitled to stay in its capital, Montevideo, for 72 hours

waiting for a kill. Indeed, he believed the mighty Renown and Ark Royal had joined the pursuit when they were, in fact, hundreds of miles away.

Langsdorff deemed the situation hopeless and asked Berlin for permission to scuttle his ship, rather than have it fall in to enemy hands. Consent duly came.

> ### Crowds had gathered on the waterfront eager to witness the great sea battle

On 17 December the Graf Spee set off slowly for the middle of the harbour. Crowds had gathered on the waterfront eager to witness the great sea battle that would surely follow. But they were disappointed. When the majority of the crew had safely disembarked, a huge explosion wrecked her and she sank to the estuary floor.

Langsdorff considered the incident a grave disgrace. Three days afterwards he wrapped himself in the flag of his beloved fatherland and put a bullet through his head.

## ■ NEUTRAL NORWAY ■

Churchill, First Lord of the Admiralty, instantly trumpeted the achievement of his navy even though it was gained by luck and misunderstanding on behalf of the enemy. Yet while Britain celebrated the triumph, it was far from the end of its troubles at sea.

Within a week in January three submarines, HMS Grenville and destroyer HMS Exmouth were sunk. There was little more by way of encouraging news for the British until February when HMS Cossack carried out a top secret raid on a German supply ship shelter in the waters of

---

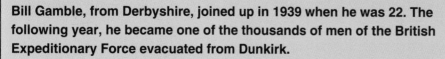

### ◆ EYE WITNESS ◆

**Bill Gamble, from Derbyshire, joined up in 1939 when he was 22. The following year, he became one of the thousands of men of the British Expeditionary Force evacuated from Dunkirk.**

❝ The Germans kept the beach under fire. I had never been under shell fire before. The Luftwaffe planes were strafing the beaches. There were rows and rows of fellows waiting to get on a boat. There was no panic because officers were there. They would have shot you if you had panicked.

I have got a vivid memory of the Welsh guards who formed the rear guard action which helped us escape. They were courageous men. I don't think I had properly fired a rifle until then. We didn't have half the equipment we should have had and there had been no training. We were just like civilians in uniform.

I was dead scared. Finally, I got on to a little barge and then on to a destroyer. When the waves came up we had to jump from one to the other. I landed in England on June 2. A few days later that destroyer got blown up. All those brave lads on the ship died.

At least when it came to D-Day, I wasn't bothered about it. By then I was properly trained. I had a job to do and I did it. ❞

---

Commodore H. Harwood guessed that it was only a matter of time before the Graf Spee was lured to the River Plate, Uruguay, attracted by the rich vein of British shipping there.

At dawn on 13 December the Graf Spee was spotted at the river estuary. Lined up before it were the ships in Harwood's force; the heavy cruiser

and the Uruguayans stoutly refused to extend its deadline.

It gave Langsdorff enough time to transfer his injured seamen to a German merchant ship. The most pressing repairs were carried out. But Langsdorff knew that outside the protection of Uruguyan territorial waters lurked a bevy a British ships

*Above:* With Hitler's consent the pocket battleship *Admiral Graf Spee* was spectacularly scuttled off Montevideo.

neutral Norway. Aboard the *Altmark*, concealed in filthy conditions in a hold, were 300 prisoners taken by the *Graf Spee*. Regardless of international regulations which banned such action, the *Altmark* was boarded and the prisoners released. Norway protested about the violation of its neutrality. Its objections sounded somewhat lame, however, in the light of the fact that Norwegian authorities had apparently already searched the ship and apparently not found the captives. The daring feat persuaded Hitler that Norwegian waters should be under German control if his navy was to get the protection it deserved.

The Royal Navy continued its efforts to contain the U-boat threat and the activities of the German fleet until May 1940 when a task of much greater importance beckoned.

At the start of May, German forces had moved into Belgium. With characteristic speed, the Reich's forces overran Belgium, Holland and northern France. The lightning pace of the attack left everyone gasping for breath, not least the British Expeditionary Force, numbering some 200,000 men, which was sent to France at the outbreak of war to bolster French defences. The British

## The Reich's forces overran Belgium, Holland and northern France

soldiers were driven relentlessly back amid some bloody fighting. With them was a section of the French forces, weary and disenchanted with apparently no hope of escape.

Commander of the BEF, General Lord Gort, had quickly realised there was no option but to withdraw his men by sea. The best and shortest route would have been from Calais to Kent, but the French port was almost in the hands of the Germans already. Dunkirk seemed to be the single remaining point from which any kind of meaningful evacuation could take place.

British and French soldiers staggered on to the beach at Dunkirk in groups or sometimes singly. All semblance of order was gone after the hasty retreat in which bands of men lost sight of their units. Communication between commanders and their men was cut inland. The soldiers, now acting on initiative, got to Dunkirk as best they could.

The French forces' commander in chief, General Gamelin, had been bemused by the German advance. His tanks, evenly spaced down the frontier, were unable to provide a striking action against the rear of the Germans. So while the Panzer armies were tiring and running short of supplies, there was no one to exploit their vulnerability.

Ironically, it was Hitler himself who called a halt to the German

*Right:* The *Altmark* lurking in Norwegian waters was holding British POWs when HMS *Cossack* attacked.

march. Concerned that vital tank divisions were at risk if they went into action against the by-now concentrated strength of the Allies on treacherous marshlands and would be unable to complete the invasion of France, Hitler stopped the key Panzer advance. He was made even more anxious by the counter-offensive of sorts that the Allies had managed to stage at Arras.

## ■ DUNKIRK ■

The strategy was perhaps sound. Hitler's decision came on 24 May when a comprehensive rout of the enemy seemed assured. Its unavoidable side effect was to give Allied troops two days' grace without which an evacuation from Dunkirk would surely have been impossible. Historians have subsequently speculated that, had the BEF been lost in northern France, Britain would have sought peace at any price as there would have been no army left to fight with.

As early as 20 May, Admiral Bertram Ramsay, the Flag Officer at Dover, had been gathering a small fleet capable of crossing the English Channel to rescue soldiers. At this stage it was believed just 35,000 men would be saved.

Still more and more men were straggling on to the beach until the ragged throng numbered 38,000. Many were by now unarmed, picking up weapons where they could which had been discarded en route or fallen from the hands of recently killed comrades. There were still rations of sorts, but many soldiers had been without sleep for days. Between periods of calm and order there was panic as the instinct of self-preservation got the better of men with

tattered nerves and a deep-rooted fear of what the future might hold if they were not rescued.

Each hour brought the Germans nearer. The shelling grew ever closer. Dunkirk itself was being blown to bits, offering little by way of protection for the British and French forces. There were attacks by the Luftwaffe, too. The low whine of oncoming aircraft followed by the clatter of its guns sent men diving to the ground for cover. Many never got up again.

### 'Operation Dynamo', the evacuation at Dunkirk, was officially begun on 26 May 1940

There was a feeling of resentment among many that the Royal Air Force was not doing its bit to aid the plight of the soldiers. In fact, its pilots were going up time and again, helping the rear guard defenders of Dunkirk or hampering the Luftwaffe high above the clouds. But the pilots' role was invisible to the eyes of the stranded soldiers – who were looking for someone to blame for their appalling predicament.

In peacetime Dunkirk had ample harbour facilities from which a major evacuation could have been carried out with ease. Now the town was rubble and the harbour installations in tatters. The only useful jetty left was wooden planking extending a mile into the sea. Yet it was valueless to the big ships for embarkation. Even the mildest wind would have blown the vessel into its concrete foundations causing damage below the waterline. As time went by it became clear that men would have to be taken off the beaches, no matter how cumbersome the task.

Operation Dynamo, the evacuation at Dunkirk, was officially begun shortly before 7pm on 26 May although in fact some support units had already been brought back to Britain. Before midnight fewer than 8,000 men had been brought home.

When the depth of the dilemma facing the bulk of Britain's army became clear, a flotilla of small boats was called upon to assist. Such boats already had to be registered with the government. Now they were recruited for the still-secret operation, with many civilian captains being allowed to stay with their ships.

The British public finally got to hear about 'Operation Dynamo' on

31 May, when about 194,000 British troops had been brought back under the guidance of the Royal Navy. When news about the crisis was broadcast, many more owners of small boats set sail immediately. This was the brave face of Dunkirk that haunts history.

### ■ CIVILIAN COURAGE ■

Their task was no easier than that faced by the Royal Navy. Bombardments by the Luftwaffe continued claiming the lives of servicemen and civilians alike. On 1 June the courage of the civilian boat owners reaped dividends when 64,429 soldiers were rescued. Having ferried their battle-worn cargo to safety, boat owners turned back to face the risks all over again in a bid to haul yet more soldiers to safety. Not least of their worries were the minefields that lay between them and their destination.

By any standards, the rout of the British army in France by Hitler's

> ## The courage of the civilian boat owners reaped dividends

forces was nothing short of outright defeat. Yet the way in which the cream of the British army slipped through the Führer's grasp and the courage of the evacuation gave an element of heroism to the event, which set it apart from other ignominious military debacles suffered by the British, and has ensured it a special place in British military history.

The soldiers who made it back were full of criticism for the army that had sent them to France inadequately armed and supplied. Yet

within a few days or weeks, most were posted again, in many cases back to France where remnants of the British contingent were still fighting with the French to keep Hitler out of Paris.

The last Allied boat pulled away from the beaches of Dunkirk on 4 June with the remnants of the 338,000 rescued British and French soldiers aboard. Each man was precious and represented the future fighting force of Britain. Yet behind the retreating force lay its equipment, without which no army could fight. Before leaving, the BEF had sabotaged 63,900 vehicles, 289 tanks and 2,472 guns.

### ◆ EYE WITNESS ◆

**Miner Wilf Cowie was 25 when he joined the army and was part of the British Expeditionary Force in France which evacuated from Dunkirk.**

❛ We were in France on the Belgian border for about six months with very little happening, just a bit of bombing and shelling.

When the retreat started, we had to make our way over fields because the Germans were patrolling the roads. The worst thing I ever saw were the refugees streaming out of Belgium pushing prams and carrying beds just machined gunned by German planes. Hundreds of them were killed.

I was one of the last to get out of Dunkirk. It was horrible on the beach. We were lying in bomb craters on the beach, expecting every day to get away. Every day seemed to take forever. Luftwaffe planes were firing at us and then there was the shelling. That was the worst thing of all. The shells screamed as they were going over the top of you and you never knew where they were going to land.

Once I took shelter in a bomb hole with three other lads. I was the only one who came out alive. The others were killed by a machine gun blast from an aeroplane.

There were hundreds of lads killed. We had to go and get the identity discs from the bodies and give them to our superiors. It was a bit upsetting but it was just a job that had to be done. We saw so many young men dead that in the end we didn't worry about it.

I came back in a trawler. It took 36 hours to reach the east coast after the skipper diverted to avoid mines. Several men on the boat died when they were hit by machine gun fire from Luftwaffe planes passing overhead. ❜

*Above:* Devastation of the beaches of Dunkirk following the evacuation.

# U-BOAT MENACE

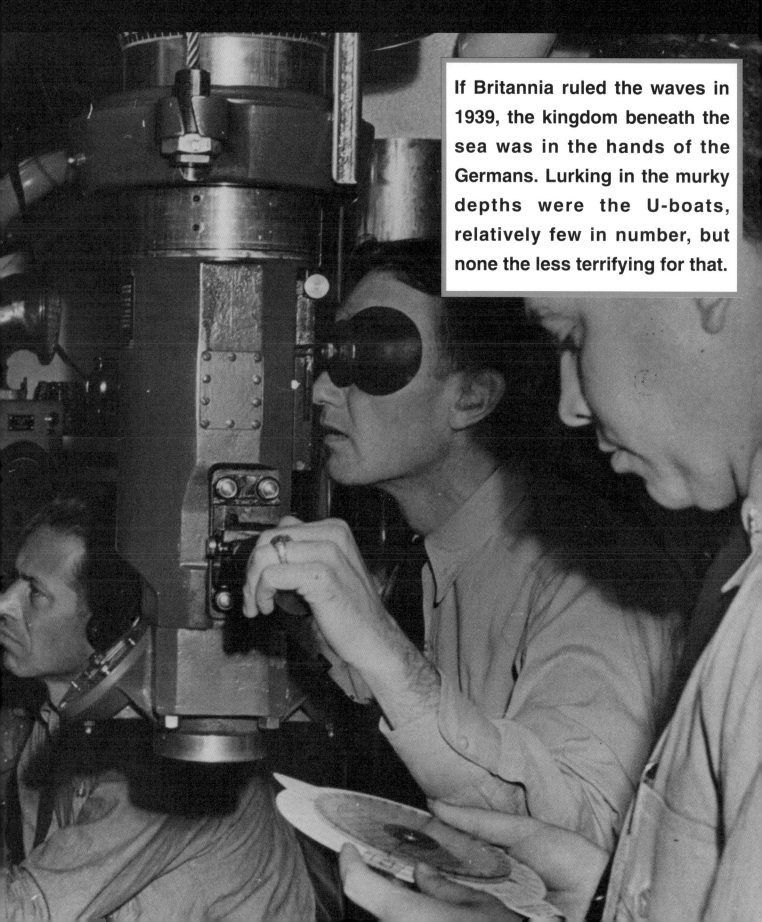

If Britannia ruled the waves in 1939, the kingdom beneath the sea was in the hands of the Germans. Lurking in the murky depths were the U-boats, relatively few in number, but none the less terrifying for that.

**J**ust a mention of the name could strike fear into the stout hearts of the English sailors. Winston Churchill confessed later that the U-boat threat in the Battle of the Atlantic was 'the only thing that ever really frightened me during the war'.

For U-boats (Unterseeboot in German) had a habit of creeping up on British shipping and sinking it without warning. At first merchant ships seemed very much like sitting ducks if U-boats were in the area. There appeared to be little opportunity to dilute the threat.

Britain, Canada and America lost thousands of tons of cargo, not to mention scores of seamen, to the prowling U-boats. Bitter experience finally taught the Allies effective defences and, later, vital offensive tactics which would ultimately neutralise the stealthy foe.

U-boats soon began to hunt in 'wolf packs', an idea thought up in

*Above:* German U-boats came close to their goal of strangling Britain.

Germany in the mid-1930s in which a group of submarines orchestrated their attacks on convoys. At first, the concept was thwarted by a lack of boats. Sometimes, in the early stages of the war, there were only a handful of submarines to put to sea, the others being in dock for repairs or in use for training. The lack of air

### By the summer of 1940 there were two 'wolf packs' operating in the Atlantic

support from the Luftwaffe to the U-boat service also slightly lessened their menace, since they were compelled to search, sometimes for days, for convoys.

However Raeder, commander in chief of the Kriegsmarine was conscious of the golden opportunity that was open to him. While finding it almost impossible to keep more than six U-boats in the sea at a time before February 1941, he devoted much time and energy to rectifying the short-coming. Before the year

was out the number of U-boats in his fleet had been increased tenfold.

By the summer of 1940 there were two wolf packs operating in the Atlantic, preying on the convoys as they made their way with precious food, goods and, later, troops to Britain from America. Submarine commanders could now pinpoint convoy positions thanks to the German Radio Monitoring Service (B-Dienst). Slung across the Atlantic, the U-boats formed a deadly chain from which the convoys could not escape. The aim was for the boat which first spotted the convoy to shadow it until other submarines could gather for a mass attack. In October, three convoys lost 38 ships to U-boats in the space of just three nights.

### ■ U-BOAT TECHNIQUE ■

The technique used by the U-boats continued to improve. At first, commanders attacked from positions both above and below the waves. Their firepower was far more accurate, however, when the U-boats were on the surface. It became

*Above:* Admiral Karl Dönitz knew the potential of his U-boat fleet. *Left:* The Allies also had submarines.

accepted procedure for the boats to sneak into the centre of a convoy, surface after dark and wreak havoc, disappearing before daybreak when the first of the Allied flight escorts arrived. On the surface, the sleek machines, powered by diesel engines, could outrun larger convoy escort vessels with relative ease.

> ## On the surface, the sleek machines could outrun larger convoy escort vessels

There followed a 'happy time', as it was known among German submariners, in which dozens of merchant ships were sent to the bottom. They were picking off targets with ease and the convoy escorts were floundering with exasperation, not knowing how to halt the rising casualty toll. In 1940, U-boats accounted for more than

*Right:* Sailors keeping watch from a surfaced submarine got a drenching.

1,000 ships while just 16 U-boats were knocked out. The following year followed a similar pattern with 24 U-boats being sunk.

### ■ AMPLE WARNING ■

Had there been a greater number of U-boats operating at that time, Britain would have been in grave danger of being throttled. Hitler was delighted with the success of the U-boats. Always sceptical of the power of his naval fleet, he became a

*Above:* One U-boat torpedo was enough to break a ship's back.

convert and lavished his favours on the U-boat arm. If he had devoted more resources to them in 1939 instead of waiting until 1941, the outcome of the war might have been very different. By the time his confidence was raised in the potential of the U-boats, it was just one of many services forced to get in line for the available resources.

As it was, technology came to the rescue for the Allies. Britain finally cracked the German radio code signals. Now operators could give ample warning to the convoys as to the whereabouts of the U-boats. Ships began to successfully bypass the waiting packs which were now forced to stretch out over huge distances, diminishing their effect.

> *Operators could give ample warning as to the whereabouts of the U-boats*

Although the sinking of the liner Athenia at the beginning of the war did serve to tighten up the rules of engagement which governed U-boats, these were soon relaxed, in part because it was difficult for submariners to abide by such rules without putting themselves into considerable danger. Stipulations like the one laid down in the 1935

*Below:* In 1942 the remains of a convoy approach beseiged Malta.

## ◆ EYE WITNESS ◆

**The following personal account of life aboard a patrolling British submarine in the Mediterranean appeared in the *Daily Express* in June 1942.**

 The captain is wearing shorts with a sweater handy in case it is chilly. His favourite dress while submerged in action is a towel wrapped around his loins.

The crew are wearing overalls, shorts, shirts, vests – anything they fancy. There are no badges of rank and it is impossible to tell the captain from the cook.

Life goes on quietly, almost dully, for some days while the submarine continues towards her patrol station. There are only seven gramophone records, some of them scratched and indistinct through constant wear. The captain tells the first lieutenant he will brain the first rating to play *Frankie and Johnnie were lovers* – he swears he has heard it 3,000 times.

At midday the next day the captain is resting in his cabin. The first lieutenant is at the periscope. He swings it, sees smoke on the horizon. Without ceasing to look he says: "Captain, in the control room". The murmur is taken up and goes around the boat. Within a matter of seconds the captain is at the periscope clothed in his towel. He looks and says: "There is smoke on the horizon – a couple of masts."

Then the orders come fast. "Diving stations, full speed ahead together, starboard 25, steer 320." The hum of the motors can be heard through the otherwise silent submarine.

There are three merchant ships escorted by six Italian destroyers. The captain grabs his slipping towel as he snaps the range – 8,000 yards.

Excitement in the submarine is terrific and suppressed. Nobody speaks except the captain. At times the silence is so intense that a movement by a rating sounds like thunder.

As the torpedoes jump from the tubes the submarine shudders a bit. The captain's towel falls off. Nearby ratings chuckle at naked authority.

Stop watches have already started to mark the time the torpedoes take to reach the target. The captain's: "I'll have a cup of tea, please," is hardly necessary. The electric stove was switched on some minutes before. It is a ritual. Everybody in the service knows that you must have a cup of tea before the depth charging begins.

In 55 seconds the explosion which means the target has been hit rocks the submarine. The captain sits on the engine-room artificer's tool box, sipping his tea. Then the first depth charge arrives.

The captain's cup leaps off the tool chest. The submarine vibrates with the clangour of charges exploding nearby.

For two hours the racket of the depth charges goes on. The men behave as if they were on tiptoe. Barely a word is spoken. As the noise of the depth charges dies away the submarine creeps to periscope depth. The captain sees three destroyers picking up survivors from the sunken merchantmen.

One of the ratings off duty has already got hold of the "Jolly Roger" skull and cross bones flag of the submarine service and is preparing to stitch another chevron to the other battle honours. They will fly it when they get back from patrol.

London Submarine Agreement that submarines must stop intended victims and order the crew into lifeboats before opening fire were soon forgotten. The hunter quickly became the hunted if he lingered too long trying to establish the identity and purpose of a ship in the Atlantic. Neutral shipping was also at risk

from German U-boats. Some vessels flying the flags of unaligned countries were hit by accident. Others, suspected of aiding the British, were rammed or torpedoed on purpose.

In November 1939 neutral countries were warned by Germany that their ships could not be guaranteed a safe passage in waters around the British Isles. Meanwhile, secret instructions to U-boat commanders gave them the go-ahead to sink tankers and other key commercial ships approaching Britain unless they were identified as Russian, Japanese, Italian, Spanish, Greek or American. To cover their tracks, the U-boat commanders were told to use only electric torpedoes which did not leave a tell-tale wake in the water. It meant the explosion could be blamed on an engine fault or a mine.

It wasn't only in the Atlantic that the U-boats plied their deadly trade. Six were broken into pieces and transported by road to Linz in Austria where the water was deep enough for re-assembly and were then launched into the Black Sea. The first to go into action there took to the water on 28 October 1940.

Operation in the Mediterranean was difficult for the U-boats – which were known by numbers rather than names – as their dark forms could be quickly spotted in the shallow, clear water by aircraft above or nearby ships. Also, the fast flowing eastern currents assisted the U-boats as they

## It wasn't only in the Atlantic that the U-boats plied their deadly trade

sailed into the warm seas but thwarted their exit.

Nevertheless, it was there that the U81 sank HMS Ark Royal on 13 November 1941, one of the prestige ships of the Royal Navy.

*Above:* Relief as a German U-boat and its crew return safely to port after a long spell on patrol.

Far easier was the task of the U-boats in the waters off America and Canada. Until Japan's attack on Pearl Harbor and Germany's subsequent declaration of war on America, Hitler had ordered that any ship bearing the stars and stripes standard be allowed freedom of the waters. There had been sinkings of US vessels before December 1941, but presumably these were in error.

When America and Germany were eventually pitted against each other, the U-boats seized the opportunity for yet another 'happy time'. U-boat commander in chief Karl Dönitz, the man who was later to take over from Hitler as Führer of Germany, knew his forces had to pounce before America became wise to the threat.

Five of the largest submarines, called Type IX boats, were dispatched from the Mediterranean

### ◆ EYE WITNESS ◆

**Stoker Fernand 'Pedro' Guinard, 69, from Halifax, Nova Scotia, served on several Canadian warships including HMCS *St. Laurent*.**

❝ My first contact with the enemy came early in the war when we picked up 27 survivors from the German submarine UB31. We were four days out of Newfoundland.

A lot of these guys were Czechs and Poles. They told me they'd been offered the chance to fight in the navy or go work in a slave camp. You couldn't really blame them for joining up. I got quite close to them because I had to detail them to hand pump the bilges.

Even that got me into trouble. When we docked and disembarked the POWs, two of the Germans came over to shake hands and say goodbye. That didn't go down well with the officers. I got warned in no uncertain terms not to fraternise with the prisoners.

We only killed one submarine in my first three years of service. But we saw plenty of attacks on our convoys. I remember one time when a wolf pack began torpedoing our boats at sunset. It was so sad to see these ships going down. There were people in the water everywhere but to be honest we didn't give a bag about them. There were guys in a life raft obviously looking for help and we just rode straight through them throwing out depth charges. All we cared about was getting the submarine.

Was I scared? I didn't have much time to be scared. I was part of a team and you just got on with your job. ❞

where they were then operating to North American coastal waters in 'Operation Paukenschlag'.

### ■ EASY TARGETS ■

Americans living along the eastern seaboard had so far been virtually untouched by the war. There were no blackouts, built-in defences, or restrictions on radio use. Even navigation lights remained helpfully in place. Not only did the U-boats have easy targets but, after the 'kill',

the pursuing submarine hunters were inexperienced and ill-prepared. There was little to stop the U-boats getting clean away. In 'Operation Paukenschlag', each boat averaged almost six 'kills' before returning to home waters. Some of the boats sunk were those who had traversed the Atlantic in a convoy to pick up a cargo only to be sunk, as the British saw it, through a reckless lack of defence on behalf of the Americans.

A further wave of 12 smaller boats did their utmost to match the grand total but, thankfully for the Americans, fell short of the target. Within a few months, America began using convoy systems in its home waters

and mimicked the successful British methods of hunting U-boats.

The tentacles of the U-boat campaign also spread into the southern oceans. There were plenty of ships carrying essential goods which

### *Within a few months, America began using convoy systems in its home waters*

*Below:* Living conditions on a U-boat were cramped and uncomfortable, with restricted fresh food and air.

were poorly equipped to deal with U-boat attack. In addition, it further stretched the Royal Navy ships charged with hunting for submarines.

Not all of the 1,300 U-boats put to see by Germany during World War II saw action. Some were used for train-

*Above:* **A U-boat in harbour is loaded with supplies before embarking on another lengthy ship-bagging voyage.**

## U-boat men got about double the rates of pay awarded to other sailors

ing, others for supplying the roving hunters. Still more U-boats were employed carrying goods from the far east to the Fatherland.

Men who served in the U-boat arm of the Kriegsmarine (German Navy) were considered the elite by their countrymen – although they were loathed and detested by the British. There can be little doubt that they had strong nerves and plenty of courage. Some were volunteers, attracted by the excitement the service appeared to offer. This was perpetuated by the public accolades awarded to U-boat aces like Gunther Prien and Joachim Schepke. U-boat men also got about double the rates of pay awarded to other sailors.

Other men who found themselves serving on the U-boats were naval recruits who had been drafted.

Yet aboard a U-boat, the day-to-day life was far from glamorous. Conditions were cramped. There was a curtained-off cabin for the captain but there were not enough beds for every member of the crew. Some men slept in hammocks, while others slept on the floor.

### ■ LIFE EXPECTANCY ■

Until hostilities began with America, the U-boat commanders had little idea of the distances their crafts were able to travel. They were pleasantly surprised to find they could cruise far further than they ever thought possible if they conserved fuel by keeping to reasonable speeds and travelled on the surface.

More supplies were needed on a long voyage, however. They took up valuable living accommodation, leaving the crew of about 50 even fewer comforts. Water was rationed

## MASCOTS

**Animals featured as mascots to the branches of army, navy and air force throughout the war. On HMS *Duke of York*, the ship's tabby cat was Whiskey who became famous for sleeping soundly through the battle which sunk the Scharnhorst. A cat called Susan made herself at home on a Royal Navy tank landing craft and even attended the D-Day invasion. A St Bernard by the name of Bamse was the mascot of the Norwegian fighting ship *Thorod*. He assured himself a place in the heart of his crew by rounding them up from shore leave by visiting their favourite bars and clubs – even boarding a bus to patrol the more far-reaching destinations.**

One of the more unusual mascots of the war was a Syrian bear by the name of Voytek, adopted as a cub by the Second Polish Transport Company in Persia. He was thought of as human by his soldier pals who watched distressed as he cried like a child when his carer, Lance Corporal Peter Prendys, disappeared from sight. His love of water led to the shower room having to be locked to prevent him from exhausting the water supply. When he discovered an Arab spy, he was acclaimed a hero and allowed a morning's free play in the bath.

It was as a hero he was greeted in Scotland at the end of the war where he served the army until 1947 when his owner was demobbed. It was then he was handed over to Edinburgh Zoo where he had to get used to a new life behind bars.

and the opportunities for washing were few. The atmosphere was squalid, sweaty and unpleasant.

Early models were even more spartan than the rest. There was inadequate heating aboard. So men soaked from taking their turn on the watch when the boat was on the surface found themselves unable to dry their sodden clothes. Men wore layers of jumpers and still felt chilled.

When the most primitive U-boats were forced to submerge, the men

*Above:* A U-boat is armed with a giant torpedo before a trip.
*Left:* Sailors stood little chance when a U-boat was blown up.

had to wear breathing masks to prevent poisoning by carbon monoxide. Later, more sophisticated air purifiers were built into the wall of the ships, so masks became obselete.

Voyages lasted for months at a time and there was little chance to

## The greatest shadow over a U-boat crewman was his brief life expectancy

breath fresh air. U-boat men operating in the darkened Arctic region during the winter months were known to queue up patiently for a glimpse of sunlight.

Perhaps the greatest shadow over the life of a U-boat crewman, though, was his brief life expectancy.

During the first two years of war, their existence was perilous due

*Left:* Depth charges were one antidote to roaming U-boats.

or fewer ships, many making no hits at all before they were sent to the ocean bed.

The U-boat force gradually became more impotent prompting the desperate Dönitz, by now admiral of the entire Kriegsmarine, to order a kamikaze-style attack by them following D-Day.

## ■ RECKLESS ATTACK ■

On 11 June 1944 he issued an order which read: 'The Invasion Fleet is to be attacked with complete reckless-ness. Every enemy vessel that aids the landing, even if it puts no more than half a hundred men or a tank ashore, is a target calling for all-out effort from the U-boat.

'It is to be attacked even at the risk of losing one's boat. When it is neces-sary to get to grips with the enemy landing fleet, there is no question of any regard to danger through shallow water or possible minefields.'

Even with the benefit of hindsight it is difficult to discern whether the U-boat captains, fired by their leader's words, carried out assaults

entirely to the shortcomings in their torpedo systems. Then, when they bore the brunt of Allied air and sea power, U-boats became an endan-gered species. Apart from torpedoes and mines, the only weapon the U-

---

### German sailors grew into the habit of calling their craft 'iron coffins'

---

boats could use against their enemies was an undersized machine gun which could do little in the face of a concerted attack. German sailors grew into the habit of calling their craft 'iron coffins'.

After attacking, there are examples of U-boat captains displaying concern for their victims, passing on food and water and radioing their position so help could be sent. Survivors were never allowed on board, however.

Equally, there were tales that abounded in Britain of men from sunken ships being machine-gunned to death by callous U-boat captains

as they lay helpless in the water. While that may have occurred, there is the strong possibility such stories were used for propaganda purposes by a Ministry of Information which depicted U-boat captains as callous, dedicated Nazis.

The most successful U-boat was U48, which came into service in April 1939 and sank a record 59 ships before being sunk itself in October 1943. Many of the submarines, particularly those commissioned in the later years of the war, sunk five

## ORAN DILEMMA

**In one of the most controversial moves of the war, Churchill turned British guns against former ally France a little more than a week after the armistice with Germany was signed.**

A British squadron led by Vice Admiral James Somerville encircled the pride of the French fleet harboured in the Algerian port of Oran on 3 July 1940 as part of 'Operation Catapult' and issued an ultimatum to the ships sheltering there to sail for Britain or America. When the order was refused, the mighty force of British ships including the ill-fated battlecruiser *Hood* opened fire.

Prestige ships, among them the *Provence*, *Bretagne* and *Dunkerque* were sunk or badly damaged and 1,300 French sailors were killed. The aim was to prevent the ships falling into German hands but it caused a major outcry in France and among French-speaking nations around the world.

Churchill said he regretted the loss of life but insisted the action was necessary. 'I leave the judgement of our actions with confidence to Parliament. I leave it to the nation and I leave it to the United States. I leave it to the world and to history.'

The French ships in British ports were confiscated with barely one shot being fired.

and were defeated or if indeed the U-boat force was already so depleted and poorly supplied that they were unable to take any meaningful action. Certainly, there is little evidence of U-boat activity in the Channel following D-Day.

Despite the Allied successes in combatting the U-boat menace, the Nazi hierarchy continued to pin great hopes on the success of a renewed campaign. Hitler, keeping faith with the U-boat service, was convinced the newest model designed by Germany was a war-winner. In his diaries, dated 6 March 1945, his loyal aide Goebbels reflected those optimistic opinions. With the Allies crossing the borders of Germany into the Fatherland itself, he wrote: 'There is considerable hope for us here. Our U-boats must get to work hard; above all it may be anticipated that as the new type gets into action, far greater results should be achieved than with our old U-boats . . .'

Later, on 28 March, barely a month before the collapse of Hitler's Germany, he noted the Allied bombing campaign against the new submarines in dock at Bremen and penned with satisfaction: 'Clearly the revival of our U-boat war has made a great impression on the war.'

*Below:* Another convoy ship falls victim of U-boats, Hitler's underused war weapon.

# BATTLE OF THE ATLANTIC

During World War I, German U-boats almost succeeded in severing the supply routes from America and Canada to Britain. Without shiploads of goods, including fuel, from overseas the prospects for Britain were dim.

**U**nable to support herself, Britain had for years relied on trade to keep her people fed, clothed and employed. If those vital links were cut during conflict, Britain would have been forced to capitulate – or see her population starve. Now in World War II the grim scenario was being played out once more. U-boats, in tandem with the German Navy or Kriegsmarine, were set to exploit the Achilles heel of the British Empire. They nearly succeeded.

Both Britain and Germany's navies had been unprepared for war. Navy chief Erich Raeder had far fewer U-boats at his disposal than he would have liked. In addition, the submarine construction programme was virtually at a halt. Hitler had little faith in his navy and earmarked only limited resources for it.

Meanwhile, Britain had a mighty fleet of Royal Navy vessels and numerous merchant ships. But the Admiralty appeared to have devoted little time or effort in the years between the wars in looking at ways to counter the U-boat threat. It still believed in the outdated notion that wars could be won with offensive action by battleships.

Putting their lives on the line alongside sailors in the Royal Navy

were volunteer merchant seamen. It was their job to ferry the all-important supplies to Britain, mostly from America and Canada across the Atlantic. Instantly, they became targets for the roaming U-boats. Their pay was £9 a month with an additional two shillings and sixpence in danger money.

Instantly, the convoy system in which merchant ships banded together and travelled under armed

---

### *The major threat in the Atlantic was always from U-boats*

---

escort was employed once again, as it had been with marked success in World War I. There were some drawbacks, however, which made shortages more acute on the homefront. For example, it took valuable time for a convoy to be assembled and some ships were compelled to travel by a longer route than they otherwise would have done. Speedier ships were impeded by the pace of slower vessels. Also,

*Left:* **Freezing weather in the Atlantic had the crew thawing out anchor chains.**
*Below:* **U-boats on far-flung missions were dependent on supply ships.**

dockyards became hopelessly congested when a glut of ships arrived all at once.

■ **ESCORT SHIPS** ■

Nevertheless, the accompanying Royal Navy ships at least offered some protection to the merchant fleet. At first, however, the short range of the accompanying ships meant that escorts could only be offered for some 200 miles out of Britain. The convoy was then on its own until it met with a reciprocal Canadian escort a few hundred miles from the other side. It offered a mid-Atlantic gap which was ideal for hunter U-boats.

Even the proximity of the armed destroyers at the outset and close of the voyages proved little deterrent to the U-boats in the opening years of World War II.

The major threat in the Atlantic was always from U-boats and sometimes from merchant ships fitted out with weaponry, known as armed

raiders. Hitler was unwilling to risk his capital ships in the open sea after the Bismarck disaster. Lacking any aircraft carriers, the Germans were unable to launch air bombardments out of range of their airfields.

If they operated at night, the U-boats often went unnoticed by the escort ships even on the surface. Low

> **By the close of 1940, more than 4,700,000 tons of British shipping had been lost**

in the water and much smaller than a surface ship, the most vigilant watch could be forgiven for letting the streamline craft slip by.

The only technology available to counter the threat from U-boats was Asdic, a sonar device which sent out underwater impulses that could, by the sound of the echoes, indicate the presence of solid objects. Not only was it almost useless used at speed or against surface objects, but early models were also unable to produce an accurate range and operators were woefully inexperienced.

In a bid to flush out U-boats during the early months of the war, Royal Navy warships attempted sweeps of convoy routes. The U-boats would simply dive and wait for the danger to pass. Even if their presence was detected, there was every chance the depth charge dropped by a pursuing vessel would fall short of its intended mark.

As the war progressed, Germany eased the way for its U-boat captains in their task of sinking trans-Atlantic shipping by providing new ports from which they could operate. The fall of Norway and France offered plenty of fresh and friendly harbours

for repairs and restocking. In port, the U-boats were housed in specially built bunkers with two metre thick walls. That meant that although the docks came under heavy fire during Allied bombing raids the U-boats remained safe. It wasn't until 1944 that the Allies found sufficient fire power to shatter these solid defences.

By the close of 1940, more than 4,700,000 tons of British shipping had been lost in the form of 1,281 vessels, about one fifth of the pre-war merchant fleet.

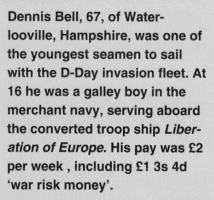

## ◆ EYE WITNESS ◆

**Dennis Bell, 67, of Water-looville, Hampshire, was one of the youngest seamen to sail with the D-Day invasion fleet. At 16 he was a galley boy in the merchant navy, serving aboard the converted troop ship *Liberation of Europe*. His pay was £2 per week , including £1 3s 4d 'war risk money'.**

❝ I spent the early months of 1944 chugging along the south coast to drop off soldiers for secret beach-storming exercises. Looking back, I was incredibly naive about the whole business of war. I was only a kid and I knew nothing. I used to think I'd be all right because I was wearing my lifejacket.

By D-Day I'd already had a taste of the Atlantic War. At 15 I was galley boy aboard a crude carrier called the *Robert F. Hind*, bringing oil from the States to Britain and North Africa. Nobody would ever tell me what was going on – they would just shout at me to get back to the galley and work.

I soon cottoned on to the fact that none of the escort ships wanted to come too close to us. Obviously a tanker was a nice juicy target for the U-boats and if we'd gone up in flames we'd have lit up the sky. ❞

*Left:* **Crewmen on board an escort warship observe the progress of a southbound convoy.**

*Above:* **Always alert, seamen knew the threat of attack was never far away.**
*Right:* **Germany housed her precious U-boats in sturdy concrete bunkers.**

In May 1941, the first convoy to receive protection for the entirety of its voyage set sail. It was an important first step towards victory in the Battle of the Atlantic.

Soon after came the introduction of radar, still far from foolproof but a huge boon to the navy ships charged with spotting predators. Radar also

> ## *Now, at last, aircraft could be brought to bear against the undersea menace*

aided Coastal Command aircraft as to the whereabouts of U-boats. Now, at last, aircraft could be brought to bear against the undersea menace and the planes posted to coastal duties appeared to be reaping a reward. Britain's Admiralty,

without a fleet air arm, was constantly battling to keep those few planes in place when many in the RAF and the war office thought they would be better employed bombing land-based targets in Europe. It took several years for the Germans in command to become fully aware of the danger posed by radar to its U-boats.

Also, the British cashed in on a fatal flaw of the wolf pack system used by U-boats, in which a handful of craft operated together during a convoy attack. To alert nearby boats of the presence of a convoy, the German commanders had to use their radios. The prospect of the British being able to track the signals was dismissed out of hand by the Germans for months. But that is just what did happen when the High Frequency Direction Finder was pioneered, affectionately known as

*Above:* A US destroyer pulls alongside
HMS *Norfolk* to refuel mid-voyage.

'Huff-duff'. When the U-boat position was fixed by the radio operators, it gave Royal Navy vessels far greater scope in their attack.

Convoy defences were reorganised so that extra escort boats could loiter above a submerged submarine for up

## 1941 proved to be a key year for the Allies in their fight against the U-boats

to two days, waiting for the craft to surface for air. Then it was an easy target. Other vessels manoeuvred themselves around the precious convoy ships to fill the gap left by the

lingering vessel for fear that another U-boat would make merry in the unexpected opening.

In the British armoury, too, was the increasing ability of the decoders to pinpoint the position of U-boats. At the start of the war, the translation of the messages sent between the German admiralty and its ships was slow and provided only retrospective information. With practice, the 'tapping' system speeded up, providing accurate and detailed assistance for convoys and British ships on the whereabouts of the enemy. While the German commanders suspected a breach in security, they never identified where the leak was.

So 1941 proved to be a key year for the Allies in their fight against the U-boats. Although 432 ships were

sunk, the total was down on the previous year. The U-boat arm lost 35 of its craft.

When the U-boats turned their attentions to the pickings off America in early 1942, the pressure on the Atlantic convoys eased. But when the U-boats returned to Atlantic waters, it was with a vengeance.

### ■ AIRCRAFT ATTACKS ■

At last U-boat manufacture was coming up to the levels hoped for by Dönitz. Every month, 20 new U-boats left the ship yards.

The boost for the Kriegsmarine was bad news for British sailors in the Atlantic who found themselves

### ◆ EYE WITNESS ◆

**Forbes Brown, from Victoria, British Columbia, joined the Royal Canadian Navy in 1941, training as an Asdic operator.**

❛ Being a Canadian ship, we didn't drink much tea. When we were docked in Londonderry, my pal Bob took me to see 'Black Dan'. He sold 'Black Dan' an enormous box of tea for £1. Bob took the money and later that night tied the box of tea to a rope and lowered it down the side of the ship to the dockside where Dan was waiting.

When I next went ashore, Bob asked me to find 'Black Dan' and offer him a bag of sugar for £1. When Dan came to collect the sugar he tasted it before handing over the money to Bob and making off.

Two nights later I was on gang plank duty when Bob was brought back with a great gash in his head. He had concussion and was severely bruised up. I went to see him later on.

He confessed there was only a fraction of sugar in the bag he had sold 'Black Dan'. The rest was salt, dirt cheap even then. I never went back to see 'Black Dan' again after that and neither did Bob. ❜

once more at the heart of a fierce battle for survival. Although the extended air patrols aided the safety of the ships and significantly improved the rate at which U-boats were knocked out, it was still a fearful fight to the death. U-boats began to attack once more during daylight hours, a sign of their boosted confidence.

During August and September alone U-boats – helped by the German advances in cracking British codes – found 21 convoys and sank 43 ships. By the end of 1942 Allied tonnage totalling 7,500,000 had been

**Below:** A cargo ship is lost amid smoke and flames following an air attack.

**Above:** When a convoy put to sea, the Atlantic throbbed with activity.

sunk, more than the combined totals for the three previous years of war.

Allied aircraft stepped up the numbers of attacks against U-boats during 1943 after the long-awaited allocation of more long-range

> *Between March 1943 and the end of the war, air attack accounted for 290 U-boats*

aircraft. Between March 1943 and the end of the war, air attack accounted for 290 U-boats alone. A surface U-boat could offer little by way of defence to an aircraft as its guns were so small as to be useless.

Suddenly, the campaign against U-boats was accelerating. That spring eight U-boats were lost in the battle to protect one convoy. During May alone 41 were sent to the bottom of the ocean, causing a concerned Dönitz to pull the ranks of remaining U-boats out of the Atlantic for a few

## The importance of the Battle of the Atlantic suddenly loomed large for Hitler

months. Still, he failed to question the security of his cipher system.

The importance of the Battle of the Atlantic suddenly loomed large for Hitler, who had previously been wholly absorbed in his bid to conquer Russia.

In January 1943 Admiral Raeder was replaced as

### ◆ EYE WITNESS ◆

**Swedish-born Nels Olson, 72, from Chicago, USA, was a gunner in the US Navy Armed Guard, responsible for manning 5-inch guns on Atlantic convoy merchant ships.**

There were 1800 of us in the Armed Guard and they split us up to around 25 per ship. I signed up in December 1942 and was assigned to the *Alcobanner*, built during World War I. Later I moved on to Liberty ships. The US built 2,700 of these during the war and it was just as well because the Germans sank so many. I guess we lost nearly 800 in the first eight months.

The Armed Guard took heavier losses than any other US naval unit. Merchant ships were a prime target because there was so little with which to defend them. We knew it was bad when we volunteered. They only took volunteers. No one was ordered to do it.

When the German submarines got in among a convoy it was a terrible sight. They always attacked at night and there was always pandemonium. I remember watching an oil tanker explode. It lit up the skies for miles around. And we had no target to fire back at.

commander in chief of the Kriegsmarine by Dönitz. Hitler saw Dönitz with new eyes after the impressive successes of the U-boat war. Now Dönitz found it impossible to achieve similar standards.

U-boat production was still relatively healthy, despite an increasing shortage of manpower in the dockyards. However, the lack of crews was becoming a dilemma for Dönitz who was compelled to send barely trained men into action despite the fact he believed the success of the U-boats lay at least in part with a rigorous training for the men aboard.

### ■ LIBERTY SHIPS ■

The Allies, meanwhile, had the bonus of Liberty ships – rapidly made craft which went to replace the mercantile fleet decimated by U-boat action. By July 1943, the number of new ships coming out of the American yards

*Left:* **Young, fit men were always needed for the fight against the U-boats.**

"SUB SPOTTED — LET 'EM HAVE IT!"

LEND A HAND – Enlist in your Navy today

was greater in total than the amount being lost.

With losses being so severe, the pack formation was abandoned in the autumn of 1943 and U-boats returned to the Atlantic hunting alone, cutting their effectiveness.

In looking at the Battle of the Atlantic, it is important to remember the contribution made by Britain's own submarines. During the war they sank 15 U-boats. Only three British U-boats were sent to the bottom by U-boats. Submarines were never sighted by their own kind until they were at very close range. For a successful attack to be presse home, the two could be no more than half a mile apart. The first U-boat fell victim to HMS Salmon as early as December 1939.

### ■ COST OF CONFLICT ■

In the last four months of 1943, the U-boats succeeded in sinking 67 ships at a cost of 64 U-boats. Clearly, the Battle of the Atlantic was lost by the Germans although it would be months before shipping in the Atlantic was completely safe from U-boat attack.

*Above:* A convoy reaches port, thanks this time to the Royal Canadian Navy.

At the end of the war, it became clear that the conflicts at sea – chiefly the Battle of the Atlantic – had been costly for both sides.

During the war, the Allies lost 5,150 merchant ships, 2,828 of them to U-boats. The number of merchant seamen who lost their lives amounted to 50,000. The U-boat tally also included 148 Allied warships.

As for the U-boat arm, 785 of its 1,131 strong fleet were lost, costing the lives of at least 27,491 crew and officers. About 5,000 were taken prisoners of war.

### ◆ EYE WITNESS ◆

**J. H. Blonk, from Eindhoven, Holland, was blinded in one eye in 1941 when he was serving as an engineer on the cargo ship *de Friesland* which was hit off the English coast.**

We knew that if we were hit, we were on our own – the other ships would not and were not allowed to turn back otherwise they would be easy targets. The ship saunk so fast that we didn't even manage to get a float from the deck.

I can still remember how the wireless operator who I shared a cabin with was standing beside me. Then the water came and I never saw him again, I just felt his hand on my leg.

I was in the water for four hours. I held on to a panel from the deck that had gone overboard. An English communications officer was holding on to the other side. After an hour or so he said to me: "I think I'm going to let myself go, I'm so tired, I can't hang on any more."

I begged him to keep going. After he went, I lost all conception of time and that is the greatest danger for a drowning man – he thinks he is bobbing around for hours when in reality it is a much shorter time.

After four hours a trawler returned from the convoy to see if there were any survivors. Thirteen members of a 27-man crew were saved.

# MATAPAN

Jostling for pole position in the Mediterranean, the tussle between the Italian and British navies was set to be of epic proportions. In the event, the British navy pulled off a tactical masterstroke which decided the debate before Italy marked its first anniversary at war.

**B**ritain had its own Mediterranean fleet. Key bases for Britain were Gibraltar, at the teeth of the Mediterranean, the hard-pressed island of Malta and Alexandria, the Egyptian port operating under Admiral Sir Andrew Cunningham, from which supplies were being shipped to Greece.

Italy had well-established ports of its home territory opening into the Mediterranean and the Aegean as well as control of Albania and Libya, on the northern coast of Africa.

When war broke out, the British had a grasp of Italian naval codes and gathered enough information to sink nine Italian submarines before the end of June 1940. But a fortuitous switch in cipher systems by the Italians in July prevented the British from cracking the codes again.

The Italian air force wasted no time in bombing the British big ships when they were at sea. Italian intelligence about British sea traffic was

## The Italian air force wasted no time in bombing the British big ships

good. It enabled her captains to circumnavigate all convoys to Libya around the British forces.

Against this background, Cunningham was determined to punish his Italian enemies and put to sea 16 times between June and October 1940. Yet he only managed to track Mussolini's ships three times.

So it was a priceless morale booster for the British when, on 11 November 1940, the Fleet Air Arm

attacked Taranto, an Italian port. In port were six Italian battleships. A dozen Swordfish aircraft from the aircraft carrier Illustrious took off at dusk and flew 170 miles to deal the blow to the Italian navy vessels, struggling to gain height with their heavy load of explosives.

They notched up two strikes with hits against the battleships Cavour and Littorio. A second wave of Swordfish arrived less than an hour afterwards, directed to their target by the blaze now roaring at the base. Together, they damaged the battleship Duilio. At a cost of two aircraft, the Italian fleet was deprived of three valuable battleships – Cavour permanently; Littorio and Duilio until the late spring of 1941.

The Italian navy was still a force to be reckoned with, however. Admiral Cunningham was determined the threat they posed to Allied shipping in the Mediterranean should be rubbed out.

At the turn of the year, Fliegerkorps X, the Luftwaffe's anti-shipping force, transferred 200 of its aircraft to Sicily. By 10 January 1941

bombers from the precision corps landed six bombs on Illustrious and also struck Warspite, although neither ship was terminally damaged.

It demonstrated, however, the need for air superiority if the Allies were to control the Mediterranean. Unfortunately, there was a shortage of Allied aircraft in the area, worsened when the Illustrious was hit again while in dock at Malta. Air attacks against Malta were so heavy and so frequent that it proved impossible to carry out adequate repairs to the much-needed aircraft carrier there. Consequently she had to be withdrawn from the Mediterranean.

### ■ ITALIAN THREAT ■

The British resolve to eradicate the Italian naval threat hardened and its objective was carried out in spectacular fashion, off Cape Matapan, the most southerly point of Greece. On 27 March 1941, a British reconaissance plane spotted a large gathering

*Above:* Italian cruisers *Fiume*, *Gorizia* and *Pola* undergoing manoeuvres.
*Left:* HMS *Revenge* sets sail from Malta in 1939, before the siege.

of Italian ships. The squadron comprised eight cruisers, the prestige battleship Vittorio Veneto and a host of destroyers. Vittorio Veneto was the pride of the Italian fleet now her sister ship Littorio had been holed by the British at Taranto. Now she was poised with her support vessels to blow convoys destined for Greece out of the water.

Cunningham was instantly informed at his base in Alexandria. To back the aircraft sighting there were messages passed through the Italian secret service cipher which had been broken by the Allies. He

*Below:* **The big guns of the *Vittorio Veneto* unleash their fire power.**

## DAKAR DEBACLE

**Among the military calamities faced by Britain in the first half of the war was the debacle of Dakar. British ships sailed to the colony of French West Africa with the aim of landing Free French Forces who would wrest control from the Vichy regime.**

As they anchored off the main port of Dakar on 23 September 1940, General de Gaulle broadcast a series of messages to the colony's governor stating his intention to land troops. All of the messages were ignored. Five messengers sent ashore with similar news were likewise rebuffed.

De Gaulle began threatening to use force. In reply, the coastal guns and ships at anchor in the port let off a barrage at the British ships, preventing the planned landing. The next day the exchange of fire continued with the British battleship *Barham* being struck. Twenty four hours later the battleship *Resolution* was hit, this time sustaining more serious damage.

At this the British commanders and de Gaulle realised that their carefully laid plans to steal a march on Vichy France was quite literally being shot to pieces. Consequently, the ships pulled out of the engagement and returned humiliated to Freetown, the capital of Sierra Leone. Apart from the damage to its ships, the British also had to endure a reprisal air raid by the leaders of Vichy France directed against Gibraltar.

grouped together three battleships, the aircraft carrier Formidable, four cruisers and as many destroyers as he could muster. If trouble was coming, the Royal Navy together with its Australian contingent were prepared.

Admiral Cunningham then made a move to protect the secrecy of the British activities which has since gone down as wartime folklore. A keen golfer, he played regularly in the same club in Alexandria as the Japanese consul who reported every move made by the British Mediterranean Fleet to its enemies. Not only did Cunningham take his clubs to play golf that afternoon but ostentatiously carried a suitcase, clearly bound for a night ashore. Having duped the tell-tale consul, he

abandoned the case and slipped back aboard the battleship Warspite in time for an evening departure. Fortunately, the British ships did not pull out until after the Italians had carried out aerial reconnaissance of Alexandria harbour which revealed all were still at anchor. Italian Admiral Iachino was satisfied the British posed no danger.

The two forces, both travelling in independent groups, first clashed in the morning of 28 March. After 40 minutes of exchanging shells, neither

> *The British launched wave after wave of aircraft to pester the Italians*

side had scored a hit and the action was broken off. The British launched wave after wave of aircraft to pester the Italians who were themselves left virtually completely unprotected by their own air forces – which were stationed in easy range.

*Above: Vittorio Veneto* was the jewel in the Italian navy crown.

Vittorio Veneto was hit by one torpedo but still managed to escape the ravages of the air bombardment. However the cruiser Pola was stopped in her tracks by British firepower. Iachino, who was without the benefit of radar and still apparently oblivious to the presence of British big ships, ordered two other cruisers to assist her. That night all three were attacked at short range. Two were quickly sunk without firing a shot. Pola and two other vessels were also sent to the bottom.

### ■ TIMED EXPLOSIVES ■

The British ships in the vicinity picked up 900 survivors before being scared off by the arrival of Luftwaffe planes. A further 270 men were plucked from the sea in the subsequent days but still the Italian casualties amounted to a devastating 2,400. The Battle of Matapan had been the biggest naval engagement of the war so far and dealt a serious blow to the Italian navy.

Vittorio Veneto was not to escape for long. A British submarine torpedoed her again in December 1941.

Despite the inferiority of Allied air cover, the Royal Navy continued to carry out admirable harrassing manoeuvres against the Italians and the Germans in the Mediterranean. Most notable were the contributions made by the cruisers Aurora and Penelope operating out of Malta who targeted convoys destined for Libya with immense success. Hitler and Mussolini were counting the cost of the contribution to the North African campaign made by the small island.

But the British didn't have it all their own way. When U-boats arrived in the Mediterranean, the fleet was deprived of the aircraft carrier Ark Royal which was sunk in November 1941, as well as the battleship Barham and two cruisers.

If the Italian navy was down, it certainly was not out as its attacks against British ships berthed in the harbour at Alexandria in December 1941 amply illustrated.

In the naval armoury were minute submarines, nick-named 'pigs' by

their crew who were clad in frogmen's suits and sat astride the 22ft long craft. The 'pigs' were carried close to their position by regular submarines. Then it was the job of the crew to go in close to the target and attach timed explosives.

The Italians had made two abortive attempts using 'pigs' against the British during August and September 1940. This time there were to be no mistakes.

## The Battle of Matapan dealt a serious blow to the Italian navy

After dark on 18 December an Italian submarine picked its way quietly and cautiously through mined seas to the approach of Alexandria harbour. There it off-loaded three 'pigs' and six crew, with a noiseless ripple on the water.

Now the Italian frogmen got to work. Beneath the waterline of the

Royal Navy battleship Queen Elizabeth, one team placed an explosive charge. Without being noticed, the two divers scrabbled ashore and posed as French sailors until they were seized by Egyptian police some time afterwards.

The second Italian team struggled to affix explosives to the side of a tanker. They were cold and stricken with sickness after spending too long underwater. But they didn't emerge from the water until their task had been completed. Egyptians arrested them as they attempted to pass the first control post of the harbour.

*Below: Vittorio Veneto smokes after attack by British Albacore planes.*

One member of the third team passed out but bobbed back to the surface and clutched a buoy until his partner finished the job in hand. The latter was having problems of his

---

## The men were still there when an explosion sent the ship lurching to portside

---

own, meanwhile, with a torn diving suit exposing him to lethal cold. Then the 'pig' plunged to the sea bed. Despite the growing effects of exposure, he dived to retrieve it,

*Above: Probably the last photo taken of the Italian big ships before Matapan.*

manhandled it 60 feet back to the base of his target, the Valiant, and set the detonator.

He and his partner, now recovered, were picked up out of the water by a British motorboat and interrogated aboard Valiant. When they refused to speak about their operation, they were sent into the bowels of the ship close to where the charge was planted. The men were still there when an explosion sent the ship lurching to portside. They witnessed the effects of the blasts on the Queen Elizabeth and the tanker, too, with satisfaction. All the vessels would be

### MALTESE CROSS

Malta was awarded the George Cross in April 1942 after four months of continuous bombardment by the Axis air forces. As the Royal Navy battled to get convoys containing vital supplies through to the island, they were hampered by U-boats and airborne attacks which wrecked merchant shipping. It wasn't until August 1942 that a convoy arrived intact. With the volley of bombs coming from the sky the people of Malta and the beleaguered defending forces were subject to the most appalling privations. Yet Malta was a key point in the Allied defences. Had it fallen into the hands of Germany, Rommel would probably have won the battle for North Africa and the outcome of the war might have been different.

out of action for some considerable time to come.

The Italian navy with Luftwaffe assistance continued to blockade Malta, the island which held the key to victory in North Africa. In December 1941 the Germans flew 169 bombing raids over Malta. In January 1942 the number rose to 262. Of course, the devastation took effect and Axis convoys began seeping through once more as Allied ships were put out of action, deprived themselves of fresh supplies.

Nevertheless, Churchill was determined to keep Malta in Allied hands at all costs.

■ **DAILY BOMBINGS** ■

It wasn't until March 1942 that a British convoy managed to slip through the Italian net bringing in vital supplies. Attempts to get supplies to the island in June failed. Yet still the vicious air bombardment continued. Much of the island was laid waste by the daily bombings as Hitler and Mussolini plotted an invasion.

In answer to a pressing need for raw materials, the Allies planned a convoy of unprecedented size and strength in 'Operation Pedestal'. Setting off from Gibraltar to guard the supply ships were three aircraft carriers, two battleships, seven cruisers, 34 destroyers and eight submarines. The US carrier *Wasp* was also in evidence to bring new air forces to the island. The convoy departed on 10 August 1942 and came under repeated air attack. Both the Luftwaffe and Italy's Regia

## *Churchill was determined to keep Malta in Allied hands at all costs*

Aeronautica launched endless attacks with dive bombers, torpedo bombers and fighter aircraft.

In the four day battle which pursued the convoy, the carrier *Eagle* was lost when it was sunk by U73, the cruisers *Cairo* and *Manchester* and the destroyer *Foresight* were sunk and ten out of the 15 merchant ships were floored. Many of the surviving escort ships were damaged. The Italian navy, denied air cover by its own airforce, refused to join the offensive and fell victim to a British submarine as it made its way back to port.

■ **CRITICAL LOSSES** ■

But even though the losses were critical, Malta was saved. Supplies that did filter through, amounting to some 30,000 tons, allowed the islanders and its battered forces to rebuild. It continued as a vital Allied base and deprived the Axis powers of a toehold which would have given them access to North Africa and the Middle East.

Woollen skull cap covered with a fine mesh camouflage net

Mouthpiece and airtube

Rubber tunic, water tight at the wrists, neck and waist

Under water breathing equipment and oxygen bottle

Rubber trousers

Frogmen feet

# SINKING THE BISMARCK

Majestic and mighty, the brand new battle-ship which sailed under the swastika for the first time in May 1941 drew gasps of admiration from friend and foe alike.

The Bismarck cut an awesome sight as it sped through the waves. More than 800 feet long and almost 120 feet wide, it was heavy with armour plating and bristled with giant guns yet was still sleek and fast. Who could blame the proud Germans for believing it was unsinkable?

It was down to the Royal Navy to send the great ship to the ocean floor and it was an urgent task which they were eager to undertake. A powerful battleship like the Bismarck posed an enormous threat to the convoys bringing essential food and materials from across the Atlantic. Without this lifeline from America and Canada, Britain would have quickly been strangled.

*Left:* On the deck of the mighty *Bismarck*. *Below:* The battleship *Bismarck* undergoing sea trials.

Then suddenly there came a more pressing desire to see the Bismarck sunk. For on its maiden voyage it confronted HMS Hood, elegant queen of the Royal Navy, and sank it with the loss of almost all the crew. It was a devastating blow to navy pride and one which had to be avenged. The humblest sailor and the most powerful admiral in the British fleet felt to a man that Bismarck's maiden voyage must also be its last.

Bismarck was built in Hamburg long before the opening salvoes of World War II were fired. The vessel was launched amid great pomp and ceremony on 14 February 1939. Nazi top brass, including navy chief Raeder, Göring, Goebbels and Hess, joined Hitler on a lofty podium when the great hull rumbled down the slipway. There to christen the ship was Dorothea von Loewenfeld, granddaughter of the celebrated German chancellor Bismarck after whom the ship was named.

After World War I, the German navy had been stripped of virtually all its assets and the Treaty of Versailles had strictly forbidden the creation of military muscle like the Bismarck. Hitler had been rebuilding the fleet and Bismarck was the largest addition to date. It was officially

> *A powerful battleship like the* Bismarck *posed an enormous threat to the convoys*

listed at 35,000 tons, some 7,000 tons lighter than it actually was.

When war came, Bismarck stayed in dock while having chunky plating affixed to its sides and decks, the 22 sealed chambers beneath its waterline made watertight and the latest technology installed on the bridge. It was being fitted out for conflict to

become, as Germany's Admiral Tirpitz put it, 'an unsinkable gun platform'.

Its first taste of sea salt came when it left Hamburg on 15 September 1940 for trials in the shelter of Kiel Bay. There were teething troubles and Bismarck had to slink back to Hamburg for modifications. It wasn't until the following May that the ship was ready to set forth.

### ■ AIRCRAFT COVER ■

Hitler arrived at Gotenhafen (now Gdynia) for an inspection of his seaborne gem on 5 May, where Bismarck was patiently waiting to embark on its first trip. He was, it appears, kept unaware that its sailing date was imminent. The Führer, distrustful of his navy and its short-comings, was wary of losing his prize vessel to the enemy and admiralty chiefs feared he would scupper their chances of getting underway at last.

Grand Admiral Erich Raeder believed it was vital to get Bismarck to sea. Germany now had the advantage of Atlantic ports in occupied France to provide bolt holes for its

### ◆ EYE WITNESS ◆

**Frank Hewlett joined the Royal Marines in 1939 when he was 20 years old.**

❝I was on HMS *Aurora*, an escort to the *Hood*. We followed her a day after she left Scapa Flow. When *Hood* was sunk we were 40 miles away. We saw a big flash on the horizon. When we heard the news, nobody believed it.

Then the *Prince of Wales* came within our sights. She was damaged and we escorted her back to Iceland. There was an unexploded shell inside her bows. If it had gone off it would have destroyed the ship. When the shell was removed, it was full of sand. It must have been sabotaged in Germany.

Afterwards, we went to Newfoundland and sank the supply ship *Max Albrecht*, sister ship to the *Altmark*. She went down with a U-boat still attached to her.❞

### *In one sense, the Bismarck was out of date even before setting sail*

ships. Likewise, there was now extended aircraft cover from the Luftwaffe operating out of France. With summer drawing near, the lighter nights would significantly reduce the cover which was needed to spirit the ship into the Atlantic through the British sea blockade. Also, there was the increasing threat of America joining the war on the side of the Allies. The United States' naval power would dwarf that of Nazi Germany.

Fleet commander Gunther Lutjens was as confident in the strength of his new ship as the rest of Germany. But he had one nagging doubt that was shared by many senior officers in the Germany navy. It was the wisdom of going to sea without round-the-clock aircraft cover. In one sense, the Bismarck was out of date even before setting sail. The days of superships dominating the sea were rapidly diminishing. The sun was rising on the fleet air arms which

*Below:* HMS *Hood*, like the *Bismarck*, was thought by admirals to be invincible.

*Left:* A confident crew parade aboard the *Bismarck* unaware of their fate.

could offer so much more by way of flexibility and accuracy. While both Japan and America were gearing up their navies for the new age, Germany and Britain were lagging behind, both caught unawares by the outbreak of war. The Bismarck had the capacity to hold just four floatplanes, which were used primarily for reconnaissance missions.

Lutjens himself was the son of a retailer who shone at naval college in

> ## It was only a matter of time before sighting of this monster was confirmed to London

Kiel after making an early resolution to combat any hurdle placed in front of him. A veteran of the sea assaults in World War I, he had already earned the distinction of a Knight's Cross during World War II through his courage in the Norwegian campaign of 1940.

Loyal to his country, 51-year-old Lutjens was nevertheless not a Nazi and refused to offer the party salute. Instead he preferred the time-honoured navy salute and wore the old fashioned insignia of the Kaiser's navy instead of a swastika.

On 19 May the Bismarck sailed under cover of darkness to begin 'Operation Rheinubung'. In the company of the 17,000-ton heavy cruiser Prinz Eugen, itself a formidable ship, the Bismarck purred off into the Baltic to be joined by other German navy vessels for its historic voyage. Its aim was to sink the battleships protecting convoys while the smaller Prinz Eugen picked off the merchantmen.

### ■ VULNERABILITY ■

Slipping down the Danish waterways and shadowing the Swedish coastline, it was only a matter of time before the sighting of this magnificent monster was confirmed to London. It was enough to spark Sir John Tovey, commander in chief of the Home Fleet, into action. At the pinnacle of his plan would be HMS Hood, 20 years old but still an inspiring sight. It was a match for the Bismarck in size and gunnery but its weakness lay in the relatively thin armour plating which covered its body and decks. It was this vulnerability that Bismarck exploited to the full.

On 22 May, just a day after news of the Bismarck arrived in London, Hood, the Prince of Wales and six other vessels set off from Scapa Flow. The following day two of the fleet, the Norfolk and the Suffolk, encountered the Bismarck in the Denmark Strait, between Iceland and Greenland. As they dashed for cover in the icy fog, the Bismarck registered their presence and fired off a warning shot.

### ■ DEADLY BLOW ■

The mood was tense among officers and men on the Hood and the Prince of Wales as the hunt for their fearsome quarry continued. All the crew were poised to strike but lost their chance when their ships slipped past the giant battleship in the darkness as it skirted the Greenland ice pack.

Bismarck continued altering its course, not greatly but enough to put the ships commanded by Vice-Admiral Lancelot Holland in a

*Above:* Following his encounter with *Hood*, Admiral Lutjens bolted for France.

# ◆ HUNTING THE *BISMARCK*

On 19 May the *Bismarck* sailed under cover of darkness to begin Operation Rheinubung. In the company of the heavy cruiser *Prinz Eugen*, *Bismarck* headed through the Skagerrak to the Norwegian coast. Passing so close to the Danish and Swedish coasts, it was only a matter of time before the two warships were sighted by British agents, and the

news transmitted to London. Sir John Tovey was ordered to get the *Bismarck*.

On 22 May, just a day after news of the *Bismarck* arrived in London, the largest ship in the Royal Navy, HMS *Hood*, and the brand-new battleship HMS *Prince of Wales* set off from Scapa Flow in the Orkneys, accompanied by six other vessels.

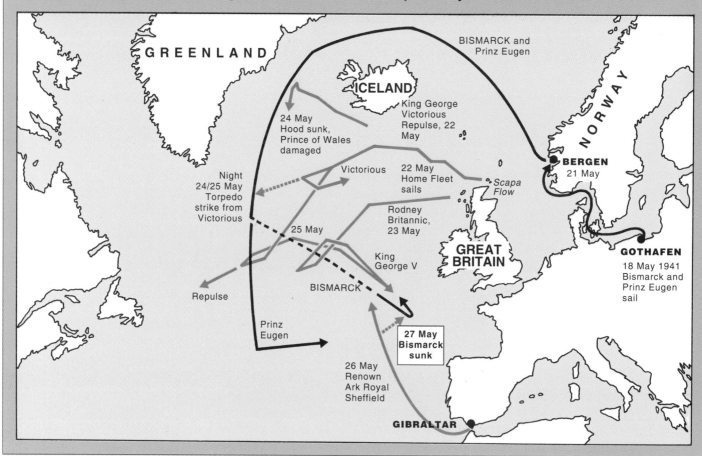

quandary. The initial plan had been to creep up on the *Bismarck* under cover of darkness in a short range strike. Now the *Hood* was forced to make a broad sweep at the enemy and would be exposed to the brunt of its firepower.

When they sighted *Bismarck*, the *Hood* and *Prince of Wales*, travelling in close formation, were about 17 miles distant. At Admiral Holland's command, both ships began a charge at the enemy.

Lutjens was under orders to engage only the escorts of convoys. He wasn't

looking for a duel and had hoped to avoid one. But now he had no choice. When the *Hood* and *Prince of Wales*

## The initial plan had been to creep up on the Bismarck *under cover of darkness*

closed the gap to 13 miles, they fired. Seconds later, the *Bismarck* and the *Prinz Eugen* replied in kind. And while

the British ships failed to find their targets, the Germans had them well and truly in range.

The second salvo from *Prinz Eugen*'s guns struck the *Hood*, igniting anti-aircraft ammunition. Another hit and then a third slaughtered many of the gun crews taking shelter. Still the guns from both sides continued firing.

It was during a manouevre by the *Hood* trying for a better angle that the deadly blow was delivered by the *Bismarck*. A shell plunged down into the heart of the ship, penetrating the

*Above: Prinz Eugen was released from escort duty to escape the Royal Navy.*

deck with apparent ease. Somewhere in the bowels, it silently sparked an ammunition store, maybe two. The effect was catastrophic. Observers from both sides were astonished to see a massive plume of fire and smoke burst from the middle of the ship when there had been no explosion. The Hood, the most prestigious

## The Hood *folded in two and plunged to the bottom of the sea*

ship in old England, folded in two and plunged to the bottom of the sea.

With it went the vast majority of the 1,400 crew, trapped in the wreckage. It was several hours before a British cruiser came hunting for survivors. It found only three, cold and near death, clinging to small rafts in the middle of an oil slick.

The Prince of Wales was soon reeling from the effect of shells. It had been hit seven times, lost two officers and 11 men and was plagued with difficulties in its gunnery, making its own attack ineffective. Moments after

its stunned crew saw the Hood ditching into the sea, it was decided to withdraw. The showdown had lasted just 21 minutes.

Britain was devastated by the loss of the Hood and its men. After the shock, the public were baying for revenge – or feared the Bismarck really was indestructible. There was no time for sentimentality among the naval officers now in hot pursuit of the Bismarck.

The battleship Prince of Wales, plus the cruisers Norfolk and Suffolk shadowed the Bismarck as it moved south. Admiral Tovey, aboard King George V, was in command of Victorious, Repulse, four cruisers and nine destroyers hoping to intercept Bismarck from the south.

Visibility was poor, however, and the radar used by Suffolk to track its movements was patchy. Bismarck had, in fact, not escaped unscathed. It was holed twice by British shells which forced it to reduce speed and lost the vessel valuable fuel.

### ■ BISMARCK HURT ■

Lutjens felt he had no choice but to head for France for repairs. He released the Prinz Eugen to make a clean getaway, firing lazily at the Prince of Wales by way of distraction. Then he set a course which he hoped would take him to friendly

France or within the torpedo range of a protective U-boat.

It was with some degree of surprise that he and his crew looked up to the skies some hours later and saw a group of circus-style planes buzzing towards them. These were the Swordfish planes which had set off from the Victorious in order to wreak havoc on the Bismarck. With

*Below: Hitler failed to share the nation's pride in the navy.*

## ◆ EYE WITNESS ◆

**Able Seaman Robert Kilburn was one of the three who survived the sinking of the *Hood*.**

❝ I was a member of the anti-aircraft gun crew but, of course, we weren't needed. There were only two other people with me at the time. The others were in a shelter deck – a shell had gone in there and killed all of them, about 200 men – but I didn't know that at the time.

One of the shells hit one of the ready-fuse lockers for the four inch guns and there was a fire on board the upper deck and the ammunition was exploding. We were laid on the deck and then there was this terrific explosion. It was most peculiar, the dead silence that followed it – I don't know if we were deaf.

One of the other men was dead and the other one had his sides cut open and all his innards were tumbling out. I went to the ship's side to be sick. I noticed that the ship was rolling over and the bows were coming out of the water so I started taking off my tin hat, gas mask, anti-flash gear, overcoat, oilskin, so that I would have a chance to swim. With the ship rolling over, I just went into the water and the water came up to me.

I was terrified. I had a small rubber life belt on which you blew up – it was partially blown up. I started swimming away from the ship. I had a right belt on so I took my knife off and cut the belt off to breathe better. The ship rolled over and the yard arms which had been broken during the action hit me across the legs and the wireless aerials tangled around my legs, pulling me down with the ship. I cut my seaboots off with the knife and shot up, like a cork out of a bottle. I must have been about 10 ft down by then. The ship was around 10 yards away from me with her bows straight up in the air – and she just sank. ❞

In 1989 a team led by Dr Robert Ballard located the crusted hulk of the *Bismarck* (above) nestling on the ocean floor. Dr Ballard, the man who found and photographed the wreck of the *Titanic*, was aboard the *Star Hercules* when he discovered the *Bismarck* three miles beneath the ocean during a 10-day expedition. Among the photographs he took with a remote controlled underwater camera were those of discarded boots, the teak deck which was still intact and a 14-inch gun with a sea anenome bursting from its barrel.

survived the hair-raising attack and landed safely back on Victorious in the dark with next to no fuel.

The damage sustained by Bismarck was enough to make Lutjens review his course. With masterly intuition he turned suddenly westwards and, in doing so, shook off the Royal Navy shadow. It took 31 hours for the British to locate the Bismarck again.

By now most of the British ships in reach had been called in to help. Yet due to a series of mishaps and misunderstandings, they were unable to find the roaming battleship, having turned

## On 26 May intrepid Swordfish planes found Bismarck *again and attacked*

in the wrong direction. In addition, many were running short of fuel and had to splinter from the body of the fleet to find more. Navy top brass was becoming increasingly nervous. Unaware that the Bismarck had been wounded, they knew its path must be taking it towards the 11 Allied convoys presently crossing the Atlantic.

On 26 May intrepid Swordfish, this time from the Ark Royal, found Bismarck again and attacked. Two torpedoes struck the big ship, wrecking the steering gear and ruining a propeller. It meant that Bismarck not only had to slow down further but also became locked on to a course which brought it directly into the path of the opposition, thanks to the jammed rudder.

The following day Bismarck came within range of the battleships Rodney and King George V. They weren't alone and soon the Bismarck was surrounded by British ships

their single propellers and stacked wings they look like something from a different age. Nevertheless, the torpedo they carried beneath their fuselage was powerful enough to

reckon with. The brave pilots of the Swordfish planes flew in low despite the barrage of anti-aircraft fire. Just one torpedo hit the mark. Yet all the eight attacking Swordfish planes

*Above:* The *Prince of Wales* was one of many ships to hunt the *Bismarck*.

firing when they could. Bismarck took punch after punch, losing men and guns with every minute of the merciless onslaught. Fires raged fore and aft while ammunition exploded all around. Yet still it stayed afloat.

Afterwards, British sailors admitted they felt little elation at seeing the enemy ship battered so badly. However, they had no option but to continue the barrage while the Bismarck still fired back.

## ■ HITLER'S OUTRAGE ■

When streams of German sailors plunged into the sea, the shelling stopped. Tovey was not only mindful of their safety but also that of his own men. Fuel and ammunition were running desperately low in his fleet. It would not be long before the lurking U-boats would turn up looking for easy pickings.

Satisfied the Bismarck would no longer menace the shipping lanes of the Atlantic, he gave orders for the British ships to withdraw. The only ship left with torpedoes, the Dorsetshire, remained to finish off the job. Controversy raged afterwards

whether it was a British torpedo or a German sailor who sank the Bismarck by opening the sea-cocks.

The situation for the men floundering in the water after leaping from the Bismarck was bleak. At first the Dorsetshire and the destroyer Maori hauled up survivors. But their goodwill came to an abrupt end following the reported sighting of a U-boat. The ships revved up and pulled away from the bobbing survivors, ignoring their cries for help and leaving them to suffer a lingering death in the waves. Two other vessels

rescued a handful of survivors between them. Only 115 of the crew escaped with their lives out of a total of 2,206.

When news of the sinking reached Hitler he was outraged. Never mind that a fleet of five battleships, three battle cruisers, two aircraft carriers, 13 cruisers, 33 destroyers and eight submarines had been involved in the execution. He bitterly regretted ever putting his classic ship to sea.

*Below:* How the incredible story of pursuit was told to the British public.

# ARCTIC CONVOYS

Manning a ship on one of the treacherous Arctic convoys was perhaps the bleakest role in the whole war. For on these storm-lashed northern routes the weather collaborated with the enemy to make each day more miserable than the last.

Arctic convoys began after Soviet Russia was invaded by Germany and became an eminent ally of Great Britain. It wasn't a matter of survival to Britain as in the case of the Atlantic convoys.

Here was an exercise designed to appease Russia's leader Stalin. To exploit the opportunities for trade between the two countries, ships had to travel in the vicinity of the north pole where, for winter weeks on end, the sun never rose.

Hidden dangers under the waves included icebergs as well as U-boats. In the air the threat lay in frostbite alongside the dive-bombing planes of the Luftwaffe. The iron-grey steel hulls belonging to the powerful surface ships of the German navy were often masked by soupy fogs or dense blizzards.

### ■ REGULAR LOSSES ■

The sailors aboard knew they were being hunted. The buzz of a German reconnaissance plane overhead was a sure indication that an attack was

being prepared. Sometimes, not often enough, the convoy skirted the edge of the polar ice and slid through the ocean without being noticed. Sole reward for the hapless mariners was the chance of arriving in one piece at their destination.

Ships carrying the precious cargoes travelled under protection of British and American warships in convoys, usually between Scotland or Iceland and Murmansk, Russia. These north-

*Above:* A U-boat crew operating in northern waters survey their iced-up weapons.

ern waters were particularly risky. After Germany invaded Norway, it meant there were ports and airfields accessible to German forces within easy range. Hitler was also dedicated

## *Hidden underwater dangers included icebergs and U-boats*

to victory over Russia. The sea battles to stop the convoys getting through to Stalin assumed greater importance given the personal interest of the Führer.

In reply the Allies did have the benefit of technology. Their grasp of the German naval secret codes was now accomplished. Yet despite re-routing to evade the attentions of the Arctic U-boats, convoys were still

*Far left:* A British convoy leaves the warmth of British waters for Russia.
*Left:* Two Valentine tanks included in the aid sent to Russia.

ALL HELP FOR RUSSIA NOW

suffering regular losses. Virtually every convoy which set sail between March and June 1942 was attacked, either by U-boat or by the Luftwaffe. In all, 21 ships were lost in addition to the cruisers Edinburgh and Trinidad. Those losses were balanced against the safe arrival of 124 ships.

Now it seemed Germany was ready to pitch its prestige big ships into the fray. Britain's Admiralty was nervous. Knowing that ships like the Admiral

> ## Virtually every convoy which set sail between March and June 1944 was attacked

Hipper and Admiral Scheer were in northern waters, biding their time in safe ports, made the prospects for any future convoys seem gloomy. Also there was Lützow formerly known as Deutschland. (Hitler changed the name because the sinking of a ship called 'Germany' would cause depression at home and would be the butt of jokes among his enemies.) Worst of all

**Forbes Brown, from Victoria, British Columbia, joined the Royal Canadian Navy in 1941 and trained as an Asdic operator.**

" My first trip was in a corvette, HMCS *Algoma*, across the North Atlantic as a convoy escort. With Asdic we transmitted a sound beam and it reflected back if there was a submarine under the water. I could hardly believe it when I picked up a contact. Action stations were sounded. It was about 600 yards ahead. About 40 depth charges were dropped.

Following the last one there was a tremendous explosion underwater. It blew out all the safety valves on the engine and there were blue flames shooting off the deck. We suspected the last charge hit a torpedo head. Still there were plenty of other U-boats about. We started off with 62 ships in the convoy and ended up with 41. It was hairy. After that trip we were supplied with sheepskins so we suspected we were going north. As usual, it was a foul up. We were off to the Mediterranean. "

was the presence of the huge battleship Tirpitz, sister ship of the Bismarck and the pride of the German fleet, with awesome firepower and astonishing capabilities.

Code-crackers revealed the large boats were preparing to depart and do battle. Convoy PQ17, sailing out of Iceland's capital, Reykjavik, on 27 June, comprised 33 ships and a tanker with an escort of six destroyers, four corvettes, two submarines and two anti-aircraft ships It was in danger of a severe mauling.

*Left:* Some of the British and US ships involved in safeguarding the Arctic convoy routes.

In London, it was clear that the enemy could pounce at any time. At sea, the convoy captains were equally expectant, wondering where and when the ferocious strike would come. Each bank of fog came as a welcome relief as the convoy made its way steadily northwards.

Information now coming out of the cipher service indicated the big ships were setting out from their base. It was enough for Sir Dudley Pound, First Lord of the Admiralty, to order the convoy ships to scatter

secret message service had been misconstrued – with devastating results. As ordered, the convoy

## Watch officers scanned the horizon, expecting to see the massive vessel looming

*Below: Scharnhorst was the scourge of convoys in northern waters.*

when the U-boats and the Luftwaffe seized the golden opportunity.

In fact, the Tirpitz did sail on 5 July but was recalled following the success the attack had already achieved. Neither did the big ships take part in action against the subsequent convoy, PQ18. Hitler once again erred on the side of caution rather than risk another humiliating loss at sea to parallel the Bismarck. Before reaching safety, PQ18 lost ten ships to aircraft and three to U-boats. The escort ships which this time

for their best protection. Little did he know that Hitler himself had intervened in the operation. He barred the use of valuable, prestige ships like the Tirpitz unless complete safety could be guaranteed. That meant British and American aircraft carriers were safely out of range.

Tirpitz was not heading for the convoy. The information from the

scattered. Armed ships pulled away from the merchant ships to search for the Tirpitz and its team. Apprehensively, the watch officers scanned the horizon, expecting to see the massive vessel looming. Nothing appeared. Now their nagging anxieties lay with the fate of the ships they had left behind, with good cause. Twenty of Convoy PQ17's vessels were lost

stayed close to their charges, claimed a number of planes with anti-aircraft fire and Allied fighter aircraft while one U-boat was sunk.

When the might of the German navy next put to sea it was at the end of the year following some intensive exercises. Their target was a 14-ship convoy, JW51B, which set out from Scotland destined for Kola on 22

*Left:* RAF Mosquitos pounced on surfaced submarines and enemy shipping at every opportunity and soon helped to tip the balance of the battle.

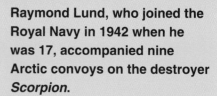

## ◆ EYE WITNESS ◆

**Raymond Lund, who joined the Royal Navy in 1942 when he was 17, accompanied nine Arctic convoys on the destroyer *Scorpion*.**

'We were never dry. And if ever you went to change your clothes you had to do it very quickly as you never knew when 'action stations' would be called. We were often at action stations 22 hours a day.

There wasn't much sleep for anyone. When I did sleep it was fully clothed on a bench with my arms wrapped around a pillar on the mess deck. I even slept standing up.

About 16 to 18 U-boats would form a line ahead of us. We used to charge through and disperse them. In the summer it was never dark, in the winter it was never light. We used to like a bit of a rough sea. It may have been uncomfortable but it kept the U-boats away.

When it was cold, it was difficult to breathe. I used to pull something wollen across my mouth to break the rush of air as it came through. Never at any time could we touch metal. It would burn and stick to your fingers and it would mean a trip to the sick bay. In the middle of winter we weren't allowed on the upper deck where the temperature could be as low as minus 50 degrees C.

The most memorable day of the war for me was when we sank the *Scharnhorst*. It was Boxing Day 1943. We were escorting a convoy to Russia when we had news that she was at sea. We were soon given orders to leave the convoy and proceeded to intercept.

The *Duke of York* came up behind. There were two destroyers to her starboard and two to port. The *Scorpion* fired torpedoes at the *Scharnhorst* which slowed her up. Her guns were firing all the time as well. We saw various hits. Then an Arctic fret obscured our view. We knew by a terrific explosion when she had gone. Our ship picked up over 30 survivors. We took them back to Scapa Flow and they became prisoners of war. '

December. It was the second leg of a convoy, the first of which had crossed the sea without being spotted. A flotilla of destroyers joined up with the convoy on Christ-

## *The weather was poor, hampering visibility and identification of ships*

mas Day. Sailing to meet them were the cruisers which had accompanied the first part of the convoy.

This time, the code-breakers let down the protection ships by failing to translate a vital enemy message in good time. Admiral Hipper and the pocket battleship Lützow, in the company of six destroyers, put to sea on 30 December. The British had no idea of the threat in the absence of deciphered enemy messages.

The weather was poor, hampering visibility and therefore the identification of ships whose shadows suddenly appeared in the mist. The first the Allied destroyers knew of the imminent danger was when the

destroyer Obdurate was fired on by one of the German destroyers.

While the convoy pulled back under the cover of a smoke screen, the destroyers set about repelling the advance. Four times the Hipper tried to break through to fire on the convoy and on each occasion the destroyers pushed it back. The only damage Admiral Hipper did was on the last attack when an eight inch shell ploughed into the Onslow. One other destroyer, Achates, was sunk along with the minesweeper Bramble before the Battle of the Barents Sea was over.

### ■ GERMAN DEFEAT ■

Hipper was forced to retire into a snow storm when it was hit three times. Lützow, although in a prime position to attack the convoy, kept its guns silent. A German destroyer which suddenly emerged from a snowstorm close to the Sheffield, by now pursuing Hipper, was soon sunk. The convoy continued on its way.

A squally, inconclusive battle, it was nevertheless a humiliating defeat for the German navy. One of its prestige ships was forced to pull away with substantial damage while the aim of the attack, the sinking of the convoy, was frustrated.

Hitler was furious at the debacle. On New Year's Day 1943 he threatened to decommission the German fleet completely and break up the big ships for scrap. Grand Admiral Raeder, he claimed, lacked the pioneering spirit of adventure that was necessary to win wars. Raeder responded immediately, by asking to be relieved of his command.

### ■ DARING PLAN ■

In his place came Admiral Karl Dönitz, hitherto commander of the U-boat service. Hitler much preferred Dönitz to his predecessor and, in turn, Dönitz was able to convince the Führer of the need to maintain the surface fleet. Nevertheless, he too was unable to find further successes, despite his efforts.

*Below:* **An X-craft, like those used against** *Tirpitz*, **with its commander on deck.**

The British Admiralty chiefs appeared to have a greater faith in the destructive power of the German fleet than Hitler himself. In northern waters, they remained wary of the threat posed by Tirpitz, Lützow and Scharnhorst. Indeed, Arctic convoys were even cancelled on the basis that the big three might sail.

By September 1943 a daring plan had been drawn up to rid the convoys of the naval menace once and for all. The aim was for four-man midget submarines armed with two one-ton charges to creep into the Norwegian anchorage at Altenfjord and place crippling explosives on the undersides of Scharnhorst, Lützow and Tirpitz. In utmost secrecy, the mission began with full-sized submarines towing the midgets to the mouth of the fjord.

Unluckily, Scharnhorst was at sea for trials when the six midget submarines went into action. The tiny undersea craft assigned to blow

up Lützow was lost as it made its way there. Another lost its tow and was forced to jettison the charges. A third caught fire and had to turn back. But the success of submarines X5, X6 and X7 more than made up for the disappointing performances of the other three.

When one of the midgets was spotted the alarm was raised. One was forced to surrender. The other

---

### Hitler threatened to decommission the German fleet completely

---

sank with the loss of two lives and the third was sunk, although it is not known when and how. But all this unfolded after at least three of the charges had been laid. Although held captive on the ship itself, the seamen

*Right:* X-craft crew got fresh air whenever they could to relieve the closet-style condition of their vessel.

who surrendered refused to reveal the whereabouts of the explosives. Finally, the Germans got their answer when the mighty Tirpitz was lifted five feet out of the water. It would take seven months to complete repairs. Both surviving submarine commanders, Lieutenants Donald Cameron and Godfrey Place, were rewarded after the war with the VC.

### ■ POOR WEATHER ■

Lützow abandoned the hunt for the Arctic convoys soon afterwards, returning to occupied Poland for operations in the Baltic. That left the last remaining danger – Scharnhorst – in Norwegian waters, fully equipped and ready for action. It was only a matter of time before she would venture forth to take on a convoy and this troubled the British commanders whose job it was to protect the merchant ships.

On Christmas Day 1943 the order to sail finally came for the expectant Scharnhorst crew, eager as they were to salvage the good name of the

## Scharnhorst *had no idea it was heading towards the Royal Navy's big cruisers*

German navy. The ship emerged from its protective fjord in the company of five destroyers that evening in search of convoy JW55B.

Poor weather once again played its part, this time to the advantage of the Allies. Scharnhorst hived away from its destroyer escorts. Lacking the superior intelligence assistance open

to the Allies, it had no idea it was heading towards some of the Royal Navy's big cruisers in the region.

First to fire on the German was HMS Belfast who picked up the enemy by radar. Norfolk then joined the battle by opening fire and scoring a hit. The British ships broke off their action, not wanting to scare Scharnhorst back into port.

Next to spy it was Sheffield some two hours later. In the spat that

followed it was Norfolk's turn to sustain damage. Yet the British cruisers did a brilliant job. They drove the unsuspecting Scharnhorst into the arms of Admiral Fraser on the Duke of York. At a range of 1,200 yards, the Duke of York opened fire with its devastating 14-inch guns. This time Scharnhorst fled to the east, making good ground against its pursuers. But critical damage forced the German ship to steady its speed. It gave

British destroyers ample opportunity to unleash some torpedoes, finally sinking the Scharnhorst at 7.45pm. Just 36 survivors were saved from a crew of 2,000.

Tirpitz was now the lone operator in the Arctic. Although it rarely saw action, its presence alone was sufficient cause to divert air and naval craft from other duties. It would not be allowed to escape unscathed for long. Nevertheless, it was to be aircraft that delivered the death-blows to this massive battlewagon.

### ■ TIRPITZ SUNK ■

The first sortie against it began from Scapa Flow on 30 March 1944 with the Duke of York, Belfast, Anson and the aircraft carrier Victorious in 'Operation Tungsten'. On 3 April, 42 Barracuda aircraft loaded with powerful, armour-piercing bombs set off after their quarry, which was at that moment in Norway's Altenfjord, preparing to go to sea.

*Above:* Wintry seas kept British sailors perpetually wet. *Left:* Proud gunners on HMS *Duke of York* posed for the camera in front of their guns after sinking the German battlecruiser *Scharnhorst.*

The action devastated the upper decks of Tirpitz and killed 122 men. Yet the supership stayed afloat, to the disappointment of the Allies.

Several other bids to sink the ship by Fleet Air Arm aircraft were thwarted by poor weather while still more failed to deliver the necessary punch to put it out of action. Aircraft were being lost in these vain attempts, forcing the Admiralty to think again. They called in the assistance of Bomber Command which had vast 'Tallboy' bombs.

Taking off from a Russian base on 15 September 1944, a cloud of Lancaster bombers rained 16 such bombs on the Tirpitz, causing extensive damage. This time it would take nine months to make the repairs.

If the crippled Tirpitz had not moved to Tromsö that October, the Allies might have been satisfied. Germany wanted it as a floating gun platform to defend an expected invasion in the region by the Allies. Yet the Admiralty was disturbed by the ship's sudden activity and feared new attacks at sea.

On 29 October, 32 Lancaster bombers in 'Operation Obviate' caused more devastation. However it wasn't until 'Operation Catechism' got underway involving the men and Lancaster aircraft of 617 Squadron – 'the Dambusters' – on 12 November 1944 that Tirpitz finally rolled over and died. About 1,000 crewmen were lost, trapped inside the great ship as it turned turtle.

# CORAL SEA AND MIDWAY

Pearl Harbor may have been the most spectacular action undertaken by the Japanese navy but it wasn't the last.

**H**ere was the world's third most powerful navy staffed by efficient, skilled commanders and loyal sailors. It was their brief to roam the seas around Japan's newly acquired territories, protecting land-based flanks by fending off attacks from air and sea.

The Japanese navy played a major role in the domino fall of Asian and Pacific lands and islands, including that of Thailand, Hong Kong, the Philippines and Burma. Indeed, the noose put around Singapore by the Japanese navy during February 1942 ensured that none of the defending British or Australian troops could escape by sea and all those who survived the fighting were consequently taken prisoner.

When the Japanese cast their eyes in the direction of Java, the jewel they wanted in their crown, an allied naval force squared up to the challenge. Under Dutch officer Admiral Karel Doorman, a fleet of heavy and light cruisers and destroyers gathered from the Dutch, American, British and Australian navies determined to keep the Japanese out of the oil-rich colony.

### ■ BATTLE OF JAVA ■

The Battle of the Java Sea began on 27 February and was one of the largest naval confrontations the world had seen since World War I.

Both sides seemed equally matched when they began a mutual bombardment with guns. But the Japanese wreaked havoc when they edged closer to the Allied fleet and opened up with torpedoes.

Hostilities ceased while the Allied ships refuelled only to resume within hours beneath the moonlight. Doorman was delighted when he once again encountered the Japanese and sought to end their plans to invade Java once and for all. Little did he realise that he was being snapped up in a tactical pincer. When

### *The Japanese wreaked havoc when they edged closer to the Allied fleet*

*Left:* Crews from USS *Lexington* go into action in the Coral Sea in May 1942.
*Below:* Carrying the wounded off USS *Marblehead* in Netherlands East docks after the Battle of Java in February 1942.

In March US planes took off from the carriers Yorktown and Lexington to attack two ports on Papua New Guinea which had just been overrun by the Japanese. Again, the results were negligible.

America determinedly began to gather its strength. US troops were sent to Darwin in Australia and were

## The US felt confident enough only to take pot shots at the Japanese

by February under the command of General Douglas MacArthur. In fact, almost four times as many troops were sent from America to the Pacific at the time than took the shorter hop across the Atlantic to reinforce the Allied armies aiming to defeat Hitler.

Australian divisions, too, were recalled from the Middle East to help defend their homeland.

And the tide of Japanese successes was set to ebb as early as May 1942 with two historic seaborne clashes between Japan and America, one in

more torpedoes blasted his force in a surprise attack from a second angle there was chaos. In just seven hours, five Allied warships were sunk, while only one Japanese destroyer sustained damage. Doorman himself was lost when his cruiser De Ruyter went down.

### ■ BATTLE OF MIDWAY ■

So far the Emperor's fleet remained virtually unscathed by the ravages of war. During all its activities in the sea-borne invasions of Pacific and South East Asian islands only a total of four destroyers had been put out of action. Meanwhile, only four US destroyers had escaped to Australia from the treacherous waters around the Dutch East Indies. It seemed as if the Japanese navy was invincible.

*Above, right, far right:* **The triumphant Doolittle raid on Tokyo. A B-25 comes under starter's orders on its way to Japan. Doolittle is pictured later by his crashed aircraft in China.**

At the time the US felt confident enough only to take pot shots at the Japanese. The first skirmish took place in January when two US task forces bombed Japanese bases on the Marshalls and Gilberts. It was a tame event but nevertheless proved a small boost for American morale, being the first strike back at the enemy.

# ◆ BATTLE OF MIDWAY

Japan wanted a base within striking range of Hawaii. It also wanted the US fleet destroyed. Yamamoto hatched a plan to secure such a base and lure the US Navy to its downfall in the process. He launched a diversionary attack on the Aleutians while he struck at Midway Island. Unfortunately for him the Americans knew he was coming and had put to sea. The

first wave of Japanese bombers caught many US aircraft on the ground at Midway. Nevertheless, enough got airborne to make a second Japanese strike necessary. It was while the Japanese were rearming that US Admiral Spruance struck. Aircraft from *Yorktown* and *Enterprise* destroyed four Japanese carriers; on the US side, *Yorktown* was sunk.

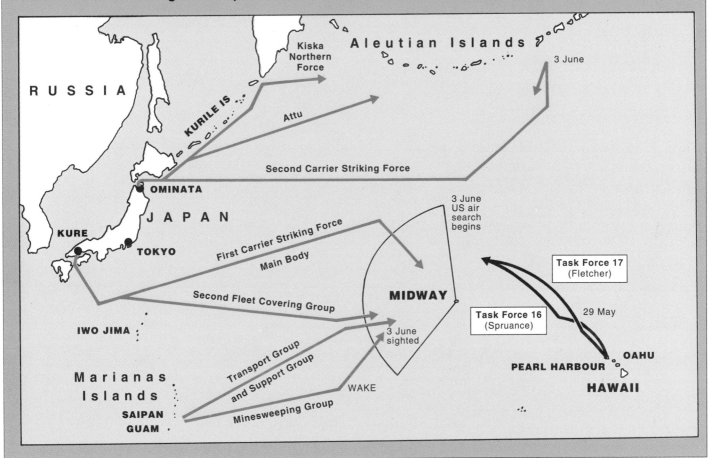

the Coral Sea and the other around the island of Midway.

The Battle of the Coral Sea was not notable for its end result as the outcome was so murky it was difficult to distinguish a winner. Japan certainly wasn't defeated but its navy was for the first time halted. However, it was the first ever confrontation at sea to take place with the enemy ships placed hundreds of miles apart.

The firepower was carried to the opposition entirely by the planes stationed on the mighty carriers

ranged against each other, capable of causing wholesale devastation.

Meanwhile, the Battle of Midway proved to be a turning point in the fortunes of war and gave America the opportunity once more to assert naval superiority.

By May, Japan had control of New Britain, parts of Papua New Guinea and the majority of the Solomon Islands. It formed the outer edge of a

## *The island of Midway was a glaring hole in Japan's line of defence*

Pacific empire which was fanning out towards Australia. The country's remaining aim was to secure the line of defence by conquering the remainder of Papua New Guinea.

Japanese priorities changed, however, with the most effective nuisance raid mounted by the Americans to date. It came with Lieutenant

### ◆ EYE WITNESS ◆

**Normand N. Silver, from Montreal, was a stoker first class. A member of the Royal Canadian Navy Volunteer Reserve, he served aboard aircraft carriers HMS *Thames* and HMCS *Punchuard* and also the minesweeper HMCS *Quatisino*.**

❝ I volunteered principally because I reckoned it was my duty. But we all guessed that if Hitler wasn't stopped then in 1945 or 1950 he'd maybe be sending his armies across to Canada.

The main action I saw was around the coast of Alaska in *Quatisino*. The Americans had a lot of their ships berthed up there and they didn't want another Pearl Harbor on their hands. So our job was to seek and destroy any Japanese subs that wanted to try their luck. It meant we were on round the clock patrol.

We were credited with killing one sub, but you could never know for sure. In the engine room you didn't get to see much anyway.

It's hard to explain the pressure you are under when you're fighting submarines. If you are a nervous person then you are in real trouble. You have to expect an attack every minute of every hour of every day. You don't know where the attack will come from and you don't know how long it will be before the next. You don't sleep much and you don't relax. I think that is the story of most men's war. ❞

Colonel J. Doolittle's bombing raid over Tokyo in April mounted through an open door from Midway. The island of Midway was held by a small garrison of American marines and was a glaring hole in Japan's line of defence. Although the damage caused during the 16-plane raid was light, it gave the Japanese hierarchy a shake up and compelled them to look again at domestic security.

### ■ FIRST BLOOD ■

Admiral Yamamoto, confident in the continuing might of his navy, was appalled at the Tokyo air raid. He felt sure the best way ahead was to knock the heart out of the American navy once again. To do it he wanted to put Midway Island under threat.

Yamamoto knew America valued the island because of its proximity to Pearl Harbor and would defend it in force with its navy, so he planned to lure the remaining big ships into action and then destroy them.

*Below:* The last gasp of the Japanese carrier *Shoho* before it sinks.

*Above:* **USS *Lexington* sustains critical damage at the Battle of the Coral Sea.**

Meanwhile, the Japanese navy would also support a new thrust into Papua New Guinea where vital new forward bases could be installed.

Intelligence experts quickly grasped details of the preparations which would lead to the attack on Port Moresby, Papua New Guinea, after decoding Japanese communications. Tempted by the presence of some of Japan's finest ships, America's Admiral Chester Nimitz hastily drew together as many ships as he could for a surprise rendezvous with the Japanese in the Coral Sea.

Australian cruisers which had gone ahead to secure a vital seaway for the heavier ships came under attack from Japanese planes but miraculously escaped damage. So first blood in the four day battle went to the Ameri-cans when a wave of planes located the light carrier Shoho and blasted it out of the water. It left the Japanese in a quandary as they had no idea where the attacking aircraft had come from.

## The US tally included three direct hits on the aircraft carrier Shokaku

As night fell, Japanese planes were launched to locate their hidden enemy but, hampered by low cloud, were forced to ditch their bombs and head back to base. En route, they happened across the USS Yorktown which sent up aircraft for a confrontation. In total 17 Japanese planes were lost that night against only three American casualties. In fact, for a while both sides suffered from the main disadvantage that this new, long-distance warfare offered. Neither could locate the enemy ships.

### ■ TACTICAL VICTORY ■

The next day both sides sent waves of aircraft in pursuit of the other. The US tally included three direct hits on the aircraft carrier Shokaku which was forced to limp back to its home port for major repairs.

Meanwhile, the Japanese struck the carriers Yorktown and

Lexington. The Yorktown escaped with comparatively minor damage while the Lexington was crippled by three bombs and two torpedoes. It was to sink days later following an internal explosion. Both admirals decided against continuing the battle

## The Lexington *was to sink days later following an internal explosion*

and pulled away from their respective battle lines.

Japan appeared to have inflicted the most damage on the opposition. In reality, however, the tactical victory belonged to the Americans. The Japanese had been contained and were forced to call off their strike at Port Moresby due to the large losses of essential aircraft.

### ◆ EYE WITNESS ◆

**Mitsuo Fuchida, who led the air strike against Pearl Harbor, was aboard the aircraft carrier *Akagi* during the Battle of Midway.**

'For Japan, the Battle of Midway was indeed a tragic defeat. The Japanese Combined Fleet, placing its faith in "quality rather than quantity" had long trained and prepared to defeat a numerically superior enemy. Yet at Midway a stronger Japanese force went down to defeat before a weaker enemy.

Not only were our participating surface forces far superior in number to those of the enemy but the initiative was in our hands. Nor were we inferior qualitatively in the crucial element of air strength which played a major role throughout the Pacific War. In spite of this we suffered a decisive defeat such as the modern Japanese navy had never before experienced or even dreamed possible.

With Midway as the turning point, the fortunes of war appeared definitely to shift from our own to the Allied side. The defeat taught us many lessons and impelled our navy, for the first time since the outbreak of war, to indulge in critical self examination.

The Japanese public, of course, was not told the truth about the battle. Instead, Imperial General Headquarters announcements tried to make it appear that both sides had suffered equal losses. The United States, however, promptly announced to the whole world the damaged inflicted on the Japanese acccurately naming the ships damaged and sunk. Thus it was clear that our efforts to conceal the truth were aimed at maintaining morale at home rather than keeping valuable knowledge from the enemy.

I myself had a rather painful taste of the extreme measures taken to preseve secrecy. During the battle I had been wounded on board *Akagi* and then transferred to hospital ship *Hikawa Maru* which brought me to Yokosuka Naval Base. I was not moved ashore until after dark when the streets of the base were deserted. Then I was taken to the hospital on a covered stretcher and carried in through the rear entrance. My room was placed in complete isolation. No nurses or corpsmen were allowed entry and I could not communicate with the outside.

In such a manner were those wounded at Midway cut off from the rest of the world. It was really confinement in the guise of medical treatment and I sometimes had the feeling of being a prisoner of war.'

*Above: Shokaku* pulled back to Japan following the Coral Sea battle.

The Japanese High Command decided to abandon that first objective in favour of the capture of Midway, a far more ambitious undertaking. While the commanders had sought outright victory in the Coral Sea, they were convinced by their own glowing track record that the US navy could still be annhilated.

Once again intelligence reports gave the United States fair warning of the Japanese plans which they had tagged Operation MI. And again Admiral Nimitz called in as much support as he could from ships and submarines in the region. Aircraft carriers Enterprise and Hornet were

## *Japanese commanders were convinced that the US Navy could be annihilated*

summoned along with the damaged Yorktown which had been hurriedly repaired so it could rejoin the action.

They sailed with six cruisers, 14 destroyers and 19 submarines to the north of Midway to await the attackers. On the island itself the garrison had been strengthened and increased numbers of aircraft brought in.

The Japanese strike force, including half the navy's aircraft carriers, came from several directions, one arm to land troops, another to tackle the American naval presence.
At dawn on 4 June, bombers took off from Japanese aircraft carriers and

### ■ SURPRISE RAID ■

blasted the land-based defenders of Midway. Aircraft from the island attempting to deflect the invaders suffered huge losses and made little impact. It seemed the Japanese navy was to escape once more intact.

But before a second wave of bombers could be launched, Japan's Vice-Admiral Chuichi Nagumo was told of the presence of enemy ships signalled by the first attack by their planes. Instead of the continuing bombardment of the already shattered small island, he decided to swing north and pursue the US Navy prey.

By now torpedo bombers from all the aircraft carriers had been

launched and began a comprehensive strike lasting 55 minutes on three of Japan's aircraft carriers. Japanese pilots supported by anti-aircraft fire defended the ships fiercely. Of the 41 US planes which set out on that

## *Of the 41 US planes which set out on that mission, only six returned*

mission, only six returned. It seemed victory was in the grasp of the Japanese. Yet they barely had time to congratulate themselves on their luck and judgement when the subsequent wave of dive-bombers sent by the Americans arrived on the scene.

As the Japanese sailors and airmen struggled to rearm in the disarray,

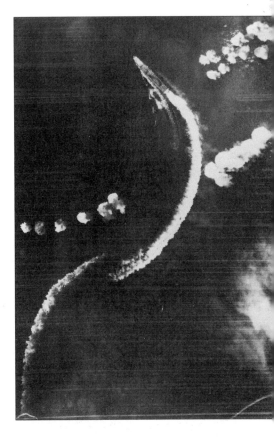

*Above: Akagi*, another Japanese navy gem, weaves its way out of fire at Midway.

bombs rained down on them and exploded on the decks crowded with aircraft. Afterwards, Japanese sailors told how the raid took them by surprise – which is why the prized planes were crowded on deck. It took a matter of minutes to reduce the

> ## It took a matter of minutes to reduce the carriers to smoking crates

carriers to smoking crates. Two of the Japanese carriers, the Kaga and Soryu, sank within hours. The Akagi drifted hopelessly and helplessly until a Japanese submarine punctured it for the last time the following day.

**Below:** US giant USS *Yorktown* lists helplessly following Midway.

Half an hour afterwards, bombers from an unscarred Japanese carrier, the Hiryu, went looking for revenge. Their target was the Yorktown on which the battle commander Rear-Admiral Frank Fletcher was based. A volley of hits during two onslaughts finally put paid to the veteran carrier which was abandoned by its crew later the same day. A Japanese submarine sent its skeleton to the bottom two days later.

It was not the end of the bloody battle, however. At 5pm, less than 12 hours after the conflict began, USS Enterprise – nicknamed the 'Big E' – launched bombers in pursuit of the Hiryu. They caught up with their target and sparked a catastrophic blaze on board. The Hiryu, Japan's fourth and final aircraft carrier in the offensive, was finally laid to rest by a Japanese cruiser.

Admiral Yamamoto continued his assault on Midway from the heavy

cruisers that remained. But when two of them collided trying to evade an American submarine, he was finally convinced of its folly.

The American navy's Rear-Admiral Raymond Spruance risked one final

### ■ HUGE VICTORY ■

foray against the Japanese, holing one of the already damaged cruisers and sinking the other. Even then Admiral Yamamoto was ready to spring a trap on the American fleet by luring them into combat with a light force and then pounce with much bigger guns.

Admiral Spruance was not to be drawn. Content with his enormous victory, he headed for home, leaving Yamamoto helpless in his wake. A Japanese submarine managed to claim one destroyer before Spruance pulled out of the region.

The decisive result was trumpeted around the Allied world. From Pearl

*Left:* Admiral Raymond Spruance, an engineer of the Midway victory.

Harbor Admiral Nimitz announced: '. . . the enemy's damage is very heavy indeed, involving several ships in each of the carrier, battleship, cruiser and transport classes. This damage is far out of proportion to that which we have received.

'The brunt of the defence to date has fallen upon our aviation personnel, in which the Army, Navy and Marine Corps are all represented. They have added another shining page to their record of achievements.'

From a position of seemingly indomitable strength, the Japanese navy had within a few short days been for the first time mauled and gored. The defeat was so terrible that it was cloaked in secrecy in Japan for the duration of the war. While scores of heroic American pilots lost their lives in the battle, they inflicted devastation on their hitherto unbroken enemy and it was their courage alone that turned the tables. Four aircraft carriers, together with more than 300 aircraft and the cream of the Japanese naval pilots were at the

## The steamroller successes of the Japanese forces had been stopped

bottom of the ocean. The steamroller successes of the Japanese forces had been stopped, Midway was saved and further plans by the Japanese to occupy other Pacific islands were shelved.

*Below:* Admiral Nimitz considers his next move from the bridge of a destroyer.

# THE SOLOMONS

The Battle of Midway sent Admiral Yamamoto and his mariners home with a bloody nose. Yet the Japanese still fostered some aggressive ambitions, among them a plan to sink the remainder of the US Navy and once again win dominance over the Pacific.

**B**y May 1942 Japanese forces occupied Tulagi, one of the Solomon Islands. The Americans were keen to keep this Pacific route open as it represented a vital line of communication with Australia. So American military planners devised a plan, 'Operation Watchtower', to rout the Japanese from the region.

Initially, US and Australian troops were to liberate Tulagi and a few other selected islands. Then their aim was to free the rest of the occupied Solomon Islands and Papua in New Guinea. The final phase of the operation would be the capture of the Bismarck Archipelago; New Britain and New Ireland.

The Americans busied themselves gathering their forces, including three aircraft carriers, a battleship, 14 cruisers and plenty of destroyers. After setting off from Wellington, New Zealand, on 22 July, there were four days of practice runs on a remote Pacific Island before the operation got underway.

Meanwhile, the Japanese were also making plans. They still harboured hopes of capturing Port Moresby in Papua, their target before the Battle of the Coral Sea. Instead of using a waterborne force this time, they would go overland. A fleet comprising five heavy and three light cruisers, five submarines and a number of destroyers was based at Rabaul on New Britain and the Japanese further tried

*Above:* A Marine's eye-view of a Pacific landing operation, this one at Tulagi.
*Left:* A Grumann Hellcat fighter returns to USS *Lexington* in the Pacific.
*Below:* US Marines practise for their invasion of the Solomon Islands.

to strengthen their position by building new airfields right across the occupied territories.

The islands they were fighting over offered little more than strategic value to either side. The Solomon Islands, discovered in the 16th century by the Spanish, had been a British Protectorate although two of

## On 7 August, 11,000 US Marines landed on the Solomons without meeting opposition

the major islands fell under the domain of Australia. They stretch for some 600 miles in two roughly parallel lines encircling a waterway called The Slot.

It was a fighting man's nightmare. The climate was damp and humid encouraging thick jungle and forest to cling to the sides of the mountains which cropped up throughout the centres of the isles alongside smokey

volcanoes. On the coastal plains there were, apart from coconut plantations, acres of dense, spikey grass, sharp as a knife.

On the morning of 7 August, 11,000 US Marines landed on Guadalcanal in the Solomons without meeting any opposition. Within 24 hours they had taken the airstrip as their own.

The three battalions that landed on Tulagi were not so lucky. The Marines encountered fierce resistance from the 1,500 Japanese defenders of the island. It cost the Marines 108 of their men before the island was theirs, in addition to many more wounded.

### ■ JAPAN ENRAGED ■

It was the work of a few days to win the islands. Ahead lay a bloody six months as they battled to keep them out of the hands of the Japanese.

The Japanese were surprised and enraged when they found out that one of their new prizes had been overrun. First response by Imperial General Headquarters was to send a convoy of

◆ **EYE WITNESS** ◆

**Despite being sunk while a soldier in North Africa, Australian George Miles went on to join the US Army Small Ships Section.**

❛ I received a medical discharge from the Australian Army in 1943 but at the time nothing much appealed in civilian life in Sydney. Within six months I joined the US Army Water Transport Division and served in a couple of invasions in Indonesia, New Guinea and the Philippines.

With the amount of casualties suffered by the US merchant navy, they were prepared to make you a seaman in a matter of weeks. The first ship I signed on was all American. These men had never met an Australian before. They called me 'Limey' and reckoned I came from London. But there were a few Aussies in the force.

For the invasion at Leyte I was on a tug patrol. The amount of sea power the Americans had was incredible. There was no way they were going to lose. ❜

*Below:* The first wave of Marines find their feet on the Solomons.

*Left:* An enemy stronghold on the Solomons is blasted by US planes.

Eleven days later the action was once again at sea when a sizeable force of Japanese soldiers charged with winning back Guadalcanal set off from Rabaul under the protection of two aircraft carriers, a light carrier, two battleships, five cruisers and 17 destroyers.

## *Allied ships were unaware their lines had been penetrated by enemy vessels*

Ready to meet them this time was an Allied task force of three aircraft carriers and a battleship. Japan's Admiral Kondo sent his light aircraft carrier ahead as a decoy. It drew the fire of the American fleet air arm and sank on the afternoon of 24 August. Meanwhile the larger carriers had also been spotted.

500 troops to reinforce the islands. However, a US submarine put paid to the plan with a single torpedo. Those troops that survived were forced to turn back to New Britain.

However, their next strike was markedly more successful. Armed with reconnaissance information about the size and strength of the enemy forces, Admiral Mikawa and a rogue squadron slipped in to The Slot unnoticed by the watching Allied ships on 8 August, their silhouettes blotted out by bad weather.

### ■ SAVO ISLAND ■

Aided by flares dropped from his carrier planes, Admiral Mikawa gleefully caught sight of the Royal Australian Navy cruiser *Canberra* and the US Navy cruiser *Chicago*, patrolling The Slot. Both Allied ships were unaware their lines had been penetrated by enemy vessels. It meant the Japanese squadron was able to open up at point-blank range with shells and torpedoes.

*Canberra* came off worse. The damage that the ship sustained was so bad it had to be abandoned. *Chicago* escaped with just one hit from a

*Right:* Japanese air power prior to the 'Marianas Turkey Shoot'.

torpedo. But before its gunners could fire back, the Japanese squadron was heading north, straight towards another Allied patrol. Three more American cruisers were set alight and sank. The Japanese squadron pulled out at speed, completely unscathed. Even though they had left the transports delivering to Guadalcanal untouched, victory in the Battle of Savo Island was theirs for the cost of 38 men, while more than 1,000 American and Australian sailors perished.

*Right:* **A kamikaze plane crashes into the sea short of its target.**

When the expected wave of Japanese aircraft arrived, there was a reception committee of US fighters to meet them, ably supported by anti-aircraft fire. Although the Japanese lost a number of planes, the Battle of the Eastern Solomons, as it was christened, was inconclusive. Both navies withdrew that night. It was the land-based bombers who later attacked the Japanese transports that forced them away from their destination.

## The sorties were nicknamed the 'Tokyo Express' by the watching Marines

Afterwards, the Japanese navy ships boldly sped down The Slot with regularity, both to fire on the American positions and to land troops and supplies. Soon the sorties were nicknamed the 'Tokyo Express' by the watching Marines.

At the end of August the US aircraft carrier Saratoga was torpedoed by a submarine and was forced back to Pearl Harbor for repairs. The

US naval strength in the area, already inferior to Japan's, continued to take a battering from both submarines and aircraft attacks.

America had to wait some six weeks before replying in kind. A squadron escorting some American transporters happened on a Japanese naval force which was preparing to fire on a US-controlled airstrip. In the confrontation that followed one Japanese cruiser and two destroyers were sunk for the cost of one American destroyer.

A major Japanese effort to recapture Guadalcanal was knocked back at the end of October but the Japanese navy was still not ready to lie down. At the ensuing Battle of Santa Cruz, the outnumbered Americans lost seventy aircraft compared to an

estimated 100 downed from the Japanese ranks. The US carrier Enterprise was damaged, along with a battleship and a cruiser. All the Japanese ships stayed afloat although five sustained damage.

### ■ SAVAGE ACTION ■

It wasn't until the three-day naval battle of Guadalcanal that the American Navy found the outright victory which had eluded it so far. It began with a savage encounter between a small American escort force against a powerful Japanese squadron. Although the US contingent was cut through during the battle, which lasted just 24 minutes, it saved the Guadalcanal airstrip from bombardment and it bought valuable time for the pursuing US task force.

Two days afterwards, the Americans unleashed their firepower at the Japanese with another close range bloody battle at sea. A Japanese battleship was so badly damaged she had to be scuttled. One Japanese and three American destroyers were sunk. The key to the American success was the attack the next day on the transports bringing an attacking Japanese force to Guadalcanal. Three-fifths of the landing troops were annihilated.

*Left:* **Japanese ships scatter as US planes open fire from above.**

The rest were rendered an ineffective fighting force, trapped as they were without supplies or food.

The final conflict in seas surrounding the Solomons was the Battle of Tassaronga, which turned out to be equally damaging to both Japan and America. The losses suffered by the Japanese navy were sufficient to persuade its leaders not to venture again into such fateful waters.

Japanese destroyers went to the Solomons just once more, to help in

seven cruisers and three more destroyers. In subsequent air battles an estimated two-thirds of the Japanese carrier aircraft were gunned down, the cream of its pilots lost forever. It finally squeezed the Japanese navy out of Rabaul once and for all.

### ■ US SUPERIORITY ■

At home Japan tried to nurture a new generation of navy pilots to replace those it had lost in the Solomons and soon afterwards. Their destination

It was known among Americans as 'The Great Marianas Turkey Shoot' after wave upon wave of Japanese planes were bagged and brought down. In total the Japanese lost 223 aircraft. Only 17 aircraft returned from an attacking force of 69 in the first wave of aircraft. In the next wave the Japanese lost 98 out of its force of 130 planes and, although a third wave returned intact having failed to find its target, in the disastrous fourth wave just nine survived

## ◆ EYE WITNESS ◆

**Swedish-born Nels Olson, 72, from Chicago, USA, was a gunner in the US Navy Armed Guard, who later served in the Pacific at the time of the Japanese surrender.**

❝ My war ended in the Pacific. I arrived on the island of Okinawa two or three weeks after the Japanese surrender. All the guys wore guns when they went ashore but there were no problems. The Japanese bowed to us whenever they saw us. It was like they went out of their way to show they did not want to fight.

For a country that caused us such problems I was amazed at how primitive some of the people were. I once had to supervise the unloading of coal from a cargo ship. They did it by sending men on board with two buckets strapped to their shoulders. It was amazing to watch. ❞

the evacuation of troops from Guadalcanal in January 1943.

With every month that passed the Americans managed to reinforce their navy and its vital fleet air arm. There was little the Japanese could do to replace its lost ships, planes or pilots.

The Japanese Navy took its next severe pounding in port at Rabaul in October 1943. Aircraft from the growing number of American carriers in the region launched two raids. The tally of damage to the Japanese was a destroyer which sank and damage to

was the Marianas, a series of islands being heavily reinforced by the Japanese to fend off US invasion.

But the students were ill-equipped to deal with intense warfare and they were lost in their droves. In the two-day Battle of the Philippine Sea in June 1944 the Japanese navy received yet another drubbing from Task Force 58 commanded by Admiral Spruance. At last the Americans had found an antidote to Japan's Zero fighter. The new US Hellcat was faster and more powerful.

out of 82. The Americans were down by just 29 aircraft. In addition, three Japanese aircraft carriers were sunk.

Afterwards the Americans had undisputed superiority at sea in the Pacific. They outnumbered the Japanese in all classes of ship, boasting 17 battleships to Japan's nine, 12 fleet carriers compared to four, 47 escort carriers against three and 155 submarines up against just 48. None of the four Japanese aircraft carriers had planes aboard and all were listing from battle damage.

# AMPHIBIOUS WARFARE

When British, Australian and New Zealand troops tried to land at Gallipoli during World War I, the sea ran red with their blood.

**B**ullets from defending Turkish guns rained down on unfortunate troops as soon as they emerged from boats just short of the shore line. It remains one of the most appalling military disasters in history in which there were more than a quarter of a million casualties on the Allied side alone.

Winston Churchill, then First Lord of the Admiralty and a keen exponent of the plan, resigned over the Gallipoli debacle and it blighted his career for years afterwards.

Though the adventure achieved little, it served to illustrate the glaring gap in military manoeuvres which reduced soldiers trying to take a fortified coast to cannon fodder.

*Left:* The Americans led the field in the development of amphibious techniques.
*Below:* LVTs and LCVPs approach the island of Aguni Shima in the Pacific.

The lesson was not lost on Major Earl Ellis in the United States. He realised the importance of safe transport of troops from ship to shore during invasion. His aim was to give American Marines the best chance of survival. As early as 1921 he had written a 50,000-word plan which was intended as a blueprint for a Marine advance in the Pacific. He argued that men should be specifically trained to overcome the hazards of amphibious warfare and that the Marines were the best task force to undergo that instruction.

■ **LANDING VEHICLES** ■

Ellis wrote: 'It is not enough that the troops be skilled infantry men and jungle men or artillery men of high morale. They must be skilled water men and jungle men who know it can be done – marines with marine training.'

By 1933 the Fleet Marine Force came into being to oversee the challenge of amphibious landings. There followed a series of experi-

ments with tracked landing vehicles able to travel in the sea, offering protection to soldiers on leaving landing boats. It wasn't until the war years, however, that an effective ship-to-shore craft was constructed, the

> *It wasn't until the war that an effective ship-to-shore craft was constructed*

LVT or Landing Vehicle, Tracked. Even then, due to its mechanical shortcomings, the 'amtrac' was mainly used to travel up beaches rather than on to them.

Boatbuilder Andrew Higgins, from New Orleans, then came to the notice of the US Marines after he built a shallow-draft vessel for crossing the Mississippi River. It beached with ease and could be pulled back into the water at speed. Here was a

craft far superior to anything else the marines had found.

Bizarrely, the US Navy's Bureau of Ships was reluctant to adopt a design from someone outside the service. Continuing its costly probes into making landing craft for years afterwards, it still failed to come up with an adequate rival to Higgins' model. The fiasco was roundly condemned by a Senate Committee during the war.

That original Higgins design finally became the father of the LCP(L)s, Landing Craft Personnel (Large) used by both Britain and the Americans during World War II. Work continued throughout the war to perfect landing craft of various capabilities; some were armed, some were ocean-going; some were tracked. They proved a formidable amphibious force.

## ■ MARINE TRAINING ■

The Japanese were also investigating the possibilities of amphibious landing craft. The Japanese army built an early version of LSDs (Landing Ships, Dock) for their operations in China during the 1930s called Shinshu Maru. Inside its cavernous interior the vessel could house a number of landing craft which rolled up a ramp and out of the ship's open doors.

In order to land troops, they had a 46ft landing craft which they modified to bear arms for the men of the Special Naval Landing Force, the equivalent of the marines.

In Britain, only fleeting interest was expressed in the dilemma. Recovering from its battering in World War I, the service chiefs in the main neglected to look ahead and

### In Britain, service chiefs neglected to look ahead and plan for another war

plan for another war. It wasn't until 1937 that Admiral Sir Reginald Ernest-Ernle-Plunkett-Drax suggested that several brigades of Royal Marines should be trained especially for amphibious landings. The eventual outcome was the establishment of the Inter-Service Training

*Below*: US troops emerge from the bowels of USS *LSM-168* in March 1945.

*Above:* **An armada of LSTs offload onto a recently captured beach.**

October 1940. It was further improved when tankers made in Britain especially to traverse a troublesome sand bank in South America were converted to carry tanks. These were fitted to carry 20 tanks or 33 trucks but were unable to come close into shore.

A new design was thought up to

> **The army lost every single tank and major piece of artillery it had committed to France**

overcome the problem. The difficulties posed in getting the ships produced in Britain's hard-pressed shipyards was overcome when America agreed to take on the contract. Shipyards across the States became involved in producing LSTs, launching the first of the new design on 7 September 1942. Before the war was over, 1,050 more came out of US yards to see action in amphibious landings across the world. They would join the Landing Ships,

and Development Centre near Portsmouth, in southern England, which involved all the defence forces and developed a policy for amphibious operations which remained key for the duration of the war.

At last staff in the unit addressed the problems of specialised landing craft, navy gunfire support, floating piers to aid the disembarkation of tanks and trucks and an array of workable tactics.

### ■ TANK SHIPMENT ■

The ranks of the Royal Marines, standing at just 12,000 when war broke out, were substantially boosted. Their role of manning guns aboard Royal Navy ships and guarding navy shore-based establishments was expanded to man commando raiding parties.

Following the evacuation of British troops from Dunkirk in 1940, the need for armoured ocean-going craft able to carry men and machines into shallow water was once again highlighted. While there was relief at the number of soldiers who got out of France in one piece, they barely managed to bring back a gun

*Right:* **Motorised equipment from an LST rolls on to a 'rhino' to reach the sand.**

between them. The army lost every tank and major piece of artillery it had committed to France at the outbreak of war. If a suitable transport craft had been available, at least some of it might have been saved.

Now Churchill's mind was concentrated on the issue. Until his men and tanks could be safely transported across the Channel, there would be no opportunity for Churchill to make up the ground he had lost in France. Tanks were a primary tool of war and shipment of them in any amphibious assault was vital.

A British prototype Landing Ship, Tank (LST) came into being in

Infantry (LSI) and Landing Ships, Dock (LSD) already in service. But although the seeds of a successful amphibious landing force had been sown, there was a long way to go before it would threaten the Reich.

## ■ DIEPPE LANDINGS ■

As if to emphasise the point, the Allied landings in Dieppe in August 1942 ended in almost complete disaster. The Allies referred to it as a raid while Hitler insisted it was a fully-fledged invasion.

The Allied force consisted of 5,000 Canadians, 1,057 British, 50 Americans and a few Free French soldiers. Setting out under the cover of early morning darkness, they ran into difficulty when the landing craft which took them from their ships to the shore were swept along the beach. Armed German trawlers happened on the scene and began shooting at one of the British sections.

Now the Germans were fully alerted and greeted the arrival of 27 light tanks with a hail of gunfire. All were destroyed while the landing forces suffered appalling casualties. It was just 9am when the troops were pulled out. More than 1,500 prisoners were taken and most of the equipment was left scattered on the beach.

## The Germans greeted the arrival of 27 light tanks with a hail of gunfire

A clutch of Allied boats was sunk and almost 100 of the aircraft dispatched to provide aerial cover were shot down. It was the largest in a succession of raids which met with varying degrees of success.

The Dieppe incident led Prime Minister Churchill and other British commanders to doubt the wisdom of making another attempt against well-fortified German positions, despite American pressure to open a second front in Europe.

However, some valuable lessons were learned from the raids in time to execute the biggest amphibious landing ever, on D-Day.

*Below:* **A few moment's relaxation by an empty landing craft for weary troops.**

## ◆ EYE WITNESS ◆

**Henry 'Marty' Martin, from Chicopee, Massachusetts, USA, stormed Omaha beach in a DD (Duplex Drive amphibious tank). He landed in the first wave aboard LCT 586.**

'My job was to drop the ramp. These men trained to get out in 30 seconds but we didn't have time to check that they all got out safely. We did four drops that day.

For our first we laid off 200 yards because it was so rough. The next one, though, we went right on to the beach. We were carrying three tanks and they had to get in close.

I watched the first tank take off to the right. He made it, but the second took a direct hit as he tried to follow. The third stayed closer to the shore and looked to be OK.

As they left a US officer came up to me literally holding the insides of his stomach in his hands. He was one of the underwater demolition experts who had gone in in advance of the landings. Those guys didn't have very good luck. I think nine in every ten were killed.

He told me we were the first ship to come right on to the beach. We got him back to the hospital ship but I never knew how he made out.

Sometimes historical accounts fail to mention the disputes and the arguments that took place. There was one officer who had it in for me. After D-Day I got a ten-day leave to Kilmarnock in Scotland and the thought of going back to work for this guy meant I decided to unofficially extend that leave for another ten days.

I served 30 days in the brig at Plymouth for that. But I reckoned that just because a man's an officer doesn't mean he can't be an asshole as well!'

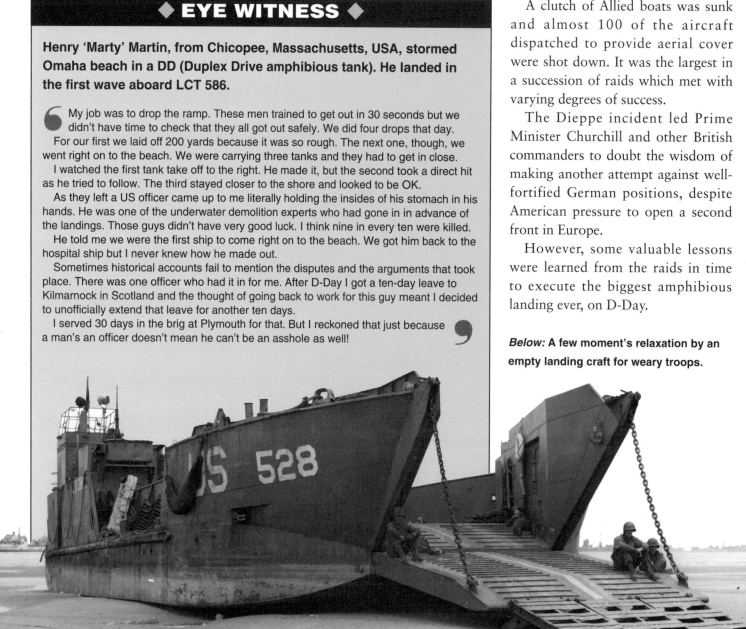

## ◆ EYE WITNESS ◆

**Ernie Marshall joined the Royal Navy at the end of 1942 aged 18. After three months training he joined a combined operations unit and was stationed on *LCT 554*.**

'When I saw it my heart dropped. It looked pretty rough. The living quarters and the engine room were at the back while the tanks were in the front. There were 12 of us aboard. I was a stoker in the engine room. I just learnt as I went, I had no training whatsoever. Eventually we sailed to North Africa. It seemed like the whole of the Atlantic was coming up at us. Then we had to slide down these huge waves. I stayed in the engine room.

We worked every port up to Tripoli. Once we carried German prisoners of war.

Then we joined the landings at Sicily. We beached at 4am when it was very quiet. Next morning the Germans really came at us. We stayed there ferrying supplies for a couple of months until we went up to Anzio. We were stuck there for three months surrounded by Germans. The beachhead was about five miles inland. Once the Germans broke through and got to within two miles of the beach. Eventually, they were pushed back again.

The long range guns were more frightening than anything. Shells just landed without warning. One morning a plane attacked us. Shrapnel from one of its bombs came right through the stern, across the mess deck, through the next steel bulk head and into the engine room. Everywhere was filled with smoke and sparks. One bloke had an injured shoulder but the rest of us survived.

That afternoon we were alongside a boat unloading supplies when a bomb from a plane went straight into the hold. We managed to get ashore. Survivors got thrown into the water and were shouting to us for help. We fished a lot out of the water but we couldn't stop because the ship was burning so fiercely. That was the worst day of the war for me.

It was two and a half years before I got home. On the whole I enjoyed the experience. The rest of the crew became like family. The captain never gave us any trouble and we had some good times. I had never travelled before so to see Arabs in their African villages was really something.'

For example, specially trained civilian aircraft recognition teams from the Royal Observer Corps put to sea with the troops on 6 June 1944. This was to cut the rate of Allied aircraft shot down by jittery comrades on the ground.

At least the design of specialised landing craft was improved. They retained their speed and low silhouettes but were substantially enlarged to carry more men. Their armament they carried was also beefed up to provide greater support for the men they off-loaded.

The beaches of Normandy, unlike that of Dieppe, were away from major towns where German defences were strongest.

Yet still some avoidable mistakes were made. In the rough seas off the Normandy coast, British soldiers were instructed to carry not only their 20lb packs but also bicycles for use in France. On arrival, they were told to ditch the cycles in order to fight for their lives – and never saw the cumbersome two-wheelers that they had lugged on to the sands again.

No amount of improvements in the technique of amphibious landings could save the 'poor, bloody infantry' from being contained in cramped vessels for hours, sometimes days, on

### Food was generally poor and home comforts were lacking

end before the final moment of invasion came. Often they suffered from sea-sickness. The food was generally poor and home comforts were lacking. Only the lucky ones got to sleep in hammocks.

Before attacking Guam in July 1944, the US 3rd Marine Division spent weeks suffering like this at sea, most of them in dreadful weather conditions. The Channel weather in on D-Day was likewise awful.

*Below:* **Australian troops boarding a beach landing ship after successful operations at Lae, New Guinea.**

# JAPAN'S LAST GASP

When America's war horse was harnessed, it galloped through the Pacific at a thundering pace. Advances made in 1944 by the combined efforts of the Army, Navy and Marine Corps mimicked those of the Japanese three years before.

By now the US strength at sea was awesome. Since the outbreak of the war with Japan a further 21 aircraft carriers had come into service capable of holding a total of about 3,000 planes.

That was in addition to a splendid array of new battleships, transports, cruisers, destroyers and landing craft newly arrived and ready for action.

On the other hand, the Japanese had suffered severe losses at sea and were continuing to do so. Apart from naval conflicts, the Japanese ships had to contend with the numerous American submarines now patrolling the Pacific in force.

Tiny Japan, so dependent on the resources it imported from overseas, was unable to replenish the fleet, with much of its merchant fleet being sunk bringing home vital war production materials. By 1944 two thirds of the tanker fleet bringing oil to Japan from the South Pacific fields had been wrecked by the Allies.

While 40 per cent of the oil produced in those fields reached Japan in 1942, only 13.5 per cent was unloaded at Japanese ports in 1944 thanks to the efficiency of the submarines and fleet ships. Oil reserves were dwindling fast, threatening to grind the war effort to a halt. Hopelessly outnumbered, it seemed on paper that Japan's navy was all but finished.

When it became clear that the US was preparing to attack the Philippines in the autumn of 1944,

## In the autumn of 1944 Japan drew up plans for one final sea battle

however, Japan drew up the plans for one final sea battle which could have tipped the balance in its favour. It was a simple manoeuvre by what remained of the Japanese navy but might have been enough to defend

*Left:* All eyes turn skywards when a Kamikaze aircraft is spotted in the vicinity.
*Below:* Vice Admiral Jisaburo Ozawa was defeated by superior US tactics.
*Bottom:* The scale of the US seapower is illustrated in this picture of Task Force 58 in the Pacific.

*Above:* Vice-Admiral William Halsey looks out to sea and draws up a winning strategy for the American fleet.

the Philippines. And it was a gamble worth risking for the Japanese. If the Americans had installed themselves on the Philippines, it would have meant the end of oil supplies from

## *The arrival of Admiral Ozawa and his decoy carriers went unnoticed*

the Dutch East Indies, now more crucial than ever before to the teetering Japanese.

After the war, Japan's Admiral S. Toyoda explained his country's actions: 'If the worst should happen there was a chance that we would lose the entire fleet; but I felt that chance had to be taken . . . should we lose in the Philippine operations, the

shipping lane to the south would be completely cut off so that the fleet, if it should come back to Japanese waters, could not obtain its fuel supply. There would be no sense in saving the fleet at the expense of the the loss of the Philippines.'

In essence, Japan's ploy was to use what was left of the carrier fleet as a decoy to lure the main thrust of the American navy away from the Philippines. Once the large ships were out of the way, a two-pronged attack from the sea was planned on Leyte, the small island in the centre of the Philippines on which the Americans had already began an assault.

### ■ AMERICAN ATTACK ■

The operation began badly for the Japanese. One arm of the fleet earmarked to blast Leyte was itself fired on by American submarines on 23 October, well before it reached its destination. Three cruisers were

## COUSINS

General Douglas MacArthur was an eighth cousin of Winston Churchill and a sixth cousin of Franklin Roosevelt. All three shared an ancestor in the shape of Sarah Barney Belcher of Taunton, Massachusetts.

badly damaged. There was a two-fold result to this action. The strength of this attacking arm was depleted and all the American shipping for miles around became focused on this single Japanese force. Despite frantic efforts to announce his presence by uncoded radio messages, the arrival of Admiral Ozawa and his decoy carriers went unnoticed by the Americans.

Now American battleships joined the attack on the hapless Japanese detachment whose brief had been to slip unobtrusively into the Philippine Sea. Japanese land-based bombers as

well as those from the distant carriers rained bombs on the American fleet, crippling the carrier Princeton.

There was a high price for this success, however. The relentless onslaught by American fighter planes finally sank the majestic Musashi, one of the biggest battleships in the world. It had been hit by 19 torpedoes and 17 bombs. Japanese commander Admiral Kurita finally broke off from the action and appeared to retreat.

## ■ BATTLE OF LEYTE ■

The absence of Japan's aircraft carriers was spotted by the sharp-witted Vice-Admiral William 'Bull' Halsey, who was in control of the American fleet. When he sent out reconnaissance planes to assess the movements of the Japanese fleet, Ozawa was finally detected. It seemed a golden opportunity to Halsey who gathered up his entire force to pursue the

*Above:* Devastation among Japanese shipping in the run-up to the invasion of the Philippine island of Leyte.

prized carriers, Japan's last surviving ship of the type in action.

Almost as soon as American backs were turned, Kurita reversed his course and began steaming towards his initial target once more, Leyte.

American sea defences were badly lacking after Halsey set off with his full complement of ships. Mostly it comprised a small force protecting the landing beaches at Leyte, just six

> ## Japan's remaining battleships were no more than sitting ducks to the enemy

escort carriers and five destroyers. In charge, Vice-Admiral T. C. Kinkaid sent a series of urgent messages to Halsey, asking him to return at once. Halsey, however, was determined to snare the carriers once and for all. He refused to turn around until he delivered some decisive damage to the carrier force. Only time would tell if his instincts were the right ones.

Meanwhile, the destroyers were defending the vulnerable section of

*Left:* The carrier USS *Princeton* is hosed after taking a direct hit from a bomber during the Battle of Leyte.

the US fleet as best they could. One escort carrier and three destroyers were lost, however, in its retreat.

Now Kurita was steaming towards the Leyte Gulf where a collection of US transports and men lay wide open to attack. Then he hesitated. As Kinkaid watched and waited with bated breath, Kurita finally pulled his forces to the north, away from the beach targets.

Thanks to confusion among the intercepted radio messages aboard Kurita's ship, he believed Halsey and his powerful ships were only 70 miles away when in fact there were hundreds of miles between them. He was also gravely concerned about the risk of attack by air when he himself had no air cover.

## ■ SITTING DUCKS ■

While the survivors of Kurita's force escaped, the fate of the carriers gave credence to Halsey's actions. All four – Chitose, Zuikaku, Zuiho and Chiyoda – were sunk, completing the effective destruction of the Japanese navy. With the long-range power of aircraft, Japan's remaining battleships were no more than sitting ducks to the enemy. There was little

## ◆ EYE WITNESS ◆

**Yasuo Kuwahara was a skilled Japanese pilot who was in a Kamikaze squadron in the final year of the war.**

'It was New Year's Day 1945 at Hiro Air Base in western Honshu. Captain Yoshiro Tsubaki, commander of the Fourth Fighter Squadron, has just called a special meeting. A silence settled over us – only the patter of rain on the roof. The captain permitted us to sit while he stands, arms folded, eyes dark and unblinking – seemingly to spear us one by one.

After a long while, he spoke sonorously: "The time has at last arrived. We are faced with a great decision."

Again, he pauses but I feel it coming – the fear, greater than I have yet known. Death is there with us, enfolding each man, lingering, growing stronger. And the words from our captain flow so strangely.

"Any of you unwilling to give your lives as divine sons of the great Nippon empire will not be required to do so. Those incapable of accepting this honour will raise their hands – now."

Once more silence and death are almost palpable. The rain has subsided to a soft drizzle. Then hesitantly, timidly, a hand goes up, then another and another . . . six in all. The decision is mine; I can choose to live or die. Hasn't the captain just said so? But somehow… Of course, I want to live. But my hands – they remain at my sides trembling. I want to raise them but I can't. I want to raise my hands, even my soul would have me do it. Am I a coward? I cannot do it.

"Ah so," Captain Tsubaki fixes those who have responded in his stare. "It is good to know early exactly where we stand." They are summoned before us. "Here gentlemen," he points to the ashen faces, "are six men who have openly admitted their disloyalty. Since they are completely devoid of honour – without spirit – it becomes our duty to provide them with some. These men shall be Hiro's first attack group."

The breath, held so long within me, struggled out. I want to draw in more air, to expel it with relief, but something clenches inside. Six men from my squadron have just been picked for death. Hiro's first human bombs.'

*Above:* **A Japanese destroyer is smashed in two at Ormoc, Leyte, by a US B-25.**

more they could contribute to Japan's war effort.

From first to last, the three-day Battle of Leyte Gulf was the largest in history. In total, 282 ships were engaged along with hundreds of aircraft. It took the title of largest battle from the World War I Battle of Jutland when 250 British and

### Those who felt disgraced in some way would commit 'hari kiri'

German ships ships had met in combat, with only five seaplanes.

At the end of it, the Japanese had lost not only four carriers but also three battleships, six heavy cruisers, three light cruisers and eight destroyers. The triumph clearly belonged to the Americans whose casualties

amounted to just one light carrier, two escort carriers and three destroyers.

Yet had the whim of the Japanese Admiral Kurita been different on the day and had he chosen to bombard the American beach positions, history might have had a different story to tell.

### ■ SUICIDE SQUADS ■

The Battle of Leyte Gulf is not only remembered as being the biggest naval battle ever. It was also the first to see the co-ordinated use of kamikazes – Japanese suicide squads.

Among the Japanese there was a strict code of honour. It had been instilled in them for centuries that death was better than dishonour or defeat. The first form of ritual suicide in Japan, called 'seppuku', was reserved by law for the samurai and was considered a privilege. Suicides could equally be carried out as a mark of respect.

Centuries later, those who felt disgraced in some way would commit 'hari kiri', literally translated to 'a cut to the stomach'. The aim for the person committing suicide was to disembowel themselves by using a ceremonial sword, an agonising process. As the years wore on, many made a symbolic cut in the stomach before turning a gun on themselves.

Surrender was abhorred by the Japanese, particularly among the troops, which explains the antipathy they displayed towards their own

Japanese victim, the latter would devote his last burst of energy to pulling the pin from his final grenade, killing both men outright.

### ■ DESPERATE ACTS ■

Others would strap explosives to their bodies and hurl themselves at tanks or enemy positions to cause as

much devastation as possible. Until now, these desperate acts were committed very much on an individual basis. But by 1944, staring into the jaws of defeat, the Japanese commanders decided to orchestrate suicide missions to cause the maximum hardship and loss of life to their enemies. Behind the enterprise

*Japanese commanders orchestrated suicide missions to cause maximum loss of life*

was Vice-Admiral Takijiro Onishi who himself committed hari kiri at the end of the war.

Kamikaze pilots in small planes would target the deck of an enemy ship. While bombs dropped by planes often fell short of the mark, the kamikazes' aim was unerringly accurate. British ships which generally boasted more deck armoury than

*Above:* USS *St Lô* takes a direct hit from a kamikaze in the Battle of Leyte.
*Right:* USS *Suwanee* gets running repairs after sustaining damage from a kamikaze.

prisoners of war. Many Japanese servicemen readily chose suicide rather than shame. High ranking officers also used to inspire courage and commitment among their men by killing themselves.

This made the Japanese particularly difficult enemies in the field. They were reluctant to be rescued if their missions went awry. In the sea, mystified Allied sailors watched in disbelief as the survivors of a wrecked ship tried to drown themselves or cut their own throats if they were armed. For if any unfortunate Allied soldier stopped to help a wounded or dying

their American counterparts were better defended against such attacks.

There were also plans for suicide motorboats to target major ships. Beneath the waves there were one-man midget submarines which would set themselves on a collision course with a much larger vessel. These were difficult tactics to counter.

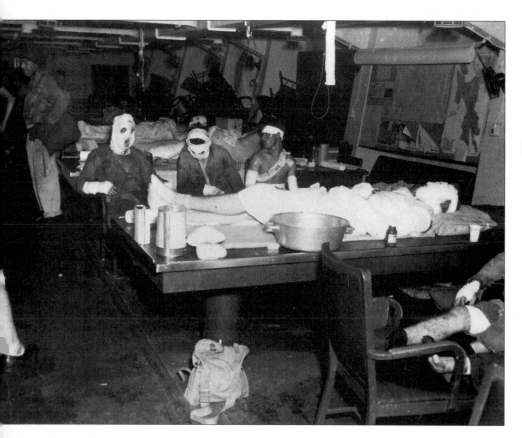

*Above:* Wardroom of the carrier USS *Suwanee* becomes an emergency sick bay after the kamikaze attack during the Battle of Leyte Gulf.

Stepping forward for these 'special' one-way missions were upright, traditional, fervent and deeply patriotic young men who thought little of laying down their lives for their country. They were, however, the elite. Despite the glory heaped on such pilots in domestic propaganda, the volunteers for the kamikaze ('divine wind') squads were drying up. Japanese commanders had no choice but to brand units as

kamikaze squads whether the men were willing to die or not.

Inevitably, it undermined the success of the squads. Those without the necessary iron nerve were just as likely to plunge themselves and their aircraft into the sea instead of a ship, representing a waste of valuable resources. In a panic, many chose the

first ships they saw to descend on. These were generally strategically less important than others in the fleet, once again wasting man and machine. Others would fly off in search of a specified target and return claiming the ship they were after could not be found. There were many accidents too, as the fuel-starved Japanese economised with all-important oil and stoked up the kamikaze aircraft with 50 per cent alcohol. If the aircraft engine failed, it was impossible to restart.

Commanders had no idea about the kamikaze success rate as there was no one left to report a result.

After the war, Japan's Lieutenant-General Torashiro Kawabe explained the reasoning behind kamikaze attacks. 'We believed that our spiritual convictions and moral strength could balance your material and scientific advantages. We did not consider our attacks to be 'suicide'. The pilot did not start out on his

## Those without the necessary iron nerve were just as likely to plunge into the sea

mission with the intention of committing suicide. He looked upon himself as a human bomb which would destroy a certain part of the enemy fleet... he died happy in the conviction that his death was a step towards the final victory.'

At the Battle of Leyte Gulf, six aircraft took off from Cebu in the Philippines on 25 October 1944. Two hours later when they arrived at Leyte the planes deliberately rammed the US carriers Santee and Suwanee, causing extensive damage. The next day one American ship, St Lô, was sunk by use of kamikaze.

### ■ BEST DEFENCE ■

In the next three months, 22 Allied naval vessels were sunk by kamikaze pilots against 12 holed in conventional air attack. A further 110 kamikaze strikes damaged shipping.

They were a hazard which was to plague the Americans, Australians and British for the rest of the war. The best defence against kamikaze was interception by fighter planes or a volley of anti-aircraft fire, but it was not guaranteed to work. A lone Japanese pilot could still bring about the deaths of many.

# Battle for the Skies

# BATTLE OF BRITAIN

When France was overrun, Führer Adolf Hitler cast his eyes across the English Channel and set his sights on Britain.

Although he never had an appetite for war with the island, he now saw it as the next jewel in his crown. He even believed its government and people would choose to make peace after the unstoppable power of the Reich had been so amply illustrated in France.

He was, of course, wrong. A peace offer made to Britain in July 1940 was rebuffed – even though the remnants of its army, hounded out of Europe via Dunkirk, were in disarray. Hitler made up his mind to invade and began gathering the necessary invasion forces in the newly acquired Channel ports of Holland, Belgium and France.

Yet while the Germans were veterans of waging attacking wars on

## *Göring pledged to the Führer that the Royal Air Force would be banished forever*

land, they had never tackled the sea before. Nor was Germany a great seafaring nation. Hitler believed the necessary arrangements for taking war across the water could be made in a matter of weeks. Given that 'Operation Overlord', carried out from Britain in 1944 to free France, took upwards of a year to plan, he was woefully shortsighted.

The effectiveness or otherwise of his plan was never revealed, however.

*Left:* Spitfires like this one proved the saviours of Britain.
*Top right:* Göring was confident his Luftwaffe aircraft could finish the RAF.
*Right:* Air crews were scrambled at a moment's notice when attacks came.

For it was clear even to the buoyant Hitler that an invasion could not go ahead until his air force had charge of the skies. It was one of the few issues that united his warring chiefs of staff, too.

'The British Air Force must be eliminated to such an extent that it will be incapable of putting up any substantial opposition to the invading troops,' Hitler told his generals. Göring, the supremo of German air power, was all ears. He blithely pledged to the Führer that the Royal Air Force would be banished forever.

### ■ IN EASY REACH ■

On paper, it seemed Göring had good reason to be confident. The Luftwaffe had a three-to-one numerical superiority against the RAF which had lost nearly half its strength during the Battle of France. German pilots were experienced, having flown missions throughout the Spanish Civil War as well as the more recent hostilities. Now they were installed in airfields in France, the Low Countries and Norway, within easy reach of Britain.

Göring believed his men would smash the Royal Air Force in much the same way as they had destroyed the Polish and French air forces before.

'Operation Sealion', Hitler's planned offensive against Britain which would bear him triumphantly to London, was set for 15 September 1940. The German navy chief Admiral Raeder had convinced Hitler his forces could not be prepared any sooner. Nor could it happen much later than that for fear of the invasion force falling foul of autumn storms.

Timing was crucial – but this did not unduly concern the Luftwaffe

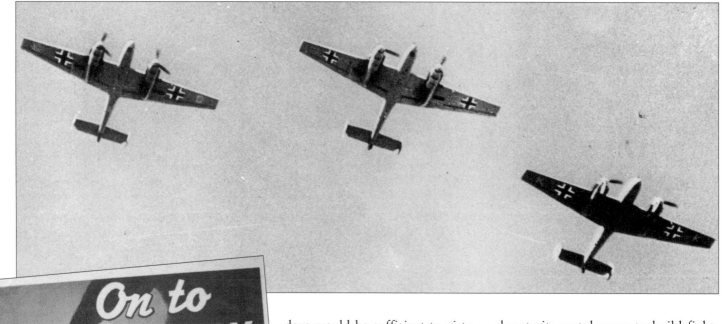

*Top:* Formations of Messerschmitt 110s became a familiar sight in the skies. *Above:* Britain and the Commonwealth countries were recruiting air crews.

chief, who was still smarting at the way the British Expeditionary Force had escaped from the French coast under his nose. When the Luftwaffe began its operations against Britain in July, Göring was sure he had time enough to fulfill his part of the bargain. Privately, he thought four

days would be sufficient to virtually annihilate his opposition. Events proved his optimism to be wildly misplaced.

For its part, Britain waited in anticipation during the summer of 1940 for the start of a battle for its very existence. Air reconnaissance teams spotted the gathering German forces. Hitler's intentions were clear.

Many of the men plucked from the beach at Dunkirk were redeployed on coastal defences. The Royal Navy played its part by attacking the collection of landing craft mushrooming at the occupied ports. Airmen joined the action and laid still more mines in the Channel to hamper a seaborne force destined for Britain.

There was a new evacuation among the children of London and the south east. As tension and expectation mounted on the home front, production doubled during June in factories working round-the-clock in a bid to help Britain's defenders meet the foe on equal terms. Lord Beaverbrook, minister of aircraft production, appealed to the public to

donate its metal scrap to build fighters. The result was mountains of old iron which could never be transformed into Spitfires or Hurricanes. But in terms of a morale-boosting exercise, it was a runaway success.

## ■ CONVOYS ATTACKED ■

As the German victory parades and celebrations died down in France there came the opening salvos of the Battle of Britain. They were quite tame affairs by comparison with what was to come, a bid to 'soften up' Britain. The targets were Britain's lifeline convoys as they reached home

*Lord Beaverbrook appealed to the public to donate its metal scrap to build fighters*

waters and the coastal ports, most notably Portsmouth and Dover. Both sides suffered losses in the air, with the English pilots, ground controllers and radar operators learning some valuable lessons.

Germany had begun with about 2,600 aircraft ready for action. They were in the main Messerschmitt fighters and Dornier, Heinkel, and Junkers bombers. They were well-organised into groups – Luftflotte 2 flew from Belgium, Luftflotte 3 from northern France, and Luftflotte 5 was based in either Norway or Denmark.

### ■ FIGHTER COMMAND ■

Lining up against them were fewer than 700 operational aircraft for the Royal Air Force. There were the legendary Spitfires and Hurricanes and some outdated Blenheim bombers.

Britain's aerial defences were divided into four groups. Fighter Command 10 Group covered south west England, Fighter Command 11 Group oversaw the south east including London, Fighter Command 12

## FINEST HOUR

'Let us brace ourselves to our duty and so bear ourselves that if the British Commonwealth and Empire lasts a thousand years men will still say, "This was their finest hour".'

(Winston Churchill
after the fall of France.)

### In the middle of August Göring opened phase two of the Battle of Britain

Irish, seven Americans, two Rhodesians, one Jamaican and a Palestinian.

Now Germany was down by some 217 planes. The losses by Fighter Command were fewer than 100 but its outlook was bleaker than that of the enemy. British aircraft reserves were tiny. Yet it was the loss of experienced pilots either by death or injury that began to concern Air Chief Marshal Sir Hugh Dowding most. Despite the acute pressure of his position, Dowding, a master tactician, did a first-class job of keeping the marauding German planes at bay during those hectic months of summer and autumn 1940. Yet Churchill unceremoniously replaced him once the threat of 'Operation Sealion' had passed.

*Above:* Göring and his staff officers survey England across the Channel, convinced the island would easily fall.

Group patrolled the airspace over the Midlands, while Fighter Command 13 Group was based in northern England and Scotland.

Britain was not standing entirely alone, as the line-up for the ensuing battle proved. Although more than 2,500 of the men who took part were British, there were also 147 Poles, 101 New Zealanders, 94 Canadians, 87 Czechs, 29 Belgians, 22 South Africans, 22 Australians, 14 Free French, ten

In the middle of August, Göring opened phase two of the Battle of Britain. His target now was RAF Fighter Command itself. Daily attacks were made on the airfields of southern England. Unlike the unfortunate air forces of crushed Allies Poland and France, the British planes

position to carry out attacks on the German formations as they crossed into Britain. Not wishing to waste vital manpower and resources, ground control never scrambled pilots until the last moment when they were sure a raid was imminent. It gave them little time to plan the most effective attack.

Both sides fell victim to erroneous propaganda. The RAF airmen were buoyed to hear that German air force losses were running at three or four times their own. In fact, vastly

*Left:* Air crews at Biggin Hill, Kent, enjoy a few moments' respite.
*Below:* Despite the dangers, pilots and crews always appeared relaxed.

were not caught on the ground. Britain's radar system, the most advanced in the world, gave early warning after seeing incoming formations of enemy bombers. There was just enough time to scramble the pilots and bring the valuable men and planes into the air.

## Smoke from planes embroiled in dog-fights was scrawled across the sky

For now the heroes of the battle were the ground crews. It was their job to patch up not only the planes which were battered during aerial spats but also the hangars and runways damaged by bombs, to keep the Royal Air Force working.

Göring earmarked 13 August as 'Eagle Day' when a preponderance of German planes would swarm over the British skies and finally subjugate the stubborn RAF. Despite wave upon wave of Luftwaffe planes, his

plan failed. Smoke from planes embroiled in dog-fights was scrawled across the sky. The British fighters held their own.

### ■ NIMBLE SPITFIRES ■

German bombers were at a disadvantage against the nimble Spitfires. Laden with bombs, they were no match for the British planes. But the RAF fighters were constantly struggling to achieve the best height and

inflated German casualty figures were broadcast, some of which were not rectified until after the war. Göring, meanwhile, was happily convinced during the early stages of the Battle of Britain that many airfields were out of action and scores of British planes were destroyed, estimates which were grossly exaggerated.

On 15 August nearly 1,800 sorties were flown by the German airmen,

# ◆ BATTLE OF BRITAIN

In the Battle of Britain, RAF Fighter Command was divided into groups distributed throughout the country. The south west of England was the responsibility of 10 Group, London and the south east was covered by 11 Group, the Midlands region was patrolled by 12 Group, northern England and Scotland was the beat of 13 Group. Against these forces were three Luftwaffe formations – Luftflotte 2, Luftflotte 3 and Luftflotte 5.

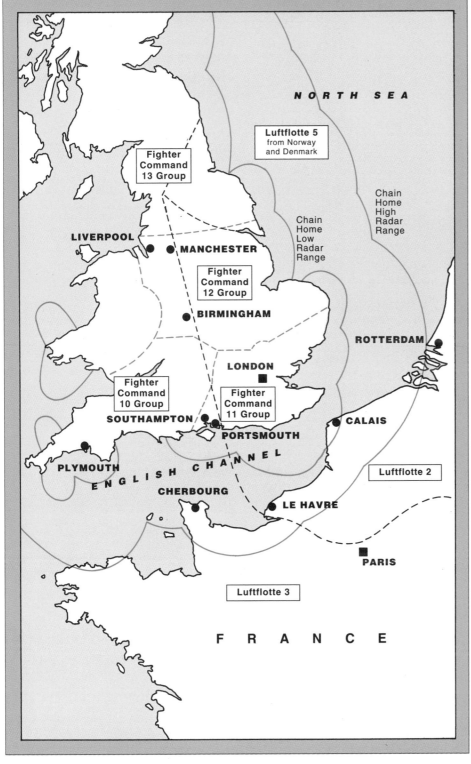

attacking targets from Newcastle to Hampshire. Britain was forewarned by radar, and each flight was attacked from the ground and the air and there were 75 German losses against Britain's 34.

The following day 1,700 sorties were made over Britain, with Göring confident the RAF would be left in tatters. Yet on that day and on many days to come, the German pilots found themselves confronted with healthy numbers of British planes and pilots.

Göring was left fuming at the apparent inability of his men to finish off the RAF. In addition, he was counting the cost of 363 lost aircraft and crew.

*Above:* A Heinkel 111 over the Thames, taken from another German plane.

Of course, the incessant demands on each and every British squadron were causing immense difficulties by mid-August. Britain had lost 181 fighters in the air and 30 more on the ground. Only 170 replacement aircraft had thus far been manufactured, while just 63 new pilots had been brought up to replace the 154

*Left:* **Temple Underground station doubled as an air-raid shelter during the Blitz.**

Now it was Hitler's turn to be furious. He pledged in turn to annihilate London, abandoning his deeply held wish to occupy the city unscarred by bomb damage. With the German campaign to obliterate the RAF clearly failing, he thought it was time for a new and different tactic. The wholesale bombing of London would not only hit at the heart of the British government but would demoralise its people. 'Sealion', he believed, would still go ahead as planned. The gloves were now off. It was the start of an arduous period of bombing raids which would test the strength of the RAF and also the people of Britain to the very limit.

lost in battle. The raiders had succeeded in knocking out a radar station at Ventnor on the Isle of Wight, which was a serious blow, although their main aim of wrecking airfields had been frustrated. How long could the casual, seemingly cheery young men in silk scarves and leather jackets who laid their lives on the line several times a day without an outward trace of anxiety hold out?

Dowding, by skilful management, contained the mounting problems. Yet he was wearied by the effort and certain in the knowledge that Fighter Command could not cope with many more all-out raids. Another change in German tack saved the force from certain defeat.

Stage three of the Battle of Britain was sparked in part by accident. On 23 August a German pilot ditched his bombs over London, not to cause mayhem in the capital but rather to speed his flight home. Churchill was outraged. In retaliation, he ordered the bombing of the German capital, Berlin.

*Below:* **The unmistakeable shape of St Paul's cathedral stands firm among the bomb damage in the City of London.**

Now the German forces were throwing their entire weight at Britain. With their losses amounting to 60 planes on 15 September, the decision to undertake mostly night bombing raids was made.

Searchlights in London were unable to track the fast-moving attackers. Night fighters in the RAF squadrons badly needed airborne interception radar to hit back, which took valuable time to provide. The demands on the men of the RAF, already weary from their exertions, were enormous, and their ability to strike back under cover of darkness was limited. They were sleeping for just a few hours in every 24 before being scrambled once more. The casualties among them continued to mount and, for the first time, their losses exceeded those of the enemy.

---

*It took hours, sometimes days, to find bodies trapped in their wrecked homes*

---

Meanwhile, on the ground, the conditions for residents of London and, eventually, other main British cities were appalling.

The London docks were among the first targets in a daring daylight attack on 7 September. Nearby residents watched in horror as scores of German bombers sparked a ferocious blaze. It took just an hour for the Luftwaffe to drop 300 tons of high explosives and countless numbers of incendiaries. Hours later several hundred more bombers returned.

At night the raging fires burned like beacons, guiding Luftwaffe pilots to their target.

Before very long, London Underground stations became shelters for

## ◆ EYE WITNESS ◆

**Fred Graves, of Swindon, Wiltshire, served in the RAF ground crews which worked on Hurricanes and Spitfires during the Battle of Britain. Later in the war he serviced Lancasters of Bomber Command and was based near Newmarket.**

'I remember the Battle of Britain as a non-stop series of dog-fights in the skies above us. Our pilots knew they had a very low life expectancy. I lost an awful lot of friends.

I was particularly impressed by the Polish airmen serving with us. Every time there was a scramble alert they would race out, usually still in their shirt sleeves, jump into a plane and take off. They were very highly motivated to hit back at Germany.

Airmen rarely if ever showed they were scared. Even the Lancaster bomber crews assigned to missions over the Ruhr somehow coped with the pressure. You could detect a reluctance among them – simply because the Ruhr industrial region was so heavily defended – but they did their duty.

I think teamwork helped beat the fear. Bomber air crews were teams. If one of them wasn't fit or well then the whole crew was grounded until he was. They also had to have faith in their aircraft and in us as ground crew. We were the last friendly faces they saw before they flew east.

Looking back it is a miracle some of these men ever made it home. Their aircraft were so shot up they were almost unrecognisable.

frightened city folk despite an immediate ban on such a use. People slept end to end in close proximity to friends, neighbours and complete strangers. Those lucky enough to have gardens and shelters in their gardens became accustomed to retiring to them in time for tea and staying put until daybreak. It was soon clear that the option of sheltering under a sturdy wooden table was not an inspired choice as house after house was reduced to rubble by the bombs.

It took hours, sometimes days, to find bodies trapped in their wrecked homes. There was trial by fire as intense blazes raged. If bombs had failed to explode, there was continuing danger for the residents and workers of London even after the planes were long gone.

On the ground fire-watchers, full-time firefighters and auxiliaries, air raid precaution wardens and the Home Guard did their best to combat the terrible ravages of the raids.

*Above:* **Coventry was blitzed in a raid code-named 'Moonlight Sonata'. The raid claimed 568 lives.**

Despite all this, the mood in London was far from one of defeatism. The spin-off planned by Hitler of grinding the British public into the ground with the incessant bombing raids was failing miserably. In the tube stations there was impromptu entertainment from singers and musicians. Cups of tea were passed around and soon people learned to pay little heed to the sound of pounding bombs above.

### ■ BUSINESS AS USUAL ■

Instead of people weeping and wailing on the streets when the harsh light of day revealed the full extent of the night raids, there was a camaraderie which no one could have foreseen. Business went on as usual in daylight hours, despite shattered windows, fractured gas and water pipes and the unnerving sight of double-decker buses upturned in bomb craters. The spirit of the people of London was ultimately symbolised in the great cathedral of St Pauls, which stood intact overlooking the battered city while smoke from incendiary fires plumed around its dome.

If anyone was demoralised by the successive and apparently fruitless attacks it was the German pilots who were patently failing in their task of bringing Britain to its knees.

The attacks came in earnest from 15 September as Göring tried to

## Hitler had no option but to call off 'Sealion' indefinitely

ground the British air force in time for 'Sealion'. That day a record 56 Luftwaffe planes were brought down. Hitler twice postponed making a final decision on whether or not to go ahead before making his decision day 17 September. As the day dawned, London was smoking. But the Luftwaffe had paid a heavy price for the privilege of setting alight this

### THE FEW

'Never in the field of human conflict was so much owed by so many to so few.'

(Winston Churchill after the Battle of Britain.)

historic capital, and the planes of the Royal Air Force were not only still challenging their fighters but also found time to bombard the Channel ports where the German invasion fleet was based.

Hitler had no option but to call off 'Sealion' indefinitely. The Battle of Britain was won and the stout little island was safe from invasion. That meant renewed hope for occupied Europe, for without Britain from which to mount an attack on Hitler's Nazi empire there would have been barely a flicker of opportunity for liberation. Churchill's words of praise and thanks for the gallant RAF, spoken back in August, echoed through the free world. 'Never in the field of human conflict was so much owed by so many to so few.'

Yet the ordeal went on for both the men of the RAF and the people of Britain. Luftwaffe attacks continued unabated. London was attacked for 76 nights in succession and failed to enjoy much more than a few hours of eerie peace until the middle of 1941.

Anti-aircraft guns boomed in answer to the rain of bombs. There was little chance of them hitting their target. Only 75 aircraft were brought down by anti-aircraft shells – when the Luftwaffe flew about 12,000

# RUDOLPH HESS

**The Führer flew into a three-day rage when his deputy, Rudolph Walter Richard Hess, flew to Britain to make peace. A full day after the flight from Germany in a Messerschmitt 110 fighter aircraft, German radio explained away the demoralising desertion by claiming Hess was suffering from hallucinations.**

British intelligence chiefs, meanwhile, were similarly at a loss to know what to make of the ace pilot who had been a loyal member of the Nazi party since 1920. On 10 May 1941, when he came down to earth at the end of a parachute and suffered a broken ankle, he claimed he had an important message for the Duke of Hamilton. This message was, apparently, a peace formula which would end the conflict between Britain and Germany.

High-ranking British officers and Churchill himself would not hear of making peace by the back door. Nevertheless, they were reluctant to trumpet the capture of such a key Nazi. Were they being duped by Hitler? Was there a further dimension to this unexpected prize which had fallen into their laps?

Even today, no one can tell whether Hess was demented at the scale of the bloodshed and hatched his plan to end the war accordingly; whether he discussed the plan with Hitler who wished to secure peace with Britain before invading Russia; or whether it was in fact the real Hess who carried out the madcap caper. Years later there were claims that the man held by the Allies was in fact an imposter, dispatched by Himmler or Göring after the murder of Hess.

What remains certain is that the man who fell to earth that night in 1941 was tried as a war criminal at Nuremberg, sentenced to life imprisonment and incarcerated at Spandau prison in Germany for 46 years until his death, apparently by suicide.

German bombers opened their doors and let 450 tons of bombs drop on the city. Its historic cathedral was ruined. Birmingham, Manchester, Exeter, Sheffield, Liverpool, Cardiff, Swansea, Bath, Plymouth, Ipswich, Norwich, Southampton, Sunderland, Hull, Middlesborough and Canterbury all also received a battering.

## ■ BITTER TRUTH ■

Countless thousands of people were made homeless by these air raids, being left only with the clothes they stood up in. During the worst of them which occurred in December 1940 and May 1941 in London, the firefighters ran out of water as they fought hundreds of blazes and were left with little option but to let them rage on. On 10 May 1941 550 German bombers unleashed 700 tons of high explosives and thousands of incendiaries, killing 1,436 people and destroying 700 acres of city. Just 14 of the attackers were brought down.

From August 1940 to May 1941, 44,000 civilians died and 103,000 were injured. The bitter truth was that the destruction and misery was no precursor to an invasion of

sorties over Britain. Post-war investigation proved that for every bomber shot down by an anti-aircraft gun in September 1940 the gun had to expend an enormous 20,000 rounds. Results did improve and by February 1941 the figure was down to 3,000. Still, the knowledge that something was being done was at least a small comfort to the population.

Göring also turned his attention to other British cities. Perhaps his aim was to eliminate great industrial centres and not simply to mete out punishment to British civilians. In fact, the lack of accuracy among bombers of the age ensured that civilians were foremost among the casualties.

In Coventry, 568 people were killed on 14 November 1940 when

> ## *From August 1940 to May 1941, 44,000 civilians died*

Britain. It was merely a camouflage for Hitler's real intentions, to expand eastwards across the Russian borders, to Moscow and beyond. Only when Luftwaffe planes were pulled out of France to concentrate on the Russian front did the attacks on Britain subside.

*Left:* **As dawn breaks, the destruction of the previous night's raid on London's docklands is revealed.**

# AIR BATTLE – BALKANS

Both Axis and Allied powers saw benefit in opening a battle-front in the Balkans.

For Hitler, there was a chance of mopping up a potentially troublesome southern flank before mounting 'Operation Barbarossa', the invasion of Russia.

Churchill and his top brass saw a successful campaign in Greece or Yugoslavia offering a possible back-door entry into Germany when no access seemed available at the front.

In the event, the short and bloody campaign in the region left both sides as losers when it illustrated both the advantages – and drawbacks – of an airborne campaign.

Mussolini had opened hostilities when he invaded Greece on 28 October 1940. It was an impetuous decision which he lived to regret. Not only did it infuriate his ally Hitler, who had fostered an amenable relationship with Greece's ruler General Metaxas and considered the country in the bag. But it served to further humiliate Mussolini and his troops in addition to their inept showing in North and East Africa.

For the Greeks, although poorly equipped for modern warfare, were imbued with fighting spirit and managed to see off the Italians, pushing them back behind their lines in occupied Albania.

Britain was determined to stand by pledges of aid made to Greece – even though it had been unable to honour promises made to Romania, which was occupied by German troops at the start of October 1940.

### ■ ALLIES IN GREECE ■

Hitler had no option but to intervene in the action. However, for a few months he bided his time.

Having dispatched several thousand men, the British were keen to send even more of their contingent presently in North Africa to the aid of the Greeks. Metaxas was unsure. Although the presence of air support was welcomed, his own men were putting up an adequate performance and the presence of Allied ground troops would only succeed in drawing the awesome firepower of an irate Hitler. Instead of men, he said, he would rather have their boots. His own soldiers were suffering greatly due to the inadequacies of their footwear.

By the end of November 1940 three squadrons of Blenheim bombers and fighters had been stationed in Greece and the numbers continued to increase. Their brief, to defend Athens.

The political outlook changed at the end of January 1941 when Metaxas died suddenly and was replaced by Emmanuel Tsouderos who was well-disposed towards the Allies.

At a meeting in February, it was agreed the 1st Armoured Brigade, the 6th Australian Division and the 2nd New Zealand Division would be stationed in Greece to repel possible German aggression. With Bulgaria to the east rapidly falling under the influence of Germany, and with Italy in the west, the fresh troops could plug defensive gaps left open by the Greeks fighting in Albania. Churchill enjoyed the idea of rescuing the

> **The Greeks were imbued with fighting spirit and managed to see off the Italians**

'cradle of civilisation', as Greece is known, from the clutches of Nazism.

Also feeling the weight of the Nazi jackboot was neighbouring Yugoslavia, a country Britain failed to support. The government, under Prince Regent Paul and Prime Minister Dragisa Cvetkovic, were given an invitation-ultimatum in March 1941. Yugoslavia was to join the Axis powers. Prince Regent Paul was unable to secure aid from the British. With a heavy heart he finally gave his

*Far left:* A ship unloading supplies for the Allies in Suda Bay comes to grief.
*Left:* Italian soldiers were held at bay when they tried to invade Greece.

## ◆ EYE WITNESS ◆

**Howard Ganly was in the US 82nd Airborne Division. He was dropped behind enemy lines before D-Day to act as a pathfinder.**

❛ I was a little bit lost. They gave us the wrong maps. I made a few mistakes. I was shot at by my own men. They had got hold of some farmers' clothes and put them on, thinking they would be good disguises in German territory. Some of them were from my own company. I could have had them court martialled but I didn't. They stuck to me close for the rest of the war.

I was looking for open fields that weren't mined and didn't have big stumps stuck in the ground so they would be suitable for landing gliders. I would signal the gliders if it was OK to come in, with special lights and flares. We didn't dare use radios too much. I was very scared, I was just 19 years old. I came into the service when I was 17. The army kept pushing me around from one place to another. I didn't have any family, I spent most of my childhood in orphan asylums. I joined up to get a job and the money was good.

I survived D-Day but ran into trouble later on in Europe. I baled out in Holland behind enemy lines. A young Dutch girl put me in a barge and hid me from the Germans. She probably saved my life. I looked for her a few times after the war but never found her. I broke my leg and back in the fall. I have been disabled ever since. I was hospitalised for two years. I worked on and off but most of the time I have been crippled up. ❜

Luftwaffe wreaked havoc on Piraeus, the harbour of the Greek capital, which was crowded with ships from an incoming convoy. As the German bombs rained down destruction, one ship at anchor, SS Glen Fraser, had its 250-ton cargo of explosives ignited by a direct hit. The roaring explosion that followed flattened much of the harbour, sank yet more

## 'It is especially important that the blow against Yugoslavia is carried out with pitiless harshness'

consent and the Tripartite Pact was signed on 25 March.

Fury against the agreement among the Yugoslav people erupted immediately. There was an internal revolt which unseated the prince regent and put 17-year-old King Peter II in his place. On 27 March the pact signed with Hitler was ripped into pieces. The sombre mood which had descended on Belgrade and beyond was suddenly lifted, to be replaced with rejoicing.

### ■ HITLER OUTRAGED ■

The outbreak of anti-Nazism outraged Hitler. He resolved to teach the people of Yugoslavia a lesson. German commanders were told: 'Politically it is especially important that the blow against Yugoslavia is carried out with pitiless harshness.' It made sense to combat the Greek problem at the same time so 'Operation Strafgericht' (punishment) against Yugoslavia and 'Operation Marita' against Greece were co-

ordinated to begin on 6 April.

Hitler's campaign to pummel Yugoslavia into submission started with a dawn raid by the Luftwaffe. The sole declaration of war was the shower of bombs which hit Belgrade at 6am. The day-long assault claimed 17,000 lives and the grand buildings of the capital crumbled.

The day closed with another disaster, this time for Greece. The

vessels and even shattered windows in Athens some seven miles distant.

German armies began driving into both countries at the usual alarming Panzer pace. Yugoslavia, which had a small army, held out for just 11 days. Much of its air force was knocked out on the ground by Luftwaffe attacks. The inglorious fortnight was compounded when Royal Yugoslav Air Force Hurricanes became

*Right:* **Germany soon won command of the skies over Greece, and this tipped the balance of the battle in their favour.**

embroiled in a dog-fight over Belgrade with some BF-109s which unfortunately belonged to the very same air force.

### ■ RETREAT TO CRETE ■

The Greek army, too, was having difficulty fending off the advance. The fighting was gruelling. British commander General Sir Henry 'Jumbo' Maitland Wilson soon saw the hopelessness of the situation and ordered an evacuation to the south. On 22 April Greece capitulated also. The initial destination of the fleeing Allied troops was the Peloponnese islands linked to mainland Greece by a bridge at Corinth. Then it was onwards to the island of Crete.

Under fire from the Luftwaffe above, the Royal Navy came in to the southerly beaches on 26 and 27 April to hoist 26,000 men to safety. Left behind were 900 dead, 1,200 wounded and something in the order of 10,000 men who had fallen prisoner to the Germans. Then there was the abandoned weaponry, amounting to more than 100 tanks, 400 guns, 1,800 machine guns and 8,000 vehicles. The RAF had lost more than 200 aircraft in total while

> **On Crete there was chaos with hundreds of leaderless men awaiting an uncertain future**

the Royal Navy had had two destroyers and about 25 other ships sunk.

On Crete there was chaos with hundreds of leaderless men awaiting an uncertain future. The only thing

*Above:* Serbs in Yugoslavia were no friends of the Germans. Many fought as guerrillas against the invaders.

of which they could be sure was that Hitler's men would not rest until Crete too fell into their grasp.

In command was Major-General Bernard Freyberg, a pugnacious New Zealander who was ready to refuse the mantle of leadership until he discovered there was a sizeable number of his own men on the island – troops he believed had been taken back to Egypt.

His force amounted to two New Zealand brigades, about 7,750 men, plus an Australian brigade, two further battalions of Australians and a field regiment of artillery, with a combined total of 6,500. There were 15,000 British troops, too, comprising a brigade of infantrymen and part

*Above: A Panzer division parades its might before the centuries-old Acropolis in Athens, after the city was overrun.*

of the 1st Armoured Brigade, complete with two light tanks. Also at his disposal were about 10,000 Greeks. The Allies also had the support of the local population, many of whom would take up arms against the incoming Germans.

Freyberg, who won the VC in World War I, set about defending the island as best he could. He focused his forces at the three airfields, Maleme, Retimo and Heraklion, and the easily accessible Suda Bay.

From North Africa he received some tanks – less than two dozen but welcome nonetheless – and some rather war-worn artillery. There was

a further injection of men, the 2nd Leicesters, who arrived on 16 May.

Crete – 136 miles long and an uneven 40 miles wide, and full of mountainous terrain – could hardly be adequately defended given the small number of men. Yet Freyberg

## From North Africa Freyberg received some tanks – less than two dozen but welcome

was determined his men would give it their best shot.

For Germany, the invasion of Crete posed some difficulties, not least in how to transport troops to the island. The Royal Navy had

established a command of the seas. Already the shortcomings of the Italian navy had been shown up and the German command did not trust its ally's sailors with the lives of crack soldiers of the Third Reich. So an all-out amphibious assault was deemed too dangerous.

Yet in the air the Luftwaffe was unrivalled. By 18 May only seven RAF aircraft were left on Crete, and these were promptly withdrawn to Egypt. An airborne assault might work. Airborne forces had been in existence since 1927 when the first was formed by Italy. The Soviet Union soon followed suit and the value of these sky-fliers was clear. They could be dropped into enemy territory either in small numbers for the purpose of sabotage or in large numbers to begin an invasion.

There were, of course, numerous hazards inherent in airborne operations, but until now the Germans had known only successes. Their use of paratroopers in Norway, Belgium and Holland during 1940 had brought striking results. The 55 men

---

*The use of paratroopers in Norway, Belgium and Holland during 1940 had brought striking results*

---

from the 'Granite' assault team who parachuted into Eben Emael, the strongest fortress in the world, on the Belgian-Dutch border, in May of that year, defeated 700 defenders in less than a day.

The Luftwaffe's airborne supremo was Kurt Student, a World War I fighter pilot and squadron leader. He had keenly studied the potential of airborne techniques in Russia during the 1930s and saw 'Blitzkreig' as an excellent opportunity to put theory into practice.

Not only did he have troops leaping from flying aircraft but also equipment-bearing soldiers carried in gliders, and 'air mobile' forces, men trained in the art of going into action straight from the door of a landed plane. He sought to use all types in the invasion of Crete.

### ■ 'MERKUR' ■

'Operation Merkur', the German attack on Crete, was to be launched following days of heavy aerial bombardment, with the landing of 36 gliders whose elite troops would knock out anti-aircraft guns and capture key locations.

The men of XI Air Corps' 1st Assault Regiment were the next penned in to see action, capturing an airfield and other key locations. At the same time, men of the 3rd Parachute Regiment would drop further up the coast and the aim was for both prongs to battle to a reunion.

Then a second wave was planned in which the 1st and 2nd Parachute Regiments were introduced with heavier arms, while two further battalions arrived by sea in fast motor-

*Right: General Kurt Student was the mastermind behind German paratroopers' triumphs – and their failures, like the ill-fated assault on Crete.*

cutters. More amphibious activity was planned when the island was in German control. First hitch for the Germans came when too few planes were provided, forcing the commanders to cut the size of the airborne assault.

Student and his men believed only a few thousand men would be there to meet them when the attack on 20 May got underway. It was a catastrophic miscalculation.

As a swarm of aircraft receded into the distance, hundreds of parachutes billowed in the breeze. The troops on the ground had plenty of time to take aim and fire, relishing a chance to get revenge on the men who had so recently chased them out of Greece. The helpless paras were picked off one by one as they all fell

Communications were poor on both sides. With telephone lines down and radios suffering patchy reception, the Allied groups felt equally isolated from assistance and exposed to the enemy. It caused one New Zealand commander to withdraw his men from a commanding position in the heights above an airfield, leaving a vital foothold open to the attackers.

## Groves and escarpments were littered with bodies, many still strapped into their 'chutes

There followed more of the bitter fighting, often at close quarters, with many Allied soldiers claiming victims at the point of a bayonet. Both sides vied for the airfields. There was an uncomfortable stalemate as both Allied and German commanders tried to land reinforcements. The Royal Navy sank the German transports while the Luftwaffe holed the British ships.

### ■ GERMAN VICTORY ■

At Maleme airfield under a barrage of crossfire, brave German pilots began to land their transport planes, some coming to grief on the runway, others colliding with planes that had preceded them. Inside were well-trained, well-armed soldiers fresh and ready for the fight.

The New Zealanders at Maleme were finally overwhelmed. Germany had scored the first victory in the battle for Crete.

And it was a key triumph, for now that the attacking troops had control of Maleme airfield, the gateway was open for supplies and still more troops to be transported in.

*Above:* German paratroopers were confident as they embarked for Crete, with good reason. Until then, they had only known success.

virtually on top of the defending Anzac and British forces. Olive groves and rocky escarpments were littered with bodies, many still strapped into 'chutes.

Some parachutists didn't even make it out of their planes. Ground fire penetrated the hulls of the low-flying aircraft, killing or wounding men while they were still inside.

The few that survived were compelled to seek cover and join up with their comrades as soon as they could. Only those who dropped away from their targets – and thus away from defensive fire – escaped being cut down. It was for them to fight their way across the rocky landscape and unite with other groups.

# OTTO SKORZENY

A scar-faced German captain called Otto Skorzeny was the action-man asked by Hitler to rescue Mussolini from imprisonment in September 1943. Skorzeny, who was frustrated in earlier plans to snatch the Duce to safety by the diligence of the Italian authorities who kept their prized prisoner on the move, planned for a German plane to land on a precarious mountain plateau while he in the company of other troops parachuted into the hotel hideaway where Mussolini was held. Italian guards at the mountain village of Assergi abided by his requests not to resist the bold German move. Mussolini was flown off in the tiny plane which battled to ascend from the plateau. On reaching Rome he was transferred to a Heinkel 111 for a flight to the safety of Vienna.

In less than a week, Freyberg assessed the situation as hopeless. He ordered the Allied troops, by now mentally and physically exhausted, to withdraw to the south where an evacuation was being launched by the Royal Navy.

Between 27 May and 31 May, about 16,500 Allied men were taken off Crete. Germany had sealed its Balkan front.

## ■ BALANCE SHEET ■

Both sides were left counting the cost, however. Left on Crete were 1,750 Allied soldiers killed in action, two thirds of them Anzacs, and 13,500 men now held as prisoners of war. The Royal Navy lost three cruisers and six destroyers in the rescue bid, along with about 2,000 sailors killed or taken prisoner. Also left behind were Greek, British and Anzac soldiers who turned guerrilla to fight a cloaked campaign against the occupiers. It was another inglorious rout for the Allies.

As for the Germans, nearly half the initial force were killed on Crete, amounting to some 3,700 men. Among them were high-ranking officers including a divisional commander, and a colonel. The number of aircraft shot to

smithereens by the Allies or junked on the island airstrips was also immense.

Hitler surveyed the results – and decided the price was unacceptably high. Matter-of-factly, he told Student afterwards: 'Of course you know, General, that we shall never do another airborne operation. Crete proved that the days of parachute troops are over.'

It was a gross over-exaggeration. Germany continued to employ parachute troops although never again in such vast numbers. Nevertheless, Hitler did decide to abandon plans to parachute men into Malta, the stepping-stone island in the Mediterranean. Had he won Malta,

Hitler might have found victory in the North African campaign, and pushed into the Middle East and India to join hands with Germany's ally Japan.

The Allies observed the German experience on Crete but also decided in favour of using airborne troops in future engagements. Paratroopers played a pivotal role in the success of the D-Day operations in 1944. Theirs was a precarious job, dropping behind enemy lines in darkness to act as pathfinders for the incoming gliders. Men of the US 82nd and 101st Airborne Divisions were also

> ## 'Of course you know, General, that we shall never do another airborne operation'

charged with hindering the enemy advance towards to the coast. But the landings did not go as planned.

A combination of inexperienced piloting and mistakes in navigation had the men dispersed over a huge

*Right:* **Captured Australian servicemen are a source of curiosity for their German guards.**

were thrown into confusion by the unexpected and unseen troops. One regiment in the 82nd Airborne Division managed to capture the town of Ste Mère Eglise.

British airborne troops were also seeing action as they seized vital bridges and knocked out a battery of guns aimed at the coast. For the British paratroopers, the ultimate test of endurance was to come later in the year at Arnhem in 'Operation Market Garden'.

Montgomery was eager to persuade Eisenhower of the wisdom

area instead of being in a concentrated group. Parachutists found themselves landing in some of the many engorged rivers in the region. Weighed down by their equipment they floundered for hours trying to get out. Others drowned in the struggle. It meant both Divisions were literally thousands of men short

## *Weighed down by their equipment they floundered for hours trying to get out*

when they went into action. All the hazards of airborne operations, particularly those carried out at night, appeared to be coming in at the Americans.

Yet success bred out of disaster. Undoubtedly, the German defenders

*Right:* Horsa gliders lie in pieces after landing men in northern France in 1944. On these gliders the fuselage is split from the wings to unload.

# ALLIED SUCCESS

**Air superiority during D-Day became the key to Allied success. While it was thought that the Luftwaffe would sent up some 900 aircraft to make 1,200 sorties on D-Day, in fact only 100 were made in daylight and a further 175 after dark. By contrast the RAF alone flew 5,656 sorties on D-Day, about 40 per cent of the total made by the Allies.**

Allied aircraft dropped a total of 4,310 paratroops and towed gliders containing 493 men, 17 guns, 44 Jeeps and 55 motorcycles without suffering harassment from enemy bombers.

As well as protecting troops and ships, Allied aircraft dropped 5,267 bombs against the coastal gun batteries.

The first German plane to fall victim on D-Day was a Ju 88, brought down by New Zealand Flying Officer Johnnie Houlton, one of 2,000 pilots in the Second Tactical Air Force who was in a Spitfire.

In the months which followed, three times as many bombs were dropped on Germany than in all the previous years.

of committing the ground troops to one hammer-blow into northern Germany. Eisenhower favoured a fan-shaped attack instead.

### ▪ 'MARKET GARDEN' ▪

'Operation Market Garden' was designed to capture key bridges in Holland through which Allied troops could be funnelled into Germany. The US 101st Airborne Division was charged with gaining land north of Eindhoven, the US 82nd Airborne Division was allocated two big bridges over the Meuse and the Wall rivers, while the British 1st Airborne Division had to seize bridges over the lower Rhine at Arnhem.

The men were carried to their targets in a total of 1,068 aircraft and 478 gliders. While the Americans experienced considerable success on their fronts, the British met enormous German resistance en route to their target. Just one battalion, the 2nd, reached the bridge at Arnhem. Soon after, they were cut off.

*Right:* Troops taken by gliders into Arnhem in a bid to short-circuit the route to Berlin. The Britons had a grim fate in store.

Unfortunately for the British paratroopers, the Germans picked Arnhem as a focal point of defence and reinforced their lines with troops, including an SS Panzer corps containing two armoured divisions. All efforts by the British to reach the men isolated at Arnhem were repelled after fierce clashes.

At the bridge, the paratroopers were pushed back into a defensive

## *It took nine days for the men to establish an escape route across the Rhine*

margin. It took nine days for the men to establish an escape route across the Rhine. Just 2,200 men got out from a force which began with a strength of 10,000. Montgomery's plan to by-pass Germany's defensive Siegfried line had failed. The thrust continued as before.

# WINGS OVER THE DESERT

The Western Desert Air Force was officially born on 9 October 1940 at Maaton Bagush in North Africa.

Here in the African desert, the theories of modern air warfare were established. For it was in North Africa that the principles of 'partnership' between air, sea and land forces were tried and tested for the first time, helping to put an end to decades of overt inter-service rivalry.

Co-operation of the kind enjoyed by air, sea and naval personnel among the Allies was unthinkable for their German and Italian counterparts, who not only fought a common enemy but were constantly embroiled in sniping against different factions on their own side. Indeed, there were plenty of hiccoughs along the way among the Allies with soldiers convinced the only worthwhile aeroplane was the one that flew protectively above their heads, regardless of the risk to the pilot and his inability to achieve results from that vulnerable spot.

The initial trials of tactical airborne operations were honed by the men of the Desert Air Force until they finally became adopted everywhere.

## Unfortunately for the Italians, early promise was soon done down by the Desert Air Force

Lessons learned in the Desert Air Force now seem rudimentary and even naive. Yet aerial combat was still in its infancy when the war commenced. Fliers in World War I had the opportunity to make only elementary trials and errors. Little was done to advance the theory of warfare in the air after 1918 as most nations were concentrating on peace.

And until the conflict in the desert got underway, the Royal Air Force was from necessity concentrating primarily on defence.

To call it simply a Desert Air Force is to vastly over-simplify the case. The men who worked under its umbrella saw action in the skies above Egypt, Libya, East and West Africa, Greece, Yugoslavia, Palestine, Italy and other hot spots in the region.

This tremendous fighting force grew from an original nucleus of some 29 squadrons – a total of 600 aircraft. These were all that were available to Middle East commander Air Chief Marshal Sir Arthur Longmore when hostilities with Italy commenced in 1940. Included in this total were a goodly number of outdated biplanes and obsolete Blenheim bombers. That summer on the home front saw the Battle of Britain reach its momentous heights. So the chances of getting top-notch replacements were slim.

In addition, the airmen faced the same shortages that cursed the soldiers on the ground, those of water, fuel and spare parts to replace those worn by the inhospitable terrain.

*Above:* Mussolini believed his air force could win the skies over Africa. *Left:* Stalwart Beaufighters played a key role in the North African campaign.

Against them was the might of the Regia Aeronautica, the Italian air force, which had proved itself already in the Spanish Civil War and Mussolini's Ethiopian campaign in the mid-1930s. The Italians were flying home-produced planes like Capronis and Fiats. Unfortunately for the Italians, their early promise was soon done down by the Desert Air Force.

### ■ MALTA ATTACKED ■

The Regia Aeronautica went into action for the first time on 11 June 1940, with 35 Savoia-Marchetti bombers attacking Malta. Pitted against them were four Gloster Sea Gladiators, constituting the island's only fighter defence force. By the end of the day, the Italians had launched seven attacks for no loss.

By way of response, 26 RAF Bristol Blenheims launched an attack against an Italian airfield in North Africa, eventually destroying 18 enemy aircraft on the ground.

*Above:* **Despite their years of experience, Italian aircraft and pilots proved no match for the Desert Air Force.**

There followed a number of skirmishes. Prime targets for the Italians were Malta, Gibraltar, the British base at Alexandria in Egypt and the British Mediterranean Fleet.

The action in Africa then forked, with General Graziani leading his contingent of Italians in the Western Desert against Wavell, while the Duke of Aosta led some 215,000 troops out of Italian East Africa and into a British dominion. To meet Graziani's men were the British 7th Armoured Division, soon to be joined by the 6th Australian Division. Meanwhile, the 4th Indian Division was dispatched to meet the threat in East Africa.

It was in the East African campaign that vital steps towards an orchestrated plan for close air support were made. At the outset in October 1940, the Italians in East Africa were a formidable enemy. Their spirits were high, their maturity in desert warfare a major advantage. But much of their buoyancy could be put down to the fact that they enjoyed air superiority. Italy had 14 bomber squadrons or gruppi in East Africa, and five supporting fighter gruppi. The over-stretched British forces, comprising nine squadrons, were happily reinforced by a further eight squadrons from South Africa, flying Hurricane aircraft.

> **Soon the battle to win supremacy of the skies began to swing in favour of the Allies**

Soon, the battle to win supremacy in the skies began to swing in favour of the Allies. Both sides fought bitterly, both on land and in the air, for command of Keren, a fortified hill top in Eritrea. At the end of eight weeks, however, the Italians were turfed out of their stronghold and, by April 1941, a corner in the war of East Africa had been turned. As the campaign toiled on, the South African Air Force formed a first Close Support Flight to co-operate with ground troops, achieving a good measure of success.

### ■ FIVE LESSONS ■

After the battle of Keren, one British observer noted five lessons to be learned. They were: the need for transport planes; the need for supplies to be dropped by air (which was to prove crucial in the jungle wars of Burma and the Pacific); the advantage lent by long-range fighters which could destroy the enemy's aircraft before they lifted off; the need for Red Cross air ambulances to evacuate the wounded; and the preference for dive bombers.

These were all points which would be brought home to subsequent

**Ern Stanton, from New South Wales, was 18 when he joined the Royal Australian Air Force and qualified as a flier on the Empire Air Training Scheme.**

Of our EATS course in Canada, about 40 per cent were later killed. It was very sad and disheartening to hear about your mates dying in action but I was really too young and conditioned too much to death to realise the more serious aspects of war

I do particularly remember one little bloke in our squadron who would give away all his personal effects before he went on a mission because he was convinced he wasn't going to come back. When he did return safely, he would go around and get them all back. But he did finally get killed.

*Below:* Hurricane pilots of 73 Squadron line up before a desert-worn aircraft in North Africa during 1941. The Hurricane was the RAF's first monoplane fighter.

senior air force officers. For now, only the immediate achievement of winning an important initial victory was noted. As the Allies took greater command of the action, Italian commanders found themselves battling not only against the Allies but also against a sapped will among their own men. A proportion of their troops were native Africans whose loyalty was suspect.

The campaign in Eritrea was to end in a complete and resounding victory for the Allies by the middle of 1941. Yet short on success though the Allies were at this stage, there was little chance to celebrate. Much as the British commanders had feared, Hitler had sent German forces into the region to assist his floundering fascist soul-mate.

Early in 1941 it was clear the Luftwaffe were installing units of Fliegerkorps X in Sicily, a specialist branch of the air force which had cut its teeth in the Norwegian campaign and specialised in picking off ships. The Mediterranean Fleet first felt its presence on 10 January 1941 when up to 40 aircraft attacked a convoy. In aerial warfare, the Luftwaffe quite simply outclassed the Italians.

At the same time, the conflict in Greece was intensifying. The only assistance actively required by the

> ### Early in 1941 it was clear that the Luftwaffe were installing units of Fliegerkorps X in Sicily

Greeks at the start was an injection of air power. Here the expanding Allied air strength had little problem asserting its authority. In one battle which took place on 28 February 1941, 16 Hurricanes and 12 Gladiators were patrolling at 14,000 feet when they were attacked by 50

Italian Fiat planes. In the two-hour clash which followed, the Royal Air Force fighters claimed 27 enemy planes for just one Gladiator lost.

The string of successes were a tribute to the ground crews who faced appalling winter conditions in the most primitive of airfields in order to keep the planes airborne. Spring saw further aerial reinforcements sent in by the British but the leaders in the field were uneasy. It was surely only a matter of months before Hitler made that battleground his own as well.

### ■ LUFTWAFFE ARRIVES ■

In April those grim predictions became reality. The Royal Air Force found its forces and those of its Greek and Yugoslav allies suddenly dwarfed by the arrival of the

Luftwaffe. Its ranks included 430 bombers, 180 fighters, 700 transport planes and 80 gliders.

By 19 April the four Hurricane squadrons in Greece could rally just 22 operational aircraft between them. All were pulled down to Athens to lend air support to the evacuation of troops from Greece to Crete and North Africa. In the end there were only seven Hurricanes left.

On Crete they were joined by four Sea Gladiators and three Fairey Fulmars of the Fleet Air Arm. The abysmally small fighting force was virtually wiped out on the ground by the marauding Germans.

Added to the boiling pot was the Iraqi uprising against the British in May 1941. The Desert Air Force was by now staffed with Australian, New Zealand, Rhodesian and Free French

*Above:* German aircraft and pilots suffered the same difficult conditions as their Allied enemies.

units, as well as British and South African. But the ceaseless demands took their toll of its strength. And the menace from the Third Reich in the

*By 19 April the four Hurricane squadrons in Greece could rally just 22 operational aircraft*

region did nothing to recede during that period. In fact, it gained momentum. Hitler was dallying with the idea of invading Malta. The little island which had found some relief when attacking forces were diverted to assist in the invasion of Greece, was once again at the top of the agenda for the Luftwaffe.

## ■ MALTA REPLENISHED ■

Its defences amounted to just four fighter squadrons as well as bombers and Fleet Air Arm forces based off the island. The succession of raids both by the Italians and increasingly by the Germans pared down the number of fighters. But the ranks were replenished on 15 June 1941 when 47 flew from the deck of the

*Below:* SS *Talbot* was one of scores of ships to fall foul of enemy planes in Malta's Grand Harbour.

Ark Royal, and a further 64 were dispatched by similar means before the month had ended.

The hectic months ahead saw the Malta-based fliers toiling to keep the convoys safe, and so deprive Hitler and Mussolini of the toe-hold they both sought. In addition, they attempted to destroy enemy convoys and hit targets in Italy – particularly Naples where, on 16 December 1941, 16 Wellingtons showered a torpedo factory with 4000lb bombs, the largest used in the Mediterranean to that date.

Between June and October 1941, 220,000 tons of Axis shipping was sunk en route to Libya, of which 115,000 tons could be marked down

to the Desert Air Force, especially its Maltese division.

The fruits presented to Churchill by the frustrated Longmore were too few and far between to impress.

### On 16 October 1941, 16 Wellingtons showered a Naples torpedo factory with 4,000lb bombs

Friction between the ground and air forces was still very much in evidence, never more so than when a reconnaissance flight reported enemy troops approaching a vital petrol dump in

## ◆ EYE WITNESS ◆

**Post Office worker Arthur Helm was one of the first New Zealanders to sign up and fight for Britain following the outbreak of World War II.**

❛ I had read a lot about the Germans and I knew how despicable they were. And I knew what I was letting myself in for.

I was a member of the First Echelon, the 6,607 men who first left New Zealand for Eygpt. Later I was in northern Greece as a member of 4th Brigade Signals. After the invasion of the Germans, we moved to fight a rearguard action at Thebes. I saw the Acropolis about four hours before the Swastika was raised over it. At Port Rafti we held a two-mile stretch of coastline and two miles inland during the evacuation. We had to throw everything overboard except for our rifles, the clothes we stood up in and a small haversack.

Author Laurence Durrell wrote that when everyone arrived in Crete they were dishevelled, dispirited and defeated – except the New Zealanders. They came up the beach with their rifles poised, their hats on and every one had a book under his arms. He was wrong – I had two books, a book of poetry and a Bible.

Spirits were high among the New Zealanders. We simply felt sorry for the Greek soldiers we left behind.

We expected the arrival of the Germans. I had just knocked off after 24 hours on duty and was having my breakfast when the first parachutes appeared.

There was a lot of deer-stalking and rabbit-shooting in New Zealand so most of us could shoot pretty straight. You knew when you had hit a parachutist coming down. He retracted his legs up as an automatic reaction.

Later I got involved at Galatas where we went in with bayonets after dark and drove out a bunch of Germans from the houses there. It was very nerve-racking but we got rid of them – even if we did have to retreat the next day.

I got out over the mountains to the harbour for evacuation. I met an English soldier at the side of the track and pointed out the way. He said: "I'm not going any further." I gave him some water and he told me he had been through Dunkirk but it wasn't a patch on this.

He just laid down on the hillside and died. He was done for, absolutely exhausted, and he had no will to live.

We lost Crete because the Germans had planes and we didn't. But we never lost heart. After being evacuated from Crete we went to Sidi Rezburgh. That was probably the worst campaign of the lot. ❜

*Above:* On Malta, air strips like this one provided constant targets for Luftwaffe pilots. *Right:* Air Chief Marshal Sir Arthur Tedder.

the North African desert. The dump was destroyed before it was discovered the troops in question were, in fact, British. Never mind that it was notoriously difficult to positively identify the nationality of soldiers from the air. The fighters on the ground had been deprived of valuable fuel for no reason. Longmore's repeated requests for more aircraft did little to endear him at home, either. Duly, Longmore was replaced by Arthur Tedder in May 1941.

### ■ AIR FLEET ENLARGED ■

The following month, Wavell was dispatched from North Africa by an irate Churchill. Happily, his replacement, General Sir Claude Auchinleck, struck an immediate harmonious note with Tedder which helped to end the bubbling army-air force discord.

Tedder, with support from the Air Ministry, helped to overhaul the repair and maintenance operations in the region which were proving so inefficient and therefore costly to the service.

Once he had enlarged the fleet of aircraft available to the Desert Air Force to beyond 1,000 in November 1941, Tedder turned his attention to the quest for new, well-trained recruits. There was a chronic shortage of training facilities in the Middle East.

## Two operations to relieve Tobruk, 'Brevity' and "Battleaxe', had failed in the early summer of 1941

Tedder fell back on his usual standpoint, which was to employ an expert – in this case Air Commodore B. Embry – who could devote the best of his time and attention to the problem.

### ■ CO-ORDINATED ACTION ■

Two operations to relieve Tobruk, 'Brevity' and 'Battleaxe', had failed in the early summer of 1941 and once again it seemed the relations between army and air force would be strained. It was in September 1941 that a satisfactory blueprint for co-ordinated action was finally drawn up to at last eliminate this problem. Drawing on the illustrations of the East African campaign, it set out the principles of close support of land forces by air forces, including pre-arranged and impromptu attacks on the enemy. Indirect air support was defined as attacks on objectives other than the enemy forces in the battle proper.

Above: Air Chief Marshal Sir Arthur W. Tedder, Deputy Supreme Commander, Allied Forces Western Europe.

An Air Support Control headquarters was created for each army corps. These were information exchanges linked by two-way radio to brigades in action. Representing the RAF at brigade was a team called a Forward Air Support Link. The RAF team could assess the action at close quarters and request air support when necessary. On receiving the request, the staff at the Air Support Control team headquarters, with its overview, could work out where best to send its aircraft during a battle for the most effective results.

The principles had already been put into practice on exercises in Northern Ireland as early as September 1940. A developmental Army Co-Operation Command had been set up by the RAF following Dunkirk when the air force received flak for not coming more visibly to the aid of evacuating soldiers.

In Africa, these close-support principles were not only rehearsed but put into action as well, and adopted thereafter to the satisfaction of everyone involved.

## THE END OF THE BEGINNING..

'This is not the end. It is not even the beginning of the end. But it is, perhaps, the end of the beginning.'

(Winston Churchill after the Allied victory in North Africa.)

# REDS IN THE SKY

No one in Russia was ready for war when it came in June 1941, least of all the unwieldy air force.

Stalin boasted of a large body of planes. But like the sizeable French air force of 1940, the Red Air Force was ineffectively used and no match for the skill and experience of the Luftwaffe. Its sole four-engined bomber at the outset of the war was the TB-3, slow, underpowered and inadequately armed. It had ten squadrons of MiG, Yak and Lagg fighters. Yet these were far inferior to the Messerschmitts so elegantly handled by German pilots.

In addition, the Russians were partway through a modernisation plan in which their outdated planes would be replaced by more competitive models. The Russian air force, like all branches of the establishment, had suffered its fair share of losses in the purges which Stalin organised to rid himself of potential opponents.

## ■ AID FROM BRITAIN ■

The pilots of the Red Air Force were trained to support the troops on the ground rather than enter into combat with other aircraft. Many ended up frantically helping to evacuate Russian industry to the east, to save it from falling into German hands – reducing the aircraft available for other duties still further. Indeed, its fighter arm had never been put to the test. The summer and autumn of 1941 brought a succession of disasters for the Red Air Force.

Still being punished by the Germans at home, the RAF neverthe-

*Above:* Britain provided Hurricanes and know-how to the Russian air force, following the German invasion.

less found the resources to send several squadrons of Hurricanes to the aid of the Russians.

It was Churchill's wish that as much aid should be devoted to the beleaguered and reluctant new ally as possible – despite the fact he was a

### *The summer and autumn of 1941 brought a succession of disasters for the Red Air Force*

lifelong critic of communism. In a broadcast shortly after Hitler's 'Operation Barbarossa', he explained how the hatred of fascism remained uppermost in his emotions.

*Left:* Much of Russia's air power was devoted to shipping industry east.
*Far left:* The TB-7 bomber that brought Russian minister Molotov to Britain.

'The Nazi regime is indistinguishable from the worst features of Communism. It is devoid of all theme and principle except appetite and racial domination. It excels all forms of human wickedness in the efficiency of its cruelty and ferocious aggression. No one has been a more consistent opponent of Communism that I have for the last 25 years. I will unsay no word that I have spoken about it.

### ■ BRITISH TEACHERS ■

'But all this fades away before the spectacle which is now unfolding. The past, with its crimes, its follies and its tragedies, flashes away. I see the Russian soldiers standing on the threshold of their native land, guarding the fields which their fathers have tilled from time immemorial. I see them guarding their homes where mothers and wives pray . . .

## 'I see the Russian soldiers standing on the threshold of their native land'

'I see advancing upon all this in hideous onslaught the Nazi war machine with its clanking, heel-clicking, dandified Prussian officers, its crafty expert agents fresh from the cowing and tying down of a dozen countries . . .

'I see the German bombers and fighters in the sky, still smarting from many a British whipping, delighted to find what they believe is an easier and safer prey.

'. . . if Hitler imagines that his attack on Soviet Russia will cause the slightest divergence of aims or slackening of effort in the great democracies who are resolved upon his doom, he is woefully mistaken.'

A British unit was sent with the aircraft to the Soviet Union to teach the Russians how to make and fly Hurricanes and to oass on tactical tips about the escort of bombers and general air operations.

*Below:* **Royal Air Force Hurricanes pictured in the air over the Russian countryside on their way back to base from escort duty.**

## ◆ EYE WITNESS ◆

**Alexander Pokryshkin, the son of a bricklayer in Novosibirsk in Siberia, emerged as one of Russia's air aces. He flew 550 operational flights, fought 137 aerial battles and had 59 victories to his credit. He became the first member of the Soviet armed forces to be awarded the title 'Hero of the Soviet Union' three times, receiving his third Hero's Gold Star Medal in August 1944.**

"I was out with pilot Semyonov as my partner flying on a reconnaissance mission to Jassy where the Germans had an aerodrome. As we approached the town I espied five Messerschmitts flying towards us, three below us and two above. Here, at last, were live Germans. They spotted us. I rocked my wings as a signal to Semyonov that I was going to attack. There were five of them and only two of us.

I was flying a MiG-3. It is a sturdy machine and well armed. It behaves wonderfully at high altitudes when its speed and manoeuvrability increase. I had my plan of action all worked out in an instant. Semyonov was to cover me as we had previously arranged on the ground. I shot up into the clouds and kept on climbing until I ran into one of the two Messerschmitts coming towards me. The German zoomed almost in my face. I did a stall-turn and found myself on the tail of the yellow, blunt-winged craft. I fired at short range. The Messerschmitt burst into flames and plunged downwards. I watched it as it fell and that almost cost me my life. The other German had crept up behind me. White ribbons of his tracers shot by and then my plane shuddered. Its port wing had been torn by bullets.

I dived to zero feet and hedge-hopped all the way home and, feeling that my aircraft was losing stability all the time, with great difficulty got back to the airfield. I made a normal landing, taxied to a stop, shut off the engine and slumped aganst the armoured back of the seat. I needed a drink. My throat was parched. That was the first German I had bagged."

Soon, the lessons of the visiting Britons and that of bitter experience began to sink in. Until the Russians became fully conversant with combat know-how and were better equipped, however, a handful of German pilots had a field day.

King of the skies at that time was Erich Hartmann, otherwise known as 'Bubi' Hartmann or the 'Blond Knight'. During World War II he scored a record 352 victories, or kills, all of which were validated, making him an 'ace of aces'. Most were made on the Eastern front.

Hartmann was born in Weissach, near Stuttgart, on 19 April 1922. As a boy, he lived in China where his father was a doctor. When the family returned to Germany Hartmann was encouraged by his mother, herself a pilot, to sample the joys of flight. First qualifying as a glider pilot and instructor, Hartmann then joined the Luftwaffe aged 18.

He revealed the secret of his success: 'My only tactics are to wait until I have the chance to attack the enemy then close in at high speed. I open fire only when the whole

---

### During World War II Hartmann scored a record 352 kills, all of which were validated

---

windshield is black with the enemy. Then not a single shot goes wild. I hit the enemy with all my guns and he goes down.'

In his beloved Me-109, he knocked out seven Red Air Force planes above the Battle of Kursk on 7 July 1943. It wasn't unusual for him to return from a sortie with more than one kill to his credit. No Allied pilot even approached such a mighty score.

### ■ HARTMANN ESCAPES ■

Operating over Russia, his plane was once shot down. Although he was unhurt, he was taken prisoner by Russian soldiers – a fate dreaded by German airmen at the time.

He pretended he was injured and was placed on a stretcher in a truck. En route to find a doctor he sprang up, overpowered his guard and leapt under fire from the lorry into a field of sunflowers. Sleeping by day and walking by night, he finally reached the German lines where he was almost shot by one of the sentries.

His outstanding success and distinctly Ayran features made him a

*Above:* Russian pilots are congratulated by their major after completing a mission on the Eastern front.

*Below:* Erich Hartmann was one of the most successful pilots of the war, scoring most of his victories over Russia.

frequently had cross words with his German superiors. Once he was even drunk enough to begin juggling with the Führer's hat but still remained a 'golden boy'.

### ■ HARD LABOUR ■

Erich Hartmann scored his last victory on the final day of the war, having flown 1,400 missions. He then came down to earth with a jolt, being captured by Russians. His sentence following the war was 25 years' hard labour – although he was offered freedom if he agreed to settle in East Germany and train their air force. He refused the deal and was finally released in 1956 following negotiations by Chancellor Adenauer of West Germany.

Hartmann resumed his air force career and learned to fly jets under

favourite with Adolf Hitler who awarded him the Knight's Cross and later added the prestigious German military decorations of Oak Leaves, Swords and, finally, Diamonds. Courageous not only in the air, he

## ACE PILOTS

In the league table of wartime ace pilots, the first five places are occupied by Germans followed by two Japanese and a Finnish pilot. The first pilot from the West to appear in the league comes in 27th place, South African J. Pattle, who is followed by Richard Bong (below) and Thomas McGuire of the US and J. Johnson of Britain.

final total of 200,000 men abandoned their air duties to become infantrymen. It left the air crews short of ground staff. They were also to suffer from lack of aircraft and fuel and a diminishing training programme.

## *Worse was to come for the German air forces remaining on the Eastern front*

Russian industry which had moved to the safety of the east was able to produce supplies for the Red Air Force – which was further bolstered by American aircraft through the Lend-Lease Act.

*Below:* **With much of Russia's powerful industrial muscle in the safety of the east, Stalin was able to provide his air force with vital replacement planes and components when Hitler could not.**

the auspices of the Americans. He was married in 1944 to his wartime sweetheart Ursula Puetsch, and the couple had a daughter. Hartmann died in 1993, aged 71.

As 1941 closed, the prospects improved considerably for the Russians in the air war. The Luftwaffe having deployed the majority of its air power in the opening stages of 'Operation Barbarossa', its strength on the Eastern front soon waned as it became overstretched and struggled to maintain its operations on three fronts.

### ■ LUFTWAFFE SUFFERS ■

Worse was to come for the German air forces remaining on the Eastern front. Luftwaffe field divisions were created to back up the ground forces as the conflict with Russia dragged on, and a

# TIGER, TIGER, TIGER

By 1941, tensions were running high between the Americans and Japan. The United States government looked on uncomfortably as Japan sought to expand its empire by waging a brutal war on China.

Although Japan's leaders pledged neutrality in the European war, alarm bells were sounding across the Western world. Both America and its future allies aided the hard-pressed Chinese.

Seizing a golden opportunity in September 1940, the Japanese pushed the boundaries of their empire back by moving into Indochina at the expense of Vichy France, the colonial rulers of the country. This was a move the European puppet state was powerless to resist. In retaliation the anxious and angry United States and Britain broke off trading relations, which meant a halt to the supply of vital oil to Japan. The exiled Dutch government did likewise. Australia was by now viewing the aspirations of Japan with trepidation.

Without oil, Japan could survive for 18 months at the most despite the huge stockpiles it had imported during the 1930s. At stake was its considerable economic might. The hawks among the Japanese hierarchy quickly argued that time was running out for Japan and that a military strike to consolidate its position was needed sooner rather than later.

### ▪ TRIPARTITE PACT ▪

In the same month as the threatening manoeuvres in Indochina, Japan joined with aggressors Germany and Italy in the Tripartite Pact, which set out a code of co-operation between the three. There could be little doubt now that the Land of the Rising Sun was poised on the brink of war. But the question which troubled the Americans was, just how would the inevitable conflict begin?

Japan had sound reasoning behind the desire to enlarge its lands. In 1939, its population reached 99 million and was increasing at the rate of five million a year. Its home islands were becoming overcrowded and overstretched. Britain, France and Holland all enjoyed the benefits of colonies. America, although ideologically opposed to colonialism,

## *In September 1940 Japan joined with aggressors Germany and Italy in the Tripartite Pact*

*Left:* An aerial view of the US Pacific Fleet's base at Pearl Harbor.
*Below:* Japan's foreign minister Matsuoka talks with Ribbentrop in early 1941.

had its spheres of influence. Japan felt entitled to the same. It was not unreasonable, the Japanese felt, for their country to hold sway over the Pacific and China.

Japan's transformation from feudal backwater to burgeoning world power had been rapid. It was only in the latter half of the 19th century that Japan had come out of isolation. After that, the Japanese followed the

## The Japanese felt cheated, unable to trust the countries they had known as friends

British and American examples and were set on a programme of industrialisation. Yet the new breed of manufacturers struggled to compete on the same terms as the Westerners. Britain had tariffs which discouraged overseas trade while America also followed a policy of protectionism.

Nevertheless, Japan joined the Allies during World War I. After-

*Right:* **Japanese pilots were hailed as heroes back home after their unannounced attack on the US Pacific Fleet's base at Pearl Harbor.**

wards, the Japanese were anxious to be accepted as part of the New World Order on equal terms with other nations. Bitter disappointment was in store.

At the Paris peace conference the Japanese proposed a clause of racial equality, with the aim of ironing out the discrimination they had previously felt, once and for all. The emissaries from Japan assumed that there would be no controversy over the clause's acceptance.

### ■ JAPANESE ANGER ■

In the event, it was barred by none other than American president Woodrow Wilson, who went on to place a ban on Japanese people entering the US when immigration by other nationalities was rife. Australia, too, had a 'whites only' immigration policy. The Japanese felt cheated and angry, unable to trust the countries they had hitherto known as friends. Western powers seemed more fraudulent than ever when the Washington Treaty of 1922 was drawn up, limiting Japan to just three capital ships for every five run by both the US and Britain.

The Japanese largely followed Western models of democracy.

*Left:* **Admiral Isoroku Yamamoto was the architect of the strike against Pearl Harbor. Yet he feared he had 'awakened a sleeping giant'.**

Although there was an emperor, he was bound by the decisions of his ministers. Yet the Japanese government differed sharply from others in one vital respect. Its civilian ministers ran civil affairs. But there were ministers from the army and navy entirely responsible for military matters. Without the co-operation of those ministers from the armed services, the government fell. It meant they wielded huge power. To further complicate matters, there was an enormous degree of rivalry between the army and the navy and the two services could rarely agree.

Aside from these wranglings, there was also the sinister threat of assassination. It became a political tool increasingly used among young patriots. Those in power became cautious, corrupt and sly. There came a feeling among the Japanese that politicians

# ◆ PEARL HARBOR

On the morning of 7 December 1941, the Japanese attacked on Pearl Harbor. As the US naval base prepared for its day, Japanese carrier aircraft swept in and tore into the US Pacific Fleet at rest. The fleet's carriers were at sea, but the battleships were in. *Arizona*, *West Virginia*, *California* and *Oklahoma* were destroyed; *Pennsylvania*, *Nevada*, *Tennessee* and *Maryland* were damaged. The Japanese lost nine Zeroes, 15 'Vals' and five 'Kates'.

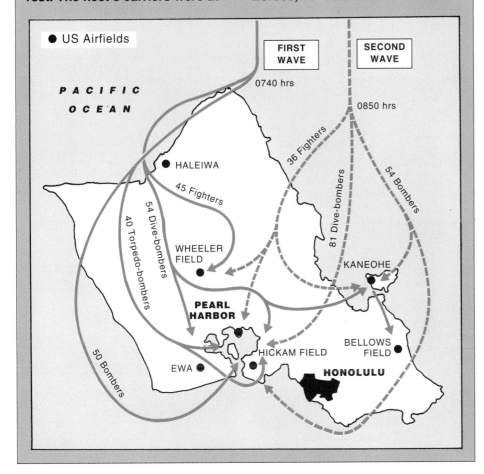

thousands of miles away. The remote islands were economically wealthy, precisely why they were incorporated into empires in the first place. Japan would become stronger than ever before if only it could avail itself of the assets there.

With Japan's vast military might, the islands were easy enough targets. But the Japanese leadership rightly guessed that America was unlikely to sit back and watch as it established a thriving Pacific or Asiatic powerbase. It would, of course, send its big ships to trouble-spots. The answer, it seemed, was to knock out the mighty American navy to obtain the necessary freedom of the seas.

> ### *The answer, it seemed, was to knock out the mighty American navy*

Conveniently, the pride of the US fleet was based in Hawaii, much closer to Japan than the inaccessible mainland of the United States. And so the infamous attack on Pearl Harbor was conceived.

It was a brilliant short-term strategy drawn up by Admiral Yamamoto. Key to its success was the element of surprise. There was a hard summer of training for the pilots of the fighters, dive-bombers and torpedo-bombers which were to be shipped in for the pre-emptive strike. Most Japanese pilots had seen plenty of action in the war with China.

To ensure the action, code-named 'Operation Z', was effective, powerful six-inch naval shells were adapted for use by the aircraft, sufficient to plough through the armour of US battleships. The Japanese also had a 24-inch torpedo known as the 'Long

could not be trusted. Not only that, there was widespread fear about the encroachment of communism. Together with a growing admiration for the achievements of Nazi Germany, Japan swung towards militarism.

Japan, still cut out from overseas trade by the policies adopted by key trading partners Britain and America, began to feel the pinch during the Great Depression of the 1930s. Japan spent much of the 1930s meddling in internal Chinese affairs. When China became unwilling and belligerent, the two countries finally went to war. In 1937, Japan withdrew from the League of Nations and denounced the Washington Treaty, privately planning to increase its naval strength to compare with that of Britain. And she sought to boost her empire.

### ■ YAMAMOTO'S PLAN ■

Casting greedy eyes at the colonies in South East Asia and the Pacific owned by Britain, Holland and France, Japanese military leaders realised the outposts were now vulnerable, with the mother countries being embroiled in problems

*Right:* Japanese aircraft warm up on the deck of the carrier Hiryu before delivering their stunning blow to the US Navy at Pearl Harbor.

Lance', containing 1,000 pounds of explosives; it was among the most powerful weapons in the world.

As early as 26 November 1941 the Japanese navy set off from its base, using an obscure route and maintaining complete radio silence. By 7 December it was in position, 270 miles north of Pearl Harbor in the Kurile Islands.

### ■ 'TIGER, TIGER, TIGER' ■

The fleet, under Vice-Admiral Chuiki Nagumo, comprised six aircraft carriers, with a capacity of 423 planes. In the attack 360 were used, the force comprising 104 high-level bombers, 135 dive-bombers, 40 torpedo-bombers and 81 fighters. In addition, the escort force consisted of two battleships, three cruisers, submarines and supply ships.

In dock at Pearl Harbor were 96 American ships. Fortunately for the US, the base's two aircraft carriers were at sea. Their destruction may have altered the course of the war.

At Pearl Harbor, a new day was beginning, clouded only by a general fear of war. Still, the beaches were silvery, the sun was warm and the majority of the servicemen based there were looking forward to a day of relaxation. Many were still in bed when the storm broke.

Although America had been forewarned that Japan was planning

## The ships in Pearl Harbor were undefended, their ammunition in lockers

a major strike, it didn't know where or when it would take place. Most thought the Philippines the obvious target for Japanese aggression. The ships in Pearl Harbor were undefended, their ammunition safely held in lockers.

The only clue to the carnage to come came in the early hours when a periscope was spotted in the harbour

*Left:* Pearl Harbor explodes under the onslaught of Japanese bombs. Fortunately, key fuel installations were left intact, so averting utter disaster.

## PEARL HARBOR

**US Losses**

18 ships, including 8 battleships, sunk or badly damaged; 164 aircraft destroyed and 124 aircraft damaged; 2,403 men dead and 1,178 men wounded.

**Japanese Losses**

29 aircraft downed; 5 midget submarines sunk; 64 men dead or missing; 1 prisoner taken.

*Below:* US servicemen at Pearl Harbor were staggered at the sight that greeted them. Japanese aggression was dubbed 'treachery' around the Allied world.

mouth. A destroyer duly went out to sink the unidentified submarine.

In fact, few people outside the navy top brass in Tokyo knew what was going on. Unwilling to announce its intentions and give its game away, Japan didn't deliver its declaration of war to America until Pearl Harbor was smoking.

At 6am the first wave of aircraft took off and headed for Hawaii. As they came in sight of Pearl Harbor Captain Mitsuo Fuchida, in command of the first wave, broadcast to his men, screaming 'Tora, Tora, Tora' – 'Tiger, Tiger, Tiger', literally translated. The message

informed them that the Americans were still unaware of what was to come. At 7.56am the first shots rang

*As they came in sight, Fuchida broadcast to his men, screaming 'Tora, Tora, Tora'*

out. In neat formations, the skilful, well-practised pilots made runs over the lines of vessels anchored along 'Battleship Row', the section of the harbour where the capital ships lay.

Far below them, braving the tell-tale shallow waters of the harbour, were Japanese midget submarines, each one hoping to bag a battleship.

## *A stunned commander ordered them to take action, bellowing 'This is no drill!'*

Ship after ship was blasted and soon the air was filled with thick, spiralling, oily black plumes of smoke. As the flaming oil from one stricken vessel spilled into the sea, it set light to another. The second wave of Japanese bombers had difficulty locating targets through the fug.

The Arizona was hit and exploded – 1,200 members of her crew died. The battleships West Virginia, Oklahoma, and California were also destroyed, and Nevada, Maryland, Tennessee, and Pennsylvania were damaged. Further casualties included the cruisers Honolulu, Raleigh and St Helena, and the destroyers Shaw, Cassin and Downs. These ships, all symbols of America's greatness, were left tattered wrecks.

In the midst of the chaos a contingent of American aircraft arrived. Their pilots must have gaped in disbelief at the scenes before them. What once was a landing strip had been set ablaze, along with most of the aircraft on it. Then they too were attacked, no match for the nimble Japanese fliers. The same fate was in store for the crews of dive-bombers from the absent carrier Enterprise who returned to base during the attack.

## ■ 29 PLANES DOWNED ■

At times the Japanese pilots screeched in so low they were clearly visible to the frantic Americans.

The men at Pearl Harbor responded to the onslaught with considerable zest. A stunned commander ordered them to take action, bellowing the words: 'This is no drill!' Despite the shock and disbelief, the Americans soon manned the guns as they had done before in training and claimed 29

*Below:* 'Battleship Row' at Pearl Harbor provided rich pickings for the carrier-borne aircraft of Yamamoto's strike force.

*Above:* **Despite the suddenness of the strike, troops rushed to man the guns. A total of 29 Japanese planes – nine Zeroes, 15 'Vals' and five 'Kates' were downed.**

Japanese planes. Others raced to rescue comrades trapped in blazing ships or operated firefighting equipment. Finally, there was calm. The surviving servicemen set about their grim tasks with one ear open for the return of the Japanese.

While the Pacific Fleet's base was extensively damaged, it was not crippled, since the fuelling and repair depots had escaped unscathed. It was to take months, however, and in some cases years, to refloat and repair the shattered bodywork of the damaged ships.

The Japanese did not return to finish off the base, as was widely feared among US servicemen and their families. Well satisfied with the results of the operation, which went better than any of the Japanese commanders dared hope, Vice-Admiral Nagumo decided a quick,

getaway was now in order, particularly as fuel was running dangerously low, and the US carriers Lexington and Enterprise might appear.

In America there was outrage and horror at the loss of life. US secretary of state Cordell Hull was still in conference with Japanese negotiators when news of the attack reached him. They had already presented him with a document purporting to set out the area of debate.

### ■ A REPEAT OF 1904 ■

Mr Hull furiously declared: 'In all my 50 years of public service I have never seen a document that was more crowded with infamous falsehoods and distortions on a scale so huge that I never imagined until today that any government on this planet was capable of uttering them.'

Although some took the opportunity to condemn President Franklin Roosevelt for his lack of readiness, most American citizens were determined to pull behind him in their fury at the Japanese action.

Ironically, the attack on Pearl Harbor mirrored a military move made by the Japanese against the Russians in 1904. Once again, without an official declaration of war, the Japanese navy carried out a surprise attack on a key Russian base, picking off some prestige targets. Back then, The Times of London hailed it as 'an act of daring' and praised the Japanese for their initiative and vigour.

In Britain, the Daily Mail now voiced the venom of many when it wrote: 'Not even Hitler has yet achieved the infamy of a stab in the back while his envoys were still ostensibly negotiating terms of agreement with his intended victim.

'This is an act which the world will never forget so long as the

> ## On 8 December, both America and Britain officially declared war on Japan

records of history are read. It will stand for all time as an example of the ultimate depths of deceit to which it is possible for any nation to descend.'

On 8 December, both America and Britain officially declared war on Japan. In response to the declaration and the wave of Japanese attacks around the region, the Royal Navy battleship Prince of Wales and battlecruiser Repulse sailed out of Singapore with an escort of four destroyers. Disastrously, 'Force Z', as it was known, ignored the threat of airborne action and left without the protection of an aircraft carrier. Their aim was to prevent the Japanese making landings on British-held territory in South East Asia. But the mission went badly wrong when the

## ◆ EYE WITNESS ◆

**Kazuo Sakamaki was the commander of a midget submarine, one of five which was sent into action at Pearl Harbor.**

❝ Something went wrong. At the moment of release my submarine nearly toppled over into the water. The trim had not worked well. I feared that if we attempted to emerge hastily enemy observers might spot the ship. I remembered that the opening of hostilities was to follow the handing of the notice of war to the US government. If by my own mistake the presence of the Japanese forces should be discovered it would create a grave problem. It would spoil the air attack and every other detail of the carefully worked-out plan. I could not cause such a blunder. No matter how dangerous the condition of my ship I could not let it emerge to the surface.

My aide and I crawled back and forth inside the submarine removing the lead ballast and filling the tanks with water to correct the trim of the craft. It had been our plan that by midnight all five submarines would be inside the harbour and would sink to the bottom and wait for the dawn. But when I looked at the watch it was midnight already. The ship righted itself.

I figured that as long as we entered the harbour during the night no damage would have been done. I drank a bit of wine and ate my lunch.

"Let's do our utmost." My comrade and I held each other's hands and pledged success. I took my position and moved forward with minimum speed.

After ten minutes I lifted the ship slightly to see through the telescope where we were going. To my horror, the ship was moving in the wrong direction.

Moving blindly because my gyrocompass was not working, the ship had gone 90 degrees off her course. If I could manage the ship with the help of the telescope we could get back on our course but this was clearly impossible.

"We must get to the mouth of the harbour" I repeated to myself. My hands were wet with cold sweat. I changed the direction three or four times, hoping against hope that somehow the ship would get going where I wanted to go. The speed was maintained at the minimum as before.

Time ticked away in complete indifference to my predicament. It was almost the moment for attack.

As we came nearer to the enemy ships guarding the entrance I was able to see the white uniforms of the sailors aboard. I concluded they were destroyers.

I pushed the midget submarine toward them, Suddenly I heard an enormous noise and felt the ship shaking. I was hit on the head and lost consciousness. This was my first contact with war.

I came to myself in a short while and saw white smoke in my submarine. I changed the speed to half gear and turned the ship around. I wanted to see if any damage had been done. My comrade was all right. My two torpedoes were all right. I did not want to waste my torpedoes on those destroyers which began again to charge against me. They threw depth charges at us. They fell near us but not as close as the first time. ❞

---

two British giants became sitting ducks for the Japanese Naval Air Arm flying out of Indochina.

The Prince of Wales, able to fire 60,000 shells every minute out of its array of 175 anti-aircraft guns, was thought to be impregnable. The cream of Japan's pilots didn't think so.

On 10 December, both ships were sunk off the coast of Malaya within an hour of each other and 800 members of their crews were killed, although 2,000 were saved by the accompanying destroyers. Among the dead was the leader of the ill-fated squadron, Admiral Tom Spencer Vaughan Phillips. There were 34 high-level bombers and 51 torpedo-bombers coming at the ships from all directions. Only three aircraft had to be ditched. The formi-

dable Japanese fliers had struck again. Winston Churchill heard the news by telephone from the Chief of Naval Staff. 'I never received a more direct shock,' he commented.

As militarily admirable as it might have seemed to the Japanese at the time, the long-term consequences of the attack on Pearl Harbor were clearly ill thought-out. Japan had a

*Left:* **Both Roosevelt and Cordell Hull were disgusted by the Japanese attack.**

magnificent navy, powerful enough to compete with that of America or Britain, with the most modern aircraft carrier fleet in the world. Its army too was large and capable.

### ■ A GIANT AWAKENED ■

Yet Japan could not have possibly hoped to complete its victory with an occupation of the US. It was a geographical and numerical impossibility. And if the leaders of Japan hoped the action at Pearl Harbor would demoralise the Americans and encourage them to capitulate, they sorely misjudged their foe. The aim seems to have been merely to cause enough damage to keep America at bay while Japan built up its strength in the Pacific.

It is likely they were then hoping for a war of attrition in which America would weary and compromise. Yet architect of the deadly war strike Admiral Yamamoto clearly had

an inclination of what lay ahead when he said: 'I fear we have only awakened a sleeping giant and his reaction will be terrible.'

*Above:* British newspapers joined the wave of indignation against the warmongering Japanese after their opening strikes in the Pacific.

## ◆ EYE WITNESS ◆

**A correspondent for the National Broadcasting Corporation gave this account of the bombing of Pearl Harbor.**

❝ The most thickly populated air base was attacked by Japanese planes a little after 8 am local time.

After machine-gunning Ford Island the Japanese planes moved to Hickman Field. Observers say that considerable damage was done there but a number of planes were brought down.

Three ships of the United States Pacific Fleet based at Pearl Harbor were attacked and the 29,000-ton battleship *Oklahoma* was set on fire.

All lines of communication appear to be down between the various Army and Navy aerodromes and the Army in the field.

The Army has issued orders for all people to remain off the streets.

The first raiders carried torpedoes and did considerable damage to shipping in Pearl Harbor and off Honolulu. They came in squadron formation over Diamond Head, dropping high explosives and incendiary bombs.

They came over Honolulu itself and were at once met with anti-aircraft from Pearl Harbor, Ford Island, Wheeler Field, Honolulu Municipal Airport, Hickman Field and the new Navy repair base.

A terrific barrage was put up but all the points I mentioned appear to have been attacked.

The chief of fire services has reported that the fires were under control and were not as bad as expected. ❞

# AERIAL WEAPONRY

Ripe for exploitation, bursting with potential, the aeroplane came of age during World War II. It could never win battles alone. But the aircraft of those troubled years undeniably made the difference between triumph and wholesale military failure. While they would never replace ground troops, they did succeed in making giant battleships obsolete and changed the face of modern conflict.

Incredibly, following World War I, British politicians, including eminent figures like Prime Minister Stanley Baldwin, were all for scrapping military 'wings'. French marshal Ferdinand Foch summed up the prevailing attitude when he said: 'Aviation is good sport but for the army it is useless.'

It was only the vociferous campaigning of Lord Hugh Trenchard, Marshal of the Royal Air Force during the 1920s, that kept the RAF in business. It was the same story across the Atlantic where sceptics failed to see a future in flight. William Mitchell, assistant chief of the US Army Air Service, faced similar negative reactions against the budding force. He managed to silence some of the critics with trial bombardments between 1921 and 1923 which sank six warships. Still, jealousies levied in America by the existing well-established branches of the military mirrored those in Britain.

### ■ SHANGHAI BLITZ ■

These were people who failed to read the writing on the wall. German air attacks by Zeppelins and aircraft in south east England during World War I claimed 1,413 lives – paltry by comparison with the casualties on the Western front but sufficient to bring the war home to people in Britain. In reply, the British fliers killed 746 Germans in a total of 242 raids.

There was a school of thought which predicted dire consequences for Britain if it was the victim of a concerted air attack during the 1920s. But its voice was ignored by those who funnelled their thinking and their actions towards peace following the 'war to end all wars'.

Only when fighting broke out between China and Japan in 1931 and parts of Shanghai were reduced to rubble by Japanese bombers did air power come back on to the agenda.

Still, the British government at the lengthy international disarmament conference of 1931 urged that military and naval air forces be abolished. The conference ended inconclusively – but not until 1934, by which time Britain was substantially behind in the rearmament race. Italy had begun to build up its military, and Germany, now led by Hitler, was doing the same despite limitations still in force from the Treaty of Versailles.

Then it was left to the people who flew for thrills to make the running in air technology between the wars.

Racing became the pursuit of playboys, which not only earned them accolades and acclaim but won the infant industry some valuable knowledge. For example, the British Supermarine S.6 racing plane – which was a winner of the prestigious Schneider Cup – was transformed into the Spitfire fighter. In Germany, the Messerschmitt 109 set a speed record of almost 470 miles per hour in 1939 and went on to father some of the Reich's most effective planes.

Although flying speed increased, the overall performance of many aircraft did not, on account of the lack of fuel capacity. New faster-than-ever trips were inhibited by the number of stops necessary for refuelling. Greater capacity was needed to increase their range.

### In 1935 the first B-17 Flying Fortress rolled onto the runway

Now it was the turn of the US to rise to the challenge. In 1935 the first B-17 Flying Fortress rolled on to the runway, with its ability to travel thousands of miles on one fuel tank. Meanwhile, the Douglas Aircraft Company unveiled the DC-3, with its top range of more than 2,000 miles. Both machines were winners.

*Left:* A pilot hauls himself from the cockpit of his Beaufighter, this one equipped with radar.
*Right:* An Italian Macchi aircraft.

Britain was seeing a revolution in air power of its own with the development at Rolls Royce of the PV-12 engine, the Merlin, in 1933. Aircraft manufacturers in 1935 had turned out the Hurricane, a stalwart fighter

**In Germany the Luftwaffe was reborn on 26 February 1935 with a total of 1,888 aircraft**

plane which even in those early days was capable of speeds of more than 300 miles per hour. In total, 12,780 were built in Britain and a further 1,451 in Canada.

The 1930s saw the development of radar in Britain, vital for both air and sea forces. After realising that aircraft

interfered with radio signals, Sir Robert Watson-Watt of the National Physical Laboratory hit on radio detection and ranging, in which a travelling aircraft reflected a radio pulse and was thus visible on a screen linked to a radio receiver. Radar gave the Allies a vital leg-up during the opening phase of the conflict. Indeed, it took the Germans some time to understand how it was that their bomber and fighter formations so rarely escaped attack during the Battle of Britain. As the war progressed, radar was fitted to planes for use against aircraft carrying out night raids on Britain, providing at last an antidote to blitz bombers.

In Germany the Luftwaffe was reborn on 26 February 1935 with a total of 1,888 aircraft and 20,000 officers and men. Powering the new air force were four companies –

*Above:* By March 1936 an early version of the Spitfire – which was based on a racing seaplane – was flying, although it was modified before becoming a battle winner.

Daimler-Benz, Junkers, BMW and Siemens-Halske. It was the designers from Daimler-Benz who dispensed with the carburettor and introduced a multi-point fuel-injection system, giving a pilot far greater control during rapid airborne manoeuvres. The rival Rolls Royce engine was prone to cutting out during dives.

### ■ BRITAIN LAGS ■

The arrival of the Luftwaffe caused consternation in Britain and was enough to spur the Air Ministry into action. New military aerodromes mushroomed on the east coast. Yet still there were crucial delays and hold-ups in the building of planes.

## ◆ EYE WITNESS ◆

**Tony Langdon-Down joined the Royal Air Force in March 1941 when he was aged 18.**

"I left school because the war started and began to read for the bar. As soon as I was 18 I joined the RAF – not for any particular desire to fly but I wanted to get into the services and there was a shortage of pilots.

For four months I was in Cambridge which is where I learnt to fly. Going solo for the first time was one of the highlights of my life. I completed my flying training and was operational by February 1942.

I was a defensive night fighter mostly serving with 219 Squadron. It was a tremendous way to grow up. After a few months I joined a Beaufighter squadron, flew out to Casablanca and from there we went to Algiers and Tunis. It was the first time I had been abroad.

We took part in the Sicily landings. I didn't see much action except for patrolling. When we returned to Britain, we left all our old planes to the Americans. They found them extremely difficult to fly.

I was an instructor when flying bombs started to fall. I volunteered to fly Tempests, single-seater night planes. The flying bombs came over on the back of Heinkels. I only shot down two. One blew up in my face which was rather unpleasant.

We didn't bring them down in built-up areas which made our job difficult. When they came to an end I rejoined a Mosquito squadron.

Although we did night flying we did tests on our aircraft in pairs during the day. I went out with another plane one day when it was very cloudy. We came down through the cloud and we were 500 feet over a port. The next minute all hell let loose. The port was Dunkirk where a pocket of German resistance remained. To my horror the other plane was shot down. We were hit but we were able to get back to Britain to land. The wife of one and the fiancée of another crew member were visiting the base for the weekend. Their deaths came as a terrible shock because there was no reason to suppose they were in any danger.

As the end of the war approached, my commanding officer asked me to make a small speech for VE day. I travelled to the BBC in London to record it. Sitting in the mess after Germany surrendered, we were listening to the radio when Princess Elizabeth made a short speech. It was followed by me. As you can imagine, there was uproar among my friends. I hardly recognised my own voice.

I didn't have a very glorious war. Flying wasn't the dangerous occupation when I joined that it had been. The main risk to me was my own flying ability. We did fly in some pretty fearsome conditions, though. I remember taking off in thick fog when I was chasing flying bombs and wondering how I would ever get down again."

---

The Wellington bomber, designed by Sir Barnes Wallis, was prepared on paper by 1932. However, its first flight was not until June 1936 and it wasn't delivered for active service for a full two years after that.

Even as late as 1938 the Royal Air Force were woefully ill-equipped. Sir Maurice Dean, Private Secretary to the Chief of the Air Staff, pointed out: 'The re-equipment of Fighter Command had barely begun. The radar chain was half completed. Of the 45 fighter squadrons deemed necessary at the time, only 29 were mobilisable and all but five of these were obsolete. The five modern fighter squadrons could not fire their guns above 15,000 feet owing to freezing problems.'

The onset of hostilities did much to speed ahead technology and cast off caution.

When war broke out the pride of Britain's flying stock were Hurricanes and Spitfires. However, there

*Below:* German Messerschmitt 109s like this one caused plenty of headaches for Allied pilots.

*Above:* **Boeing B-17 Flying Fortresses ready for action. The enormous capabilities of these classic aircraft were a tremendous boon to US airmen.**

### *At sea, the slow Sword-fish still earned their colours despite their advancing years*

were also Fairey Battles, Gloster Gladiators, and Bristol Blenheims, all hopelessly outdated. In September 1940 the first Bristol Beaufighters were introduced, complete with radar sets to combat night attackers. At sea

there were slow Swordfish – which still earned their colours despite their advancing years, both in sinking the Bismarck and in the successful raid on the Italian fleet in Taranto.

During the war came the Handley-Page Halifax, which was progressively bettered, the subsequent Halifax Mark III, known for its versatility, and the heavy-duty Avro Lancaster. Best-loved of all was the wooden Mosquito, fast enough with its two engines to outrun many of its German adversaries on bombing runs.

### ■ ESCORT FIGHTERS ■

Ranged against them were Henschels, old-fashioned but nevertheless effective, the Ju.87 'Stuka', an ideal

Blitzkrieg weapon thanks to its terrifying siren wail, Junkers, Heinkels, Dorniers and Messerschmitts. One of the most successful late arrivals in the German air fleet was the Focke-Wulf 190, which preyed on bombers. However, the Germans never found a successful formula for a heavy bomber, preferring instead fast bombers like Heinkels.

The best of Japan's aircraft were carrier-borne. They included the Mitsubishi A6M, better known as the Zero, torpedo-armed Nakajimas and dive-bombing Aichis. It came as a mighty shock, but the Japanese, when they entered the war, had the best air force in the world both in terms of agility and range.

## ◆ EYE WITNESS ◆

**E. Rickman, who had been building model aeroplanes since he was a child, opted to join the Fleet Air Arm in April 1942. By 1944 he was based on HMS *Illustrious* and flew Grumman Avengers, US-made aircraft and the pride of the British fleet.**

In January 1945 we were told the twin oil refineries at Palembang in Sumatra which provided the Japanese with nearly half the aviation fuel they needed in South East Asia had to be put out of action. One of the refineries was successfully bombed despite a barrage balloon protection. Three days later we were told the next one was our target.

During the briefing, our commanding officer Lieutenant-Commander Charles Mainprice, told us: "I consider this operation to be highly dangerous . . . I consider this strike to be so dangerous that if anyone would prefer not to fly, I shall respect his wishes and I shall not, repeat not, think any the less of him for so doing."

The next day at about 4.45am as we approached Palembang, I could see the target ahead and the balloons. Just before I made our dive an enemy plane got on our tail. Suddenly, the Browning gun jammed. Fortunately, it was our turn to get in line for attack. I trimmed the Avenger for the dive and put the stick forward and the enemy plane broke off its engagement. There were three aircraft ahead of me. I could see one balloon cable between us and the pump house which was our prime target.

The commanding officer who went in first didn't see it. To my horror, he hit the cable with his port wing, cutting off two thirds of it as clean as a whistle. His plane went into a spin and exploded on impact seconds later.

The senior pilot next in line saw the cable and steered around it. But I could hardly believe my eyes when the third plane in line hit the same cable and suffered the same fate as the CO. I felt sick and angry but I didn't have too long to think.

It was my turn to go in. I went around the cable and met a huge smoke cloud which was obliterating the target. I had no choice but to go through it. The plane bucked in the turbulence and emerged from the smoke on its side at 500 feet.

I levelled out, went to tree-top level and headed around the coast, blasting away with my front guns at any target I could see.

On my way back I saw another Avenger which looked all right. But before my eyes I saw it descend into a shallow dive and blow up as it hit the sea.

At the end of the attack we were told there were 18 direct hits on the target and we did not need to return again.

common target with the support of fighter escorts did the British find some success.

Throughout the war, aircraft design was refined to provide faster fighters and better bombers. The latters' capacity for bombs was continually increased. Also, aircraft which were 'jacks-of-all-trades', such

> ### *Aircraft design was refined to provide faster fighters and better bombers*

as bombers that could act as transport planes or were able to fly low-level missions to drop supplies, were now in demand as aircraft began to take a broader role in the war.

*Below:* **Sir Robert Watson-Watt was a pioneer of radar, which became crucial during World War II.**

In their aircraft arsenal, the Americans had the invaluable Boeing B-17 Flying Fortress heavy bomber, and later the North American P-51 Mustang long-range escort fighter. On the other hand, they had problem planes, too. Captain Philip White was in a squadron of Brewster Buffaloes – heavy with armour plating and lightly armed – which was virtually wiped out by Japanese Zeros. He later wrote: 'It is my belief that any commander who orders pilots out for combat in a Brewster should consider the pilot as lost before leaving the ground.' The Australians who were given 154 Brewsters with which to defend Malaya. Within three months every one was destroyed.

A welcome addition to the US ranks during the war was the P-51 fighters, which had enough range to protect bombers on long-distance missions deep into Germany. In the bomber fleet, as well as Flying Fortresses, there were Liberators, less effective but with the supreme advantage that one rolled off the assembly line every 50 minutes back at the Ford Motor Company in Michigan.

### ■ LACK OF TACTICS ■

At the start of World War II, British tactics were virtually non-existent. Planes merely took off and headed in the general direction of their target. It was only when aircraft formations ascended in unison heading for a

Fortunately for the Allies, the Luftwaffe fell into disfavour with Hitler and many new German innovations were scuppered. Nevertheless, Hitler maintained a lively interest – which ensured a financial lifeline – in the development of rockets and jets.

From test centres of the Third Reich came the ME-163 Komet, capable of speeds of 600 miles per hour. Still in its infancy, it did not cause the headaches for the Allies that it promised.

Its fuel was a combination of C-Stoff (hydrazine hydrate in methanol) and T-Stoff (hydrogen peroxide and stabilisers). When the two fuels were mixed they transformed into an explosive hot gas, sufficient to kill any members of the ground crew who accidentally combined the two on the ground.

*Below:* **The military version of the Douglas DC-3, the C-47, entered service during 1941. The aircraft was known as the Dakota in the RAF.**

Inside there were only five engine controls for the pilot to consider. These were off, idle and thrusts one, two and three. His mind was often taken away from the business of flying by the incredible agonies of

## *In fact, the Komet was too fast to be effective against the much slower Allied planes*

extreme G-forces not to mention the high possibility of death by fire should the plane explode.

After the flight came the hazardous and problematic landing, done in a gliding skid on the undercarriage. In fact, the Komet was too fast to be effective against the much slower Allied planes. Swooping down on Flying Fortresses, for example, the target was only in range momentarily before the Komet shot past. They also became targets themselves for

Mustang fighters who took to patrolling near Komet bases to pick them off as they landed.

Britain was not far behind. Sir Frank Whittle, an RAF officer, piloted its first jet-propelled aircraft as early as May 1941 but Britain failed in the race against the Germans to get it into service.

### ■ DEATH RAY ■

There were other ideas being knocked around in Britain which failed to come to fruition. One, originating in World War I, was to freeze the clouds and mount gun emplacements on them. Another was to freeze stretches of sea and use them as landing strips – which was a project taken seriously enough to be given a code-name, 'Habbakuk'. Thirdly, there was the much-loved idea of the death ray. No matter how hard scientists tried, they found it only worked when the chosen victims had first been thoroughly poisoned.

Despite the odd flight of fancy, aviation science and skills moved on

*Above:* **The Junkers Ju.87 'Stuka' dive-bomber was a terrifying aircraft.**

apace on both sides during World War II. However, it can be assumed that the Germans were a step ahead of the Allied countries as far as technology was concerned. Many

*Many German scientists were enticed to America...many on a 'no questions asked' basis*

German scientists were enticed to America following the war, many of them on a 'no questions asked' basis. There was an outcry years later when it was discovered that people regarded by some as war criminals were harboured in the US.

## ◆ EYE WITNESS ◆

**Hilda Richards, from Cardiff, Wales, joined the ATS in 1941 when she was 21 and worked on the radar which guided one of the biggest 'ack-ack' guns in London.**

There were only three gun sites like us in the country. One was on Wimbledon Common, one in Regent's Park and ours was outside Eltham. Most guns measured 3.5 while this had a 5.25 specification. It came from an abandoned cruiser.

I was one of six girls on radar. I still keep in contact with four of them. There was a lot of comradeship. For most of us it was our first time away from home. I wouldn't have missed it for anything – even when we counted 108 buzz bombs passing over us in just one night.

We worked any time the sirens went off at a post about 100 yards away from the gun itself. Rotas were 24 hours on duty, 24 hours on standby and 24 hours off. It sounds tough but we got used to it.

If we were on standby we could get some rest until we heard the siren. Then we would slip our trousers and battledress over our army pyjamas and run. The majority of us smoked because we had to keep awake.

We were tracking in south east London and on the edge of the Kent fields on circular radar screens. We could recognise the Germans as our own used to carry a signal. Then we could take height, distance and bearing and relay these to the command post.

I can remember when Hitler's rockets came down. They didn't make a sound. They would land and two houses would suddenly be gone. Every man and woman who wasn't doing anything would run to pull people out. It was just an unwritten law.

Looking over towards Woolwich one night, I saw all the huge oil drums on fire after an air raid. It was like daylight even though it was miles away.

I was in London, my sister came to join me and my brother went over to Burma. I never even considered what my mother went through at the time until I had children of my own.

# FIRES IN THE NIGHT

While German bombers were pounding Britain during 1940 and 1941, the British people huddled night after night in stuffy, cramped shelters and comforted themselves that Royal Air Force bombers were delivering similar punishment to the citizens of the Third Reich.

Sadly, they were mistaken. While British bomber crews were full of sterling young men with an iron resolve, their success rate in the first half of the war was low – and for very sound reasons.

Night bombing was far safer for the aircraft and crew, as the Germans had illustrated in their raids over London. RAF Bomber Command was keen to conserve these valuable assets too and favoured night-time bombing raids instead of exposing its forces to daylight risks.

But the Luftwaffe was operating from occupied airfields a short hop over the English Channel. For the Royal Air Force to strike at the heart of Germany, its pilots and planes had to fly many more miles than their German counterparts, in aircraft that were ill-equipped for long-distance flying or bombing. It took time and investment for new, heavier bombers to be commissioned for the task.

The already limited resources of Bomber Command were also stretched in many different directions. Not only were there the demands of bombing raids over enemy territory but Coastal Command was in constant need of planes to combat the U-boat menace in the Battle of the Atlantic. With Britain under threat of isolation and annihilation if the U-boat peril was not seen to, the need to have planes available for maritime duties was paramount in 1940. In addition, the Middle East and North Africa required a complement of bombers, together with crews and parts – all of which required regular replacements. For a while, night bombing raids over Germany were abandoned altogether so the force could focus on its duties elsewhere.

### ■ EARLY PROBLEMS ■

Operational shortcomings put the Royal Air Force at a disadvantage, too. For the first sorties were flown, rather informally, on an almost individual level. Following a joint briefing, each aircraft would depart at five-minute intervals following a course chosen by its own navigator to the target. Often, the crews would not catch sight of another plane until after their return. Given that each

> ## For a while night bombing raids over Germany were abandoned altogether

would offload its bombs over a wide area, the effect of single bomb drops on the ground were, of course, much less than an orchestrated raid involving greater numbers.

Added to this, the navigational aids available on planes at the time were wildly inaccurate. Crews conforming to their instructions were sure their bombs were away right on top of the targets. It was not the case. While bomber crews scored hits on clear nights in easily located target areas, bombs dropped on blacked-out Germany or on targets shrouded with industrial haze as often as not fell short. After the war it was discovered that 49 per cent of the ordnance released by the British crews between May 1940 and May 1941 exploded in open countryside.

Navigators used maps, a sextant and a procedure of 'dead-reckoning' to work out their position, all of which could be fouled up by poor weather conditions. It meant that precision bombing by the RAF at night could be successful only on clear, bright, windless nights of which

*Left:* German planes on a daylight raid of London before night-time tactics were introduced. *Far left:* The Renault works at Billancourt after bombing by the Allies.

*Above:* A Wellington bomber and its crew pepare for an arduous night's work over Hitler's 'Fortress Europe'.

◆ **EYE WITNESS** ◆

David Greig, of the Royal Australian Air Force, was 19 and second pilot on a Wellington bomber when his aircraft was shot down in a night raid over Germany.

❝ We were already on fire when a night fighter pounced on us. My heart was in my mouth. I knew the situation was grim. We were facing death, that's all there was to it. I saw a piece of shell come out of nowhere and it hit me. I was furious that a German had wounded me and scared at the same time. I was knocked out for a moment. When I came to, I was by the rear escape hatch. The flames had really taken a hold now. The smell was acrid. Mechanically, I clipped on my parachute. Then another crewman shoved me out. I was injured in the arm and chest.

The Germans had no trouble capturing me. The pain was both mental and physical. I felt I had not much longer to live. ❞

there were precious few. Once again, it took many months before the difficulties of finding targets under cover of darkness were resolved.

Bomber Command was continuing to sustain losses from the missions over Germany, in exchange for precious few results. It soon became clear a new tactic was in order.

The principles of precision bombing – a technique almost impossible to execute successfully given the constraints of the era – were abandoned for 'area bombing'. For this, not only was the target itself carefully chosen but also its neighbourhood. Thus a large factory producing vital components in the middle of open countryside would be overlooked in favour of a smaller factory among other small factories and industrial workers' housing.

That way enormous damage could be caused for the same amount of effort and risk as was required in precision bombing. It gave a twofold purpose to bombing missions. Not only was there the clear-cut intention of halting Germany's industrial output but, in addition, the chance to demoralise the people by bringing the war to their doorstep, making them homeless or otherwise hampering their daily existence.

The concept was fostered by Air Marshal Sir Richard Peirse, in charge of Bomber Command during 1941. Unfortunately, the failure of his forces to destroy three German warships, Scharnhorst, Gneisenau and the heavy cruiser Prinz Eugen, while they were in dock at Brest, northern France, did little to enhance the ebbing reputation of the force.

### ■ BREST RAIDS ■

While these three sea monsters roamed, the British suffered terribly. Between them they were responsible for the loss of HMS Glorious, HMS Ardent, HMS Acasta as well as the armed merchant cruiser Rawalpindi and something in the order of 115,600 tons of merchant shipping.

In the spring of 1941, Bomber Command flew 1,161 sorties against the ships, scoring just four direct hits, none of which caused substantial damage. All this for the loss of 43 bombers. Even when the three ships left the dockyard to slip back to

*Below:* Air Chief Marshal Sir Arthur 'Bomber' Harris, commander of the RAF's Bomber Command.

home ports, the 242 planes sent to destroy them as they sailed failed to dent the pride of the German navy.

It signalled the departure of Peirse and the arrival of Air Chief Marshal Arthur Harris, who adopted the idea of area bombing as his own.

Afterwards, Harris summed up his position. 'I had to prove, and prove quickly, to the satisfaction of those who mattered that the bomber force could do its work if it was large

> ## The historic town was engulfed in a firestorm which swallowed up 200 acres

enough and if its efforts were not frittered away on objectives other than German industry as a whole.'

His first priority was to bolster the stocks of planes available to carry out attacks, particularly heavy bombers of which there were fewer than 70 when he arrived.

An opportunity to prove the ability of himself and his men came just a matter of weeks after he was installed at Bomber Command. On 3 March 1942, Harris sent a force of 235 bombers across to Billancourt, France, where a giant Renault factory was turning out tank components for the German war effort.

The planes set off in three waves and now Harris mimicked a successful German tactic. The first wave carried not only bombs but a large number of flares which would light up the target for subsequent attackers. With the River Seine acting as a brilliant marker, 223 of the aircraft found their targets within the space of two hours. This concentrated attack had the desired effect. Enough machinery was put out of action to

## SUICIDE BOMBERS

Germany formed its own squadron of suicide bombers known as the Sonderkommando Elbe. They first went into action in April 1945 and engineered mid-air collisions with laden Allied bombers. The 300 volunteers were told they could parachute to safety if possible.

stop the factory working for several months. As a happy spin-off, many completed products were wrecked.

It appeared to Harris that Bomber Command had received the change of fortune it so urgently required. With a new directional aids now in use among navigators, he felt that Germany's industrial heartland of the Ruhr was his for the taking.

Five days after the Renault raid, 211 bombers took off and headed towards the city of Essen. Once again, the technique of using flares and incendiaries was employed. But this time, many had burnt out before the second wave of bombers had got the measure of the area. It finally bore the hallmarks of the haphazard raids which Bomber Command were now known for. Another three attacks made on ensuing nights also failed to produce the spectacular results Harris yearned for although there was widespread damage caused in the city.

Harris had to wait until the end of the month for the next feather in his cap, a raid carried out against Lübeck, a Baltic port comprising many ancient timbered buildings.

When almost 200 aircraft dropped 300 tons of high explosives plus 144 tons of incendiaries on the night of 28/29 March, the historic town was engulfed in a firestorm which swallowed up 200 acres.

### ■ ROSTOCK RAID ■

At the end of April another Baltic port, Rostock, was given similar treatment. The targets for the bombers were specifically a factory which produced the Heinkel 111 aircraft and in general the town itself. An estimated 70 per cent of the old town was turned to rubble with direct hits being scored against the factory too. Of the 168 bombers that set off for the mission, all but 12 returned safely.

Harris noted with satisfaction that, yard for yard, the destruction wrought in Germany by Bomber Command in those two raids equalled that caused by the Luftwaffe in Britain in 1940 and 1941.

*Below:* **The Renault works at Billancourt was destroyed after Bomber Command was fired with fresh resolve.**

The Nazi hierarchy was riled by the savage encroachment into the Fatherland. In a fury, Hitler ordered raids against Britain's historic cities to even the score. He picked the targets from a tourists' book of Britain called the Baedeker Guide. Among them were Bath and Exeter.

### ■ 'MILLENIUM' ■

For one daring raid against a factory producing U-boat parts, Harris was persuaded to return to daylight attack. New Avro Lancaster heavy bombers were brought in for the assault on Augsburg in southern Germany. Together with their fighter escorts they flew in low over enemy territory to avoid radar detection and then began a breathtaking roof-top scrap with Luftwaffe fighters before hitting their target. The cost was high. Seven out of 12 bombers were lost. The crews of the returning battle-scarred aircraft were decorated for their bravery.

It confirmed the general view that daylight raids were unacceptably risky given the aircraft available. In any event, Harris became far too preoccupied with his latest tactical trailblazer to consider further daylight sorties. The continued all-out efforts to obliterate the Ruhr were proving frustrating. With the lack of truly efficient navigation and the industrial smog it was impossible to co-ordinate a successful mission. He had pondered long and hard about pulling off a single operation which would earn the admiration of those doubters at home and the trepidation of the Germans.

The answer, he decided, was a thousand-bomber raid against a prime target in Germany. But, given that the most he had been able to rally for an attack to date was 235 bombers, it seemed this was nothing more than a flight of fancy. That was until Harris's deputy Air Vice Marshal Saundby got to work.

With the use of borrowed aircraft from Coastal Command and the entire stock of his reserves flown by trainee pilots and instructors alongside existing crews, it was conceivable that 1,000 bombers could be summoned for an epic raid.

Code-named 'Operation Millenium', the first thousand-bomber raid took place against Cologne on 30 May 1942. All the planes were to strike within an hour and a half.

The raid represented a new departure in aerial warfare. The largest force of aircraft dispatched to Britain at any one time had numbered 487 while the British had never been able to gather together more than 235 bombers at any one time.

Churchill himself was captivated by the idea of such a mighty strike. He

*Below:* An RAF Wellington bomber is loaded with bombs before setting off on another mission.

was under pressure from fellow politicians who saw the largely inconclusive night raids against Germany as a waste of time and effort. Stalin was also waiting in the wings, always demanding a decisive attack by the British

> ## Ground crews worked flat out on damaged aircraft to furnish Harris with the required number

against Germany. It was realised that there would be too few German fighters in the air to halt the impact of the raid. The possiblity of collision was to be diminished by dividing the planes into three groups operating in parallel lines against different targets. Despite the immense commitment, it seemed the risks were calculated. The raid could not end up as the swansong of Bomber Command.

### ■ 1,046 BOMBERS ■

For a while, 'Operation Millenium' appeared under threat when Coastal Command refused to release the 250 planes it had promised. Its chiefs had got cold feet. They decided the risk of releasing their aircraft was too great. Saundby was left scraping the barrel

to fill the ranks for the raid. A spell of poor weather which caused the operation to be postponed proved a saving grace. Ground crews worked flat out on damaged aircraft to furnish Harris with the required number. On the morning of 30 May the magic 1,000 was surpassed.

The 1,046 bombers departed from 53 airfields across Britain and assembled in a 70-mile convoy across the North Sea. Before them went 50 fighter planes ready to duel with the defending Luftwaffe.

Mechanical difficulties accounted for 100 planes in the force even before it had reached the target and they turned back to base.

Still, the first bombs and incendiaries were dropped at 12.47am on 31 May. The rest of the operation went according to plan. Land-based defences and intercepting Luftwaffe fighters were overwhelmed and the last bomber dropped its load over Cologne at 2.25am.

As they flew homewards, rear gunners could see the city burning from 150 miles away. The night's work destroyed 18,432 buildings, killed nearly 500 people, injured 5,000 more and rendered almost 60,000 homeless. Forty bombers did not return, which meant the loss of 40 instructors and 49 pupils.

*Above:* **Sir Barnes Wallis, inventor of the bouncing bomb, which proved a huge morale-booster in Britain.**

At home it was hailed as a triumph. Yet the success in itself put pressure on Harris to produce more of the same. Now the British public expected many more raids of similar dimensions to lambast the enemy.

An attack against Essen on 1 June involving 956 bombers failed to achieve the same degree of destruction. Key industrial centres escaped from the raid unscathed.

It wasn't until 25 June that another large-scale attack was attempted, this time against Bremen. Poor weather once again hindered the 1,006 bombers as they sought their targets. It was a resounding success except for the higher number of casualties claimed by Germany. This time 49 aircraft didn't come home.

The Luftwaffe, in charge of ground defences as well as airborne, quickly realised the intention of Bomber Command. Now it set about denying the British an opportunity to hammer German industry.

To combat the upsurge in Luftwaffe fighters and improve the success of the night bombing raids, a

### ◆ EYE WITNESS ◆

**Dennis Golding, of Gosport, near Portsmouth, England, was a British rifleman with the King's Royal Rifle Corps. As a light infantryman he was engaged in hand-to-hand combat with German troops throughout the 1944 advance across Western Europe.**

❝ On VE day we marched into Hamburg to find everything devastated except the roads. The Germans had cleared them and stacked up all the re-usable bricks they could salvage. It was typical German efficiency and I suppose it also helped improve their morale.

The civilians were more or less glad to see us. There was certainly no hostility and, like our own people, they were just glad it was all over. We weren't allowed to fraternise with them at first. If you were caught you were put on a charge. That rule soon broke down. When they spoke to you you felt you had to talk back. ❞

Pathfinder force was created. In charge was Australian Group Captain D.C.T. Bennett, a first-class pilot and skilled navigator.

Their aim was to fly 'finder' aircraft over the target on parallel tracks two miles apart dropping flares, creating a 'runway'. Behind them came 'illuminator' aircraft, dropping further flares picking out the target area precisely. Then came the 'marker' group which started fires with incendiaries to pinpoint the targets for following bombers. When it was cloudy the Pathfinders dropped 'sky-markers', parachute flares which lit up the target beneath the cloud cover. In response the Germans used fires on the ground as decoys in much the same way as the

## The Air Ministry favoured a plan to knock out three giant dams

British did during the Battle of Britain. The Pathfinders proved a massive boon to the night bombing raids, with the additional attraction that their loss rate was a smaller-than-average three per cent.

At the end of 1942 Bomber Command diverted resources to the 'Torch' landings in North Africa and provided valuable support. At the same time it carried out some successful raids over Italy, finding the air defences there far lighter than those in Germany.

Still, Harris was determined to kill off German industry in the Ruhr. By March 1943 he was set upon a concerted attack on the region. The Battle of the Ruhr got underway on the night of 5 March with a 442 aircraft raid and continued for six

weeks more or less relentlessly. During the battle the famous Dambusters raid was carried out. Although Harris himself was opposed to it, the Air Ministry favoured a plan to knock out three giant dams which would deprive the region of vital hydroelectric power. To do it, Wing Commander Guy Gibson and his squadron had to drop new 'bouncing bombs', designed by engineer Barnes Wallis.

### ■ DAMBUSTERS ■

Each bomb weighed five tons, measured five feet in length and four feet across. Carried in a special cradle beneath a Lancaster bomber, it went into action with backspin imparted, which would cause it to skip along the surface of the water until it met the dam wall.

The targeted dams – the Möhne, the Eder and the Sorpe – were 150 feet high and their concrete walls were almost the same again in thickness. The skill required by Gibson and his crews was enormous. They had to fly in at low altitude to evade German radar and drop their bombs at

*Above:* A Lancaster of 617 Squadron, loaded with its 'bouncing bomb' before heading for the German dams.

precisely 60 feet above the water and exactly 425 yards from the perimeter of the dam.

On the night of 16 May 1943 the 19 Lancasters took off in three waves. In the first wave of nine planes, headed by Gibson, one plane was lost to flak and several bombs went astray before three explosions ripped through the Möhne Dam and a flood poured down the valley.

In the second wave just one of the five Lancasters reached the Sorpe Dam, under the guidance of Flight Lieutenant McCarthy, an American serving with the RAF. His bomb load damaged the dam but failed to breach it. Meanwhile, the third wave scythed a gap in the Eder Dam.

Eight of the Lancasters together with their 56 crew members failed to return. And, although it was a feat of undoubted heroism, the damage took the Germans just three months to repair. Perhaps it was most successful in capturing the public's imagination

George Funnell joined the 55th Kent Regiment in 1939 aged 17, after lying about his age. He witnessed the Blitz in London when he was stationed at an anti-aircraft battery – and later saw the destruction caused by air raids in Germany after fighting his way through Normandy, Belgium and Holland to Hamburg in 1944.

 In Hamburg there was mile after mile of devastation. I lived through the London bombing but it was nothing like as bad as that over Germany.
Even when we got to Hamburg, long after the air raids had taken place, there was still the stench of death coming from crumbled buildings. It took ages to find some of the buried remains.
On the streets we only found a few old men and young boys. The rest of the male population had been called up into the army. The vast majority of the people we met were women struggling to survive as best they could. '

in terms of a morale-boosting coup and depriving the Atlantic Wall in northern France of some labour. This was redirected instead to the Ruhr to repair the damage there.

Harris returned to his bombing campaign, this time picking Hamburg as the target for prolonged attack . 'Operation Gomorrah' began on 24 July with the first use of aluminium foil. It had been known for years that a simple device like this would fog the German radar screens. But the Air Ministry held back from using it in case that same device was used in retaliation. In fact, Germany was well-acquainted with the technique and also refrained from using it, for the same reason. Called 'Window', it was brought in to play on the orders of Churchill in a bid to counter the Luftwaffe defences.

### ■ HAMBURG HORROR ■

At midnight 740 bombers dropped 92 million strips of tin foil, creating the desired effect. The planes went on to deliver almost 3,000 tons of bombs. Subsequent attacks made by night and day virtually unremittingly devastated the city's defences. Fine weather had left the city dry as paper. As new fires were sparked by existing blazes, the perpetual heating of the

air which funnelled into the sky caused a firestorm, akin to a tornado with wind speeds of 150 miles per hour. Delayed detonators on some of the bombs wrought havoc among the rescue workers as they attempted to deal with the blazes.

The melting temperatures achieved in the raid scorched buildings and bomb shelters, water mains and electric cables. Hamburg endured the horror for nine days by which time ten square miles of the city was laid waste. In total 2,630 bombers unleashed more than 4,300 tons of incendiaries and a similar amount of high explosives, creating in total three firestorms. The death toll was an estimated 42,000.

Harris continued to work through the list of German cities he hoped to destroy. His armoury now included a 12,000lb bomb and some excellent new nagivational aids and target-finders. Now his sights turned towards Berlin. The German capital was a far-distant target from British airfields across hostile territory. The Battle of Berlin opened in November 1943 and a further 15 attacks were launched against it. Although the demands on the participating crews of Bomber Command were eased when airfields were opened in Europe

following D-Day, those raids cost no less than 587 aircraft together with 3,640 men killed or missing. When reconnaissance photographs proved little was being gained from the attacks, they were suspended.

If Harris hoped to end the war with his tactics bathed in a blaze of glory, he was disappointed. At last, public opinion both in Britain and overseas began to question the wisdom of saturation bombing. (The phrase 'terror bombing' was constantly rebuffed by air chiefs.)

On 30 March 1944 a night raid by Halifaxes and Lancasters was sent awry by a strong wind which sent them into the arms of defending Luftwaffe fighters. Out of the 795 aircraft that set off, 95 failed to return and another dozen crashed in England. Night bombing raids afterwards came to an end.

*Below:* A reconnaissance photograph reveals the damage done to the Möhne Dam by Wing Commander Guy Gibson and his Dambusters.

# CARRIERS AND KAMIKAZES

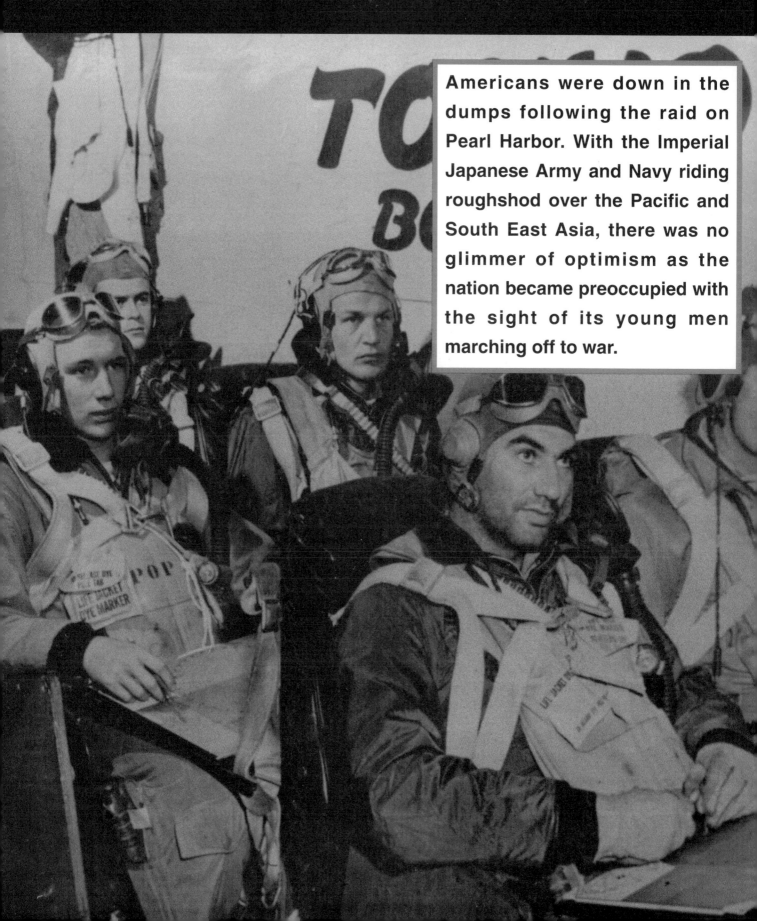

Americans were down in the dumps following the raid on Pearl Harbor. With the Imperial Japanese Army and Navy riding roughshod over the Pacific and South East Asia, there was no glimmer of optimism as the nation became preoccupied with the sight of its young men marching off to war.

Finally, on 18 April 1942, there came some small consolation for the folks back home. It was provided by a daring air raid into the heart of Japan itself. American airman Lt-Colonel Jimmy Doolittle, a veteran of glamorous pre-war air races, delivered a small but significant strike back against the aggressor.

The newly commissioned aircraft carrier Hornet, bearing 16 army bombers, in the company of fellow carrier Enterprise and a body of cruisers set off from Midway Island towards Japan. Some 650 miles short of the Japanese coastline, the fleet stopped so the B-25s could be launched. Despite the stiff wind, the planes took off at dawn, heading for Tokyo and other major cities.

At noon, 13 of the aircraft unloaded their cargoes of bombs over Tokyo. The other three dropped incendiaries on Nagoya, Osaka and Kobe. In fact, little was achieved in the exploit and many Japanese people remained unaware that it had even taken place at all. Its main effect was to shock the Japanese commanders who had until now considered themselves somewhat impregnable.

It now seemed vital to the Japanese to take control of Midway Island, a gap in the extended front line they had created in the Pacific. Those who doubted the wisdom of pushing Japanese lines still further were persuaded that the vulnerability of the home islands warranted the new push.

As for the attacking American B-25s, they did not have the range to return to the aircraft carriers which were by now high-tailing it for home. Their orders were to seek out friendly airstrips in China.

■ **JAPANESE REPRISALS** ■

All made it out of Japanese air space without a problem although one crash-landed in Russian Vladivostok. Only four of the planes actually touched down while the rest ditched after their crews baled out. Three of the men were captured by Japanese troops operating in China and shot.

A further five died but 72, aided by Chinese peasants, made their way to Chungking and eventual freedom.

The most terrible effects of the raid were probably felt by the Chinese. When Japan realised the escape route taken by the fliers, troops exacted revenge against the native Chinese, slaughtering anyone suspected of aiding the airmen.

It was some 30 months before Japan was once again in range of American bombers. This time the aircraft were far more fearsome, their capacity for wreaking terror much greater than in 1942.

Even from airfields in India and China in the summer of 1944, the American fliers found it difficult to carry out effective missions over Japan. The only island within their

## *At noon, 13 of the aircraft unloaded their cargoes of bombs over Tokyo*

range was Kyushu, the southernmost Japanese home island.

It took victory in Saipan, freeing the Marianas Islands and their airfields, before a more comprehensive bombing campaign could begin. On 24 November 1944 110 B-29s took off with the aim of knocking out Japan's aircraft industry in Tokyo, Nagoya, Kobe and Osaka. They were to do it by dropping 500lb bombs from high altitudes. But cloud cover obscured the targets and at the end of it, only one factory out of nine had been struck.

*Left:* Lieutenant-Colonel Doolittle ties a medal to a bomb bound for Japan.
*Far left:* US Navy pilots receive a final briefing before a raid on Tokyo.

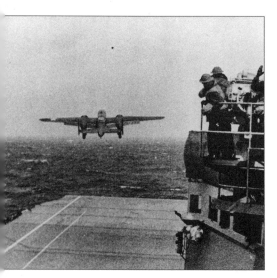

At the start of 1945 Major-General Curtis LeMay was brought into 21st Bomber Command. He had an inkling that the flimsy wooden shacks which filled Japanese cities were a major fire hazard. He pinpointed incendiaries as the best weapon with which to attack them.

On 4 February his theories were proved right when a force of 70 Boeing B-29 Superfortresses dropped

## To add to the effect of the bombs, a fresh wind fanned the flames

160 tons of incendiaries on the centre of Kobe. A tenth of a square mile was burnt out and that included several factories.

The ploy was repeated on 25 February, this time against Tokyo. Now 172 B-29s dropped nearly 450 tons of incendiaries, devastating a square mile. An estimated 28,000 buildings were razed.

*Right:* Kobe, Japan's sixth-largest city, comes under attack with incendiaries dropped by US B-29s. Fires have already been sparked in the industrial areas.

*Left:* A B-25 heavy bomber takes off from the USS *Hornet* to deliver its load to Japan. The Doolittle Raid sparked Japanese reprisals in China.

Interrupted by the call for aid in Okinawa, LeMay had time to consider his options. The use of incendiaries had proved itself beyond question but the effect was far more widespread when the bombs were dropped from lower altitudes. It pointed to the need for night raids.

In advance, a single plane would pinpoint targets with marker bombs and the rest of the bombing party would follow at intervals of every couple of minutes.

On the night of 9 March 334 B-29s took off and showered a 12-square-mile industrial area of Tokyo with 1,700 tons of oil incendiaries. To add to the effect of the bombs, a fresh wind fanned the flames until it seemed the entire city was on fire.

## ■ RAIDS CONTINUE ■

Anti-aircraft fire claimed 14 of the planes but their mission was an outstanding success. No less than 16 square miles of the city had been burned out, with 267,000 buildings flattened and 84,000 people killed. An official Japanese report noted: 'People were unable to escape. They were found later piled upon the

## ◆ EYE WITNESS ◆

**Masuo Kato was a reporter in Japan throughout the war and detailed the terror by fire inflicted by US bombers.**

' For more than three years my small nephew Kozo Ishikawa, who was about five years old when the war began, held an unshakeable faith in Japanese victory. To his small world it was unthinkable that the Emperor's armies could suffer defeat or that the Japanese navy should endure any fate other than glorious victory.

After his home was burned to the ground during a B-29 raid, destroying almost every familiar material thing that had made up his existence, he told me with great gravity: "We cannot beat the B-29." The psychological effect of the loss of his home went deep. He had been one of the happiest and most carefree of children. He became thoughtful and serious and it was seldom that he laughed. He became ill and died shortly after the war was over. A nervous breakdown, the doctor called it.

The B-29s had brought the war to the Japanese people in a real and personal sense and each man had begun to form his own opinion on whether Japan was winning or losing. My nephew's experience was repeated many thousands of times in every part of Japan. To each family that watched its home and belongings go skyward in a rush of smoke and flame, the news from Okinawa, true or false, meant little. For them, their personal war was already lost. '

bridges, roads and in the canals. We were instructed to report on actual conditions. Most of us were unable to do this because of horrifying conditions beyond imagination.'

Two nights later 285 aircraft dropped 1,800 tons of incendiaries at Nagoya. Without the wind, the fires were more contained. One aircraft was lost and two square miles of the city laid to ruin.

On 13 March Osaka was the target for 274 B-29s. About 13,000 people died, 135,000 homes were

*Below:* **A large area of Osaka was levelled by sustained fire-bomb attacks carried out by the Americans.**

*Above:* **Tokyo became a patchwork city following the destruction delivered by the incendiary raids, with much of its industry and housing flattened.**

burned down and 119 factories were knocked out. Once again, the American losses were light, with just two aircraft lost and 13 damaged by anti-aircraft fire.

The heaviest attack yet was made against Kobe on 16 March, this time using 2,355 tons of mixed oil and thermite bombs. More than 300 planes launched the onslaught and three were lost, an outstanding one per cent loss rate. At Kobe 2,669 people were killed, with 66,000 houses and 500 industrial centres eradicated. A fifth strike was made against Nagoya three days later, in which high-explosive bombs were among those used.

In 11 days 21st Bomber Command had notched up 1,595 sorties and

*Right:* **Major-General Curtis LeMay (left) believed the policies of 21st Bomber Command – the obliteration of key centres – would bring about Japan's defeat.**

dropped more than 9,000 tons of incendiary bombs, proving that Japan was exposed to complete devastation. As important to the Americans was the low level of losses the bomber command had sustained. Only 20 aircraft were destroyed, mostly by anti-aircraft fire and only one per cent of the crews had been lost.

The rate of attacks was kept up, some made by day but all those against the heavily fortified Tokyo were at night. In the summer bad weather hampered the airmen but still they rained fire on the major Japanese cities, week in, week out. When these had all been substantially ruined, LeMay turned his planes' attention to the secondary Japanese cities.

## ■ LEAFLETS DROPPED ■

Now he became involved in psychological warfare, too, with the dropping of thousands of leaflets prior to the raids, naming 12 cities which were going to be hit and urging the civilian population to evacuate. Not only did this spread confusion but helped to demoralise the battered, war-weary population.

At the same time, 21st Bomber Command was involved in a mine-laying programme to complete the blockade of Japan. Between the end of March and the middle of August about 12,000 mines were dropped into the waters around the islands. It meant that in May mines were responsible for more losses to Japanese shipping than submarines were.

Submarines were then able to move into the Sea of Japan, looking for the occasional ship which had escaped the blockade and organising lightning sabotage raids.

## ◆ EYE WITNESS ◆

**Geoff Michael, from Perth, was 18 when he joined the Royal Australian Air Force in 1942 and trained under the Empire Air Training Scheme, launched in 1939 to train Allied pilots. He went on to complete 32 missions with Bomber Command and retired from the RAAF after 37 years' service, as Air Commodore.**

❝ Even though it was a hectic and sad time, one is inclined to remember most of the good things – the great time I had on leaves etc.

But I also recall vividly having my aircraft shot up by ground fire and fighters. The fortunate part was that I was never wounded and never lost a crew member.

However, I did lose a close mate who was killed in a daylight raid over Germany. I saw the plane go down but didn't realise at the time it was my mate's plane.

It was a time when we were conditioned to death. Every morning you expected not to see the next one. So all you did was to read the operations board, see if you had been rostered on a missions and, if your weren't, go out and relax and have a good time. ❞

With the Japanese Imperial Navy now completely impotent and the majority of surviving Japanese aircraft in hiding, American aircraft carriers also sailed close to the home islands, their aircraft launching attacks at regular intervals. Freed by the end of the war in Europe, Royal Navy warships joined the US Navy in the waters off Japan, and combined attacks were launched, before the typhoon season made air attack impossible.

In August a Japanese plan to launch 2,000 kamikaze planes on the 21st Bomber Command bases in the Marianas was discovered. The carrier fleets moved to within range of the airfields on the northern island of Honshu where the heavily camouflaged planes were being gathered for the covert operation. For the first time since the end of the Okinawa campaign, a Japanese fighter counterattacked and a kamikaze aircraft struck an American destroyer. Still, the Japanese airfields came in for heavy bombing.

### ■ DEVASTATION ■

In Japan itself the people were enduring appalling hardship. Homelessness caused by the effective incendiary strikes left many in dire straits. If their factories had also been destroyed they were in an even worse situation. There were few building materials on hand in the devastated city and little food. Inadequate rice rations were sometimes being boosted by sawdust. The wounded were also receiving scant attention. But if the population went to the countryside to scavenge food where it could, who would man the remaining factories and workplaces?

## *By August, Japanese ministers had called for a collection of acorns to turn into food*

Natural disasters, including extensive flooding, added to their problems. By July 1945 an estimated 25 per cent of all housing in Japan had been destroyed, leaving 22 million people without a roof over their heads.

By August, Japanese ministers had called for a collection of acorns to turn into food. Yet despite their difficulties, the people spoke of surrender only in whispers. An inherent will to serve the Emperor prevented an uprising. The Japanese would struggle on regardless.

LeMay was delighted with the success of his aerial bombing campaign and was convinced that it alone would bring Japan to the point of surrender. His confidence was somewhat premature.

# DAYLIGHT RAIDING

By the time America entered the war, the British had some fixed ideas about aerial combat.

The Royal Air Force had learned the hard way that aircraft employed on daylight raids were more vulnerable to the enemy, that bombers had a better survival rate when they were accompanied by fighters. Harris and the other British air supremos thought it best that the US fliers reinforced the existing night bombing expeditions being carried out by the RAF.

Novices at warfare in the air they may have been, but the Americans had thoughts of their own on the issue. US pilots were untrained for night missions. Not only that, they had a different bombing philosophy from that of their British counterparts, that of precision bombing.

### ■ FIRST ACTION ■

Given that their Flying Fortresses were, in their opinion, well defended and that the aircraft were equipped with a revolutionary new bombsight called the Norden which 'could drop a bomb into a pickle barrel from 20,000ft', it was their preferred plan to fly during the day. No amount of friendly persuasion from the British could dissuade the US air chiefs from their stated aims.

The Royal Air Force held Flying Fortresses in low regard. During experiments with the new aircraft in 1941, pilots felt they became large targets for German defences. For their part, the US air chiefs believed the RAF had used the Fortresses wrongly, sending them out in twos and threes instead of in a large formation when they performed best.

First taste of action for the US pilots came on 17 August 1942 when a dozen Flying Fortresses flew out of Grafton Underwood aerodrome, heading for Rouen, northern France.

With protection from four squadrons of RAF Spitfires, they made the flight, dropped the 18.5 tons of bombs on railway targets and returned home intact but for slight damage on two Fortresses caused by flak.

On the mission was Ira C. Eaker, a brigadier-general, and superb pilot, who set up the headquarters for the US 8th Air Force in Britain and was soon given command of its European flight operations.

There followed a succession of small-scale bombing raids. The success of precision bombing was trumpeted by Eaker although, like the number of victories claimed against the Luftwaffe on such outings, the statistics had to be

---

*The Norden bombsight 'could drop a bomb into a pickle barrel from 20,000 ft'*

---

treated with caution. Nevertheless, in 13 missions, just two planes were lost – an enviable record.

Still, their operations had been strictly 'local' on missions regarded as workaday 'milk runs' by the British pilots.

*Left:* A US Flying Fortress carries out a daylight bombing raid over Germany.
*Below:* By the middle of 1942, US aircraft were a familiar sight in Britain.

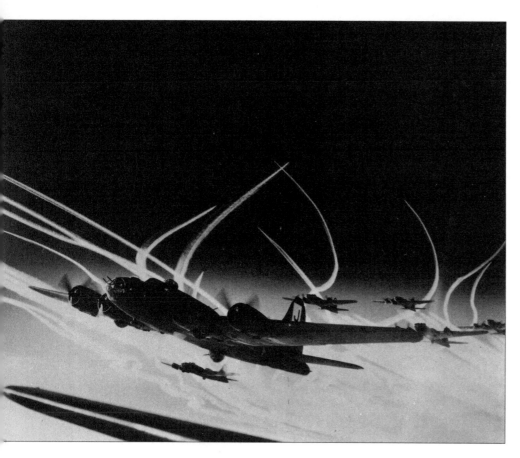

*Above:* US B-17s plough on towards their targets while fighter escorts fend off marauding enemy interceptors. The range of escorts increased during the war.

Then poor weather began to not only hamper the efficiency of the Norden bombsight – which had earned its colours in the cloudless skies above New Mexico and frankly struggled in the cloud- and smog-filled heavens above Germany – but brought about the wholesale cancellation of planned raids.

Like the RAF, the USAAF had to do its bit for the 'Torch' landings in North Africa in late 1942, which cut aircraft and crew stocks by a third.

Then the Luftwaffe hit on a new tactic which took its toll among the American fighters. Canny German pilots spotted the Achilles heel of the Flying Fortresses, which was head-on attack. There were no defences on the nose of the plane and the Germans had enough guts to mount

daring frontal assaults despite the obvious risk of collision. It appeared that the 8th Air Force, clinging to its belief in daylight raids, was on a hiding to nothing.

Churchill was among those who strongly objected to the Americans going their own way. He believed that precision bombing being executed by the Americans, which needed daylight to succeed, was the height of folly. Area bombing under the cover of darkness appeared a far better bet and might encourage the Americans to venture for the first time over German territory.

At the Casablanca Conference of January 1943, the British leader was hoping to persuade Roosevelt that daylight bombing raids should be dropped in favour of night bombing operations by both air forces.

Eaker had one chance beforehand to convince Churchill otherwise. Finally, it only took one sentence. His proposal in favour of the continua-

tion of daylight raids contained the words: 'By bombing the devils around the clock we can prevent the German defenses from getting any rest.' The idea instantly caught Churchill's imagination. He vowed to give Eaker the opportunity to prove his point.

## ■ THE B-24 ARRIVES ■

Afterwards there came the Casablanca Directive, backing orchestrated day- and night-time bombing raids and listing top targets, namely centres of German industry.

On 27 January that year the US airmen were at last sent to Germany to produce the goods. Their target was Wilhelmshaven on the North Sea, where U-boats were made. By now B-24 Liberators had joined the Flying Fortresses in the ranks. Of the 53 which left for Wilhelmshaven, three were lost and the remainder had to battle at close quarters with Luftwaffe fighters while achieving only moderate success in their mission. The difficulties of daylight raids over hostile territory were crystallised for the Americans.

Danger from flak and enemy fighters was not the only problem faced by the Americans on their daylight raids. To stay out of reach of the enemy, they flew at high altitudes, usually above 20,000 feet. The chill of the air

## *Area bombing under cover of darkness appeared a far better bet*

numbed their faces, crammed as they were in small cockpits. Tension mixed with boredom as another lengthy mission got underway. For a while each member of the crew remained vigilant for the enemy, but there were long hours when the Luftwaffe didn't

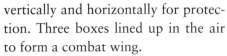

## ◆ EYE WITNESS ◆

**Burdsall D. Miller, from Sacramento, California, joined the US Army Air Force, aged 24, following the Japanese raid on Pearl Harbor. Based in Sudbury, England, he became a colonel and flew 32 missions.**

' I flew ten missions in a B-24 Liberator and then switched to B-17s for a further 22 raids. Most of them were daylight raids over Germany although we also hit Italy and Norway. I got shot up but never enough to bale out or crash land.

As command pilot, I sat in the co-pilot's seat and made all the decisions as far as the group or squadron were concerned that day. I was scared but I was trained to do a job. The thing that made the biggest impression on me was flying in formation and seeing a wing man shot down in flames. It was very upsetting.

But we all got fatalistic and figured when our time came we were going to get it. Perhaps that made us seem like we had nerves of steel. Otherwise we would not have lasted. We had some men who didn't last. They refused to fly, but it was very few out of a considerable number of men.

As soon as we dropped our bombs we got out of the target area as most were heavily defended. As we turned we could see bombs hitting and we could usually tell if we had hit the target.

I have a big picture at home. It was taken on a raid over Germany on one of the most heavily defended targets. We had turned to start our bombing run. We just opened our bomb bay doors. To the left of us, another plane was doing the same when some flak went right into the bomb bay. The plane just exploded. Nobody got out alive. At the moment the plane blew up, my waist gunner took the picture. '

appear in which there was little to do but study the clouds.

Every US airman wore a steel chain vest to protect himself from flak. His flight suit was thick to protect him from the cold. Each wore a parachute and an oxygen mask, itself deeply uncomfortable. Despite the elaborate precautions, there was at least a one in ten chance of dying.

Americans adopted different flying patterns to suit the daylight nature of the raid. Up to 21 planes would form a box which was staggered both vertically and horizontally for protection. Three boxes lined up in the air to form a combat wing.

To improve the accuracy of bombing, the most skilful men were placed in the lead planes and gave the signal for the rest of the aircraft in the box to drop their bombs.

### *Historically the US Army Air Corps was treated as the poor relation by the White House*

On the ground, Eaker had his own problems. Historically, the US Army Air Corps, as it was first known, was treated as the poor relation by the White House. Priorities changed only slowly during the war and Eaker spent many fruitless hours harrying his bosses in America for extra planes and crews. It wasn't until mid-1943 that his efforts paid off. The US 8th Air Force could at last increase the size and effectiveness of its attacks.

■ **DANGEROUS GAME** ■

Perhaps the biggest bonus of all to the US airmen was when fighter aircraft increased their range, although it was late in the conflict when a combat aircraft which could escort bombers into the heart of Germany and back came into use.

Daylight missions were stepped up in 1943 and the heavy bombers recorded some admirable successes. Assisting their cause was the decision to scale down Luftwaffe defences in France by withdrawing two groups back to the Reich to improve air security there. The Allies were now

*Left:* **Despite damage from a German rocket in the Battle of Berlin, this US B-17 still managed to land safely.**

making a concerted effort to draw the Luftwaffe aircraft into the sky at every available opportunity, trying to shoot down as many as possible. Of course, a considerable number of Allied planes fell victim while playing this dangerous game.

### ■ PLOESTI RAID ■

The US medium bombers fared less fortunately. A flight of B-26C Marauders which set off from Great Saling on 17 May was virtually wiped out during a raid on Haarlem.

And raids later in the year proved yet again the perils of daylight raiding. On 1 August 1943 the target was Ploesti, the oilfields in Romania which fed Germany's war machine. The Americans had planned a surprise attack, keeping radio silence and flying at low altitudes to avoid radar detection. Their approach was to be over a lightly defended sector and their escape route was to North Africa. Alas, the planes were picked up in Germany as soon as they left the runway. Navigational errors brought them in over the thickest of the anti-aircraft gunfire. Fifty three of the Liberators on the raid were shot

down in enemy territory. A further 55 reached Libya in such appalling condition that they were fit only for scrap. The results were disappointing, too, with only a small dent being made in the oil production levels.

In the same month, the Americans tackled Regensburg and Schweinfurt, key centres for aircraft manufacture and the production of that tiny but indispensible engineering component, the ball bearing. The raids would be without fighter escorts. So deep were the targets inside Reich territory the

> **The German pilots were under no illusions. They were no longer the favoured elite**

existing fighters did not have the capacity to fly there and back.

When the 146 Flying Fortresses dispatched for Regensburg crossed the German border they met a hail of fire from a host of defending Luftwaffe planes. The German pilots were under no illusions. They were

*Above:* A German tank factory is ruined and its new stock in tatters following a daylight raid by the United States Army Air Forces. The Americans specialised in precision bombing by day.

no longer the favoured elite. Hitler was once again frustrated at the lack of success brought home by the Luftwaffe which once had seemed invincible. Now fewer resources than ever were being ploughed into aircraft manufacture and the training of crews. Without this investment, the entire force would surely be strangled. Luftwaffe production chief Ernst Udet had already committed suicide in despair at the plight of the force. The pressure was on to prove the worth of the air force before the unpredictable Führer sought his own revenge against it.

Those Flying Fortresses that survived the arduous 90 minutes to Regensburg dropped their bomb loads and made off in haste towards Algiers, saving themselves a possibly fatal return journey.

Now it was the turn of 230 Flying Fortresses to run the gauntlet across Germany en route to Schweinfurt.

The fierce firepower of 300 Luftwaffe fighters battered and buffeted the American planes. While the Germans lost 25 fighters that day, the US bombers were down by 60 and another 47 were so badly damaged they could not be salvaged.

The figures were bleak for the USAAF. In October 1943, 153 aircraft were lost in a single week. It led to the halt of bombing raids without fighter escort.

### ▪ DROP TANKS ▪

Fortunately the drop tank appeared, a suspended fuel tank which could be jettisoned when empty. This was attached beneath the wing to vastly increase the range of fighters. Hot on

its heels came the P-51 Mustang, a fighter with an 850-mile range. It helped tip the balance of the air war over Europe in favour of the Allies.

By 1944 the Allies were producing twice the number of aircraft as the Reich was. The Luftwaffe's difficulties were compounded by the damage each fighter was sustaining which wasn't being repaired. Hitler was punishing the disappointing Luftwaffe by depriving it of essential materials to stay alive.

Yet the theories adopted by 'Bomber' Harris for the RAF and Eaker for the USAAF cannot be said to have been an outright success. Harris hoped to defeat the Third Reich by saturation bombing, destroying the will

of the German people. The question of the morality of carpet-bombing civilian centres, including the ancient city of Dresden late in the war, raged long after the conflict had ended.

Eaker targeted industrial centres, certain that concerted bombing raids would cause Hitler's regime to topple. Despite the bravery and commitment of the pilots, the principles were flawed. In fact, Hitler illustrated only too well over Britain in 1940 that air power by itself was not sufficient to win a war. Bombs from above failed to break the will of the Germans in just the same way as they had failed to crack the British. And damage sustained by industry could inevitably be repaired – particularly in Germany with the use of forced labour.

The liberation of Europe came with the arrival of the ground troops, albeit with priceless assistance from their colleagues in the air forces.

---

### ◆ EYE WITNESS ◆

**Lieutenant Harmon Cropsey, a former state senator from Decatur, Michigan, served with VB110, a US Navy squadron, navigating Liberators on 12-hour anti-submarine patrols into the North Atlantic. He was based at Dunkeswell in Devon under RAF Coastal Command.**

❝One of my fellow officers was Joe Kennedy, John's elder brother. We used to meet quite regularly in the mess and swap notes. He was flying the same aircraft as me.

It was Joe who volunteered for one of the most dangerous missions of the war. The idea was to strip everything out of one of the Liberators and pack it full of TNT. He was to fly this out over the North Sea to a prearranged navigational point and bale out. The plane would then be radio controlled to crash-land on its target – a 40-foot layer of reinforced concrete around some U-boat pens in Holland.

But something went wrong and the plane exploded in mid-air over England. We never found out what the problem was, and obviously there was nothing left of his body. He was a very brave man.

Our base lost an awful lot of airmen. The other two squadrons, 103 and 105, had around two-thirds of their crews killed in the first few months of our arrival in 1943. There was a German advanced training base at Brest and they were sending up the twin-engined Junkers 88 which had a 50-knot advantage on our planes. If you got caught out over the sea on a clear day you were a dead duck. Your only hope was to find cloud cover.

I know of only one plane, flown by a Free Czech crew, which made it home after being attacked. We were just fatalistic about it.

Every mission you were handed a top secret chart showing where all the Allied subs and ships were supposed to be. It was absolutely vital. One day I'd got this thing spread out inside the plane with the door still open. Suddenly the engines start and the whole thing blows right out into a field. I go haring after it and my flight suit gets caught on some barbed wire. As a result, I fall and dislocate my shoulder.

That really extended my war. You were allowed to go home after 25 missions but because of my injury I stayed behind when all my chums left. Then they decided they needed an experienced navigator to show the new crews what to do. I ended up flying 42 missions.❞

---

> ***Hitler was punishing the disappointing Luftwaffe by depriving it of essential materials***

# THE ULTIMATE WEAPON

In Japan, the people were preparing for all-out war against invading Americans.

As early as November 1944 all Japanese men aged between 14 and 61 were conscripted. Women between the ages of 17 and 41 were on standby for military service, too. This new militia was being schooled in beach defences and guerrilla warfare. Those that were left unarmed – the vast majority – were told to practise martial arts skills as a form of defence. The message from the rulers of Japan was to be seen on giant posters hung around towns and villages. 'One hundred million will die for Emperor and nation!'

Key installations in Japan had been destroyed by the American bombing campaign. Much of the Japanese shipping had been sunk already by US ships, aircraft and submarines, which were now operating a tight blockade of the island coastlines. Japan was being starved of everything she needed to survive – yet still there was no sign of surrender.

In fact, various feelers had been extended by the Japanese through Swedish and other neutral sources for a negotiated peace, all cloaked in secrecy. Finally, the Japanese foreign ministry approached Russia to act as an intermediary, partly in a bid to divert Stalin from opening another battlefront with the war-weary country. But Japanese demands were unacceptable to the Allies who would agree to nothing less than an unconditional surrender.

Not for the first time, the lack of a cohesive war leader in Japan was keenly felt. Emperor Hirohito was a figurehead who could apparently do little without the say-so of his government. Prime minister Admiral Suzuki was eager to sue for peace but there still remained in opposition hardliners who were willing to fight to the death. No one, it seemed, was in outright control and nobody dared utter the word 'surrender' without the prospect of assassination, political retribution or military uprising looming large. So Japan struggled on as best it could in a vacuum of indecision.

The losses among the American troops in the landings around the Pacific islands had horrified and shocked the commanders. By now painfully aware of the Japanese resilience to attack and reluctance to surrender, they viewed invasion of the home islands as a tall order. The estimates for the number of US casualties appeared virtually open ended.

### Later Truman confided that America had developed a new bomb which could end the war

When Truman met with Churchill and Stalin in Potsdam in July 1945, they discussed the inadequate peace overtures from the Land of the Rising Sun. Later Truman confided that America had developed a new bomb which could finally end the war.

### ATOMIC POWER

He was referring to the end result of the Manhattan Project, begun back in 1942, in which a band of elite scientists, the most admired brains of the free world, had got together to probe the possibilities of atomic power.

By December of that year, the scientists under the leadership of Professor Enrico Fermi made a significant breakthrough in understanding how to spark a man-made chain reaction.

At two big plants – Oak Ridge, Tennessee, and Hanford, Washington – work continued in the bid to extract the essential substance known as U-235 from uranium for the manufacture of plutonium.

It wasn't until 5.50am on 16 July 1945 that the theory was finally put into full-scale practice. In the scorched sands of the New Mexican

*Far left:* Scientists knew they had created the ultimate weapon when it was tested.
*Left:* Truman confided in Churchill about the bomb at Potsdam.

*Above:* A weapon similar to that detonated at Nagasaki. Its weight was 10,000 pounds and it was equivalent in power to 20,000 tons of TNT.

*Below:* Dr Albert Einstein (left) was the initial innovator. Dr Robert Oppenheimer (right) took up his theories and made them reality.

desert the plutonium bomb called 'Fat Man' was detonated. (It won the name by having a passing resemblance in profile to Churchill.) Observing scientists could barely hide their awe at the intense power man had created.

Dr Robert J. Oppenheimer, the physicist directing the project, instantly realised the shattering effect it would have on the world.

### ■ TRUMAN INFORMED ■

A telegram detailing the precise results of the 'Fat Man' experiment was sent to the Potsdam Conference for the consumption of President Truman – who himself had only found out in April the full scope of the Manhattan Project.

Two further atomic bombs were made and dispatched to the Pacific while the politicians pondered. Was the world ready for the atomic age? Once unleashed, would this mighty new force return to act as a Sword of

> *Observing scientists could barely hide their awe at the intense power man had created*

Damocles poised over the heads of free and fair countries?

Churchill for one was in no doubt that it should be used. Afterwards, he wrote: 'To avert a vast, indefinite butchery, to bring the war to an end, to give peace to the world, to lay healing hands upon its tortured peoples by a manifestation of overwhelming power at the cost of a few explosions seemed, after all our toils and perils, a miracle of development.

'British consent in principle to the use of the weapon had been given on 4 July, before the test had taken place. The final decision now lay in the main with President Truman, who had the weapon. But I never doubted what it would be nor have I ever doubted since that he was right.'

In his memoirs, Truman wrote: 'Let there be no mistake about it. I regarded the bomb as a military weapon and never had any doubt that it should be used.'

Still, there was debate about whether Japan should be warned about its terrible fate. A chain of events finally overtook these talks.

The Potsdam Conference finally closed on 26 July with an ultimatum for Japan. It called for unconditional surrender. In the absence of such a surrender, Japan would face complete destruction. Just two days later Premier Suzuki announced his country would be ignoring the Allied threat.

Such belligerence was enough to confirm an order sent to Lieutenant-General Spaatz, commanding general of the US Army Strategic Air Forces to prepare a B-29 to carry the newly fabricated atomic bomb.

*Below:* Smoke rises more than 60,000 feet into the air following the explosion of the atomic bomb at Nagasaki.

### ◆ EYE WITNESS ◆

**Dr Michihiko Hachiya was at home when the first atomic bomb – 'Little Boy' – fell on Hiroshima from the bomb bay of B-29 'Enola Gay'. He recalls the moment of impact in his eye witness account *Hiroshima Diary*.**

' The hour was early, the morning still warm and beautiful. Shimmering leaves reflecting sunlight from a cloudless sky made a pleasant contrast with shadows in my garden as I gazed absently through wide-flung doors opening to the south.

Clad in vest and pants, I was sprawled on the living room floor exhausted because I had just spent a sleepless night on duty as an air raid warden in my hospital.

Suddenly a strong flash of light startled me – and then another. So well does one recall little things that I remember vividly how a stone lantern in the garden became brilliantly lit and I debated whether this light was caused by a magnesium flare or sparks from a passing tram.

Garden shadows disappeared. The view where a moment before all had been so bright and sunny was now dark and hazy. Through swirling dust I could barely discern a wooden column that had supported one corner of my house. It was leaning crazily and the roof sagged dangerously.

Moving instinctively, I tried to escape but rubble and fallen timbers barred the way. By picking my way cautiously I managed to reach the roka and stepped down into my garden. A profound weakness overcame me so I stopped to regain my strength. To my surprise, I discovered that I was completely naked. How odd. Where were my vest and pants. What had happened?

All over the right side of my body I was cut and bleeding. A large splinter was protruding from a mangled wound in my thigh and something warm trickled into my mouth. My cheek was torn, I discovered, as I felt it gingerly with the lower lip laid wide open. Embedded in my neck was a sizeable fragment of glass which I matter-of-factly dislodged and with the detachment of one stunned and shocked I studied it and my blood-stained hand. '

*Left:* Colonel Paul Tibbets, pilot of 'Enola Gay', waves from his cockpit before take-off on his epoch-making mission on 6 August 1945.

growing up and we watched it blossom. And down below it the thing reminded me more of a boiling pot of tar than any other description I can give it. It was black and boiling underneath with a steam haze on the top of it. And, of course, we had seen the city when we went in and there was nothing to see when we came back.'

On 8 August further pressure was exerted on Japan when the Soviet Union declared war and launched an invasion of Manchuria.

> **'We had seen the city when we went in and there was nothing to see when we came back'**

A day later a further atomic bomb dropped, this time on Nagasaki. It came from the bowels of another B-29, this one christened 'Great Artist', under the command of Major Charles Sweeney. About 40,000 people died this time with a further 60,000 injured.

It is doubtful whether the introduction of atomic weapons had a huge effect on the people of Japan. The scale and horror of the previous bombing campaigns had claimed victims by the thousand and caused acres of destruction. Wholesale killing, burns and homelessness was nothing new for them. The only fresh aspect was the radiation sickness spread among the survivors, the wide-ranging effects of which were not immediately apparent.

For the rest of the world, the double bombing was like a macabre sideshow

On 6 August 1945 the first atomic bomb, called 'Little Boy', was released over Hiroshima. A mammoth 120 inches long and weighing 9,000 pounds, beneath its shell it contained the power equivalent to 20,000 tons of TNT. It was carried to its target in a B-29 called 'Enola Gay' which took off from the Marianas. In command was Colonel Paul Tibbets.

The uranium bomb exploded 2,000 feet above the centre of Hiroshima. Four square miles of the city was instantly wiped out. Those at the epicentre of the bomb were reduced to ashes along with buildings and cars. Beyond that immediate area, many more died and tens of thousands were horribly burned.

### ■ SHOCK WAVES ■

The authorities could only estimate the numbers of people who had perished in the ferocious cauldron. The final figure was put between 70,000 and 80,000 persons.

Colonel Tibbets later described how his plane was shaken by the shock waves as it sped away and told of the scene of devastation he left behind: 'There was the mushroom cloud

## ◆ EYE WITNESS ◆

**Tsutomu Yamaguchi worked in the Hiroshima yard of the Mitsubishi shipbuilding company and was on his way to work when the bomb dropped more than a mile away.**

'Suddenly there was a flash like the lighting of a huge magnesium flare. As I prostrated myself there came a terrific explosion. I was lifted two feet from the ground and I felt a strong wind pass my body.

How long I lay in the road dazed, I don't know, but when I opened my eyes it was so dark all around me that I couldn't see a thing. It was as if it had suddenly become midnight in the heat of the day. When my eyes adjusted to the darkness I perceived that I was enveloped in an endless cloud of dust so thick it was black.

As the dust blew away and my surroundings became visible I saw what seemed to be thousands of tiny, flickering lamps all over the street and in the fields. They were little circles of flame, each about the size of a doughnut. Myriads of them were hanging on the leaves of the potato plants.

I looked toward the city and saw a huge, mushroom-shaped cloud rising high into the sky. It was an immense evil-looking pillar. It seemed to be reflecting every shade in the spectrum turning first one colour then another.

Feeling terribly weak and suffering intense pain from the deep burns on my face and arm, I stumbled into the potato field. There was a big tree out in the field and I headed for that. Sometimes I could only crawl, creeping from bush to bush. When I finally reached the tree I had no more strength to go on. And I had acquired a terrible thirst.

I saw a group of teenage boys unclothed except for torn underpants. As the boys came near I saw that they were pale and shaking severely. I had never seen such a horrifying sights as those five shivering boys. Blood was pouring in streams from deep cuts all over their bodies mingling with their perspiration and their skin was burned deep red like the colour of cooked lobsters.

At first it seemed strangely that their burned and lacerated backs and chests were growing green grass. The I saw that hundreds of blades of sharp grass had been driven deep into their flesh, evidently by the force of the blast.'

with people riveted by the footage and photos of the vast mushrooming cloud that rose up some 20,000 feet as the bomb was detonated.

### ■ JAPAN SURRENDERS ■

In any event, it was clear that Truman's pledge to 'obliterate' Japan was no empty threat. Hirohito himself was sickened at the sight of the suffering among his people. Finally, he found the leverage inside his government to bring the conflict to an end.

The day after Nagasaki was bombed, Japan broadcast a willingness to surrender 'on the understanding that it does not comprise any demand which prejudices the prerogatives of the Emperor as Sovereign ruler.'

Yet still the hawks in the regime dragged their feet. A flight of US Navy carrier-borne planes flew over Japan on 13 August dropping leaflets spelling out the surrender so the people would understand that it was all over.

> *The following day at 11pm the Emperor himself told his people the war was over*

The following day at 11pm the Emperor himself told his people the war was over. Even at this late stage, 1,000 militant soldiers stormed the Imperial Palace in a bid to prevent the surrender. They were beaten off by the Emperor's own guard.

VJ day was then declared on 15 August. The pockets of Japanese resistance around the Pacific and

*Left:* The atomic bomb scarred the landscape of Nagasaki so deeply it was beyond recognition.

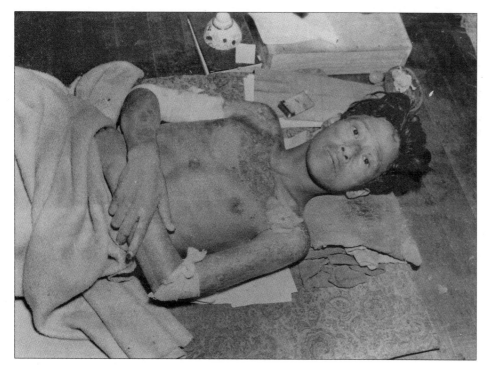

conclude a solemn agreement whereby peace may be restored. The issues involving divergent ideals and ideologies have been determined on the battlefields of the world and hence are not for our discussion or debate.

### ■ PRAYER FOR PEACE ■

'Nor is it for us here to meet representing as we do a majority of the people of the earth in a spirit of distrust, malice or hatred. But rather it is for us both victors and vanquished to serve, committing all our peoples unreservedly to faithful compliance with the understandings they are here formally to assume. It is my earnest hope... that from this solemn occasion a better world shall emerge... a world dedicated to the dignity of man... Let us pray that peace be now restored to the world and that God will preserve it always.'

South East Asia surrendered through the following month, ending with Hong Kong on 16 September.

In the meantime the official ceremony marking the outbreak of peace came on 2 September aboard the USS Missouri in Tokyo Bay. The Japanese delegation was led by the

Sailors squeezed into every available inch of the deck to witness the historic moment.

After the signing was over, General MacArthur gave a stirring speech opening the door to a new order.

'We are gathered here, representatives of the major warring powers, to

## *'Let us pray that peace be now restored to the world'*

one-legged foreign minister Mamoru Shigemitsu, who wore a top hat for the occasion. The military wing of the country was represented by General Yoshijiro Umezu. There to receive them were dignitaries from all the countries that had taken part in the war against Japan – America, Britain, Australia, New Zealand, Canada, China, France and Holland.

**Right:** Servicemen greeted news of the atomic explosions with relief. The blasts probably saved thousands of US troops.

# Horrors of War

# NANKING MASSACRE

On the pretext that the Chinese had kidnapped a Japanese soldier, a momentous conflict between two brother nations was sparked in 1937.

China and Japan shared much by way of culture and history. Yet when hostilities broke out in 1937 each country fought the other with a tenacity and barbarity scarcely witnessed on a battlefield. The missing soldier at the heart of the dispute turned up some hours later, by the way, and was thought to have been biding his time in a brothel.

In the ensuing violence one of the worst atrocities ever committed by uniformed soldiers took place in an incident over which tensions still run high even today.

The scene of the horror was Nanking, a Chinese city serving as a makeshift capital following the fall of Beijing, whose population of some 200,000 was swollen with refugees trying to escape the onslaught of the Japanese army.

### ■ NANKING ATTACK ■

It was five months after the first shots of the war were fired that the Japanese army came within sight of Nanking. The government, led by Generalissimo Jiang Jieshi, evacuated leaving a determined Chinese army to fend off the invaders.

The first bombardment of the city walls came on 9 December 1937 after Chinese military leaders ignored a call for surrender. Within four days the Japanese with their superior mechanised weapons had blasted their way into the city. An estimated 40,000 Chinese had perished in the battle – yet that was only the start of the population's suffering.

First, there was turmoil as the desperate Chinese tried to flee through a rear city wall. Inside the 70ft tunnel which led to the gate, two vehicles had collided and burst into flames. There was chaos as a surge of Chinese people turned to run from the flames and faced a tide of incoming city residents who were themselves followed by machine-gun toting Japanese soldiers. Countless scores died in the melee, suffocated, trampled under foot or fatally wounded by Japanese bullets.

Doubtless Nanking's refusal to surrender was an irritant to the Japanese. Yet nothing could explain the appalling acts which took place after the fall of the city.

In the words of one Swedish observer: 'With a blindness and absence of psychological judgement that astonishes the westerner who is at all familiar with Chinese mentality, the Japanese soldiers sullied their march to victory with repeated acts of cruelty, ruthlessness and bloodshed on innocent people.

'[These were] actions unparalleled in modern times and perpetrated by no civilised nation.'

During their approach to the city gates, two Japanese officers had a competition to see who could kill the most Chinese. It was a race to reach 100 but when confusion reigned over the body count, they amicably decided to make their final target 150. Later, it was reported: 'Mukai's blade was slightly damaged in the competition. He explained that this was the result of cutting a Chinese in half, helmet and all. The contest was "fun", he declared...'

> **The Japanese officers had a competition to see who could kill the most Chinese**

Any Chinese who turned and ran from the Japanese was doomed to die. While observing the rights of the international community, the Japanese then embarked on their debauched and disgusting campaign against the locals.

Where they could, the European doctors, welfare workers and writers

*Left*: **Chinese refugees fleeing Japanese troops.** *Below:* **Cities like Chungking were left in ruins by Japanese bombs.**

*Above:* **Chinese army supremo Chiang Kai Shek lectures officers at a training camp. He was destined never to rule China.**

sheltered the Chinese and pleaded for tolerance on their behalf. Without this moderating presence, even more would have died.

### ■ MULTIPLE RAPE ■

For seven weeks, the women and girls of Nanking were subject to repeated rape by the rampaging Japanese soldiers, often many times in a single night. The soldiers knew no bounds and picked on pregnant women, the elderly and children as young as ten. Degrading sexual assaults were also carried out in broad daylight, by ordinary soldiers and officers alike. Although women were the main victims, there were also cases of attacks on young boys.

Anyone who tried to intervene was stabbed or shot. There were frequent

cases of civilians being used for bayonet practice. Others were disembowelled for sport.

There were many massacres in which the victims first had to dig their own grave. They were then lined up at the edge of the pit and shot or bayonetted or both.

At least 2,000 Chinese were buried alive in Nanking, several were

roasted over a fire and still more killed in a bath of industrial acid. There were cases of soldiers being tied up and then blown up by hand grenades. Ferocious dogs were also used to kill Chinese prisoners and wild stories circulated about Japanese soldiers sating themselves on the hearts and livers of dead Chinese.

Official estimates for the number of dead vary between 155,000 and 300,000. The orgy of raping and killing last for seven long weeks.

## General Matsui admitted 'the Japanese army is... the most undisciplined in the world'

In charge of the men was General Matsui who was himself apparently devastated at the conduct of his men. Matsui, who once admitted that 'the Japanese army is probably the most undisciplined in the world today', reserved a tirade of abuse for the officers under his command who had permitted their troops to run riot. In common with other Japanese generals, he considered the rank and file men to be uneducated, illiterate and akin to barbarians.

### ◆ EYE WITNESS ◆

**In 1994, Prince Mikasa, brother of Emperor Hirohito, recalled what he described as 'truly horrible' scenes while he was a cavalry officer serving in China during the war. In an interview with the 'Yomiuri' newspaper, he described seeing film of Chinese prisoners being gassed and shot.**

That could only be described as a massacre. I was shocked at one battlefront when a young officer told me: "The best way to train new recruits is to have them undergo bayonet practice using prisoners of war. It helps them acquire guts." The issue is not about the numbers killed but killing people in a cruel manner. The prime factors contributing to the tragic consequences were China's geographical proximity to Japan... also the strong disdain that Japanese held towards the Chinese.

*Above:* **Bodies litter the streets after the Japanese army made gains in the key Chinese city of Shanghai.**

After the scandal of Nanking General Matsui was recalled to Tokyo. Soon afterwards, he retired and devoted himself to building a temple in which to atone for the misdeeds of the army in Nanking.

Two missionaries from Nanking had a very different view of the dilemma. 'The common soldiers are all right if they are not drunk. The Japanese, in general, are very easily intoxicated, however, and then the trouble begins.'

Japanese people have since tried to excuse the actions of the army in those dark days. There were cases of Chinese mutilations of Japanese soldiers both before and after death in the war but none to match the terrorism which took place in Nanking.

For years, the formula explanation for Japan's actions was that it was 'liberating' its neighbours from Western influence. This explanation has been accompanied by a marked reluctance to apologise or reparate for the events which took place in the name of the Emperor.

Even as late as 1994, a Japanese government minister, Mr Shigeto Nagano, denied the war against China had begun through his country's aggression and denied the Rape of Nanking had even taken place. In a newspaper interview, he said: 'It's a mistake to call [the Pacific War] a war of aggression. It's not true that [it] was carried out with invasion as an objective. We sincerely believed in liberating the colonies.'

*Left:* **Captured Chinese soldiers were ruthlessly slaughtered by the score by blood-thirsty Japanese invaders. Killings took place all over China.**

### ■ MILLIONS DEAD ■

Although he retracted his remarks and resigned, there is little doubt his opinion reflects a body of thought still widely believed in Japan today.

Naturally, such blunders inspire fury and resentment in those neighbouring countries which suffered under dominance of the Rising Sun. Abuse of Chinese prisoners particularly occurred all over the country, not just in Nanking.

Before the end of the Sino-Japanese war in 1945, at least two and a half million soldiers on both sides had died and there were many million more civilian deaths, particularly in China.

Whether the Japanese warmongers sincerely believed they were freeing Asia from its colonial ties or not, their commitment to war with China was ultimately a disastrous one. It kept an enormous number of troops tied up for years as they tried to conquer a land that proved to be unconquerable.

# THE WARSAW GHETTO

The clampdown on Jews in Poland began almost as soon as the first shots of World War II were fired.

Following the brief conflict, occupying German soldiers at first contented themselves with ritually humiliating any Jews they encountered on the street.

A punch was thrown here, a beating administered there. Crowds gathered as the crowing, cocksure military men publicly shaved off the whiskers which marked out an orthodox Jew. Few Jews fought back. The punishment for striking a German officer was torture and frequently death. And not just for the perpetrator of the alleged crime. The concept of mass punishments for one single misdemeanour soon brought the population to heel.

Laws were hastily introduced to formalise the new official attitude to Jews. They were forbidden to work in certain jobs, to bake bread, for example, or sit at the desk of a government office. No Jewish worker was allowed to earn more than 500 zloty a month – at a time when the price of bread was as high as 40 zloty per loaf.

All Jewish wealth was confiscated and no longer could they ride on trains, trams, wear gold jewellery or leave their own district without official permission. From 12 November 1939, every Jew aged 12 years and above was compelled to wear a white arm band with a blue Star of David displayed on it.

### ■ EASTER POGROMS ■

From this the situation deteriorated. During the Easter holidays of 1940, old-fashioned pogroms took place with Polish thugs in the pay of the Nazis wreaking havoc in the Jewish quarter of Warsaw. For the first time, the Jews retaliated. There was a collection of Jewish militants who refused to tolerate any further

subservience to the aggressor. They gave a good account of themselves in the ensuing street battles.

However, this token resistance could do litttle to halt the German roller-coaster in Warsaw. In November 1940 the Germans finally established the Warsaw Ghetto. Now the entire Jewish population numbering some 300,000 was confined to a specially designated area. Poles who lived within its boundaries were compelled to move out.

Walls were built around it and security was made even tighter with vicious barbed wire. By the middle of the month the Warsaw Ghetto had been entirely isolated from the outside world.

Inside, the existence was a sordid and miserable one. Now there was little opportunity to earn even a crust. Jews had already been brought to the depths of poverty by the actions of the Nazis, and they had nothing left to fall back on.

## Jews were transported from all over Poland into the Warsaw Ghetto

Daily, the population of the Warsaw Ghetto increased with the arrival of more Jews deported from other cities and towns around Poland. There to greet them were the malnutrition, disease and hopelessness that were all mirrored in the bleak faces of the inhabitants.

To the people of the Ghetto, the war was now a distant issue. The effect of the segregation on their minds together with their physical hardships left them able to focus only on the day-to-day survival of themselves and their closest family.

Ghetto dwellers for the most part relied on soup kitchens and a meagre ration of bread, plus whatever they could scavenge or beg. Six-year-old boys were dispatched by their parents through holes in the barbed wire to steal food from other areas of the

*Left*: Bleak-faced German soldiers taken prisoner by the Polish Home Army.
*Below*: Poland's Home Army attracted enthusiastic recruits.

city. Occasionally they were shot in the process. If they returned, their haul was seized on by starving siblings and parents.

Food was smuggled in from the Ayran sections of the city by the burgeoning numbers of black marketeers who preyed on the snared Jews. Jewish businessman seeking to make a living were equally at the mercy of these rogues. The final vestiges of wealth remaining among the Jews were spent in this way during the first few months.

Within months people began to die of hunger in the streets. Corpses were covered over with paper which was weighted with stones until the daily round of the burial cart. Desperate families would dump their own dead in the streets to save the cost of a funeral. Often, the bodies were naked, stripped of rags which had now become a valuable commodity.

Disease was raging through the over-crowded and squalid conditions, with admissions to the hopsital exceeding 150 a day.

*Below:* Polish children ready to risk their lives to deliver underground newspapers around the occupied capital.

*Above:* Starving Poles reach for Red Cross bread as it is distributed across the divide in occupied Warsaw.

Instead of feeling pity or self-disgust in the face of this unmitigated horror, the delusion of the Germans continued. A German major who witnessed what was happening in the Warsaw Ghetto put the blame on Jewish barbarism:

### ■ CORPSE CARTS ■

'The conditions in the ghetto can hardly be described . . . The Jew does business here with the others also on the street. In the morning, as I drove through in my car, I saw numerous corpses, among them those of children, covered anyhow with paper weighed down with stones. The other Jews pass by them indifferently, the primitive "corpse carts" come and take away these "remainders" with which no more business can be done.

## The Germans claimed the Jews had brought the horrors of the Ghetto on themselves

The ghetto is blocked by walls, barbed-wire and so forth... Dirt, stench and noise are the main signs of the ghetto.'

There were continuous executions carried out on real or fanciful notions by the Germans. Those who worked on underground newspapers, for example, were targeted as were those whose illegal trading came to the notice of the authorities. Anyone found on the Aryan side of the divide without the necessary papers was returned and shot.

Yet there were also examples of killing without the remotest provocation. Three children sitting outside the hospital were slaughtered and a pregnant women who tripped and fell was continually kicked down by a German soldier who finally shot her. Every resident of the ghetto knew of horror stories such as these.

## ■ MASS DEPORTATION ■

In July 1942 events took an even more sinister turn with the start of mass deportations, with a German quota of 6,000 people per day. Their destination was the extermination camp at Treblinka in Poland. There was panic among the ghetto dwellers. Their options for escaping the round-ups taking place were limited. Each house and street targeted for the expulsions was thoroughly searched by German-sponsored officials who would shoot anyone they found cowering inside.

The spate of deportations eventually slashed the population of the ghetto to an estimated 60,000. Many of those that remained either worked for the Germans or the Jewish Council. Their conditions were barely improved by the reduction in

### When mass deportation to Treblinka began, the Jews finally decided to fight back

population but there began a subtle change of mood among the ghetto Jews. They decided to fight back. Covertly, they gathered together what arms they could, various

*Below:* Men and women from the Ghetto are marched off to camps. Their destination was probably Treblinka.

◆ **EYE WITNESS** ◆

**Leo Heiman was a young Jew rounded up in Russia who later wrote a book about his wartime experiences.**

❛ On that morning Janek and I walked once again down the main street when we saw a big crowd of Byelorussians and Poles surrounding something. Naturally, we pushed right throught the crowd and saw three Germans kicking an old Jew in his belly and pulling him up by his beard each time he fell down. I recognised the Jew who was a cantor at one of the local synagogues. His two sons, both rabbinical students, were being hanged from a nearby lampost, the crowd applauding and cheering the Germans.

'What did the dirty Jew do?' I asked a Polish kid standing nearby. The kid laughed and told us that the Germans tried to take the Jew's two daughters away to a military brothel and the Jew was arrogant enough to slap one of the Germans. ❜

*Above:* During the Warsaw uprising members of the Home Army, two carrying flame-throwers, seek the enemy in the wrecked city.

ancient guns from bygone conflicts and a few more modern models that had been smuggled in by Polish freedom fighters on the German side. A system of underground tunnels was dug to aid Jewish resistance.

By 1943, it was no longer safe for Germans to enter the ghetto. Lone Germans or those in twos and threes found in the streets of the ghetto were killed. Terrible retribution was also wreaked on those Jews who collaborated with the Gestapo to save their own skins.

On 19 April 1943 the Germans decided to 'liquidate' the ghetto once and for all. In charge of the operation was General Jurgen Stroop who had been promised honour and accolades for his men if the operation was carried out quickly and efficiently.

## ■ GHETTO UPRISING ■

Stroop dispatched 2,000 troops from local garrisons, dressed as if for battle. They went in on armoured cars with grenade launchers and flame throwers. It was their aim to flatten the ghetto and kill all those who got in the way.

The Jewish resistance had been tipped off and was waiting.

Short of guns and ammunition, the determined fighters still halted the German advance and even stymied the tanks with their home-made grenades. The ghetto which was once a prison now became a fortress.

The bold action of the Jews took Stroop by surprise. He had branded them 'sub-humans and natural cowards'. Every day, increasing numbers of Germans were sent into the ghetto. They found a canny and determined opposition inspired by its

## *The Jews decided that it would be better to die fighting than to die in Treblinka*

leaders, fighting with the conviction that death by defence was far better than death at the hands of the Germans in an extermination camp.

When all their buildings were flattened or burnt out, the resistance took to the sewers – until they were flooded by the Germans.

It took six weeks and thousands of German troops to quell the Warsaw uprising. German casualties were put at 1,200. Most of the Jewish fighters died in action. In the middle of May, when all hope had finally gone, 55,000 Jews remaining in the ghetto surrendered. More than 7,000 were shot immediately. A further 15,000 were sent to Majdanek camp and 7,000 to Treblinka where they were

*Left*: Following its initial success the Polish Army proudly flies its flag from the back of a captured German vehicle.

*Above:* A casualty is tended by his comrades. Despite their dedication, the Poles could not crush the German enemy.

killed in the gas chambers. Only a few hundred of the total population of the Ghetto escaped to the safety of 'Aryan' Warsaw.

But this was not the last time that the people of Warsaw gave vent to their anger against the Germans. In August 1944 the Polish Home Army under the command of General Bor-Komorowski seized the Old City

## The Polish Home Army seized the Old City of Warsaw which was shelled by German tanks

which was subsequently shelled by the Germans using Tiger tanks.

Numbering an estimated 40,000, the Polish soldiers fought determinedly for each building and every street. They were doubtless bucked by the

sound of gunfire from the approaching Russians and with pride and optimism raised the Polish flag over the city for the first time in six years.

The cause was a hopeless one. Assistance from the Russians failed to materialise and the Germans, better equipped and in greater numbers, fought back tenaciously. For two months the battle raged, once again inflicting immense hardships on the residents of Warsaw who were confronted with starvation. But by October Warsaw was once again under German control, its population decimated by the revolt.

Nevertheless, the Poles were defeated in the knowledge that they had proved a costly diversion for the Germans. The Red Army was indeed close by, ready to press ahead once more against the Third Reich. That Russia

*Right*: Heavy-hearted Bor Komorowski surrenders to German SS commander Erich von dem Bach-Zelewski.

stood by and did nothing to aid the beleaguered Poles gave rise to accusations later that the Polish Home Army was sacrificed by Stalin. He had chosen his own men to lead Poland – and the fighting men were not among them.

In the event, Warsaw didn't fall to Soviet and Polish troops until mid-January 1945.

# THE CAMPS

Внхд в лагере
через проволоку воспрещён
под угрозой РА

Internment has long been used to curtail the activities of so-called 'undesirables' by countries across the globe.

In this respect, concentration camps – although the very name now chills the heart – were nothing new in the Thirties. Unsavoury though the idea appears, they were to pen people without trial on account of their race or beliefs.

Indeed, during World War II both Britain and the US used similar devices to curb the movements of potential enemies on the home front. In Britain those with German ancestry or Fascist sympathy were targeted while in America the residents of Japanese descent were rounded up. In Russia, dissidents were put in Gulags.

The argument for such action in times of war is that of national security and it is a valid one. Concentration camps in Germany were different entirely because of the barbarity that became inextricably associated with them.

Concentration camps became a covert fact of life in Germany soon after Hitler came to power. The first was Dachau which opened on 22 March 1933 just 12 miles outside the centre of Munich.

### ■ ANTI-SEMITISM ■

Their main purpose was to cage 'enemies of the state'. Into this category fell Communists, Socialists, homosexuals, gypsies, pacifists, opposing politicians and intellectuals – and just about anyone else conceivably opposed to the Nazi regime. They were to become most notorious for housing Jews.

Anti-semitism was not invented by Hitler. He merely made a stake in a middle Europe movement which flourished among the ignorant and was expounded in pamphlets.

Some have suggested that Hitler's own vociferous brand of Jew-hating

was inspired by him having caught venereal disease from some dubious sexual relations with a Jewess.

The theory has never been proven. But certainly there is not a single fact contained in 'Mein Kampf' and his anti-semitic rantings which give the remotest credibility to his arguments. His depictions of Jewish people were so far-fetched as to be laughable. Perhaps it was this very extremism that captured the imagination of his supporters, who were tunnel-visioned people looking for a scapegoat in society on which to vent their otherwise aimless fury.

In 'Mein Kampf' Hitler wrote of his hatred of Jews: 'Thus I finally discovered who were the evil spirits leading our people astray... My love for my own people increased correspondingly. Considering the satanic skill which these evil counsellors

> ## Hitler claimed that the German people had been tricked by the Jews in World War I

displayed, how could their unfortunate victims be blamed?'

So Hitler sought to excuse the weaknesses as he saw them of the Social Democrats and trade unionists, whom he had previously despised, at the expense of the longtime scapegoats, the Jews.

The steps taken against Jews increased gradually from 1933 and did so with the full force of law. By the time the 1935 Nuremberg Laws were passed, German Jews were

*Left:* **Russian children, parted from their parents, were among those caged by the Nazis. Right: A prisoner at Buchenwald after liberation by the Americans.**

stripped of their citizenship and the many still remaining at liberty endured a precarious existence.

### ■ NAZI SADISM ■

Following 1933, violence against minorities and dissidents became an accepted part of German society. The government itself was not beyond imposing law by terror and intimidation. There was a wide range of potential targets and many of the acts of thuggery carried out by Nazi bully-boys were pure acts of revenge or sadism. Too many people in the battered and buffeted state of Germany construed this to be a hallmark of strong government and favoured it.

*Above:* Britain also had its concentration camps, like this one at Ramsey on the Isle of Man.

*Below*: Himmler (*second right*) visits Dachau. He personally engineered much of the suffering.

### ◆ EYE WITNESS ◆

**Alf Toombs was a German prisoner of war for five years after he survived the Normandy barn massacre of British troops shortly before Dunkirk.**

❛ For the first two and a half years the treatment was really bad. After that we got Red Cross parcels. If it hadn't have been for them, many of us would not be alive today.

All we got was a cup of coffee in the morning. For lunch there was a loaf of brown bread between five of us. We had to take it in turns to have the small end of the loaf. We worked until 6pm when we were given soup, usually potato. Once we had cods' heads which was disgusting. The cooks were German and they didn't give them much to do.

The Poles were very good to us. Women took bits of bread and food to us while we worked. But when we got back we were searched so we had to be careful. ❜

When they could, German Jews fled. In the Thirties some 250,000 Jews left Germany, abandoning all hope of a peaceable existence when daily they read slogans and posters bearing the messages 'Let Judah perish' and 'Jews not wanted here'.

## *Inmates worked from morning till night, usually on futile tasks, always at jogging pace*

Sooner or later, those who remained were destined to be sent to a concentration camp. Joining them were the much-despised Slavs, particularly the intelligentsia.

The first inspector of concentration camps was SS recruit Theodor Eicke who made it his business to breed out any signs of compassion in his men

*Top right:* Hitler's 'Mein Kampf', heralded around Germany, was full of anti-semitic rantings without a shred of fact.

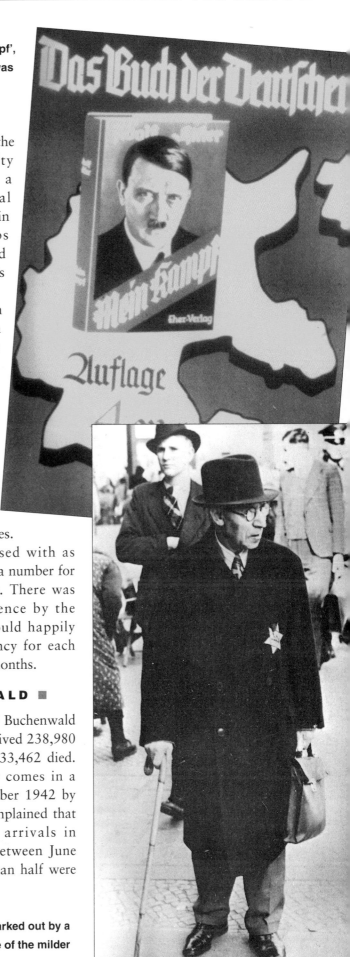

who would be guarding the camp prisoners. Cruelty and sadism became a matter of professional pride. SS men involved in the running of camps boasted of their work and named themselves Death's Head units.

Helping the SS to run the camps were German criminal prisoners dressed in blue and white striped uniforms and just as willing to mete out beatings as their legal overlords. In fact, they were frequently more vindictive to impress their SS masters and avoid a beating themselves.

Names were dispensed with as each detainee was given a number for identification purposes. There was little attempt at pretence by the prison guards who would happily reveal the life expectancy for each prisoner was but three months.

### ■ BUCHENWALD ■

Between 1937 and 1945 Buchenwald concentration camp received 238,980 prisoners out of which 33,462 died. A grim note of reality comes in a letter written in December 1942 by an SS official which complained that out of 136,870 new arrivals in concentration camps between June and November, more than half were already dead.

*Bottom right:* Jews were marked out by a yellow star in Germany, one of the milder measures taken against them.

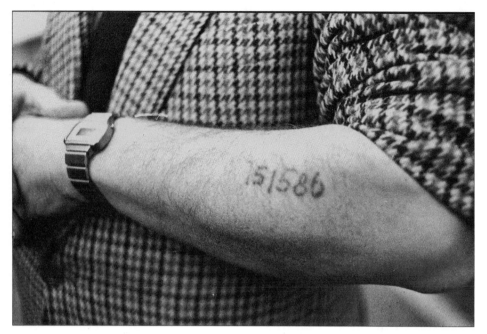

*Above:* Concentration camp survivor Maurice Goldstein reveals the number he was identified by as an inmate.

Discipline was harsh and the beatings regular, particularly for the old or infirm. Frequently the sadistic lashings carried out by the guards were enough to kill. Medical treatment for those who survived was a case of make-do-and-mend by fellow prisoners with a modicum of training.

Inside the wooden huts that housed the prisoners, beds were made of straw and their occupants were crammed together, forbidden to speak. In the summer the huts were acrid and airless, in the winter, damp and cold.

For inmates, the days were filled, morning until night, with unrelenting work. The tasks chosen by their captors were frequently pointless or futile. Nevertheless, all the jobs had to be done at a jogging pace.

In addition to all this, there were regular singing lessons in German complete with beatings for those who were judged to have performed poorly because they were too tired, too scared or because they couldn't speak sufficiently good German.

Inmates were colour-coded to denote the reason for their incarceration. Jews wore yellow stars. The others wore tags which were coloured pink for homosexuals, orange for political prisoners, purple for pacifists, green for criminals and black for those found guilty of anti-social behaviour.

Escape was rare – which was fortunate for the prisoners, because the retribution dished out to those left behind was terrible and merciless. For a single escape, hundreds of prisoners might be made to stand in the compound naked and still for an entire night, summer or winter. It was enough to claim the lives of those growing increasingly frail with the everyday rigours of camp life.

### ■ HEINRICH HIMMLER ■

The atmosphere bred tension, fear and despair. The terrorised inhabitants forced to witness the punishment of others and suffer the endless, undeserved beatings themselves felt their spirits crumble. Many had never seen a dead body before going into a concentration camp. Now they were seeing many each day who gave up the fight for survival.

There were those who collaborated with the Germans in a bid to save their own skins. At first they were despised and killed by the guards or exposed and slaughtered by fellow prisoners. Finally, the guards relied on such assistance and the inmates had no energy to strike back at the traitors.

Now inmates dreamed of dying a peaceful death in a comfortable hospital bed rather than be killed in such sordid surroundings. There seemed little hope of this small dream coming true.

Amid the despondency were a few glimmers of hope. Working parties sent outside the boundaries of the camp sometimes found local people bearing food and drink for them. When the residents of local towns were in evidence, the harsh treatment from the guards usually diminished for a while.

In 1942 Himmler drew labour from the camps to prop up German

> **'We Germans are the only people in the world who have a decent attitude towards animals'**

industry. Some prisoners, he maintained, could be worked to death.

'Whether 10,000 Russian females fall down from exhaustion while digging an anti-tank ditch interests me only in so far as the anti-tank ditch for Germany is finished. We shall never be rough and heartless when it is not necessary, that is clear.

'We Germans, who are the only people in the world who have a decent attitude towards animals, will also assume a decent attitude towards these human animals. But it is a crime against our own blood to worry about them and give them ideals thus causing our sons and grandsons to have a more difficult time with them.

'When someone comes to me and says: "I cannot dig the anti-tank ditch with women and children, it is inhuman, for it would kill them",

## 'If the anti-tank ditch is not dug German soldiers will die and they are the sons of German mothers'

then I have to say "you are the murderer of your own blood because if the anti-tank ditch is not dug German soldiers will die and they are the sons of German mothers. They are our own blood." We can be indifferent to everything else.'

### ■ FINAL SOLUTION ■

By the end of September 1944 there were a staggering 7,500,000 civilian foreigners in harness for the Reich alongside two million prisoners of war. Often, the civilians who had been rounded up, herded on to insanitary railway trucks and shipped miles from their homes and families, were housed in concentration camps.

As the numbers deemed suitable fodder for concentration camps grew, so did the number of camps across Germany, Austria and, later, occupied Poland. The tentacles of the Reich spread still further, across the Low Countries, France and Norway, bringing in ever larger crowds of prisoners. When the camps could hardly cope with the daily influx, there seemed little option for the authorities. Tough measures were needed to deal with a tough situation. A systematical extermination would be necessary.

### ◆ EYE WITNESS ◆

**Ron Tansley, a pacifist volunteer doing humanitarian work with the Friends Ambulance Unit, helped to clear Belsen and Neuengamme concentration camps.**

'We took the victims from there to various hospitals. It really was shocking. The atmosphere, the stench of death, the dead bodies, the poor victims on their last legs. The barbarity of it all was in each person who existed there. When we had cleared Belsen we were sent to Hamburg.

The worst people I met the entire time I was in Germany were in the Gestapo. They were not all Germans, there were Rumanians, Latvians, Hungarians and all nationalities. They couldn't care less about what had happened in the concentration camps.

From Hamburg we went past Lubeck to Neuengamme concentration camp. All the victims had gone but there were still piles of bones 10ft high and bones left partly in the furnace.

We had to get the camp ready for 5,000 Russian labourers on their way back to their homeland. I went down to the nearest town and asked for the mayor. He had run off so I spoke to the priest instead. I wanted 100 local people to help clear out this camp.

I told him: 'I'm surprised that you, a man of God, could allow that (the events at the camp) to happen'.

He turned up his sleeve and there was a concentration camp number tattooed on his arm. He had spoken out against it and a few days later he was inside the gates himself.

Then he turned to me and asked: 'What would you have done?' I have often thought about that since.

The Russians duly arrived. We fed them as best we could on cabbage and potatoes. On the day we had order papers saying the Russians were to go back, we posted notices and prepared them. The next day half of them had disappeared. They knew they would be killed in Stalin's Russia. All the Allied leaders knew it too.'

# NAZI MURDER SQUADS

A ruthless, merciless, murdering maniac. That's a description not of Hitler but of Joseph Stalin which might well have been levelled at the Russian despot by his own people.

For years they had suffered under his harsh and barbaric rule. Thousands had died as the 'man of steel' had sought both forcibly to improve Russian industry and eliminate possible opposition. Crude Gulags, state-run labour camps which were the forerunners of Germany's own concentration camps, housed thousands of dissidents.

All the passion so evident in the Russian Revolution of 1917 had evaporated. Society had been dulled by fear and repression together with a sense of helplessness.

A clever man determined to invade Russia might have made capital out of this, portraying himself as a liberator and winning the support of the downtrodden masses. Given the vast area to conquer, widespread support of the people would have made the task considerably easier.

### ■ NAPOLEONIC PLAN ■

Hitler wasn't smart enough to see the golden opportunities he was passing up. Blinded by his rabid racism which extended to Slavs, he ignored the easy path in favour of the outright hostility necessary for an ideological war of destruction.

> ## *The Führer considered Russia a stronghold of Jewry and Bolshevism, his twin loathings*

His plan was to incorporate the Crimea into the Reich along with the Baltic states. Further mineral-rich areas were ear-marked for the Fatherland. Germany would dominate Russia as far as the Urals and would

tolerate no armed resistance in the entire area. It was an ambitious plan, one which the Emperor Napoleon had found impossible to achieve. Much taken with the pint-sized despot of the previous century, Hitler was determined to retrace his steps but emerge as victor.

*Left:* **Partisans were usually hanged as an example. Above: These starving Russian soldiers were later executed.**

The Führer considered Russia a stronghold of Jewry and Bolshevism, his twin loathings. There is even a school of thought which says he

---

### ◆ EYE WITNESS ◆

**Vera Inber, trapped inside Leningrad when it was under siege by the German army, kept a diary of the city's sufferings.**

**25 Jan 1942**
'Our position is catastrophic. Just now a crowd destroyed the wooden fence of the hospital grounds and carried it away for firewood. There is no water and if the bakery stops even for a single day, what happens? We have no soup, only porridge. In the morning there was coffee but there won't be any more to drink.

**26 Jan 1942**
For the first time I cried from grief and fury. Inadvertently I overturned the saucepan of porridge on the stove. We nevertheless swallowed a few spoonfuls mixed with the ashes. There is still no bread.

**27 Jan 1942**
The bakery did not stop work after all as we were afraid it would. When the water mains packed up, eight thousand Young Communist League members – weakened like everyone else from starvation and chilled to the bone – formed a chain from the Neva to the bakery tables and passed to them the water from hand to hand.
   Yesterday there were enormous queues at the baker's shops. Bread wasn't delivered till the evening but still it was there.

*Above:* **Russian citizens were murdered in cold blood by rabid Nazis as they forged through following Barbarossa.**

carried out 'Barbarossa' not to provide 'Lebensraum' or 'living space' for his people as he professed but merely as a major thrust in his policy to rid Europe of Judaism. The diabolical excesses of Hitler and his forces surely saved Stalin's bacon.

Russia's vast Jewish population which in its history had already known so much about bully boy authorities was to be subjugated again. Although the task was immense, it became a military consideration for Hitler. The Slav people were equally unworthy and were to be extinguished as necessary.

### ■ KILLING SQUADS ■

Hitler gave his troops an amnesty for atrocities committed on the Eastern front before they even left German soil. Soldiers – and not just SS troops – were encouraged to treat Russian people, prisoners and Jews as nothing better than vermin. However, there was a special role for the SS.

Almost immediately after invasion, more Einsatzgruppen were formed, special killing squads which had cut

### ◆ EYE WITNESS ◆

**Russian schoolmistress Genia Demmianova tried to negotiate with invading Germans who were in search of food when they occupied her home village of Povsk in August 1941. Her attempts to speak for an old man found herding his calf on the outskirts of the village were frustrated.**

' I was seized by two soldiers. I fought to get free but I could not even move. I was screaming all the time but suddenly I stopped. It flashed into my mind that this was just a nightmare and that I should wake up in a minute. My eyes fixed on old Serge. He looked horrible. One of his eyes looked terribly big and staring and he was whimpering just like a young puppy dog. His face was one mass of blood and there was blood dripping from the gnarled hands he was holding up in front of it.

Two Germans tore the shirt off Serge's back, pulled down his trousers and topboots and left him standing half naked with is bloody hand covering the staring eye. The sergeant picked up a short whip from the table and stepping up to the old man he bawled: 'For the last time, where is the food depot?'

The interpreter quickly translated this. The old man tried to speak but only brought out a hoarse grunt.

All the Germans stepped aside. They knew what was coming. The sergeant raised the whip and brough it down on the old man's back with terrible force. It made Serge's dirty shirt split. The next blow and the next cut it to ribbons which were dyed crimson at the same time. The old man fell to one knee, with on bare bloody arm held in front of his face then he just collapsed on the floor.

The sergeant kept repeating with horrible gentleness: 'Where is the food?'

Two soldiers entered with a tub of water. They flung the water over old Serge. He made a faint movement and moaned once or twice but that was all.

'Take him out,' ordered the sergeant, 'and hang him on that tree.' He spoke casually without the slightest expression in his voice and asked the interpreter to explain why.

The sergeant forced me to look out of the window. The interpreter said old Serge was charged with food smuggling and would be hanged unless the people revealed where the food was hidden. I saw people being driven along to the school by soldiers from all directions. The interpreter kept talking on and on but I knew that the people did not quite understand him not only because his Russian was bad but also because they were dazed. They only began to understand when a German soldier came out with a long rope and tied it on a branch of the chestnut tree.

Immediately poor Serge was brought out. I do not think he was conscious. When people saw his battered bloody old body there was a murmur, then an old woman gave a scream, an old man shook his fist at the Germans and someone threw a stone. The old man was at least ninety.

The stone thrower could only have been a boy. But the Germans responded like beasts. They used their rifles blindly hitting out right and left like mad dogs. It all happened in a few seconds. The air was full of screams, groans, brutal curses. The people ran in all directions. '

their teeth in occupied Poland. They moved eastwards in the wake of the front line rounding up Jews and Bolseheviks and shooting them. Those Jews involved in the state or party machine were most at risk.

One Einsatzgruppe leader Otto Ohlendorff estimated that his unit alone killed 90,000 men, women and children in southern Russia in a year. Later, at the War Crimes Trials at Nuremberg, he explained his orders:

'The instructions were that Jews and Soviet political commissars were to be liquidated; the Jewish population should be totally exterminated.'

In the north, another Einsatzgruppe boasted of killing 135,000 victims in just four months. Adolf Eichmann once said that over the course of the war these killing squads claimed two million lives, probably a slightly exaggerated estimate but nevertheless a shocking one.

**Above:** SS men didn't hesitate to mete out summary justice to those suspected of anti-German activities.

As the idea of efficient extermination in order to achieve the Final Solution gripped the Nazis, mobile gas vans were eventually supplied for use around Russia.

### ■ THE WINTER WAR ■

For the first time, German soldiers became involved in atrocities which in the west had been the preserve of the Gestapo and the SS. At first, the army were simply encouraged to

*In White Russia, the German 707th Infantry Division shot 10,431 prisoners out of 10,940*

trigger action by the local communities against their leaders. This was soon set aside. Although commanders feared individual action by

soldiers against the Russians would result in a catastrophic break-down in discipline, they did little to curtail the killings.

The invading German soldiers themselves were experiencing trying conditions, which were to become more acute in the winter months.

They found Russia to be a primitive country compared to their own. And they found actions by the rapidly expanding partisan movement which claimed many German lives almost intolerable. Before long, German soldiers were no longer able to tell the difference between partisans, Jews and communists.

In White Russia the 707th Infantry Division shot 10,431 people in one month, out of a total of 10,940 taken prisoner. Partisan action had inflicted just two dead on the division and five more men were wounded.

**Below:** Russian citizens standing before a deep pit are gunned down by a German army firing squad.

## ◆ EYE WITNESS ◆

**Herman Graebe, a German civilian engineer building roads in the Ukraine, witnessed the modus operandi of an Einsatzgruppe. His account to a rapt courtroom at Nuremberg portrays the misery brought about at the whim of the 'master race'.**

'Armed Ukrainian militia were making people get out, under the surveillance of SS soldiers… The people in the trucks wore the regulation yellow pieces of cloth that identified them as Jews. I went straight toward the ditches without being stopped.

When we neared the mound I heard a series of rifle shots close by. The people from the trucks – men, women and children – were forced to undress under the supervision of an SS soldier with a whip in his hand. They were obliged to put their effects in certain spots, shoes, clothing and underwear separately.

I saw a pile of shoes, about 800 to 1,000 pairs, great heaps of underwear and clothing.

Without screaming or weeping, these people undressed, stood around in family groups, kissed each other, said farewells and waited for the sign from the SS man who stood beside the pit with a whip in his hand.

During the 14 minutes I stood near I heard no complaint or plea for mercy. I watched a family . . . . an old woman with snow-white hair was holding a child of about one in her arms, singing to it and tickling it. The child was cooing with delight.

The parents were looking on with tears in their eyes. The father was holding the hand of a boy about ten years old and speaking to him softly: the boy was fighting back tears. The father pointed to the sky, stroked his head and seemed to explain something to him.

At that moment the SS man at the pit started shouting something to his comrade. The comrade counted off about 20 people and instructed them to go behind the earth mound. Among them was the family I have just mentioned.

I well remember a slim girl with black hair who, as she passed me, pointed to herself and said : 'Twenty-three'.

I walked around the mound and stood in front of a tremendous grave. People were closely wedged together and lying on top of each other so that only their heads were visible. Nearly all had blood running over their shoulders from their heads.

Some were lifting their heads and moving their arms to show that they were still alive. The pit was nearly two thirds full and I estimated that it contained about 1,000 people.

I looked at the man who did the shooting. He was an SS man who sat at the edge of the narrow end of the pit, his feet dangling into it. He had a tommy-gun on his knees and was smoking a cigarette.

The people, completely naked, went down some steps which were cut in the clay wall of the pit and clambered over the heads of the people lying there to the place to which the SS man directed them. Some caressed those who were still alive and spoke to them in low voices.'

The SS Cavalry Brigade clearing the Prypiat Marshes in August 1941 shot 699 Russian soldiers, 1,001 partisans and 14,178 Jews. All this killing was in retaliation for 17 dead and 36 wounded Germans. A report from the Second Army revealed it shot 1,179 people out of the 1,836 arrested between August and October 1941.

German soldiers readily believed tales of Jewish and Bolshevik barbarity. One story circulated about innocent Lithuanians having their homes burned, their hands and feet chopped off, their tongues torn out and their children nailed to the walls.

### ■ RACIST SENTIMENT ■

In letters home, the German soldiers who were anyway programmed by years of Nazi propaganda revealed their racist sentiments.

German Captain Hans Kondruss wrote: 'Here clearly a whole people has systematically been reared into subhumanity. This is clearly the most Satanic educational plan of all times which only Jewish sadism could have constructed and carried through.'

Lance-Corporal Hans Fleischauer wrote: 'The Jew is a real master in murdering, burning and massacring…

**Left: On Wulecka Hill in Lvov, eminent scientists were shot by the Nazis.**

These bandits deserve the worst and toughest punishment conceivable. We all cannot be thankful enough to our Führer who had protected us from such brutalities and only for that we must follow him through thick and thin, wherever that might be.'

Another soldier described Russian prisoners of war. 'Hardly ever do you see the face of a person who seems rational and intelligent. They all look emaciated and the wild, half-crazy look in their eyes makes them look like imbeciles.'

He went on: '[It is] almost insulting when you consider that drunken Russian criminals have been set loose against us. They are scoundrels, the scum of the earth!'

It wasn't until after the war that many soldiers questioned the brutality which occurred on the Eastern front.

## 'The Russian fights today... for nothing more or less than... his human dignity'

One junior officer who had served in Poland and Russia explained: 'Well, of course, what they [the Nazis] did to the Jews was revolting. But we were told over and over again that it was a necessary evil. No, I must admit, at the time I had no idea we had fallen into the hands of criminals. I didn't realise that until much later, after it was all over.'

One man in Germany spoke out about the folly of the campaign. Dr Otto Brautigam, a diplomat who became deputy leader of the Political Department of the Ministry for the Occupied Eastern Territories, pinpointed the mistakes being made in a 13-page memo written in October 1942. 'In the Soviet Union

we found on our arrival a population weary of Bolshevism which waited longingly for new slogans holding out the prospect of a better future for them. It was Germany's duty to find such slogans but they remained unuttered. The population greeted us with joy as liberators and placed themselves at our disposal.

'...The worker and peasant soon perceived that Germany did not regard them as partners of equal rights but considered them only as the instrument of her political and economic aims...

'...Our policy has forced both Bolshevists and Russian nationalists into a common front against us. The Russian fights today with exceptional bravery and self-sacrifice for nothing more or less than recognition of his human dignity.'

### ■ NAZI INVASION ■

The invasion of the Nazis wasn't entirely unwelcome. Ethnic Ukrainians, Lithuanians, Latvians and Estonians were thrilled to be free of Stalin's choking communist yoke. They even held parades and sported the Swastika. At least for them the German slogan of 'Liberation from Bolshevism' had some credibility.

*Above*: **After liberation, women work to identify bodies.**

Their young men rushed to volunteer for the SS and became in many cases some of its most ardent and hardline members.

Predictions that the Red Army would be beaten in ten weeks turned out to be wildly optimistic. Although it took two years, Stalin's men got the upper hand against the invaders and began pushing them back into their own territory and beyond. Here was their opportunity to pay back in kind the treatment their own people had endured.

German troops were now faced with the appalling prospect of giving themselves up to the Red Army and went to elaborate lengths to surrender to American and British forces instead.

British soldiers released from prison camps by the Russians were appalled at the behaviour the liberators displayed towards German civilians, little realising the horrors that had gone before on the Eastern front.

The horror inspired by senseless Nazi doctrine that had taken place in Russia makes up yet another shameful chapter in history from which neither side could easily recover.

# FINAL SOLUTION

June 1941 did not only spell disaster for Russia, which was invaded by Hitler. It also marked a turning point in the treatment of European Jews.

The drive against Jews had escalated with dynamism. As each new European territory was incorporated into the Reich, there were thousands more shipped in cattle trucks to the concentration camps of Germany, Austria and Poland.

As they saw the countryside race by through the slits and cracks in the uncomfortable carriages, they knew they were facing their doom. The existence of concentration camps where only the supremely fit could survive was now no secret. Yet few could have been prepared for the state-sponsored horror which awaited them.

## The death squads in Russia went about their task with the fervour of the zealot

Concentration camps and ghettos which by now had become the chosen route to 'free' Europe of Jews were both haphazard methods which took time to win results. The emigration of Jews to freedom, both voluntary and forced, had been curtailed in Palestine and was occurring at little more than a dribble. (It was finally brought to an end by the Germans themselves.)

Now the sheer volume of 'Untermenschen' or 'sub-humans' being deported into the Reich was multiplied many fold. The satellite death squads which went into Russia went about their task with the fervour of the zealot. Although as many as half a million died in total, it wasn't sufficient for the barbaric regime. Ideas of the 'Final Solution' were formulating

in the heads of the most ardent Nazis; that is, the wholesale extermination of the Jewish people in Europe.

There is no exact date for the start of the Final Solution, though operations against the Jews were stepped up after the end of July 1941.

To that end, a range of experiments were tried. The first guinea pigs at Auschwitz were the much-despised Russian prisoners of war, who, alongside 300 Poles, were herded into a sealed cellar one night in September 1941. Through a grating, the callous guards pumped poison gas, oblivious to the screams of the men inside. It took hours for the cries and groans to stop. At dawn, other camp inmates were ordered to carry the bodies from the chamber to the crematorium.

In November 1941 another experiment in mass killing took place, this time in Berlin. The victims were Jewish slave labourers taken from Buchenwald concentration camp whose destination was the infamous Euthanasia Institute where they were gassed to death. The experiment was once again deemed a success. The answer to the Nazi problem was by now apparent.

On 8 December 1941 several hundred Jews were taken from three Polish towns to a wood outside the village of Chelmno and gassed in a specially constructed building.

The Wannsee Conference scheduled for 9 December 1941 was a top level debate on what to do with Jews in the Third Reich. It was sponsored by SS-Obergruppenführer Reinhard Heydrich, one of the authors of Nazi policy against the Jews.

### ■ WANNSEE ■

In fact, the conference was postponed after Japan's attack on Pearl Harbor. It didn't take place until 20 January 1942 when the representatives of seven high offices – including the Ministry of the Occupied Eastern Territories, the Interior Ministry, the Ministry of Justice, the Foreign Ministry and SS departments – gathered to hear about the Final Solution.

Heydrich made no secret of his desire to deport the entire Jewish

*Left:* Hopeless and helpless, inmates at Auschwitz concentration camp wait for the end. *Below:* Windowless huts in the Auschwitz camp housed thousands.

Historians have since debated long and hard the significance of the Wannsee Conference. Today it is regarded as little more than a platform sought by Heydrich to broadcast his radical views. It was, nevertheless, the precursor to genocide and the holocaust for which

## Mass murder was now sanctioned as an official Third Reich policy

population into the east where they would be quite literally worked to death. Those who remained would be 'dealt with'. Here, the policy on procreation was acidly clear. It was the germ that led to the sterilisation programme later brought in by the Nazis to stop the spread of the Jewish population. Among those present at the Wannsee Conference were Himmler, Adolf Eichmann and Ernst Kaltenbrunner.

the Nazis are best remembered today. The mainly localised examples of mass murder carried out on the initiative of individuals was now sanctioned as a Reich policy.

In a speech given by Hitler at the end of January 1942, he told the German people the war could only end when the Jews had been 'uprooted' from Europe.

Hitler said: '...The war will not end as the Jew imagines it will, with the uprooting of the Aryans, but the result of this war will be the complete annihilation of the Jews. 'Now for the first time they will not bleed other people to death but for the first time the old Jewish law of "an eye for an eye, a tooth for a tooth" will be applied.'

It seems clear, therefore, that not only the Nazi officials but also the general public knew of Hitler's desire to kill off Jewry in Europe.

There has been much debate since about the passive acceptance of the German people to this sickening policy. Yet it is clear that the Germans had suffered a degree of brainwashing by Hitler. Thrilled at the emergence of a strong state in which their personal fortunes had improved tremendously, most

*Above:* **Zyklon-B was the gas used to kill thousands in Auschwitz after they were herded into fake shower rooms.**

Germans accepted the arrival of concentration camps as necessary to suppress revolutionaries and to house the mentally deranged. There was confusion in the minds of many people who felt being anti-Hitler was tantamount to being anti-German.

As the activities against those targeted minorities like Jews, gypsies, the mentally or physically handi-capped and homosexuals increased, the brutalised Germans were already

*Left:* **In Auschwitz camp the inscription on the main gate read 'Work brings freedom'.**

well-practised in turning a blind eye. The punishment for showing any kindness to Jews was severe. Victims of an expert Nazi propaganda machine, native Germans believed they themselves were at risk from a resurgent Jewish force.

## ■ NO FREE SPEECH ■

If lively discussion of the Jewish question and the extreme measures taken by the regime had been permitted, perhaps a group of people

### ◆ EYE WITNESS ◆

**Peter Strachan, in the 147th Brigade Company of the Royal Army Signals Corps, was an army driver in Europe.**

❝ I got a message to pick up a civilian. He never spoke, just gave me directions. As we neared the place, I saw this white stuff on the ground. I thought, has it been snowing? We drove in some massive gates. There were steel ovens on the left hand side. I thought they were bakers ovens.

   The air fill filled with this awful smell. Only later did I realise I was in Belsen and these were the ovens used to kill its inmates. The white stuff I saw on the way in was the residue of the quicklime they had put in mass graves. We had to wear gas masks because of the threat of diphtheria and other diseases. I didn't go in any of the huts. I could see the people inside were covered in lice and sores. Quite a lot were still alive but many of them could not be made right. I reckon my brain stopped working while I was there. ❞

opposed to exterminations would have found expression. But free speech was impossible. A Berlin butcher who whispered to a customer that Hitler had started the war was sentenced to death and dispatched to a concentration camp. Germany was, after all, a militarised state which would brook no opposition.

People were subject to the same tools of terror as the so-called 'enemies' of the people. The German underground could operate with only the same degree of effectiveness and in much the same sphere as those resistance movements set up in occupied countries. Veterans of the

Eastern front were no longer shocked by extermination and were even convinced of its necessity.

After the war, American interrogators discovered a broad sense of guilt about the fate of the Jews among everyday Germans. But generally people feared revenge, blocked out

# KRISTALLNACHT

**German citizens chuckled and cheered when Jewish businesses were smashed and businessmen were beaten during a night of horror in November 1938.**

Organised by propaganda chief Goebbels, a wave of anti-Semitic attacks took place across Germany apparently in reprisal for the killing of a German diplomat in Paris by a young Jew. On account of the amount of plate glass shattered it was dubbed the Kristallnacht, or Crystal Night.

More than 7,000 Jewish shops were looted and scores of synagogues were set ablaze. An unknown number of Jews died with many more suffering appalling injuries at the hands of thugs employed by the Nazis. Yet as the terror unfolded, middle-class passers-by stopped to applaud the actions of the bully boys and even held up their babies to see the violence administered to Jews.

In order to prevent a recovery by the Jewish faction, the government plotted to confiscate insurance cash paid out following the Kristallnacht and return it.

unsavoury information and put the blame squarely on the shoulders of the Führer.

Abroad, governments had long known about the threat to the Jewish population. There was, however, an unwillingness to believe that systematic murder of a race was taking place. Allied leaders were unwilling to use the facts as they knew them in the propaganda war against the Axis powers. The stories of extermination seemed too terrible to be true. Surely no modern nation could be that vile and cruel? Horror stories about Germans had been circulated during World War I which had later been shown to be false.

Torn by political considerations, the British government even went as far as restricting Jewish immigration into Palestine, a vital escape route, to pacify the Arab populations of the Middle East. By 1942 the Swiss authorities also closed their borders, barring the way to freedom for scores of Jews in Vichy France. Despite its reported independence from Germany, the anti-semitic measures common to the rest of the Reich were also instituted there.

There was enormous sympathy for the plight of the Jews in Britain, reflected in pontifications by the politicians who urged that Britain house more than seven million dispossessed Jews at the end of the conflict. The fact that, given the savage Nazi actions against them, far

*Below*: **One of the devices which was used to boil human remains down to soap by the Nazis.**

> **By August 1942 news of the mass killings in the Reich reached the free world on a daily basis**

fewer Jews than that would remain alive at the end of the war appeared to have escaped them.

Britain's Foreign Office first began hearing about the use of gas chambers in February 1942. A Swedish doctor returned from a visit to the Third Reich confirming that asylums were being cleared by the use of poison. Further reports leaked out of Germany to the same effect. By August 1942 news of the mass killings reached the free world on a daily basis.

## ■ RIGA MASSACRE ■

On 19 August the Foreign Office in London received via the Belgian Embassy an eyewitness account of a massacre that had taken place outside Riga in Latvia.

'The order was given for the Jews to undress completely. There followed a scene impossible to describe; men and women weeping, falling on their knees, beseeching the German executioners to desist. But all in vain.

'These unfortunate people, among them young children, were lined up at the edge of the trench and machine-gunned. The execution over, the trench was searched to ensure that there was no one alive among the victims. One of the Latvian officers present was unable to stand it and went suddenly mad.'

### ■ AUSCHWITZ ■

Now some concentration camps had turned into extermination camps, the largest of which was Auschwitz, with its annexe camp of Birkenau. The rate of killings here far exceeded that in other camps of Treblinka, Sobibor, Lvov, Kaunas, Minsk, Vilnius, Riga and Belzec. It was into here that vast numbers of people snatched from their homes in occupied territories disappeared, never to be seen again.

Train loads of deportees arrived to be gassed immediately. On 2 Septem-

---

### *Everything of value was stripped from them, including gold fillings from the teeth*

---

ber 1942, 957 Jewish men, women and children arrived from Paris in the early hours of the morning and 918 were gassed before sunset. The same story with victims taken from the length and breadth of Europe was repeated daily on an ever-increasing scale for almost uninterruptedly for three years.

Following the removal of the bodies from the crematoria, everything of value was stripped from them, including the gold fillings from the teeth, and was shipped to the Reichsbank in Berlin where it was paid into an SS account opened in the bogus name of 'Max Heiliger'.

*Right*: The gas chamber, with its door on the right, and the crematorium at Mauthausen concentration camp where thousands died.

Soap was made of the fats drained from the bodies processed in the enormous crematoria, fertilizer concocted from human bones while hair was kept for stuffing mattresses or for making cloth.

In addition to gassing, people were also shot, usually with a bullet to the back of the neck, received fatal injections or were shot and thrown on a fire while still alive.

When the trainloads of people arrived at Auschwitz, their fate was decided at the flick of an eye. Blinking at the sudden daylight after hours or days penned up in an insanitary boxcar, the fittest that emerged were filed in one direction to work the rest of their useful days as slaves to the Reich. Included in this work was the everyday policing of the camp and the gruesome task of carrying and disposing of bodies. This was carried out by a group called Sonderkommando who enjoyed certain privileges including better rations and quarters. Yet every four months the Sonderkom-

mando were liquidated on the basis that they knew too much of how Auschwitz worked.

Those herded into shacks and sent out to work began their day at 3am when there was a cruel roll call. Each had to stand for four hours in the cold and dark while camp's sadistic criminal 'officials' and then the SS guards counted and re-counted their

---

### ◆ EYE WITNESS ◆

**Commandant Rudolf Hoess, a veteran of concentration camps, investigated the most efficient way in which to carry out his grim task.**

‘ After the war in his affidavit to a war crimes trial, he explained: 'I was ordered to establish extermination facilities at Auschwitz in June 1941. At that time there were already three other extermination camps in the Government General: Belzec, Treblinka and Wolzek.

I visited Treblinka to find out how they carried out their extermination. The Camp Commandant told me that he had liquidated 80,000 in the course of one half year. He was principally concerned with liquidating all the Jews from the Warsaw ghetto. He used monoxide gas and I did not think that his methods were very efficient.

So at Auschwitz I used Zyklon-B which was a crystallized prussic acid dropped into the death chamber. It took from three to fifteen minutes to kill the people in the chamber, according to climatic conditions.

We knew when the people were dead because their screaming stopped. We usually waited about half an hour before we opened the doors and removed the bodies. ’

## ◆ EYE WITNESS ◆

**For her 13th birthday, Anne Frank received a diary in which she recorded the silly and sentimental, the childish and the charming aspects of her life. And it was no ordinary life. For Anne was the daughter of Jews living in occupied Holland in 1942. Soon the charade of wearing yellow stars to indicate their Jewishness, segregation and harassment was not enough for the Germans. They began transporting Jews to far off concentration camps.**

'Rather than risk the unknown, Anne went into hiding with her parents and her sister Margot. Within days they were joined by the Van Daans, who had a 15-year-old son called Peter, and then a dentist called Dussel. Dutch friends kept the hideaway near the centre of Amsterdam a secret. But the Germans finally discovered the secret rooms shut off at the back of her father's former business and her cat-and-mouse game with the Germans was abruptly over.

On 4 August 1944 Anne was sent to Bergen-Belsen concentration camp where she died of typhus in March 1945, three months before her 16th birthday. Her diary was discovered after the family's arrest by a cleaner and given to her Dutch friends. They were able to hand it back to her father Otto Frank when he returned at the end of the war. In her last entry into the diary, made on Tuesday 1 August 1944, Anne echoes many other teenagers with her thoughts and her dreams.

'I never utter my real feelings about anything and that's how I've acquired the reputation of being boy-crazy, a flirt, know-all, reader of love stories. The cheerful Anne laughs about it, gives cheeky answers, shrugs her shoulders indifferently, behaves as if she doesn't care, but, oh dearie me, the quiet Anne's reactions are just the opposite. If I'm to be quite honest, then I must admit that it does hurt me, that I try terribly hard to change myself but that I'm always fighting against a more powerful enemy.'

*Below:* **Nazi crematoria were built to cope with vast numbers of bodies. Those at Auschwitz worked ceaselessly to cope with the victims.**

until it was finally collected by wheelbarrow for disposal. Given the physical degeneration in their condition during a long journey with little water and no food, many failed to endure the working life for long.

---

### *On the walls of the camps were posters which read 'Cleanliness brings freedom'*

---

The rest who arrived by train went another direction, to their doom. This group were informed by loudspeaker that they were going for a shower and delousing before being reunited with their loved ones. Curiously, the camp staff appeared to revel in a charade which never once gave away the fact that people were about to be killed. Every effort was made to convince people of the legitimacy of the 'delousing' including posters which read 'Cleanliness brings freedom'.

### ■ CHILD KILLINGS ■

This was probably because any signs of panic or dissension from the victims would have seriously disrupted the production-line efficiency of the operation, including the orderly collection of clothes and valuables. Children were always exterminated because they were of little value to the Reich. Their mothers frequently faced the same fate on the basis that loving mums who knew their children had been killed made poor workers.

In a long wooden hut they were forced to strip, their heads were shaved and then they were marched into giant shower rooms. But instead of water, these humiliated, boney figures were gassed to death.

numbers. Absurdly, anyone who died in the night was equally required to attend the roll call. It was up to two inmates to support the naked corpse

Rudolph Hoess explained the finer points: 'Still another improvement we made over Treblinka was that at Treblinka the victims almost always knew that they were to be exterminated while at Auschwitz camp we

## The gas chambers at Auschwitz regularly slaughtered between 6,000 and 12,000 a day

endeavoured to fool the victims into thinking that they were to go through a delousing process.

'We were required to carry out these exterminations in secrecy but… the foul and nauseating stench from the continuous burning of bodies permeated the entire area and all of the people living in the surrounding communities knew that exterminations were going on at Auschwitz.'

Although the gas chambers at Auschwitz housed 2,000 people at a time and they regularly slaughtered between 6,000 and 12,000 people a

day, the camp was unable to cope with the demand it was put under during 1944 when the killings were at their peak. By now Jews in the Yugoslavian states, Greece, Hungary, Rumania and France were deluging into the east. As German successes dwindled in the field, the hierarchy became more focused on its stated aim of killing Jews in which they were achieving greater success. Thanks to the personal attentions of Adolf Eichmann, trains ferrying the victims to Auschwitz and other death camps were given priority above those carrying troops needed for national defence. Until the bitter end, the authorities refused to liberate the inmates of Auschwitz, choosing instead to kill them or march those who were still

*Above:* Hitler's elite, the Waffen-SS, burgeoned during the war and was responsible for scores of killings.

*Below:* Emaciated corpses piled up at Buchenwald. The sight shocked and sickened the liberating Allied soldiers.

able-bodied to further camps deeper inside the Reich.

### ■ WAFFEN SS ■

In charge of the extermination programme for the most part were members of the Gestapo or the rapidly expanding Waffen SS. At the start of the war, this elite band numbered just three divisions. By its end, there were 35 containing more than half a million men. They were pitched by Hitler as a tough state police force against the army and as a reward for their efforts they were promised powers and increased status after the end of hostilities.

The power and prestige of the Waffen SS units didn't appeal to

Germans alone. Many foreigners were enlisted into its ranks and happily carried out the most gruesome and grotesque of its chores. Of the 900,000 men who passed

## The most feared of the 900,000 men in the Waffen SS were the Ukrainians

through the Waffen SS, less than half were Reich Germans. A further 300,000 were racial Germans from outside the boundaries of the Reich, 50,000 were from other Germanic

races while 150,000 were foreigners. The most feared of the SS guards were the Ukrainians.

### ■ FREE AT LAST ■

Their master, SS Reichsführer Heinrich Himmler, urged them to show no restraint. He told them in October 1943: 'One basic principle must be the absolute rule for the SS men; we must be honest, decent, loyal and comradely to members of our own blood and nobody else. What happens to a Russian and a Czech does not interest me in the slightest. What the nations can offer in the way of good blood of our type we will take, if necessary, by kidnapping their children and raising them here with us.'

Such was their enthusiasm that up to 90 per cent of incoming prisoners went immediately to their deaths, depriving the Reich of the slave labour it needed to replenish its armaments and food supplies. This became a source of some dissatisfaction among the Nazi hierarchy.

Battle-hardened soldiers who arrived to liberate Auschwitz and other extermination camps were sickened at what they found. Those who remained alive were little more than skin and bone, their enormous sunken eyes glazed, their heads

*Below:* **Freedom for the children of Auschwitz. This picture was taken just hours after the camp was liberated.**

*Above:* The funeral procession for victims of the Nazis at Auschwitz held in January 1945 stretched as far as the eye could see.

shaven, capable of little movement on their own account.

Conditions by then were abominable. There was widespread disease as well as infestations of lice and other bugs. Those who witnessed the terrible scenes, together with the gas ovens and the overworked crematoria, all spoke of the odour of death emanating from the camps. To be passing nearby and remain ignorant of the killings there was surely impossible, they questioned.

At last, the Allies were convinced beyond doubt of the scale of the killings. Although detailed figures across the board were not kept, it seems upwards of five million died. Some claim that fully one third of the Jewish population in Europe was murdered in the Holocaust. The decision not to bomb Auschwitz and smash the operation now seemed to have been made in error.

One man who suspected the truth all along, the most ardent of anti-Nazis,

## HOLOCAUST

**Although six million is the most quoted figure for the death toll of Jews during the Holocaust, it remains impossible to apply an exact figure. There could have been fewer – or far more – killed as Hitler and his henchmen implemented 'the Final Solution'.**

There were only six extermination camps, the largest being Auschwitz, but killings were carried out at most of the concentration camps, too. Rudolph Hoess, commandant at Auschwitz until December 1943, admitted after the war that at least two and a half million people were executed during his time at the camp and a further half million died from hunger and disease. This comprised not only Jews, but Russians, gypsies, homosexuals, dissidents and the disabled. However, the most terrible measures taken against the Jews came after his tenure was finished.

*One man who suspected the truth all along was the most ardent of anti-Nazis, Winston Churchill*

was Winston Churchill. As early as July 1944 he wrote to Anthony Eden to say: 'There is no doubt that this is probably the greatest and most horrible single crime ever committed in the whole history of the world.'

# DOCTORS OF DEATH

For centuries people have been fascinated by twins. Two identities from the same womb who may even be the spitting image of one another were worshipped by some ancient races, feared by others.

To the rabid Fascists of Nazi Germany twins were a short cut to peopling the Third Reich with blond-haired, blue-eyed super specimens of the master race. This noble breed of Aryans so adored by Hitler would have the run of Europe at the expense of the Czechs, Poles, Slavs and Jews.

Women in Germany were already being encouraged to produce as many children as possible. If only every good German woman could produce multiple sets of twins with the requisite physical qualities, that problem of populating the expanding empire would be cut at a stroke.

In order to achieve a larger incidence of twins, there was the need to do detailed medical research. The man who came forward to lead this investigation was Dr Josef Mengele. The place to do it was the notorious death camp, Auschwitz.

*The investigation was led by Dr Josef Mengele at the notorious death camp Auschwitz*

Here, Mengele worked long and hard to establish the special characteristics of twins. Any that were transported to the camp were set aside for his special attention.

First came the rigorous medical check-ups on them while they lived. Each was examined together and separately in the quest to break new ground. Then Mengele played his

*Left*: A prisoner in a pressure chamber is the subject of a painful experiment.
*Right:* No pity was shown to children.

trump card. Until now, it was rare that twins ever died together. So medical probing into their inner likenesses was severely curtailed.

Mengele, with the aid of his pistol or a fatal injection of chloroform to the heart, could personally dispatch twins to their maker within moments of each other – although frequently he got one of his faithful entourage to do the dirty deed. The still-warm bodies of the ill-fated twins would be the subject of postmortems to reveal whether or not the similarities of twins was more than just skin deep.

Internal organs removed in the dissection thought to be of particular interest were pickled in alcohol and sent to the Anthropological Institute at Berlin-Dahlem for further study. His aim was to clone the perfect Ayran and he would stop at nothing to fulfill this warped dream.

■ **HUMAN GUINEA PIG** ■

Using live humans, he would attempt to change hair and eye colours. It is said he once returned a gurgling tot to the arms of his anxious prisoner mother with a bloodied red cavity

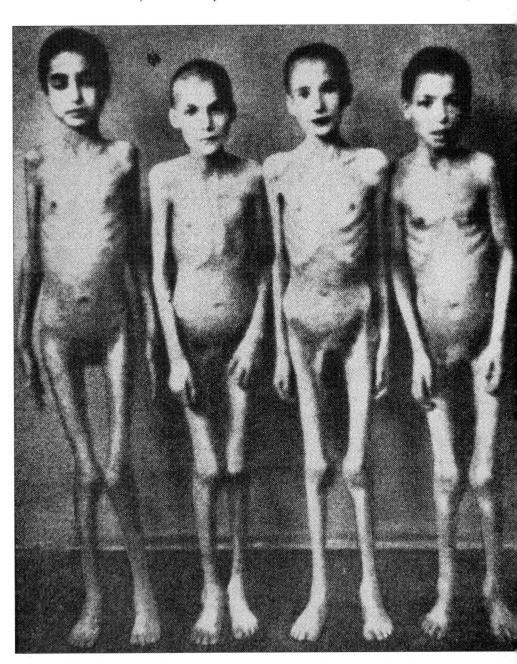

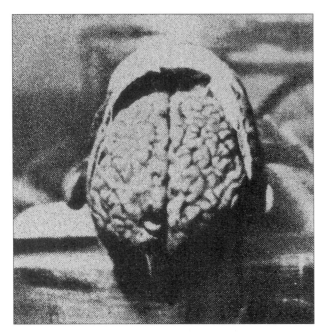

*Left:* **This opened-up skull provides a hideous record of the obscene methods used by Nazis in their quest to discover the workings of the human brain.**

where an eye used to be. He was blatantly unconcerned that many of his patients died, were crippled or blinded during his experiments.

## ■ DOCTOR OF DEATH ■

Mengele was without any doubt dedicated to his work. The eldest son of a Catholic German industrialist, he went to the University of Munich where he secured a doctorate in philosophy and proceeded to medical school at the University of Frankfurt. At both places of study it appears he was infected with virulent anti-Semitism which was rife in Germany at the time.

A former member of the discredited SA, Mengele joined the Nazi Party in May 1937 and embraced the SS a year later. Injured on the Eastern front in 1942, he recovered from his wounds, received the Iron Cross for his actions against the Red Army and then volunteered to be camp doctor at Auschwitz despite a marked lack of experience in practical doctoring.

Although short in stature, he was suave, sophisticated in conversation and graceful in movement. Associates at Auschwitz, even inmates, remember him still with a certain awe and occasionally even adoration. Ironically, while he laboured to perfect the blond-haired, blue-eyed image of true Ayrans, he was himself dark and could pass as a Mediterranean.

Speculation about how Mengele got out of Germany at the end of the war is rife. Some claim he was

> **Speculation is rife about how Mengele got out of Germany at the end of the war**

smuggled out by a Jewish mistress and was kept in hiding in various European cities until he could safely be spirited away to Argentinian shores. Others maintain that he was captured by the Allies but slipped through their fingers in the chaos of newly-won peace.

*Below:* **To halt the population, Nazi doctors carried out painful sterlisiation operations on Jewish and Slavic women.**

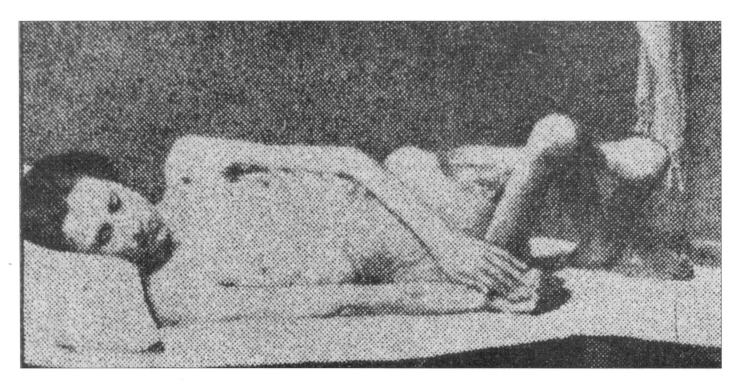

Still, he certainly made it to Argentina and felt so secure in his new home that he used his real name to apply for an Argentinian passport in 1956. He also won permits to visit Germany and Switzerland. An extradition bid failed in 1959 on a technicality, by which time Mengele was concerned in a pharmaceutical company in Buenos Aires.

## ■ DEATH IN BRAZIL ■

He left Argentina for Paraguay in 1960, apparently to work on a cattle cloning project for which he was eminently qualified, thanks to his time at Auschwitz. From there he travelled to Brazil where it is almost certain that he drowned in 1979. His death was cloaked in secrecy for six years. In the early Eighties, Dr Simon

## ALDERNEY

**Alongside the names of Dachau and Belsen in the annals of horror ranks Alderney, one of the Channel Islands which became the site of three harsh work camps for slave labour and a fourth, fully fledged concentration camp called Sylt.**

All four camps, in particular Sylt, became living hell for hundreds of prisoners, particularly Russians, who were sent there to be literally worked to death for the Third Reich.

In charge was the Todt Organisation, tasked with building the defences for Hitler's Fortress Europe. Food was short, the working days long and the beatings meted out by the Germans in control were cruel beyond belief.

One Russian recalled how a fellow countryman died in one of the work camps. 'In Alderney camp, I saw a Russian beaten for half an hour until he bled to death. Willi, a cook, did it. The Russian had taken some potato peelings.'

One Todt officer beat at least one Russian prisoner to death for picking up discarded cabbage leaves.

Officially, the death toll on Alderney is 530 although the real figure is thought to be much higher. Alderney stands out not only because it is on British soil but because the atrocities associated with the Third Reich are normally thought to have been committed by the SS while in this case it was the Todt Organisation building the Atlantic Wall which was responsible. The British government has decreed that records linked to the events on the Channel Islands will be kept under wraps until 2045, probably to save the face of islanders who collaborated.

---

### *It is almost certain that Dr Josef Mengele drowned in an accident in Brazil in 1979*

Wiesenthal had drawn up a list of 10 prominent Nazis whom he wished to see brought to justice. At the time he said: 'If I could get all ten, it would be an achievement. But if I could get only Josef Mengele, I think my soul would be at peace.'

Wiesenthal, among thousands who yearned to see Mengele brought into a courtroom to face his crimes, was cheated by the apparent fluke death of the 'Angel of Death'.

In addition to his forays into medical experiments, Mengele was also guilty of vicious beatings. Afterwards, he would meticulously clean the blood from his hands using perfumed soap.

His research into the incidence of twins was not the end of the

grotesque activities which took place in the name of medical advances at Auschwitz and other camps throughout the Reich.

Bacterial cultures were grown in live humans afflicting them with the ravages of terrible disease no matter what the pain and suffering that went with it. 'Volunteers' were injected with all manner of vile germs to see what effect they would have.

Surgical operations were carried out by SS doctors without anaesthetics in their crazed attempts to establish the precise effects.

A 'cause celebre' of the manic medic was to sterilise women from the 'sub-human' races around Europe to prevent them procreating further. One technique was to subject each woman to an X-ray for minutes on end to wither the reproductive organs. Poisonous injections were

**Right:** Tests at high-altitude on pyjama-clad prisoners revealed new information to German scientists about the effects of decompression on human beings.

also administered into the womb, their effects being carefully monitored as the 'guinea pig' female writhed in agony.

In one of the most callous experiments, Jewish people were lined up to be shot so German scientists could assess how many bodies a bullet

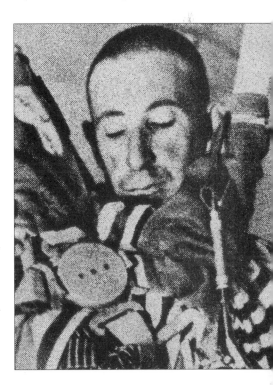

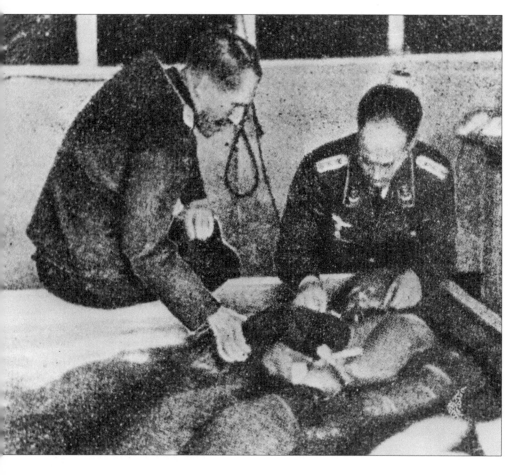

**Left:** Dr Sigmund Rascher used inmates at Dachau concentration camp for immersion experiments like these, deep in chilling ice water.

In the past, the government has claimed the bones belonged to victims of the Allied bombing raids. Marks on them suggest otherwise but all attempts to analyse the bones have been blocked.

At the head of Japan's grotesque probes beyond the bounds of medical science was Lt-General Shiro Ishii. He oversaw experiments in which prisoners were infected with bubonic

## *Lt-Gen Ishii oversaw experiments in which prisoners were infected with bubonic plague*

could travel through before finally coming to rest.

News of the medical research carried out by the Nazis caused worldwide distress and distaste when details emerged following the war. Yet that stark fact didn't stop medics making full use of the research material gathered by the Nazis amid such appalling anguish and pain.

For more than 40 years British university lecturers showed X-rays taken by the Nazis of their mad work to students. The remains of death camp victims have also been used for teaching purposes.

### ■ TEACHING AIDS ■

One Cambridge University doctor defended the controversial use of such heartbreaking material in the years following the war by saying: 'It was excellent teaching material. It was used here for over 30 years and served a valuable purpose. There was

obviously a degree of revulsion felt but at least the suffering of those involved was of benefit.'

The X-ray film was in use as recently as 1987. Continued observation of the findings of SS doctors has caused outrage among holocaust survivors who have urged doctors to now give the remains in question a decent burial.

Medical experiments also took place in Japan, an issue which has for years been a source of embarrassment and denials by the government.

Circulating today in Japan are severed skulls and thigh bones. The skull bones contain drill holes, some of them square, indicating brain surgery has taken place.

The bones were discovered in 1989 buried in the grounds of an army medical college where medical experiments are thought to have been carried out following the outbreak of the Sino-Japanese War in 1931.

plague and other fatal diseases and then disembowelled to see the effects on their inner organs. It was his practice to perform autopsies while the 'patients' were still alive. Ultimately, his aim was to perfect a biological weapon which would win Japan's war.

### ■ COLD EXPERIMENTS ■

Another of his quests was to find a cure for frostbite. Prisoners had their hands dipped in iced water and were then forced outside into freezing winter weather until the hand was thoroughly affected.

The most notorious venue was Unit 731 in occupied China where some 3,000 were killed.

After the war, staff used on the trials admitted the knowledge they gained during these experiments was used after the war. Some felt they had been cheated out of due credit for their endeavours.

A Japanese professor who spoke to these scientists after the war reported: '[They] felt they were victims because they felt they had spent a golden time in fruitful research but the work at 731 would not be recognised by ordinary scientists.' He found only one man who expressed any guilt about what had happened.

He used predominantly Chinese, Korean and Russian guinea pigs but some British and Americans are also thought to have been involved.

*Below:* **The 'Anatomy Institute of the Academy of Medical Sciences' in Danzig received this human skin.**

## SMOKING

**Vegetarian, teetotaller and non-smoker, Hitler was keen to use his propaganda machine to spread the word about clean living and good health. When links between smoking a lung cancer were detected by German scientists in the Twenties, he became one of the first anti-smoking campaigners in the world.**

Magazines and newspapers contained warnings about the dangers of smoking. Women were forbidden to buy cigarettes in cafes, smoking was restricted among soldiers and banned in scores of public places. It was illegal to use tobacco in advertising to advocate manly qualities and those who abstained were awarded shining qualities of good Aryan citizens.

Despite his iron grip on the propaganda system, his move to cut smoking failed. The number of smokers rose in Fascist Germany in much the same way as it did in other European countries. The shortcomings of preventative medicine in a totalitarian regime where everyone is subject to the message has cast doubt among some doctors on its value in democratic states today.

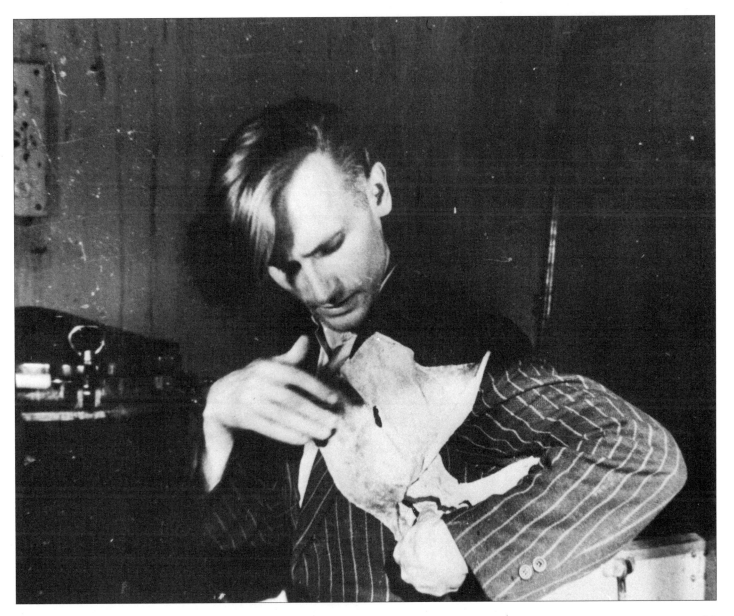

# ATROCITIES

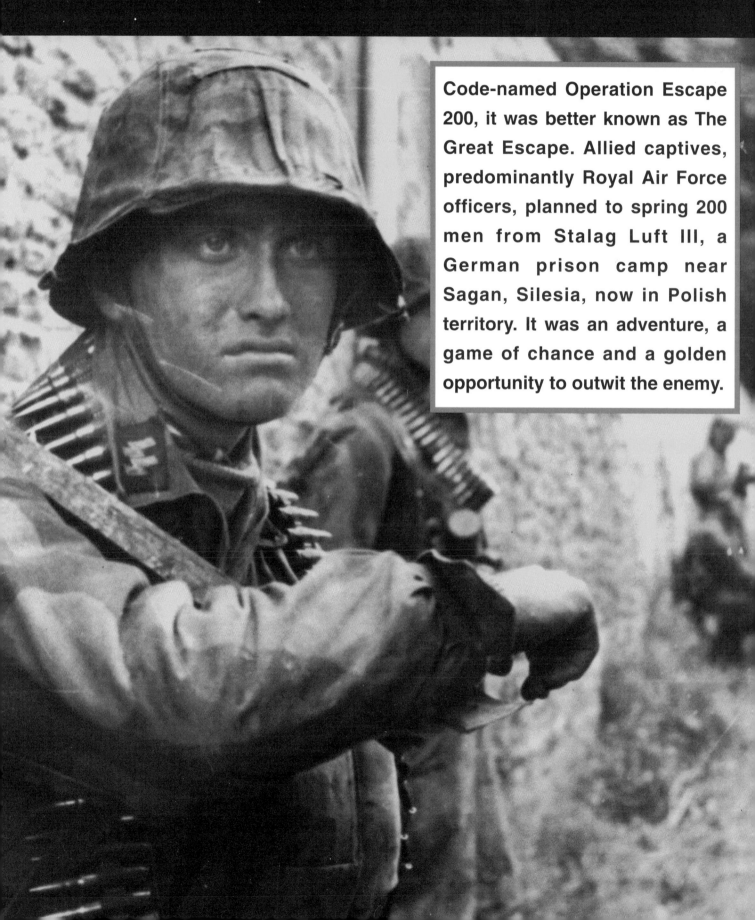

Code-named Operation Escape 200, it was better known as The Great Escape. Allied captives, predominantly Royal Air Force officers, planned to spring 200 men from Stalag Luft III, a German prison camp near Sagan, Silesia, now in Polish territory. It was an adventure, a game of chance and a golden opportunity to outwit the enemy.

**B**ut the men who slaved to pull off the most memorable prison breakout ever were to be sorely disappointed. On the night of the escape, 24 March 1944, a conspiracy of events allowed just 76 men to flee the barbed wire and watchtowers of the Stalag. And of those, only three made it to freedom, two Norwegians and a Dutchman.

Worst of all, 50 RAF servicemen chosen at random were shot by the Gestapo as a reprisal for the daring plot, to satisfy Hitler's fury. The Nazis committed an atrocity which the men of the Royal Air Force would never forgive and forget.

Stalag Luft III was built in 1941 on the orders of Hermann Göring, head of the Luftwaffe, to house the increasing numbers of Allied airmen shot down in raids over Germany.

It was a far cry from the concentration camps for which Hitler and his henchmen became famous. Although 12 men were forced to share a room, some days around the clock, they were allowed to play games like rugby and football and enjoyed reasonable rations. The prisoners of war totalling 5,000 were even allowed to build their own theatre where they staged productions twice weekly.

It was an indication of the sneaking regard in which Göring held the courageous airmen – as was the treatment dished out to them if they escaped. Until 1944, when the tide of war had turned against Germany, British airmen had to endure only a verbal lashing and a spell in solitary

*Left:* By 1944, Waffen-SS troops were battle-hardened desperate men.
*Right:* Stalag Luft III, the camp from which RAF officers planned a daring breakout.

confinement if they were recaptured. They were treated to applause and cheers when they emerged to rejoin their comrades.

### ■ ESCAPE COMMITTEE ■

Stalag Luft III was constructed on sand. It wasn't long before enterprising airmen housed in the officers' compound desperate to escape to Britain and resume the battle against Hitler had dug a maze of different tunnels from inside the complex. The escape committee run by Senior British Officer, Wing Commander Harry 'Wings' Day, a veteran of the Great War was active if something of a shambles.

Only when South African Roger Bushell, an experienced escapee, took charge did the plans for The Great Escape take shape. He believed the best way to harry the Germans was to have scores of their internees turned loose at one time. To do it, he hit upon the idea of having three tunnels only for escaping purposes, nicknamed Tom, Dick and Harry. Work started in the summer of 1943 but was dramatically halted when the existence of Tom was discovered in October. It wasn't until January 1944 that work resumed. This time the

intention was to complete Harry as quickly as possible.

Its entrance in Hut 104 was disguised beneath a heating stove. Digging with usually nothing more than empty tins, a team of two men squeezed into a tiny shaft scooping away the sandy earth and propping up the extending tunnel with wooden supports taken from the prison bunk beds. Engineers among the prisoners designed and made a trolley running on wooden rails large enough to

> *The entrance to the tunnel in Hut 104 was disguised beneath a heating stove*

carry a man on which the diggers and their sand were eventually ferried. At first the operation was lit by fat-burning lamps. Later however, a supply of electricity was filched from the camp itself by means of some stolen cable. There was also an air pump made of a kit bag and piping constructed of old food tins which provided fresh oxygen to the tunnel while digging was in progress.

Beyond the designing and digging, there were teams of prisoners involved in scattering the dug-out sand. One technique was to fill two sausage-like containers with sand to wear down each trouser leg, releasing it slowly during a trudge around the campsite. The sand bags were the ingenious idea of another escape organiser, Captain Peter Fanshawe, taken prisoner during the Norwegian

> ## There were teams of prisoners involved in scattering dug-out sand during exercise

campaign. Nicknamed 'Hornblower' by his comrades, he was dispatched to another camp shortly before the breakout and so, to his immense disappointment, was unable to take part. Following liberation, he was later put in command of the sloop

Amethyst during the Korean War and died shortly before the commemoration of the 50th anniversary of the Great Escape in 1994, aged 82.

Those who made friends with camp guards elicited further tools and even cameras for forging the documents that would be needed outside the camp. Yet another group set to work making service suits look like civilians' garb using dye concocted of boot polish or ink.

### ■ 200 TO ESCAPE ■

More than 500 officers worked frantically on the project – although not everyone in the camp chose to get involved. Many thought the end of the war was imminent and considered that it would be foolhardy to risk lives at this belated stage. They had a point. The notion that the men were escaping to freedom was quite wrong. They were escaping from the camp into German territory from where it would be a long and dangerous haul home.

*Above:* RAF men held in Stalag Luft III enjoyed many privileges, thanks to the esteem of Göring.

Nevertheless, when the 330 ft tunnel was completed by 14 March there was no shortage of volunteers to go through it. Bushell selected the first 25 himself. The rest were drawn out of a hat. Astonishingly, guards noticed nothing as the 200 men converged silently on hut 104 before dusk when the doors were locked. Three men went down the tunnel to complete the last two feet of digging. With horror, when they finally pierced the crust of snowy, frozen ground above them, they discovered the tunnel fell 30ft short of the forest which would give them essential cover. It was in clear sight of the watchtowers and their guards. Quickly, the determined bunch devised a rope alarm system, in which a man in the forest would signal the all-clear to the next in line to escape by giving two tugs.

Below ground, things were not going well. The electric lights rigged up to aid the men in the tunnel cut out due to an air raid on Berlin. The troops of men sweeping through on the trolley caused landfalls which had

> **Disaster struck. A German soldier happened on the tunnel exit and raised the alarm**

to be repaired. In the end, it was decided only 80 men would escape that night before the tunnel had to be sealed. Then disaster struck. A German soldier accidentally happened on the tunnel exit and raised the alarm.

Those in the tunnel had to beat a hasty retreat, gorging their rations and burning their papers and money before being discovered. Seventy-six men who had made it to freedom had to scatter at speed. While they were mostly British, the number included some Canadians, Australians, New Zealanders, Poles, Czechs and Norwegians as well as one Lithuanian and one Greek. Although there was help and support given by Americans in the construction of the tunnels, all were moved to other camps before the date of the escape.

In the national alert that followed, most of the escapees were picked up almost immediately. With appalling weather conditions, anyone who remained on the loose soon suffered the effects of exposure. Only three made it to freedom, including Norwegian Jens Muller. He described being on the run in the Third Reich as 'just as exciting as the film [The Great Escape] but not in that wild cowboy fashion.'

Fifty officers were chosen by the local Gestapo for execution. With the exception of Bushell, the selection appears to have been made randomly. Bushell, the barrister and bon viveur, had been warned that if he broke out again he was a prime target for the Gestapo who were irritated by his escape artistry. His sadly ill-advised response was merely to say: 'I am not going to be caught.'

### ■ SHOT IN THE BACK ■

In groups of twos and threes, they were driven into a forest and shot in the back of the head after being invited to leave the car they were travelling in for a 'pinkelpause' or toilet break. Their bodies were cremated and the ashes taken back as an example to the men left in Stalag Luft III. There, news of the merciless killings was greeted with disbelief.

A poster went up in the camp stating: 'The escape from prison camps is no longer a sport!' It went on: 'Urgent warning is given against making future escapes! In plain English, stay in the camp where you will be safe! Breaking out of it is now

*Above:* Equipment needed by tunnel builders who burrowed their way through sandy soil beneath barbed wire fences.
*Left:* A trolley used to move sand then men sits in the entrance of Harry, the escape tunnel.

## ◆ EYE WITNESS ◆

**Alf Toombs was a German prisoner of war for five years after he survived the Normandy barn massacre of British troops shortly before Dunkirk.**

For the first two and a half years the treatment was really bad. After that we got Red Cross parcels. If it hadn't have been for them, many of us would not be alive today.

All we got was a cup of coffee in the morning. For lunch there was a loaf of brown bread between five of us. We had to take it in turns to have the small end of the loaf. We worked until 6pm when we were given soup, usually potato. Once we had conds' heads which was disgusting. The cooks were German and they didn't give them much to do.

The Poles were very good to us. Women took bits of bread and food to us while we worked. But when we got back we were searched so we had to be careful. '

a damned dangerous act. The chances of preserving your life are almost nil! All... guards have been given the strictest orders to shoot on sight all suspected persons.'

*Below:* **A diagram of the escape tunnel and its route out of the Stalag Luft III prison camp.**

### ■ SENSELESS MURDER

For many, it merely hardened the resolve to escape. Of the survivors of The Great Escape, at least two tunneled out of the next prison camp they were sent to and as punishment for that spent a soul-destroying five months in solitary confinement until the end of the war.

The feat of the men was immortalised on film in 'The Great Escape' made in 1963 with stars James Garner, Steve McQueen, Richard Attenborough, Donald Pleasance and James Coburn. A warm if glorified account of the breakout, it differed from fact because there were no Americans in the escape itself.

## *The feat of the men was immortalised in the film 'The Great Escape'*

However, throughout the Second World War there was no shortage of senseless killings like these which offended against all the common laws of humanity.

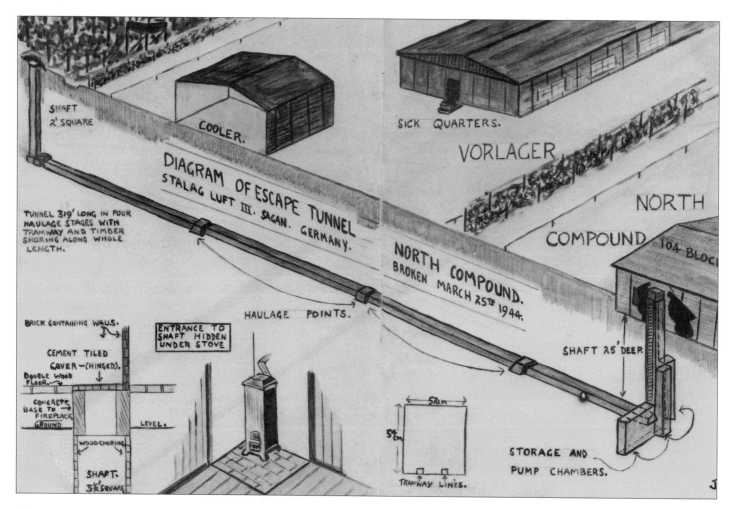

British servicemen once again bore the brunt in an appalling slaughter which took place as the Germans powered into Europe during the spring of 1940. After an unexpected period of calm following the declaration of war, British troops sent to France to bolster defences suddenly found themselves embroiled in a fast-moving conflict. Their only hope of escape was to reach Dunkirk from where a massive evacuation would take them to England.

It was those soldiers prepared to sacrifice their own chance of escaping to mount a rearguard action who were caught up in the bloodshed.

### ■ DUNKIRK ■

Men of the 2nd Royal Warwicks dug in at Wormhoudt, 12 miles southeast of Dunkirk, to confound the enemy. Little did they realise that they would encounter the 2nd Battalion of the crack SS-Liebstandarte, Hitler's favoured troops.

The British soldiers put up a brave resistance, claiming clutches of casualties including the commanding

> *British soldiers have testified that prisoners were shot in cold blood by the Germans*

officer of the army group in opposition, Schutzeck. Many German soldiers were already stoked up to fury by the continuing backlash from the British troops. When word of their commander's head injuries spread, the SS men became inflamed. In place of the injured commander came Wilhelm Mohnke.

British soldiers have since testified that prisoners of war, including those who were injured, were shot in cold-blood by the Germans as they advanced on the retreating enemy.

By 28 May, much of the organised resistance by the British had been knocked out, with only pockets of

*Below:* A poignant photographic memorial to 25 of the men shot after 'The Great Escape'. All these men were taken in twos and threes to a forest and shot in the back of the head.

```
26. Langford, P.W.
27. Leigh, T.B.
28. Long, J.L.
29. Mc Garr, C.A.
30. Mc Gill, G.E.
31. Marcinkus, R.
32. Milford, H.J.
33. Mondschein, J.T.
34. Pawluk, K.
35. Picard, H.A.
36. Pohe, P.P.
37. Scheidhauer, B.W.
38. Skanziklas, S.
39. Swain, C.D.
40. Stevens, R.
41. Stewart, R.C.
42. Stower, J.G.
43. Street, D.O.
44. Tobolski, P.
45. Valenta, E.
46. Walenn, G.W.
47. Wernham, J.C.
48. Wiley, G.W.
49. Williams, J.E.
50. Williams, J.F.
```

## ARMY JAIL

**Army jails, named 'glasshouses' because the first military prison at Aldershot had a glass roof, were notoriously barbaric.**

They were the destination of those evading military service by faking illness, men who overstayed their leave or were guilty of behaviour which was otherwise interpreted as 'malingering'. During the war a string of jails was established across Britain and across the world in the wake of the British advance.

During the week, inmates had to get up at 6am for a day of strenuous physical activity, deprived of all comforts including razors, knives, forks and plates and performing every task 'at the double'. Talking was often banned for hours on end, as was smoking. At weekends, men were often locked up for hours at a time. There were frequent accusations of beatings from sadistic prison guards although this was denied by the army.

Punishments for misdemeanours inside the jail included three days on bread and water and the withdrawal of bedding so that men were forced to sleep on bed springs.

men remaining to stem the tide of Germans. At Wormhoudt a posse of prisoners about 50-strong had been taken, not only from the 2nd Warwicks but also the Cheshires and the Royal Artillery.

Ominously, they were forced to hand over their dog-tags, personal papers and other identification before being marched through the town to the Germans' Battalion Battle Headquarters. As they trudged on, they spotted with horror the bodies of British soldiers by three burnt-out trucks. The corpses themselves were smouldering. One man saw 20 men lined up and shot by the Germans beside a town's building.

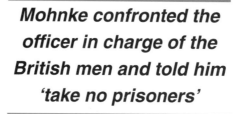

*Mohnke confronted the officer in charge of the British men and told him 'take no prisoners'*

A further 50 prisoners including men from the 8th Battalion of the Worcestershire Regiment and the 20th Anti-Tank Regiment joined their ranks at the HQ where Wilhelm Mohnke was now in charge. It is now believed that a raging Mohnke left the HQ, confronted the officer in charge of the British men and told him: 'Take no prisoners'.

The meaning of the order filtered through to a few of the British men,

*Left:* **Wilhelm Mohnke, the war crimes suspect, meets with his commanding officer Sepp Dietrich.**

who were scarcely able to comprehend what grim fate awaited them.

Now a new guard of higher ranking SS men marched with them over fields and in double time. The panting prisoners who fell by the wayside were beaten or bayonetted. Their destination was a wooden barn with a straw roof, about the size of a garage, mucky and airless.

Herded into the barn, four men found their way out through a back door and escaped. Still, there remained about 100 men inside under the eagle eye of the SS men gathered around the main entrance. As one British captain complained about the deplorable conditions the men were forced to endure, there came a taste of what was to come. The irate guard, weary of the Britisher's complaint, suddenly hurled a grenade into the crowd of men.

### ■ IN COLD BLOOD ■

Two men took their cue and tried to escape in the mayhem. One of them, the vocal captain, was shot dead soon afterwards as he tried to hide in a pond. A private with him was injured and left for dead.

Back at the barn, more grenades were thrown, killing and maiming the men as they exploded. The carnage stopped as suddenly as it had begun when the senior SS men decided on a different approach. They demanded five volunteers to step outside. After a brief hesitation, five brave men stepped forward.

They were marched outside, forced to turn their backs to a five-strong firing squad and shot in cold blood. A further five men marched off to meet the same grisly end. Just as the firing squad pulled the triggers, they turned around to look their executioners square in the eye.

Now the men in the barn were not only frightened but belligerent as well.

*Right:* US troops advance towards Malmedy, Belgium where 30 vehicles were ambushed and 140 men massacred.

As rain deluged down, the SS men stepped inside the barn and began shooting their prisoners by the score. Those who survived were pinned beneath the bodies of their dead comrades. Some died holding photographs of their loved ones, others reciting the Lord's Prayer. Bodies were piled high around the walls of the flimsy shack in which about 90 people had died. Survivors amounted to perhaps 20, some of whom were so badly wounded they would die of their injuries before receiving help.

## Some died holding photographs of their loved ones; others recited the Lord's Prayer

The SS men pulled out, content with the success of their operation. There was no help at hand. Some of the men, in groups or separately, tried to escape. They were to a man all picked up by the Germans although one managed to stay on the run for five months. Their luck had changed, however, and they were captured by patrols of the regular German army who treated them decently and accorded them their rights. When the appalling tale of their plight emerged, many German soldiers expressed their disgust.

The injured who were too ill to move were finally rescued by members of an Austrian Red Cross team. One badly wounded man, Richard Parry, recalled the moment of rescue. 'The one thing which stands out is that their handling of me was ever-so gentle. There were six or seven of us taken from the barn wounded but alive, thank God. I remember the great feeling of relief which came over me as I was placed in the ambulance. Inside the vehicle, I fell asleep.'

It wasn't the last wartime massacre to bear the mark of Wilhelm Mohnke. Four years later disarmed members of the Canadian invasion forces at his mercy were to be killed at his command.

On 8 June 1944, the Battle of Normandy was centred around Caen with Canadian forces making repeated attempts to take the city's environs. Striking back was the 2nd Battalion of the 26th Panzer Grenadier Regiment, Mohnke's regiment, who managed to take about 40 prisoners. The prisoners were marched towards the German lines, pushed into a field and then shot by their guards who were brandishing machine guns. Only five escaped by making a run for it.

The same SS group are believed to have murdered six more Canadians who were attending a first aid post. Their bodies were discovered when the area was finally taken by the Allies – they had suffered various wounds to the body and fatal gun shot injuries to the head.

There were other scattered examples of military terrorism in those frenzied days following the invasion in which Mohnke's men are implicated. Then Mohnke himself becomes a leading player in the killing of three more Canadians.

### ■ WILHELM MOHNKE ■

As Regimental Commander, he stalked out to interrogate the three prisoners who had been captured laying mines and taken to his headquarters at Forme du Bosq. Bellowing and snorting, Mohnke quizzed the men through an interpreter for some 20 minutes. At the end of the interrogation the prisoners were searched and stripped of all their identification.

Abruptly, the questioning ended and the men were marched across a meadow to a bomb crater. As they approached it, they were shot in the back at close range by an SS man – while Mohnke stood and watched.

*Left:* **Bodies of men, women and children await formal identification before burial after the massacre at Malmedy, Belgium.**

Mohnke was not alone in overseeing bloody murder following D-Day. Kurt Meyer, who commanded the 25th Panzer Grenadiers, dispatched his prisoners in much the same manner. His headquarters were in the Abbaye Ardenne, near Caen, where 11 Canadian prisoners were killed on 7 June 1944, seven were murdered on 8 June and two more died on 17 June.

According to witnesses, the Canadians killed on 8 June were fully aware of what was about to happen. From a place of interrogation in a stable, each man was summoned to his death by name. He shook hands with his comrades and bade them farewell before walking up the steps to the garden – where a German guard was waiting to put a bullet in the back of his head.

Others who died at the Abbaye were battered to death or cut down in a hail of bullets.

This was not the end of the story, either. Mohnke handed down an order given by Hitler himself, that during the Battle of the Bulge – Germany's last ditch effort against the Allies – soldiers were to fight with zeal and commitment and to do what it took to achieve victory.

Taken with regard to Mohnke's men and their unenviable past record, the results were not altogether surprising. There was spasmodic violence in the treatment

## Christmas 1944 was scarred by one of the worst German excesses of the war

of prisoners of war, this time from the American forces. Yet the German campaign at Christmas 1944 was scarred by one of the worst excesses of the war.

It occurred when an American convoy of 30 vehicles and about 140 men was ambushed at the town of Malmedy on 17 December. Overwhelmed by Germans, a substantial number of Americans surrendered.

After being searched, the men were lined up in eight rows in a nearby field with their hands held above their heads. There were some 120 men in the field when two armoured vehicles pulled out of the German columns to take aim at the unarmed prisoners. A pistol shot claimed the first victim. Then the machine guns on the vehicles burst into life, killing many before they could even raise their voices in protest.

The bodies collapsed in a heap, some dead already, others dying and still more feigning death in the hope they would escape. Blood oozed from the bodies on to the frosted ground, soaking those still alive who could feel the life ebb from their comrades.

### ■ EYES BAYONETTED ■

Their agony was far from finished, however. For when the armoured cars moved on, others passing by opened up with a rattle of gunfire at the human debris in the field.

Men began strolling among the bodies, kicking them over and shooting where they saw signs of life. All the time they were laughing hysterically. In common with the other massacres carried out by Mohnke's SS-Liebstandarte men, the perpetrators of the killings were wild-eyed and cackling as if they had been drinking or taking drugs.

Some victims were battered to death. Others had their eyes bayonetted while they were still breathing.

When the coast was clear, the living rose from the dead. About 20 survived. But fortune was not on their side because they were spotted staggering to a nearby cafe by the German rear guards. The Germans set the building ablaze – and fired on the Americans as they dashed out to escape the flames.

Amazingly, 43 Americans survived the Malmedy massacre while an estimated 86 perished. And the rampaging Germans continued to shoot US soldiers and Belgian civilians as they tried to break through to Antwerp and the Belgian coast.

Colonel Jochen Peiper was in charge of the unit which had so savagely murdered that day.

After the war a military tribunal heard from German Corporal Ernst Kohler about the scope of the operation. 'We were told to remember the women and children of Germany killed in Allied air attacks and to take no prisoners nor to show mercy to Belgian civilians.'

Peiper was sentenced to hang among others deemed responsible for the bloodshed. The case, however, caused disquiet because there was evidence that confessions were beaten out of some of the SS prisoners by vengeful American officers and men.

### ■ TRIGGER-HAPPY ■

And a question mark hung over the fairness of the trial in view of the lack of action taken against US soldiers who committed a similar atrocity in shooting unarmed prisoners of war as they made they way up Italy. Indeed, there is ample evidence to suggest that Allied soldiers were criminally trigger-happy following D-day. The spoils of victory apparently stretched to immunity from prosecution. Peiper was finally sentenced to 35 years in jail and was released after 11 years.

Mohnke, the man who linked the massacres of Wormhoudt in 1940 and those of Canadian soldiers in 1944, was also alleged to have handed specific orders requiring a

barbarous response to prisoners down to Peiper before his thrust through Malmedy.

He fell into Russian hands at the end of the war and served 10 years in a Soviet jail. Afterwards, he returned to Germany and lived in Hamburg. He has never been brought to court to face charges on account of the deaths of the Allied prisoners.

Authors Ian Sayer and Douglas Botting compiled a detailed dossier about Mohnke called 'Hitler's Last General'. It outlines the disgraceful

---

## The disappearance of 15,000 Poles in Russia remained a mystery for 50 years

---

massacres linked with Mohnke, finding proof against the general in the words of men who were there. They maintain: 'It shows beyond all reasonable doubt that a prima facie case exists against Wilhelm Mohnke on a number of counts; and it urges that the American, Canadian, British and Belgian governments should take action now or prevail upon the West German authorities to pursue the case with the utmost vigour in order that justice might take its proper course before it is too late.'

The disappearance of some 15,000 Polish officers in Russia after the division of their homeland remained a mystery for almost 50 years until secret files revealed the grim truth. The men had been liquidated on Stalin's order by his secret police, the NKVD. Their unmarked resting place was Katyn Wood.

*Right:* Jochen Peiper photographed in 1943. He was to serve 11 years in prison for his part in the Malmedy massacre.

Each man was killed by a single shot in the nape of the neck. It took from 3 April to 13 May to transport the men from three different camps and complete the grisly task.

### ■ KATYN WOOD ■

Their bodies fell into sandy pits alongside those of their companions. It wasn't until 1943 that the mass graves were uncovered by German soldiers. The shocking story appeared to have all the hallmarks of a German propaganda coup. Instantly, Stalin's regime counterclaimed that Nazis were responsible.

In 1990 the truth was revealed when a box containing NKVD files was handed by the Russians to Poland. It detailed the actions of the violent men who ran the secret police, the forerunner of the KGB,

and revealed they themselves had fallen victim to Stalin's ruthlessness and were later killed. While the shroud of mystery had at last been lifted, nothing could erase the grief of the families whose young men were killed so meaninglessly.

### ■ LIDICE ■

Atrocities in wartime were not confined to fighting men. Civilians in the occupied territories saw many unspeakable horrors, like the ill-fated residents of Lidice. The village outside Prague may have had its fair share of those keen to see the Nazis thrown out of their land and a return to independence. Every village in

*Below*: At a war crimes trial in 1946, a Malmedy survivor identifies the man who fired the first shot of the massacre.

### ◆ EYE WITNESS ◆

**Chester Wilmot reported the words of an anonymous Frenchman on the BBC in April 1945 which revealed another German atrocity carried out against slave labourers travelling by train away from the Allies.**

On Sunday evening the train stopped in the yard at Celle while the engine filled up with water and coal. Our carriages were left standing between an ammunition train and a petrol train and we hadn't been there long when some Allied bombers came over. We heard them coming and we tried to get out of the train, but as we jumped down on to the tracks the SS guard opened fire on us with machine guns. Then the bombs began to fall and they hit the train. The ammunition and petrol began to explode. Many must have been killed. But those who survived tried to get away from the fire and explosions. Some of us reached shelter but most of the rest were shot down by the SS guards. After it was all over, there were only 200 left out of the 4,500 and we 200 were rounded up by the SS and herded into a stable – a filthy stable, and there we lay on straw that barely covered the manure underneath. Many of us were wounded or burnt but they left us there for four days without medical attention, food or water. We were rescued only when the British came.

Czechoslavakia, taken by Hitler by force in 1938, had the same. It was no more of a thorn in the side of the German rulers than any other.

Yet on 10 June 1942 it was surrounded by German security police prepared to carry out a massacre. All

*Lidice was surrounded by German security police prepared to carry out a massacre*

the men and boys of Lidice and a neighbouring village Lezaky, amounting to 199, were shot dead. Their wives were shipped off to Ravensbruck conentration camp and 90 children were dispatched to other camps around the Reich. The entire village was then burned to the ground. Its name was even erased from German maps. In addition, there were the usual round-ups in reprisal, bring-

> ## The atrocity was carried out as a reprisal for the assassination of Reinhard Heydrich

ing the total dead to some 2,000. The village of Lidice was paying dearly for the death of one German. Reinhard Heydrich, one of the arch exponents of the Final Solution, died on 4 June from injuries he received when his car was blown up.

### ■ BUTCHER ■

Heydrich, the Governor of Bohemia, was a particularly loathsome Nazi who had well earned his nickname of 'the Butcher of Moravia'. From the velocity of the revenge thought up by Himmler, one might have thought the killers were from Lidice or were in hiding there.

In fact, the assassins were two members of the Free Czech movement, Joseph Gabcik and Jan Kubis, native Czechs who joined the French Foreign Legion and the 1st Czech Brigade in Britain. They had trained for their mission in Britain, were in the pay of the British army

*Right:* **Weeping Polish wives and mothers flock to identify the bodies of their loved ones cut down in Katyn Wood by Stalin's secret police.**

and were parachuted onto their home territory from an RAF plane.

After tossing a bomb in Heydrich's car on 27 May, they sought sanctuary in a church but were eventually killed following a gun battle. The name of Lidice was found in the papers of a third Free Czech agent, unrelated to the pair who carried out the killing. The razing of Lidice was nothing more than a crude kick-back

by the Germans to repay the death of one of their own.

### ■ ORADOUR ■

One of the best remembered civilian slaughters of the war took place at Oradour-sur-Glane, near Limoges, in south-west France. One summer's afternoon in June 1944 the streets of this quiet village ran red with the blood of its inhabitants.

## ◆ EYE WITNESS ◆

**Stanislaw Mikolajczyk, successor to Sikorski as leader of the Polish government in exile, recalled how a Soviet bureaucrat explained the Katyn Wood massacre. It happened following rumours that the Polish officers would join the Red Army.**

'Senior commanders were aware of such talk but had nothing specific to go on. The staff officer was sent to get Stalin's clarification. The staff officer saw Stalin and briefly explained the problem. Stalin listened patiently. When the staff officer finished, Stalin supplied him with a written order. Such orders were common, often requested by subordinates as a matter of self-protection. In this case, said the informant, Josef Stalin took a sheet of his personal stationery and wrote only one dreadful word on it: 'Liquidate'. The staff officer returned the one-word order to his superiors but they were uncertain what it meant. Did Stalin mean to liquidate the camps (housing the officers) or to liquidate the men? He might have meant that the men should be released, sent to other prisons or to work in the Gulag system. He might also have meant that the men should be shot or otherwise eliminated. No one knew for sure what the order meant but no one wanted to risk Stalin's ire by asking him to clarify it. To delay a decision was also risky and could invite retribution. The army took the safe way out and turned the whole matter over to the NKVD. For the NKVD, there was no ambiguity in Stalin's order. It could only mean one thing: that the Poles were to be executed immediately.'

Every one of the village's 254 buildings was reduced to rubble as the population looked on aghast. More than 200 men were locked into a barn and cut down in a hail of bullets. Women and children were herded into the church and the doors were locked behind them. Then explosives rained down into the building, all thoughts of its traditional use as a sanctuary forgotten by the bloodthirsty killers.

If the 450 women and children were not dead from suffocation through the choking smoke, they

*Below*: **It is thought that NKVD men murdered these Polish officers at Katyn Wood rather than query an ambiguous order from Josef Stalin.**

were killed by grenades thrown through the blasted windows. To ensure the massacre was done thoroughly, however, the doors were finally opened and bullets from a machine gun were pumped inside. Anyone who tried to run or was too sick or old to leave their home was mercilessly shot.

Today Oradour looks exactly the same as it did at the moment when the murdering German troops pulled out. Although the smell of fear, death and spent explosives has long since faded, the walls of the wrecked church are still scorched and the doctor's car remains in the street in the same spot it was when he was pulled from its seat and taken away for execution. Visitors come to pay homage to those 642 innocent people who died and wonder at the barbarity of those responsible.

Indeed, the reason behind this most brutal of repressions has perplexed and intrigued observers of

*Above*: **The funeral of Reinhard Heydrich. His death led to the razing of the Czech village of Lidice.**

## Today Oradour looks exactly the same as it did when the murdering German troops left

subsequent generations. For years it was believed the action was carried out as a reprisal following the deaths of three German soldiers at the hands of the French resistance.

However, another explanation has come to light which better explains the severity of the massacre.

A truck allegedly containing plundered loot intended to line the pockets of three SS commanders was attacked by the resistance on its way to being hidden in the Loire valley. Only

one German soldier who fled with his clothes aflame escaped the ambush. And the return of fire killed five out of six of the French attackers. The remaining member of the Maquis could hardly believe his eyes when he cautiously probed the back of the truck and discovered it packed with gold.

Known only as 'Raoul', the wide-eyed peasant hurriedly buried the boxes of treasure at the roadside before himself fleeing. When the three German officers heard about the ambush and the subsequent loss of their booty, they were furious. Recent intelligence pinpointed Oradour as a centre of the resistance. General Heinz Lammerding and his cohort Major Otto Dickmann decided here would be a good place to start their search for the missing gold. In addition, the third member of their conspiracy Helmut Kampfe had co-

incidentally been taken prisoner by the resistance. His prospects for survival were not good.

Consequently, Lammerding sent troops from the Waffen SS under the command of hardline Nazi Captain Kahn into Oradour to extract from its residents the whereabouts of the gold. When they professed ignorance, Kahn simply shot them.

### ■ SHOCKING TALE ■

The shocking tale of what happened at Oradour-sur-Glane only emerged much later when an entrepreneur called Robin Mackess met the mysterious and still unidentified Raoul long after the war during some dubious business transactions. Mackess was unable to prove conclusively the validity of Raoul's story when he was arrested for customs irregularities and jailed for 21 months. But in his book 'Oradour – Massacre and Aftermath' he outlines his amazing theories for the appalling events that took place.

# DEATH RAILWAY

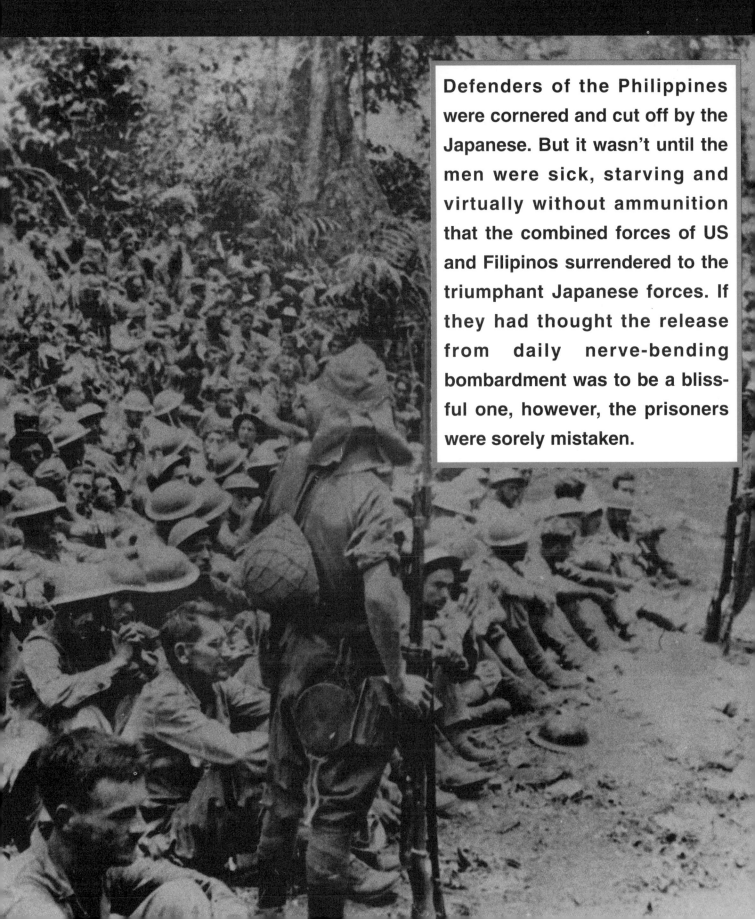

Defenders of the Philippines were cornered and cut off by the Japanese. But it wasn't until the men were sick, starving and virtually without ammunition that the combined forces of US and Filipinos surrendered to the triumphant Japanese forces. If they had thought the release from daily nerve-bending bombardment was to be a blissful one, however, the prisoners were sorely mistaken.

Immediately, the captured forces of 12,000 Americans and 63,000 Filipinos were compelled to embark on a 60-mile trek to a prison camp. Heat, hunger, thirst and barbaric treatment from the Japanese guard soon won the gruelling expedition a new title, that of 'Death March'.

Up to 10,000 died as they made their way along the jungle track, victims who were already dangerously weak from the deprivations of fighting on the island peninsula for so long.

Afterwards, men told how they were pushed past cool streams and plentiful wells even though they were parched. Sadistic guards would club men who stumbled. Little or no food was handed out to men who became faint with desperate hunger. Many who fell by the wayside were summarily shot.

US Air Corps pilot William Dyess was among the prisoners. His account of the march, published in 1944, gave an insight into the sufferings endured.

### ■ STARVATION ■

'I heard a cry, followed by thudding blows at one side of the paddy. An American soldier so tortured by thirst that he could not sleep had asked a Jap guard for water. The Jap fell on him with his fists then slugged him into insensibility with a rifle butt...

'...Troop-laden trucks sped past us. A grimacing Jap leaned far out, holding his rifle by the barrel. As the truck roared by he knocked an American soldier senseless with the gun's stock. From now on we kept out of reach if we could...'

Following a day without food, the prisoners came to a camp where they found bubbling cauldrons of rice and hot sausages.

'They ordered us out of the patio and lined us up in a field across the road. As we left, grinning Japs held up steaming ladles of sausages and rice. The officer followed us to the field then began stamping up and down, spouting denunciations and abuse. When he calmed enough to be understood we heard this:

> ## 'When you came here you were told you would eat and be let to sleep. Now that is changed'

'"When you came here you were told you would eat and be let to sleep. Now that is changed. We have found pistols concealed among three American officers. In punishment for these offences you will not be given food. You will march to Orani [five miles to the north] before you sleep."

### ■ MENTAL TORTURE ■

'The accusation was a lie. If a pistol had been found, the owner would have been shot, beaten to death or beheaded on the spot. Besides, we knew that the searchers hadn't overlooked even a toothbrush, to say nothing of a pistol. The Japs simply were adding mental torture to the physical.'

Not all the men on the march received the same treatment. Some arrived in poor physical shape at the other end following their exertions but were nevertheless unaware that brutalities had taken place en route.

*Left and below*: Two scenes from 'The Death March' from Bataan which claimed the lives of 10,000 men.

*Above:* **Mean Japanese guards staged a picture of a lavish prison camp Christmas dinner before removing the food from the hungry men.**

Some men even rode in trucks. For those still able to summon up the energy, there was ample opportunity for escape. Yet the death toll was a shocking one.

### ■ CAMP O'DONNELL ■

Those that did arrive at the destination – Camp O'Donnell – had further nightmares to counter. Four out of ten men inside the primitive camp died of disease, starvation or cruel treatment during the first three months of their stay.

There is evidence that the Death March won its inglorious name thanks to the actions of a few barbaric guards, that the orders from Lt General Homma, now in charge of the Philippines, were to treat the prisoners humanely, to supply food, water and medicines along the way.

Yet the cruelty and viciousness of the guards were symptomatic of the treatment dished out to US, Australian, Canadian, British, New Zealand and Dutch prisoners of war all over the Japanese empire.

The range of obscene abuses which were time and again revealed to prisoners stemmed from their culture which viewed fighting men who surrendered as dishonourable. For them, truly brave men would die in battle rather than lay down their arms to the enemy. Consequently, few Japanese soldiers were ever taken prisoner and those that were often tried to commit suicide.

Japan was a signatory of the Hague Convention of 1907 which decreed that prisoners of war must be treated humanely. Alas, the convention went on to rule that prisoners should be treated similarly to the men in the army of the state which

> **The Japanese were brutal even to their own men, and prisoners got even worse treatment**

held them. The military regime in Japan was brutal even to its own men. Captains frequently lashed out at sergeants who in turn would bash rank and file soldiers. There was to be little respite for the unfortunate men who fell into the clutches of the forces of the Rising Sun.

Red Cross officials were hindered and hampered in their attempts to observe what was happening in the Japanese-run prisoner of war camps. Despite enormous efforts, they were blocked by a deluge of red tape. When Red Cross officials did gain entry to camps, they were closely

*One Red Cross delegate was executed after being charged with conspiracy against the Japanese*

chaperoned, their access to prisoners severely restricted and their questions stonewalled. One Red Cross delegate was himself executed after being charged with conspiracy against the Japanese government. Few, if any, parcels of aid were received by the men in the camps.

*Below:* Though General Homma, the victor in the Philippines, was thought 'too soft' by Japanese High Command, he was still condemned by a war crimes trial.

## ◆ EYE WITNESS ◆

**Ken Gray, of the Australian 8th Division, was one of the few to survive an epidemic of cholera when he was a 22-year-old Japanese prisoner of war in the Far East.**

❝ I finished up in a camp called Sonquari. The number of deaths that occurred in that camp during the height of the cholera far outweighed deaths that occurred in others. There were no medical supplies. On one day alone 38 men died.

I saw a doctor on one occasion weep over the body of a dead Allied soldier, saying he could have saved the man with a sixpenny packet of Epsom Salts.

One of my mates was about the first to die from cholera. Within 36 hours he had gone from a man weighing perhaps 10 stones to five stones. The normal body fluids ran out of him from the bowels and the mouth. His body just shrivelled up. Unless cholera is arrested in three to four hours, that is the end.

I was delirious for seven days. Apparently I was given a saline solution in a home-made injection kit which saved me.

The survivors were not strong men, they were lucky men. Those far more robust than I went down like ninepins. I feel the public today cannot possibly comprehend how shocking conditions were. ❞

## ■ TORTURE ■

The worst treatment was meted out to Allied airmen who were kept blindfolded and bound until they were tortured, usually until they died.

It has left the names of Japanese prisons including Rangoon Central Gaol in Burma, Changi and Selerang Barracks in Singapore, Padang on Sumatra, Kuching in Borneo, Karenko in Formosa and Mukden in Manchuria haunting the annals of wartime horror. Perhaps the most appalling memories among survivors are those evoked by the building of the Burma-Siam railway.

**Above: Changi jail, 'home' for thousands of British and Australian servicemen following the fall of Singapore.**

Japan was looking for a means of transporting supplies to its posts in southern Burma other than the sea route which was subject to attack by the Allies. Only when this route was complete could the Japanese consider extending their imperial tentacles into India.

On 14 May 1942 a 3,000 strong force left the confines of Changi prison to begin work on the massive project. Before the main building force left Changi, however, the camp commander Major General Fukuye insisted that all prisoners sign the following statement. It read: 'I, the

## Japan was looking for a means of transporting supplies to its posts in southern Burma

undersigned, hereby solemnly swear on my honour that I will not under any circumstances attempt escape.'

British troops under the authority of Lt Colonel E. B. Holmes and Australians under Lt Colonel 'Black-jack' Galleghan flatly refused to make the undertaking.

Outraged, Fukuye ordered the men from Changi into Selarang Barracks, cut their meagre rations to a third and allowed the 15,000 men to get water from just two taps. It meant endless hours of queuing in the heat of the day. The overcrowded conditions were a sure indicator that disease epidemics would follow.

The Japanese commander was finally convinced to make his request for prisoners to sign an outright order. Leaders of the prisoners decided this meant the men could sign the document but were not obliged by it.

There was little to inspire the men to escape. Deep in Japanese territory, they could not rely on local assistance nor, with their Western appearance, could they disappear into a crowd. The penalty for escape bids was death.

Four men who had slipped away from an island working party were brought to Changi in order that senior Allied commanders could witness the executions. Two of the men were British, two Australians. The older of the two Australians pleaded for the life of his young accomplice, maintaining he had only been obeying orders. It was to no avail.

### ■ FIRING SQUAD ■

All four came before a firing squad manned by Sikhs who had joined the Japanese. Their aim was awry and round upon round had to be let off before the bullets found their targets. The courageous older Australian, Corporal R. Breavington – who had refused to be blindfolded – finally bellowed: 'For God's sake, shoot me through the head and kill me.' It was a deeply scarring experience for those forced to watch.

Four more Australians who later attempted to escape from Burma were killed in the same grotesque way. The brigadier who witnessed their executions wrote in his diary: 'They spoke cheerio and good luck messages to one another and never showed any sign of fear. A truly courageous end.'

## JAPAN

**When Japan attacked Pearl Harbor, there were about 126,000 people of Japanese ancestry living in the US, about 93,000 of whom were resident in California.**

Those born in America were called Nisei while those born abroad were known as Issei. Roosevelt authorised the removal of 112,000 Japanese Americans to so-called relocation centres which, with armed guards, barrack huts and barbed wire, were little more than prison camps. The first people to be released from them did not return to freedom until 1944 by which time most had lost homes and jobs. Later, Justice Frank Murphy called it: 'One of the most sweeping and complete deprivations of constitutional rights in the history of this nation in the absence of martial law'.

### The courageous Australian bellowed: 'For God's sake shoot me through the head'

The nightmare of those sent to build the railway began almost immediately. Travelling to the site was deeply unpleasant. For example, the men who first left Changi were crammed into the hold of two rusty tubs for 12 days during which time the only food given to them was rice. Dysentery was rife and rats had the monopoly on the floor space and the health of the men plummeted.

#### ■ SLAVE LABOUR ■

Still, when they arrived they were put to work as slaves of the Nippon empire. The Japanese, eager to complete the ambitious task and armed with strict schedules and quotas, brought in more and more prisoners to speed up the rate of progress. Suddenly, life in the harsh prison camps seemed positively bearable set against the appalling conditions which faced men in the camps along the railway. Each new batch of men was horrified at the sight of those who had been working there for weeks or months before.

Malaria, dysentery, infestations, biting bugs and all manner of other jungle afflictions plagued the working men. Eventually, when monsoon rains had turned camps into mires, the dreaded cholera spread, shrinking men's bodies through painful dehydration.

As their clothing deteriorated, men were reduced to wearing only under-pants or home-made loin cloths, battered hats and often no footwear at all. At night there were few mosquito nets available, exposing the

men to all the dangers of the tropics. Often, they had little more than a blanket or rice sack with which to cover themselves.

As previously, the lack of proper nutrition brought its own miseries for the men who had to battle with problems brought about by vitamin and calorie deficiencies. Every day, the toil made huge demands on the

*Below:* **Two bridges built over the River Kwai with the sweat and blood of Allied prisoners of war.**

# ◆ THE JAPANESE IN BURMA

The Japanese invasion of Burma began in mid-December 1941 in the south of the country. General Iida's Southern Army seized the region's airfields and began bombing Rangoon. On 20 January 1942, the main ground assault began from the direction of Raheng. The Allies struggled to hold back the tide but on 8 March Rangoon fell. The British and Empire forces, reinforced by Chinese troops, then carried out a fighting withdrawal to India.

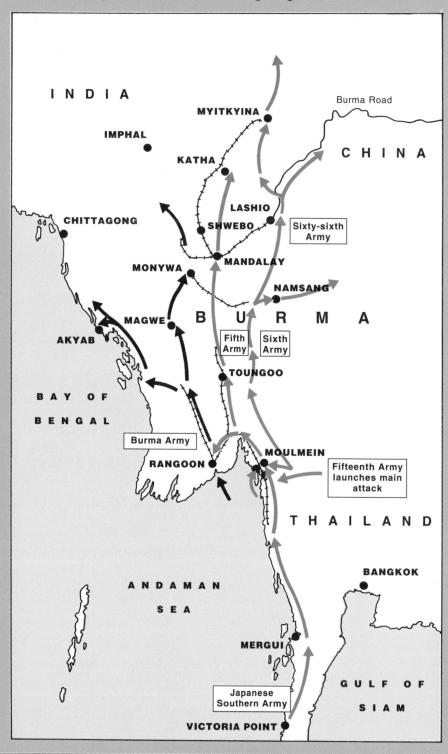

men's bodies which grew ever more emaciated and unfit for work.

Work began at both ends of the railway and the parties were to join up in the middle. It entailed clearing vast tracts of jungle, felling giant trees and constructing cuttings. The tools they had were primitive and all the clearance of rocks and stones had to be done by hand. Men worked by day and night, when their labours were lit by bamboo fires. Even the elephants brought in to assist in the heavy work lost their health.

There were stories of extreme mental torture as well as physical hardship. Sometimes the guards threw rocks and boulders at the men working below. Others forced individual prisoners to push mighty

## *Men worked by day and night in the light of bamboo fires; even the elephants fell ill*

rocks up a steep gradient. It would take every ounce of the victim's strength to stop the rock from crushing him and others below. Those who perished by plunging down the forested ravines or being crushed by rock falls were considered by their comrades to be the lucky ones.

In total, more than 60,000 Allied prisoners were used on the project alongside 270,000 forced labourers from China, Malaya, Thailand, Burma and India. These conscripted civilians enjoyed even fewer comforts than the prisoners with no medical facilities at hand and less concept of hygiene and discipline.

It was undoubtedly the commitment and enterprise of the medical men which saved many Allied lives. One such hero was Lt Colonel

*Right:* Printed leaflet dropped by B-29s on 28 August 1945 into POW camps in Japan, Taiwan, Sumatra and Malaya. The drop killed three and seriously injured two.

Edward 'Weary' Dunlop. His dedication to the survival of his fellow men never wavered nor did his courage in the face of the tyrannical Japanese. The plucky Australian wrote in his secret diary: 'I pledged myself to face them unflinchingly.'

### ■ WHIRLING SWORD ■

Dunlop was in Java before he and his men were moved to work on the railway. During his time in captivity he leapt between a Japanese soldier charging with a bayonet and one of his crippled patients; stood almost unblinking while an enraged Japanese commander whirled a sword around his head; defied Japanese orders to force patients into work and carried one of his men like a baby across to a sadistic commander, pronouncing: 'This man can't walk, Nippon.'

He kept a radio set, an offence punishable by death in Japanese eyes.

*Dunlop was chained to a tree trunk; four men fixed their bayonets and prepared to charge*

In the absence of the necessary evidence, an officer screamed at him: 'We know all about you and your set. You will be executed but first you will talk.'

When he refused to co-operate, Dunlop was chained to a tree trunk and four men with bayonets fixed prepared with the customary screeches and yells to charge.

'Have you a message for relatives? I will convey,' barked the officer.

'Conveyed by a thug like you? No, thanks,' said Dunlop. Only after several hours was he cut loose.

Dunlop devised a system to treat men dying of cholera. The steam from water boiled in petrol cans was funnelled through a lorry feed pipe and mixed with rock salt. The saline solution was then stored, filtered through cotton wool, fed into bamboo pipes and into a syringe. It helped to save countless Australian lives.

Afterwards, Dunlop, who died in 1993, said: 'I can say that the Australians outworked and outsuffered any nationality on that accursed river [Kwai]. I hardly ever saw a man refuse to go out in another's place or a man's spirit break until the time came to turn his face to the wall.'

Work was for the most part completed by September 1943 when the two ends met near Three Pagodas

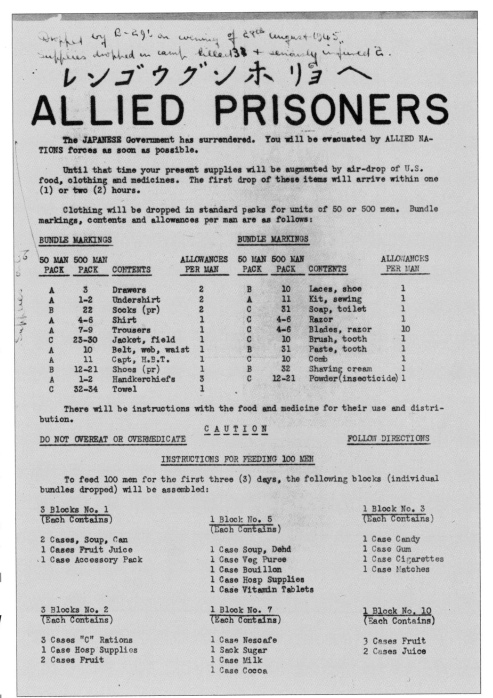

*Dropped by B-29's on evening of 28th August 1945. Supplies dropped in camp killed 3 & seriously injured 2.*

# レンゴウグンホリョヘ
# ALLIED PRISONERS

The JAPANESE Government has surrendered. You will be evacuated by ALLIED NATIONS forces as soon as possible.

Until that time your present supplies will be augmented by air-drop of U.S. food, clothing and medicines. The first drop of these items will arrive within one (1) or two (2) hours.

Clothing will be dropped in standard packs for units of 50 or 500 men. Bundle markings, contents and allowances per man are as follows:

BUNDLE MARKINGS

BUNDLE MARKINGS

| 50 MAN PACK | 500 MAN PACK | CONTENTS | ALLOWANCES PER MAN | 50 MAN PACK | 500 MAN PACK | CONTENTS | ALLOWANCES PER MAN |
|---|---|---|---|---|---|---|---|
| A | 3 | Drawers | 2 | B | 10 | Laces, shoe | 1 |
| A | 1-2 | Undershirt | 2 | A | 11 | Kit, sewing | 1 |
| B | 22 | Socks (pr) | 2 | C | 31 | Soap, toilet | 1 |
| A | 4-6 | Shirt | 1 | C | 4-6 | Razor | 1 |
| A | 7-9 | Trousers | 1 | C | 4-6 | Blades, razor | 10 |
| C | 23-30 | Jacket, field | 1 | C | 10 | Brush, tooth | 1 |
| A | 10 | Belt, web, waist | 1 | B | 31 | Paste, tooth | 1 |
| A | 11 | Capt, H.B.T. | 1 | C | 10 | Comb | 1 |
| B | 12-21 | Shoes (pr) | 1 | B | 32 | Shaving cream | 1 |
| A | 1-2 | Handkerchiefs | 3 | C | 12-21 | Powder(insecticide) | 1 |
| C | 32-34 | Towel | 1 | | | | |

There will be instructions with the food and medicine for their use and distribution.

### C A U T I O N

DO NOT OVEREAT OR OVERMEDICATE                     FOLLOW DIRECTIONS

INSTRUCTIONS FOR FEEDING 100 MEN

To feed 100 men for the first three (3) days, the following blocks (individual bundles dropped) will be assembled:

3 Blocks No. 1
(Each Contains)

2 Cases, Soup, Can
1 Cases Fruit Juice
1 Case Accessory Pack

3 Blocks No. 2
(Each Contains)

3 Cases "C" Rations
1 Case Hosp Supplies
2 Cases Fruit

1 Block No. 5
(Each Contains)

1 Case Soup, Dehd
1 Case Veg Puree
1 Case Bouillon
1 Case Hosp Supplies
1 Case Vitamin Tablets

1 Block No. 7
(Each Contains)

1 Case Nescafe
1 Sack Sugar
1 Case Milk
1 Case Cocoa

1 Block No. 3
(Each Contains)

1 Case Candy
1 Case Gum
1 Case Cigarettes
1 Case Matches

1 Block No. 10
(Each Contains)

3 Cases Fruit
2 Cases Juice

Pass. The railway was peppered with graves of men who died as they worked. An estimated 12,000 British, American, Australian and Dutch men died. In addition, 70,000 of the Asian labourers perished.

### ■ DIET OF RATS ■

Life had not improved much in the camps during this period. Officers were tortured in order that the Japanese might elicit military information. Hospitals were periodically cleared so that the ailing patients could join work parties. Food was reduced to snails, rats and snakes as the tide of war turned against Japan and supplies were sunk at sea.

*Scores of prisoners were shot, stabbed or died from exhaustion during the forced marches*

In Borneo there were a series of forced marches inflicted on the captive Allies as the liberating forces

*Above:* In the Japanese prisoner of war camps, men had to queue in the heat of the sun to collect their meagre rations. This is the officers' mess at Kanburi.

closed in. This claimed the lives of scores of prisoners who were shot, stabbed or died from exhaustion en route. Prisoners installed after just such a march at the Ranau camp were subsequently massacred in August 1945 before the arrival of Australian forces. Only six Australians who escaped on the march or from Ranau itself survived.

It wasn't only captured troops who suffered at the hands of the Japanese. There were an assortment of Dutch women who had been residents of the invaded Dutch East Indies, Australian nurses and British women snared in Singapore and an assortment of Western children and other refugees. They, too, were victims of forced marches, food shortages and disease.

The Japanese showed their disregard for the fairer sex when 22 nurses were washed up on an island beach after their boat was sunk off Singapore. All the surviving ship's crew were bayonetted and the nurses were herded into the sea where a machine gun was turned on them. Just one survived.

In 1994, Prince Mikasa, brother of the Emperor Hirohito and a cavalry officer in China in 1943 and 1944 admitted Japanese responsibility for war crimes. Besides talking of atrocities committed on the battlefield, he also spoke of an incident in 1931. That year a team of investigators from the League of Nations led by

◆ **EYE WITNESS** ◆

**English-born Dickson Smith, who emigrated to Western Australia, recalls some of the horrors of being a captive of the Japanese.**

“The main thing about the tropics is the insects and small animal life. There are barking lizards, croaking bull frogs, red ants, black ants, flying ants, dragonflies measuring four inches across the wings, wasps, hornets and cockroaches. in addition there are mosquitoes, some big and black, others white, and bugs which latch onto your skin. I kept wondering what my family was doing at home. Each month of the war seemed like an eternity. News from the outside world was sadly lacking and we felt totally isolated. I came to realise it was probably the most eventful period of my life, an adventure without pleasure filled with new and unimagined horrors and the terrible uncertainty of when it would all end. ”

the Earl of Lytton had visited Japan to analyse who was to blame for the start of the Sino-Japanese conflict. There was apparently an attempt to poison them. The Prince claimed that 'fruit laced with cholera germs' had been administered to the high-ranking officials in their food although none of them died.

The bitterness felt towards Japanese camp guards by those who came home is still very much in evidence on four continents, even today.

*The bitterness felt towards Japanese camp guards is still very much in evidence, even today*

**Left:** When they were released, PoWs were shadows of their former selves. Years of deprivation took their toll on previously strong, healthy men.

# JUSTICE AT NUREMBERG

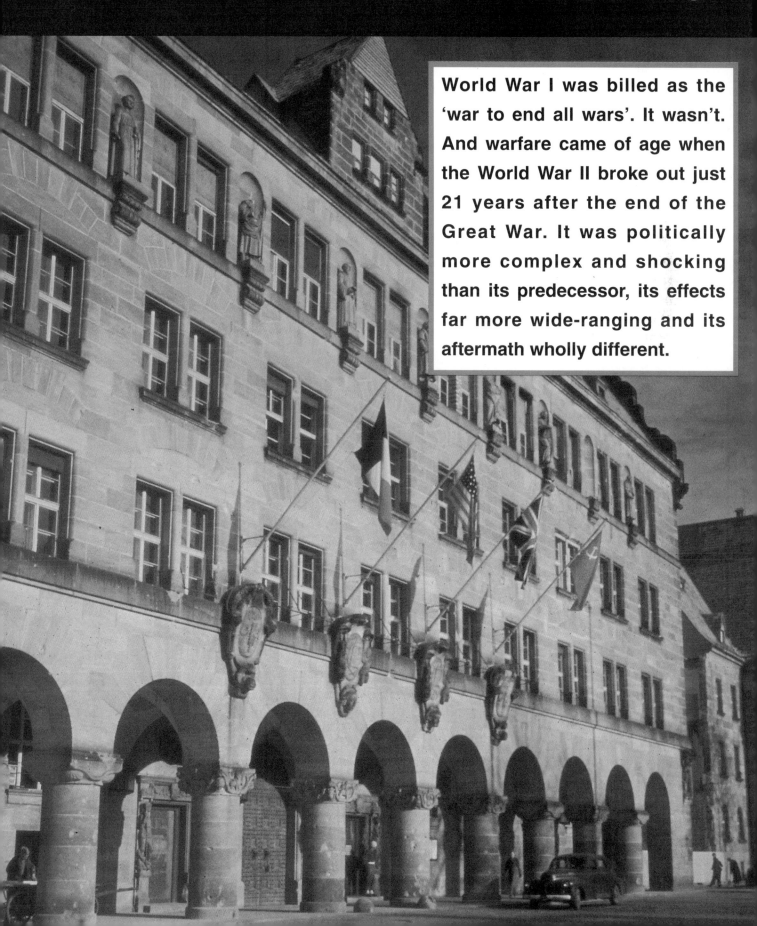

World War I was billed as the 'war to end all wars'. It wasn't. And warfare came of age when the World War II broke out just 21 years after the end of the Great War. It was politically more complex and shocking than its predecessor, its effects far more wide-ranging and its aftermath wholly different.

For the victors there was the dilemma of how to lay the foundation for tomorrow's world and build a lasting peace. More immediately, in their custody were some of the architects of Hitler's Third Reich. What would be their fate now?

Some believed that with Hitler, Himmler and Goebbels dead (all three committed suicide) the arch villains were already dispatched. There were a series of other trials taking place simultaneously in Germany dealing with those at the dirty coal face of the concentration camps. Their obscene activities amounted to murder of the worst degree for which suitable charges and penalties already existed.

Many felt the high-profile men held, including diplomats and banking chiefs, could essentially be absolved. There was at least a

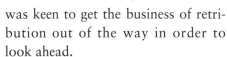

*Left:* The Palace of Justice at Nuremberg housed the most momentous trial of the century. *Below*: Tojo, the Japanese Prime Minister, was brought to justice in 1948.

question mark over whether or not these men truly had blood on their hands. In addition, it would be wrong to punish a military man – soldier, sailor or airman – for doing his job during times of war.

Others thought the only good Nazi was a dead one and that those held by the Allies should be shot, the sooner the better. With so many lives lost and families in mourning, it was wrong to allow these types to posture and pedal their propaganda ever again.

## ■ TRIALS OF NAZIS ■

Yet there was a different school of thought, equally enthusiastic about wiping the slate clean, which won the day. The captured Nazi leaders should face a trial and answer for their crimes. The Americans particularly among the Allies felt the application of the rule of law was fair and correct and would define once and for all who was guilty by association. Here was the opportunity of laying the blame for the disaster that befell Europe in the early Forties on the heads of those responsible and freeing the German people as a whole of guilt. The trials held at the end of

World War I were nominal, inconclusive affairs which barely reflected the carnage that had gone before. This time it was going to be different.

Once the British, French and Russian allies had been persuaded, there were a host of difficulties to unravel which would make the difference. Firstly, no statute books held charges which befitted the appalling crimes carried out in the name of Nazism. There was the clear danger that if the prosecutions were bodged, the world's best-known killers could end up getting away with murder.

The legal brains of the victorious countries got to work in creating charges which reflected the crimes which had taken place, identifying and closing possible loopholes at the same time as creating a scrupulously even playing field, fair to all sides. All this had to be done swiftly. Everyone

> *There were four main charges at Nuremberg, including Crimes Against Humanity*

was keen to get the business of retribution out of the way in order to look ahead.

Afterwards, there were accusations that the charges had been worded to fit the crimes and so offended the principle of justice. Yet as early as November 1945 the groundwork was laid for the most sensational trial of the century, Nuremberg, an astonishing feat by any standard.

There were to be four main charges which broadly covered a variety of individual acts. They were Crimes Against Peace, which covered the planning and waging of aggressive war; War Crimes, including the execution of prisoners of war; Crimes

responsibility. The Americans sought prosecutions on the conspiracy count in addition to probing the criminal organisations like the SS. The British proceeded with the charge of Crimes Against the Peace. The Russians and

> ## The trials created the precedent that acts of war were the individual's responsibility

the French dealt with the remaining two charges for Eastern and Western powers respectively.

Due to the complexity of the conflict, it remained an irony that Russia was prosecuting Germany for war crimes when it was also involved in waging aggressive wars against Poland and Finland.

### ■ WHY NUREMBERG? ■

The army of occupation in Germany was almost rivalled in size by that of lawyers, interpreters, researchers, clerks, prison guards, journalists and other observers linked to the Nuremberg Trial. Hearing the case were two judges from each of the main Allied countries, any four of whom would sit together at one time.

From America came Francis Biddle and John Parker, the British judges were Sir Geoffrey Lawrence and Norman Birkett. Professor Henri Donnedieu de Vabres and Robert Falco represented France while Russia sent Major-General I. Nikitchenko and Lieutenant-Colonel A. F. Volchkov. Prosecuting was

Against Humanity, dealing with the the genocide of Jews and other minorities; and finally the Common Plan or Conspiracy.

The final charge was defined as follows: 'All the defendants, with divers other persons, during a period of years preceding 8 May 1945, participated as leaders, organisers, instigators or accomplices in the formulation or execution of a common plan or conspiracy to commit, or which involved the commission of, Crimes Against the Peace, War Crimes and Crimes Against Humanity... and are individually responsible for their own acts and for all acts committed by any persons in the execution of such plan or conspiracy.'

An important precedent was being created, that acts of war were the responsibilty of the individual not just the state.

Each of the four countries on the winning side had their realms of

### ◆ EYE WITNESS ◆

**Seaghan Maynes was a journalist working for Reuters who attended the Nuremberg trials. In 'Eyewitness at Nuremberg', a book by Hillary Gaskin, he recalls his impressions.**

'The trial to me was a showpiece. It wasn't a juridical process; it was a revenge trial. This is my opinion and I think it was shared by a lot of other correspondents. It doesn't say that they shouldn't have been held because the purpose was to show crime followed by punishment, as an example to the other. But the legal process was very suspect. They made a charge to fit a crime after the crime had been committed. In that atmosphere, as distinct from now, I can see good reasons for having the trial because public opinion all over the world had been convinced that an example must be made. But take the case against Schacht. If Germany had occupied Britain, would our Minister of Transport, or somebody, be on trial for his life? Should Ribbentrop, the German foreign minister, have been executed? He was a diplomat; he didn't take part in any killing. I had niggling doubts about these things at the time. "What did he do to deserve death? After all his country was at war." In hindsight, I can say that the winner calls the shots and fixes the charges and the vanquished haven't as much of a chance as they should have. I wouldn't have missed it but I wouldn't want to see it again.'

## ◆ EYE WITNESS ◆

**Following the armistice, John Gorman, VC, a 22-year-old captain in the Irish Guards, was put in charge of a German prison camp housing 500 men suspected of war crimes.**

"The camp was at Sieburg, near the Dutch border. The majority of men were Germans but there were some French, Belgian and Dutch collaborators who had been denounced in their local communities. They were accused of various crimes including slaughter and other atrocities.

I had six officers to help me. We were superimposed on a structure which already existed with an administrator, who was not thought to be a criminal, and his team of warders.

Our job was to run the prison as humanely as possible and to produce these people for trial before the war crimes commissions. We did what we could and organised football matches, sport and encouraged them to help in the prison garden.

I was given a platoon of Belgian soldiers to help me who had previously been members of the resistance. They didn't like the inmates at all. I was away for a weekend in Brussels when I received a frantic telephone call from the officer in charge. The Belgians had decided they couldn't stand the prisoners having the freedom to look out of the window. Every time one of them had the temerity to show his face, the Belgians tried to shoot him.

I rushed back, thinking I would find a pile of corpses. Fortunately, the Belgians were bad shots. All we had was a badly pock-marked wall. They didn't hit any of them.

As for the British officers there, we prided ourselves on our discipline. We ran the prison on orthodox lines. We certainly didn't want them to say we were doing to them what they had been doing to others.

For their part, the prisoners were very servile and obsequious. They would have kissed our boots if they thought it would do them any good. The bully, when bullied, becomes a coward. They were not nice people.

It was very difficult finding enough to eat. Everybody was hungry. The Dutch had been eating their bulbs, the seedcorn of their future, to keep themselves alive.

We had to order the German authorities in the local town to produce food for the prison. The inmates had diet of soup, rice and occasionally meat.

One man died while I was there. He was terribly thin and a doctor told us he was severely undernourished. That gave the idea that something was amiss.

I used to patrol the prison at all times of day and night. Early one morning I happened on the German prison administrator leaving the kitchen with a large suitcase. When I ordered him to open it, I found it was fulll of meat. He was stealing meat from the prison kitchens to sell on the black market and had made a fortune. It was most underhand when you consider that the majority of the prisoners were his fellow countrymen. He went straight into a spare cell. "

Justice Robert Jackson from the United States, Sir Hartley Shawcross from Britain, Francois de Menthon of France and General Roman Rudenko of Russia.

The location of the trial was not a random choice. Few could forget the impressive and sinister rallies held by Hitler and his Nazi followers at

*Right:* **US soldiers mounted a heavyweight guard outside the Palace of Justice during the trial.**

Nuremberg before and after the outbreak of hostilities. And it was there in in 1935 that a special session of the Reichstag unanimously approved the Nuremberg Laws, depriving Jews of German citizenship and associated rights.

## ■ PALACE OF JUSTICE ■

The session went on to agree further anti-Jewish legislation which prevented marriages between Germans and Jews and forbade the employment of German servants by Jews. Nuremberg represented the fiery heartland of the Nazi doctrine and it would be here that the evil light would be extinguished.

Symbolically, the notorious city, in the American zone of occupation, was by now in ruins, the victim of the saturation bombing so potently used by the Royal Air Force in the last few years of the conflict.

The courtroom of its Palace Of Justice was now to house the momentous – and frequently monotonous – proceedings that were designed to

*Above:* Flamboyant Göring refused to be cowed. Here he is quizzed by journalists shortly after being captured.

turn the page on one of the worst periods of Europe's history.

In the dock were 20 by-now infamous characters from Hitler's hierarchy. Hermann Wilhelm Göring had been a long time cohort of Hitler and was best known as Commander in Chief of the German air force. In addition, he was a general in the feared SS and the Reich Hunting and Forest Master.

Next to him sat the enigmatic Rudolf Hess, a co-author of 'Mein Kampf', the book by Hitler explaining his dubious philosophies. A question mark remained over his sanity following his mysterious flight to Britain in 1941, apparently to seek

a peace settlement with King George VI. He had been held by the British since then, latterly in an asylum.

Joachim von Ribbentrop was next in the line-up. A Nazi party member since 1932, he rose quickly to become Hitler's adviser on foreign affairs. His devotion was rewarded with the post

## It was no coincidence that the trials were held at Nuremberg, the site of the great Nazi rallies

of ambassador to London between 1936 and 1938 and finally with the plum job of foreign minister.

World War I spy Alfred Rosenberg took part in the abortive 1923 putsch

when Hitler tried to seize power in Germany. The anti-semitic Reich Minister for the Occupied Eastern Territories wrote 'Mythos des 20 Jahrhunderts', a tome reflecting the Fatherland's distasteful philosophies under Hitler.

Lawyer Hans Frank had been Bavarian Minister of Justice and was in 1939 made Governor General of occupied Poland. Ernst Kaltenbrunner, born in Austria, coupled his own legal talents with those of commanding key SS units. Wilhelm Frick was also legally trained and strongly associated with the SS. When the war ended, he was Reich Protector.

Former schoolmaster Julius Streicher was a well-known anti-Semite who had been editor of the Fascist newspaper Der Sturmer and honorary leader of the thuggish SA force.

Wilhelm Keitel was a Field Marshal and held the title Chief of Oberkommando der Wehrmacht. His loyalty to Hitler was never in question.

Dr Walther Funk, paymaster of the Reich machine in his post as President of the Reichsbank, sat beside another economist Hjalmar Schacht, latterly out of favour with the Führer.

leading light in the propaganda machine. Tried in his absence was Martin Bormann, Hitler's personal secretary who went missing in the chaos of the Reich's last days. Only in 1973 was it established that, despite various post-war sightings of him, he had probably committed suicide in May 1945.

'In the prisoners' dock sit twenty broken men... their personal capacity for evil is forever past. Merely as individuals their fate is of little consequence to the world. What makes this inquest significant is that these prisoners represent sinister influences that will lurk in the world long after their bodies have returned to dust.

### *Ex-teacher Julius Streicher had been editor of the anti-semitic newspaper Der Sturmer*

The second row of defendants began with Karl Dönitz, the U-boat supremo who had become Commander in Chief of the Kriegsmarine and, on Hitler's death, Chancellor to the ruins of Germany.

Beside Dönitz sat longtime Hitler Youth leader Baldur von Schirach, who wrote songs and verses which inspired the country's youth to lay down their lives without question.

Fritz Sauckel was an eminent Reich Defence Commissioner assigned to the organisation of slave labour who sat in the shadow of charismatic Albert Speer, the man responsible for arming Germany's forces.

Diplomat Franz von Papen was seated beside Alfred Jodl, Chief of Staff in the High Command of the Wehrmacht, who in turn was next to Constantin von Neurath, an eminent member of the Reichstag and SS General.

### ■ MARTIN BORMANN ■

Dr Arthur Seyss-Inquart was an SS general, Reich minister without portfolio and President of the German Academy. Erich Raeder, the former Commander in Chief of the German navy, was next to him and beside him sat Hans Fritzsche, a

The defendants were charged with all or a combination of the charges. The trial opened on 12 November 1945. Making the opening speech was Justice Robert Jackson, the American attorney:

'The privilege of opening the first trial in history for crimes against the peace of the world imposes a grave responsiblity. The wrongs which we seek to condemn and punish have been so calculated, so malignant and so devastating, that civilisation cannot tolerate their being ignored because it cannot survive their being repeated.

'That four great nations, flushed with victory and stung with injury, stay the hand of vengeance and voluntarily submit their captive enemies to the judgement of the law is one of the most significant tributes that power ever has paid to reason...

*Above:* Top Nazis on trial *(front row, left to right)* Göring, Hess, Ribbentrop, Keitel, Rosenberg. *Back row (left to right):* Dönitz, Raeder, Shirach, Sauckel, Jodl.

### *Martin Bormann went missing at the end of the war but was tried in absentia*

We will show them to be living symbols of racial hatreds, of terrorism and violence and of the arrogance and cruelty of power.'

It was for the prosecution to prove that the primarily frail, vacant and occasionally quivering men lined up in the dock should be held responsible

Jackson's examination of Göring drew crowds into the courtroom expecting to see this swaggering man scythed to pieces. In fact, gloating Göring turned the tables and batted off questioning from the American prosecutor with ease. Jackson, hindered in no small part by inaccurate translations of evidence against

## *Guilty of racial hatreds, terrorism, violence and the arrogance and cruelty of power*

*Above:* Lt Thomas F. Lambert, Jr presents the case for the US prosecution against the absent Martin Bormann, who was sentenced to death but never caught.

for the calamities of wartime Europe. One of the first problems facing the prosecution was that posed by Hitler's one-time deputy, Rudolf Hess.

Hess was showing the signs of a disturbed character – and had been since his escapade to Britain back in 1941. Was it right for a man in this state to stand trial? The decision to press charges against him came in December 1945 when he admitted that he faked amnesia to fool British interrogators and Hess chose to conduct his own defence. Many privately felt that he was nevertheless a man devoid of many of his senses.

### ■ HERMANN GÖRING ■

For different reasons Hermann Göring caused the Allied prosecutors a major headache, too. Göring was a somewhat glamorous and charismatic figure, the last commander of

*Right*: Hermann Göring conducted his own defence at Nuremberg and made mincemeat of US prosecutor Jackson.

the Richthofen Fighter Squadron of World War I known for his unscrupulous and amoral behaviour. He relished the luxuries of life including good wines and flashy cars and had acquired a magnificent collection of art during his tenure, pilfered from the cultural capitals of Europe. Even in the courtroom, he could not contain his lustful gaze which appraised young women on the staff. More than that, he was witty, razor sharp and intelligent as Justice Jackson discovered to his cost.

Göring, had to appeal to the court to control the defendant and finally retired flustered and frustrated. It was left to the cool-headed Briton Sir David Maxwell-Fyfe who was assisting with prosecution to compromise the German.

Despite his straitened circumstances, Göring was always ready with a quip for the interpreters, an insult for witnesses or a putdown for his fellow defendants as they tried to wriggle out of some damning evidence as it was presented against them. He

## PATTON

US General George Patton won his reputation for revelling in warfare after making comments like: 'Compared to war, all other forms of human endeavour shrink to insignificance. God, how I love it.' He also wrote to his wife: 'Peace is going to be hell on me.'

remained a dominating force roundly unapologetic for his beliefs.

For the most part, the other defendants sat listening raptly to the evidence, occasionally aloof but for the most part displaying little or no emotion. Hess would read from a book of fairy tales by the Brothers' Grimm. Those with sufficient English occasionally corrected or aided the interpreters. Others simply sank into a murky silence. Stripped of their braid and regalia, they were grey-faced men who knew they faced a bleak future.

### The prosecution relied heavily on documentary evidence – and there was plenty of it

Kaltenbrunner suffered a stroke early in the proceedings but recovered sufficiently to appear in the dock again later on. Streicher suffered a heart attack in January 1946 but later returned to the stand.

Finally, tension gave way to tedium as each day passed. The

*Right:* The Japanese war crimes trial went on for three years after the end of the war and lacked the drama of Nuremberg.

prosecutors relied heavily on documentary evidence – and there was plenty of it. With characteristic Germanic efficiency, the Nazi regime had noted many of its activities down for its own future reference. Even in the grimmest of the concentration camps details of the exterminations were put into writing. The worst of the massacres were often filmed and now provided excellent evidence. Although there were many German witnesses to the Holocaust, it was felt their testimony could be unreliable because they might try either to ingratiate themselves with the victors or else to settle old scores with the defendants in the dock.

### ■ DEATH SENTENCE ■

The trial ended on the last day of August 1946 and the International Military Tribunal, as it was also known, began delivering its judgement a month later.

A dozen of the men on trial were sentenced to death. Hess received a life sentence, six more were also jailed and three were acquitted.

On 16 October 1946 the gallows were prepared in the prison gymnasium at Nuremberg. In a final

flourish, Göring cheated the executioner by taking a cyanide pill smuggled in to him, perhaps by his Swedish wife Karin.

### Julius Streicher screeched 'Heil Hitler' before the trap door opened beneath him

First to the rope at 1.11am was Hitler's Foreign Minister Ribbentrop. As the black hood was placed over his head, he called out: 'I wish peace to the world'.

Next to the gallows was Field Marshal Wilhelm Keitel. His final words were: 'More than two million German soldiers went to their death for their fatherland. I follow now my sons – all for Germany.'

Filing up the steps after him were Kaltenbrunner, Rosenbrug, Frank (a recent convert to Roman Catholicism), Frick, Streicher (who screeched 'Heil Hitler' before the trap door opened beneath him), Sauckel, Jodl and Seyss-Inquart. Martin Bormann was sentenced to death in absentia.

Funk and Raeder were jailed for life, Doenitz for 10 years, Speer for 20 years, Neurath for 15 years and Schirach for 20 years. Fritzsche, Schacht and von Papen were acquitted.

It was far from the end of the story. The Subsequent Proceedings dealt with a further 182 Nazis from the doctors who set up experiments in the concentration camps to industrialists, government ministers, military men and SS officials.

Twenty-six were sentenced to death while the rest received various prison sentences, forfeited property or were acquitted. The last of the Subsequent Proceedings ended in October 1948.

When Japanese Emperor Hirohito came before General Douglas MacArthur on the surrender of Japan in September 1945, he told him: 'I come to you to offer myself to the judgement of the powers you represent as the one who bears sole responsibility for every political and military decision made and action taken by my people in the conduct of the war.'

Yet despite his frankness, he was not charged as a war criminal. It wasn't until December 1948 that General Tojo, one of Japan's prime ministers during the war, was hanged along with six others. He had tried but failed to kill himself even though a Japanese doctor refused to treat his wounds.

### ■ ATROCITIES ■

The accused were convicted of 'crimes against peace and responsibility for atrocities'. The sentence was carried out by the American Army at Sugamo Prison in Tokyo. A further 16 men were jailed for life their roles in the war.

Among those executed for war crimes was Lt General Homma, the Japanese commander victorious in

## ◆ EYE WITNESS ◆

**Hugh Trebble, a clerk with the Royal Air Force, was taken prisoner by the Japanese on Java after fleeing Singapore.**

❛ I was taken prisoner at the beginning of March. We were rounded up in Dutch Air Force hangars at Tasek Malaja and dispersed all over the island. I was sent to Surabaya, the principle port on the north coast to help repair bomb damage – by scraping burnt sugar coating the jetties into the sea. We dug air raid shelters – which was against the Geneva Convention – and then began planting castor oil plants.

A party of about 30 was taken to a walled garden. Our guard was a Korean, built like a barn door. He was a Christian. He produced an English bible, selected me to read it and I started with verse one, chapter one of Genesis. While the others worked I sat beside him reading the bible, interpreting what I could for him.

Soon after we were lined up in a playing field with a manned Japanese machine gun post in each corner while they decided whether to shoot us or not.

The Japanese were very ready with their fists and their rifle butts.

I contracted malaria and eventually dysentery in two forms. I was finally sent for treatment at a hospital staffed by Dutch medics. After I recovered I was sent by boat to Singapore then on to Sumatra to build a railway. We managed to wreck three full-sized steam locomotives in the process!

We had to work 16 hours a day, seven days a week. We had a bowl of rice in the morning and a bowl of rice at night and it was all we had to live on. At our base camp we used to bury about 16 men a day.

The Japanese were utterly ruthless and they were all the same. It was impossible to find anything good about them. The only mitigating circumstances were that they treated their own troops in the same way they treated us.

One of the native soldiers pushed a Japanese guard while he was being beaten with a rifle butt. He was tied up with wire, put in a bamboo cage with no roof and kept there for days. Every time a guard went past he would poke his rifle butt in to give him a thump. Eventually, the bloke died. There was nothing we could do about it. We would squirm every day when we had to file past him – but that kind of treatment was commonplace.

When we were building the railway, we were beaten with rails and spanners. The thing to do was to stay concious. If you fell over and blacked out you were beaten and could get badly injured. One of the guards was so short he would make you stand in a monsoon drain in order to beat you.

When I was released in 1945 I was 6 stones 7lb instead of my usual 12 and a half stones. I was blown up like a balloon and as yellow as a guinea fowl. ❜

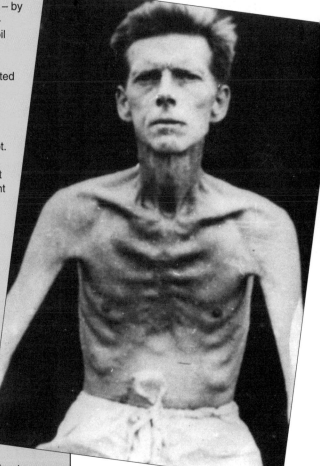

*Above:* **A PoW of the Japanese displays the classic signs of malnutrition.**

the Philippines who was removed by his overlords for being too soft. He ordered his men to treat the Filipinos as friends and refused to distribute propaganda criticising US rule. It was General MacArthur, whose forces had been routed in the Philippines, who ordered the trial of Homma.

## The trial of Lt Gen Homma was ordered by US General Douglas MacArthur

*Below*: In the dock, those accused of carrying out war crimes on behalf of Japan listen intently to proceedings.

# HITLER'S BODY

**After Hitler shot himself in his Berlin bunker alongside his wife Eva Braun who had taken poison, his body was taken out and burned by the few remaining faithful in his entourage.**

Yet Russian dictator Stalin was convinced that his arch enemy had somehow cheated death by using a double and staging the suicide. When the bodies were recovered by a Russian soldier in the rubble outside the bunker, it seems Stalin's crack troops from Smersh, a trusted security team, took over. The charred bodies of Hitler and Braun underwent not one but two post mortems as Stalin quested to know for certain whether they were the genuine articles.

After that, the fate of the bodies and their final resting place is subject to controversy. Some ex-Russian soldiers have claimed that Hitler and Braun, together with the Goebbels family, are buried at Magdeburg in a garage. A few historians are convinced the body is buried in the grounds of a Moscow prison. Others believe it to have been destroyed following Stalin's death.

Even if it was turned to dust, at least a few remnants remain. In 1993 a Russian journalist claimed she had held some of the the skull of Hitler in her hand after she discovered parts of it in the Moscow state archives. The two sections were believed to have been discovered in Berlin following the removal of the bodies. It is also thought that Hitler's jaw bone and that of Eva Braun are kept in Moscow where they were taken for identification purposes.

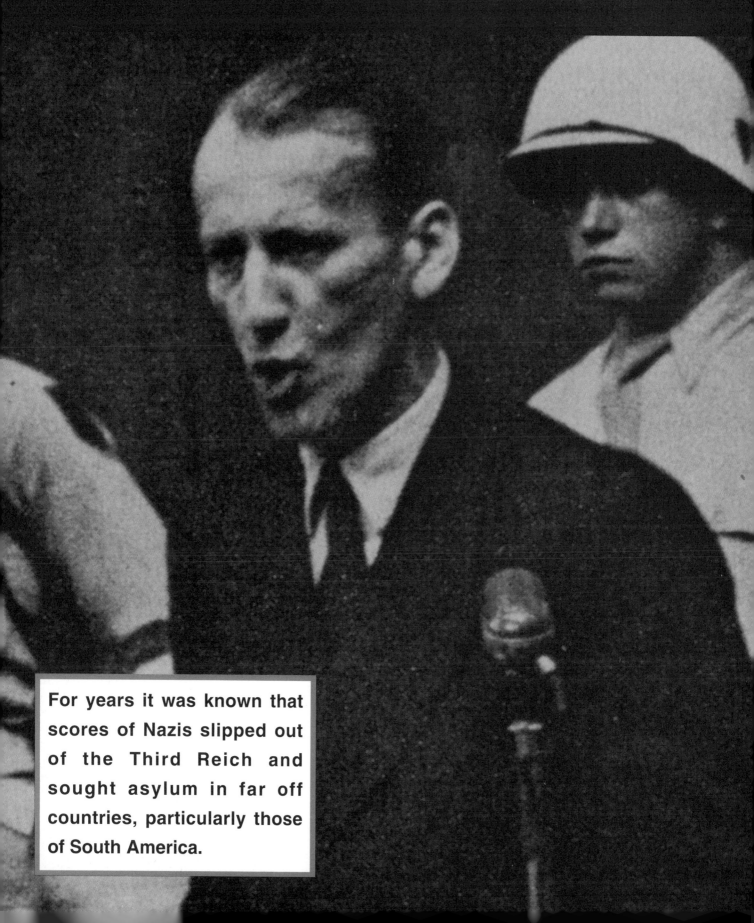

# NAZIS ON THE RUN

For years it was known that scores of Nazis slipped out of the Third Reich and sought asylum in far off countries, particularly those of South America.

To smuggle themselves out of danger, they used the services of the sinister and infamous ODESSA – the Organisation of Former Members of the SS – which provided the necessary cash and papers. Sometimes they donned the robes of priests to avoid detection. There are even cases of submarines bringing fugitives to the coast of South America.

Much of the finance came from treasures looted up and down Europe and from the victims they had murdered, converted through Swiss bank accounts.

From their bolt holes Hitler's henchmen were able to escape retribution for the horrible war crimes they had perpetrated. For the most part their host governments refused to hand them over to either the Allied governments wishing to proceed with a trial or the Jewish groups in search of justice.

Josef Schwammberger, commandant of the concentration camp at Przemysl fled to Argentina along with the notorious Adolf Eichmann

## Eichmann and Mengele fled to Argentina where they were sheltered by President Peron

and 'doctor of death' Josef Mengele. Less well-known figures took shelter in Argentina with the apparent complicity of its President Juan Domingo Peron. They included Ludolph Von Alvensleben, adjutant to Himmler, who escaped Germany in 1946 and died in Cordoba in 1972. Gestapo chief Heinrich Muller was sighted in the Fifties, also in

Cordoba, and could still be alive there today. Rudolf Mildner, held responsible for numerous Jewish deaths at Auschwitz, may also be living in peace there.

SS commander Walter Kutschmann, who entered Argentina dressed as a Carmelite priest, became director of sales of a German-owned light bulb company. He died in 1986 before efforts to extradite him came to fruition. Lung cancer claimed the life of Walter Rauff in 1984, an SS officer who also went into hiding in South America, running a meat-freezing plant in Chile under his own name.

### ■ REFUGE IN SYRIA ■

Alois Brunner, designer of the mobile gas chambers and the man responsible for the death of many Greek Jews, found the protection he needed among the Arabs in Damascus.

Some were finally brought to trial after protracted arguments. Others died in their hideaways. The fight continues for still more to be brought before the courts, despite their extremely advanced years.

But only recently did the Nazi hunters begin to realise the scale of their task. Files released from Argentina show that more than 1,000 suspected war criminals and Nazi collaborators fled there after the war. Previous estimates put the number at less than 100.

The news stunned the Jewish groups which had long been pressuring the Argentinian government to come clean on its shadowy involvement with Nazis. Until the recent attempt by Argentina to rid itself of Nazis and the unsavoury image accompanying them, just two were

extradited, Nazi doctor and lawyer Gerhardt Bhone in 1966 and Josef Schwammberger in 1988.

In the files was further evidence that Martin Bormann survived the collapse of the Reich and was among those who slipped into South America, possibly carrying a stateless

## Bormann escaped to South America on a stateless passport in the name of Goldstein

**Right**: Martin Bormann. Did he commit suicide in 1945 or escape to South America? **Left**: Ernst Kaltenbrunner, chief of security police, sentenced to death.

## ALESSANDRA MUSSOLINI

**The name of Mussolini has survived in Italian politics through his grandaughter Alessandra. In 1992 she was elected to the Italian Parliament under the banner of the neo-fascist party, the MSI.**

Alessandra, married to a financier, has had a chequered history. Before entering politics, she was a nude pin-up, an actress, a TV chat-show host and a graduate in medicine. Her aunt is actress Sophia Loren.

Her policies are often at odds with those of the party which is anti-divorce and anti-abortion, for the death penalty and in favour of sending immigrants to their country of birth. For her part, Alessandra supports increased independence for women, including state payments for housewives. Not surprisingly, the voluptuous blonde is employed mostly by her party in travelling around the country as an emissary to drum up new votes.

person's passport in the name of Eliezer Goldstein. Sightings of him reported in 1947 and 1948 were never conclusively proved and the Argentinian government of the day refused to co-operate in a search for him. Other historical detectives are convinced he died in the Berlin

*Below:* **Adolf Eichmann was kidnapped from his new hideaway home in Argentina by the Israelis to stand trial in Tel Aviv for his role in the Nazi atrocities.**

bunker with his beloved Hitler or soon afterwards.

Adolf Eichmann slipped through the fingers of the Allies even though he was arrested in May 1945. Eichmann was one of the architects of the Final Solution who devoted himself to transporting large numbers of Jews to death camps as quickly as possible. Dressed as a Luftwaffe pilot, Eichmann was not recognised and managed to slip away from his preoccupied interrogators.

It wasn't until 1957 that the men who dedicated themselves to hunting down stray Nazis received a confirmed sighting of the man they were so keen to interview.

## A man named Nikolaus Klement bore a striking resemblance to the wanted Eichmann

A former internee from Dachau who had emigrated to Argentina following the war became suspicious of a man by the name of Nikolaus Klement. Not only did Klement bear a striking resemblance to Eichmann but his son had been heard making offensive anti-Jewish remarks.

The Argentinian government was not convinced. It took all the persuasive powers of the Israeli agents to get permission even for surveillance. When it finally came, they took snaps of the suspect entering and leaving the family home at 4261 Chacabuco Street, Olivos, Buenos Aires. Blurred and indistinct, it was impossible for camp survivors back in Europe to use

them to identify him positively as Adolf Eichmann.

It wasn't until Klement was seen carrying a bunch of flowers on 21 March 1960 that the Israelis were convinced they had got their man. It was the same date that Eichmann celebrated his wedding anniversary.

### ■ EICHMANN TRIAL ■

The slick Israeli operators went into action at once. On 11 May they pounced on Eichmann as he got off a bus, bundled him into a car and spirited him off to a safe house. When he was stripped, bodily scars and a giveaway SS tattoo confirmed their suspicions.

To smuggle him out of Argentina, he was drugged with his captors posing as the caring relatives of a helpless car crash victim. With ease they boarded the El-Al jet which took them to Tel Aviv. Eichmann was to face the justice he richly deserved.

His trial began on 12 December 1961 and he faced 15 charges emanating from his activities in Nazi Germany. In his defence, Eichmann claimed he tried to promote Jewish emigration and bore no responsiblity for the 'Final Solution'.

Yet voices of the past returned to condemn him, including that of a trusted lieutenant Dieter Wisliceny, executed soon after the war in

## REMAGEN

**American troops were delighted when they found the Remagen Bridge across the Rhine intact and finally crossed in their droves. However, just 10 days after the first soldiers edged their way across under enemy fire, the vital link crumbled forcing 400 men in the US 1st Army, who were on it at the time, to scramble to safety.**

Czechoslovakia for his part in war crimes. He revealed to the Allies the extent of Eichmann's evil by recounting a comment made by him as the end of the war beckoned.

'He told me in 1944 that he did not care what happened if Germany lost the war. He said he would leap into his grave laughing because the feeling that he had five million Jews on his conscience only filled his heart with gladness.'

Eichmann was hanged shortly before midnight on 31 May 1962 at Ramleh Prison near Tel Aviv.

Argentina was also the destination for hundreds of Jews after the war.

### After the war many Jews went to Argentina, and they often went there on the same ships as Nazis

They even travelled alongside Nazis to the promised land of Argentina, whose Jewish population thrived every bit as much as the Fascist one.

Jose Jakubowicz, a Jew who had been held in Dachau and Auschwitz, arrived in Argentina in 1948 aged 23.

'We sailed from Le Havre and at the table in the evening we were eight. A Jewish woman and myself and six Nazis. You must remember there were not only German Nazis on board but Hungarian, Romanian and Croat Nazis too.

'One day, one of the Nazis said to another at the table: "I hear you killed 5,000 Jews during the war. It is a pity that you did not kill them all."

'At that point we asked to be moved to another table.'

Another runaway who was also eventually returned to answer for his crimes was Klaus Barbie, a notorious Gestapo chief in Vichy France. Barbie earned his nickname as 'the butcher of Lyons' due to his harrowing exploits both with local Jews and members of the French resistance.

### ■ BUTCHER OF LYONS ■

It was Barbie who discovered a refuge for Jewish children high in a mountain village near the Swiss border. Instead of turning a blind eye in common with other German commanders, Barbie had the house raided and the children as well as their minders sent off to Auschwitz. Not a single one survived. On his orders, young men were shot in the street while scores more men and women were rounded up and machine-gunned in cellars.

His headquarters in the Ecole Sante Militaire were kitted out with chains, spiked coshes and whips and resembled a medieval-style torture chamber. He relished watching prisoners being dunked alternately in boiling hot then freezing cold baths. He experimented with the effectiveness of acid injections, amateur electric shock treatment and burning by blow torch.

One of his most famous victims was Jean Moulin, the courageous leader of the French resistance who was so fiercely beaten by Barbie that he died soon afterwards from his injuries. Moulin had refused to utter a word despite the barbaric excesses of his tormentor.

Barbie's sadism reached such extremities that he would oversee the most agonising tortures – with a naked woman seated on his knee.

He too disappeared at the end of the war, fleeing to Frankfurt where he lived covertly for some years until in 1951 he and his family emigrated to La Paz, Bolivia.

### ◆ EYE WITNESS ◆

**Concentration camp survivor Simon Wiesenthal devoted his life to hunting down Nazis who fled from justice at the end of World War II.**

When I was liberated from the last camp I felt that as a man from the intelligentsia my duty was bigger than the duty of the others to find those responsible for the atrocities.

I was very naive. I thought it would be completed in a few years. Yet the moment I started, I could not finish. I feel it is a moral duty that is never ending. 'I am satisfied that I have done it because I was the only one who stood up and asked people not to forget and said 'tell all this to your children'. If this does not happen history will repeat itself.

During the early Eighties, Bolivia was no longer a safe spot following the resolution by a new President to clear his country of Nazis. France had maintained its case for extradition. On 4 February 1983 Barbie was finally arrested and sent back to France. During his trial France was gripped by revelations about the extent of French collaboration with the Nazis and Allied complicity with his freedom.

Heinrich Muller, head of the Gestapo, has proved a mysterious case. Although his hand was never on the trigger, he was undoubtedly the man responsible for thousands of Jewish deaths, killings that were carried out on the orders of the Nazi. Despite every attempt made by Simon Wiesenthal and other eminent Nazi hunters, the trail on Muller went cold too quickly after the war.

### ■ IVAN THE TERRIBLE ■

Others that vanished after the war include Friedrich Wartzog, commander of the Polish Lemberg-Janowska camp, where guards used prisoners for target practice; Dr Aribert Heim, director of Mauthausen concentration camp in Austria where prisoners of war were among the thousands who died; and Richard Gluecks, Inspector General of all concentration camps.

Yet the passing years pose increasing problems for Nazi hunters. This was richly illustrated in the case of John Demjanjuk, a Ukrainian-born car worker in America thought to be a cruel concentration camp guard nicknamed 'Ivan the Terrible'.

## Demjanjuk was sentenced to death then acquitted because of doubts about his identity

Demjanjuk was extradited from the States where he emigrated following the war to face charges in Israel. Despite his advancing years, he was sentenced to death. However, he was subsequently acquitted because of doubts over his identity. The case crystallises the dilemma for those still

seeking justice following the atrocities of the Nazis. The testimony of witnesses appears ever more doubtful as the years go by while public sympathy for frail old men in the dock of a hostile court increases.

British authorities considering the prosecution of at least 10 alleged Nazi war criminals have been delayed as they search for irrefutable evidence against the suspects to eliminate all possible confusion.

Simon Wiesenthal, who has devoted his life to hunting Nazis, is

well aware of the difficulties: 'When you have a man aged over 80 in the dock, the whole sympathy of the audience is for him. Let this old man die in peace, they say. They don't realise that through his crimes, he has lost the right to die in peace.'

Wiesenthal admits that as time goes by he is looking for a smaller

*Below:* Nazi-hunter Simon Wiesenthal has scoured the world for escaped Nazis because he believes they have forfeited their right to a peaceful retirement.

and smaller number of criminals who played lesser roles in the Nazi Holocaust. 'Most of those people who gave the orders are not alive today. They committed suicide or were living in old age homes under a false name until their deaths.'

One of the last remaining key figures in the Nazi hierarchy who

Brunner lived in Syria. He even gave interviews from there boasting that 150,000 Jews were killed on his orders. The Syrian government continually claimed it was unable to trace him even though he was believed to have a police guard around his house. Rumours have reached the Wiesenthal Centre in

Vienna that his death occurred in 1992 or early 1993.

Wiesenthal explains that the hunt for Nazis was irreparably damaged by the Cold War.

'During 12 years of the Cold War between 1948 and 1960, nothing happened. Both sides were more interested in harassing each other than the

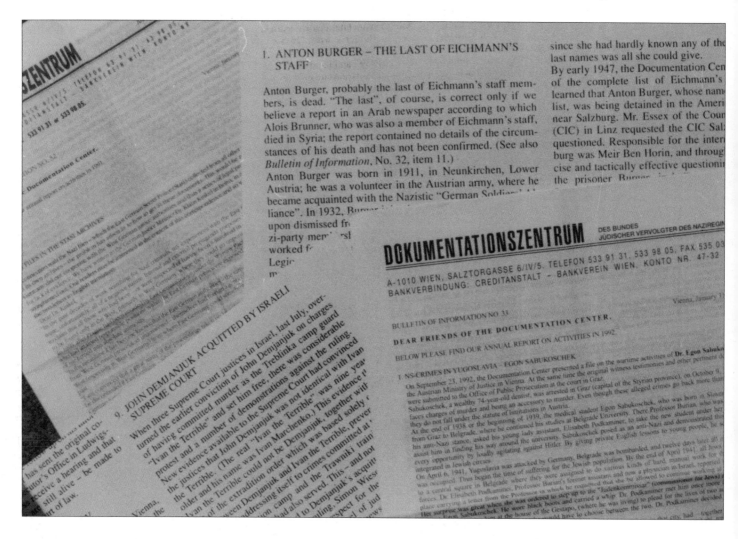

had still to be accounted for was tracked down recently. Anton Burger, a leading member of Eichmann's staff, was found to have died in 1993 in Germany. He had adopted the common German surname of Bauer. 'Even though we knew the false name he used, every telephone directory had many pages of the same name,' sighs Weisenthal.

He is intrigued to know if Alois Brunner, has now died. For years

*Above:* **Some of the documents produced by Simon Wiesenthal and his workers from their Vienna headquarters. Each wanted man has been closely tracked.**

## Simon Wiesenthal is deeply troubled by the neo-Nazi groups that exist today

war criminals. The only winners of the Cold War were the Nazis.'

Simon Wiesenthal's mission to bring fugitive Nazi war criminals to justice still goes on. The fact that neo-Nazi groups are tolerated today by nations that ought to know better troubles him greatly. He cannot understand why governments allow them to exist: 'This is a slap in the face for all the people who survived,' he says with deep feeling.

# Countdown to Victory

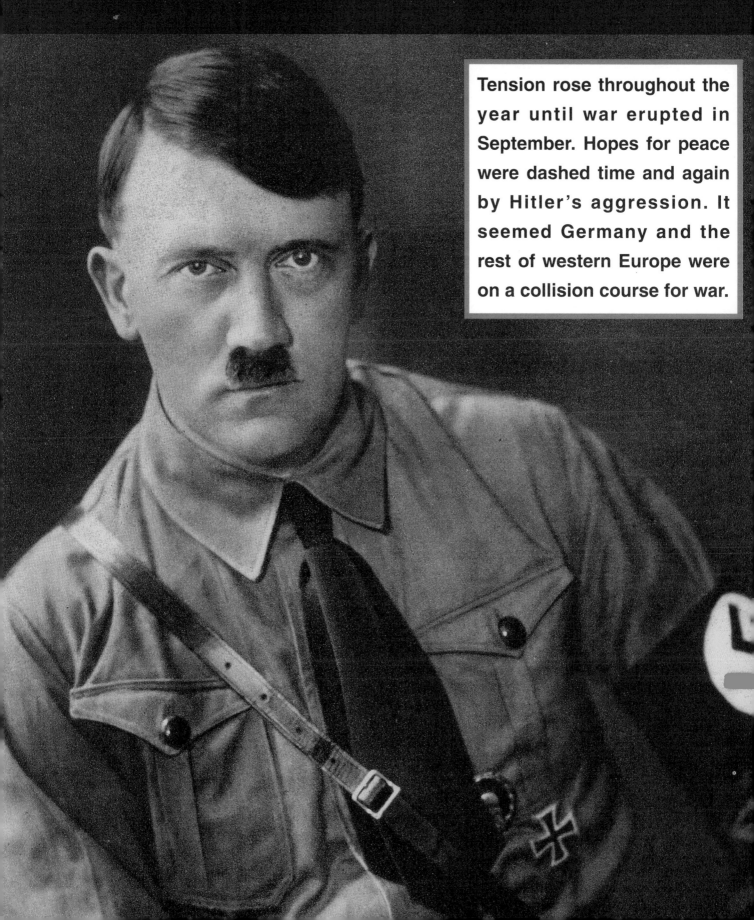

# 1939

Tension rose throughout the year until war erupted in September. Hopes for peace were dashed time and again by Hitler's aggression. It seemed Germany and the rest of western Europe were on a collision course for war.

**Thursday 26:** General Francisco Franco and his troops arrive in triumph in Barcelona.

**Saturday 28:** Irish poet William Butler Yeats dies, aged 73.

■ **FEBRUARY** ■

**Thursday 9:** The Home Office announces its blueprint to provide thousands of at-risk homes with air-raid shelters.

**Friday 10:** Pope Pius XI, a bitter and influential opponent of Nazism, dies, aged 81.

**Tuesday 28:** Britain recognises the fascist government of General Franco in Spain.

■ **MARCH** ■

**Wednesday 15:** German troops cross the Czech frontier.

**Tuesday 28:** Madrid surrenders to Franco to bring an end to the Spanish Civil War.

## Hitler rips up a non-aggression pact signed with Poland in 1934

**Wednesday 29:** As part of its preparations for war, the government has announced plans to double the size of the Territorial Army.

**Friday 31:** France and Britain declare a guarantee of the independence of Poland against aggressors.

■ **APRIL** ■

**Friday 7:** Italian troops launch invasion of Albania.

**Thursday 13:** France and Britain guarantee the independence of Greece and Romania.

**Saturday 15:** US president Franklin D. Roosevelt invites Hitler and Mussolini to give an assurance that

*Above:* Spain's General Franco eventually refused to join Hitler against the Allies.
*Left:* Hitler revelled in the pomp of his position as Chancellor of Germany.

they will not attack 29 named countries for a decade at least.

**Wednesday 26:** British prime minister Chamberlain announces conscription into the armed forces. The first call-up is 1 July.

**Friday 28:** Hitler rips up a non-aggression pact signed with Poland in 1934. He further demands the free city of Danzig is handed to Germany – and rejects President Roosevelt's appeal for restraint.

■ **MAY** ■

**Monday 22:** Italian and German foreign ministers Ciano and Ribbentrop sign the 'Pact of Steel', a document which identifies joint interests between the fascist states. Although it gives an outward appearance of unity, there were in fact many misgivings about forging links on both sides.

*Below:* At the outset of World War II, Italian forces fighting overseas found tremendous success, to the delight of their long-established leader, Il Duce, Benito Mussolini. It was Il Duce's ambition that Italy should have an empire.

## ■ JUNE ■

**Sunday 4:** Newly launched British submarine Thetis sinks during trials in Liverpool Bay, costing the lives of 71 men.

**Friday 16:** The coastal town of Littlehampton is put up for sale by owner the Duke of Norfolk.

## ■ JULY ■

**Tuesday 4:** In Vienna Archbishop Cardinal Theodor Innitzer is beaten up by young Nazis.

**Saturday 29:** The British government begins a purge on all IRA suspects, following an explosion which killed one person and injured 18 more. An emergency law is introduced that allows arrests without warrants.

*Below:* **Inner-city children are filled with trepidation as they await evacuation. For some, it was a joyous adventure. For others, a terrifying nightmare from which they would soon flee.**

## ■ AUGUST ■

**Wednesday 23:** German and Russian foreign ministers Ribbentrop and Molotov sign a non-aggression pact in Moscow, reversing Stalin's previous policy of courting France and Britain. The change of heart by Stalin was brought about by the option of

### *At dawn, Germany invades Poland with a blitz of bombs and artillery fire*

territorial gains for Russia after the German invasion of Poland. France and England are left reeling.

**Friday 25:** The guarantee given to Poland on 31 March is converted to a formal alliance. It forces German Führer Hitler to cancel plans to invade Poland that day.

**Wednesday 30:** More than 1.5 million British children are evacuated to safe areas of the country. In an operation that began at dawn and will last for several days, children taking no more than one spare set of clothing, a toothbrush, handkerchief and comb are being dispatched from cities to the countryside. Historic treasures like the Coronation Chair are also being moved from the capital to secret strongholds elsewhere.

**Thursday 31:** Hitler receives Polish ambassador Lipsky, ostensibly to resolve the differences between the two countries. The meeting breaks up after only a few moments, with the Germans claiming their 'generous offer' had been rejected by the Poles.

## ■ SEPTEMBER ■

**Friday 1:** At dawn, Germany invades Poland with a blitz of bombs and artillery fire. Moving at lightning speed, 1.25 million men in six

# HITLER

**He was the world's most loathed and feared dictator yet German Führer Adolf Hitler's origins were, to put it kindly, unremarkable.**

His book 'Mein Kampf portrayed a rough and even deprived childhood. Not so. He was the son of a minor civil servant, the family was comfortably off, and Adolf was no more emotionally neglected and deprived than the next child.

Born in 1889 in Braunau, a small town on the Austrian and Bavarian border, Adolf was the sole surviving child of Alois Hitler and Klara Polzl. The two were second cousins and needed special dispensation from the church to wed. Alois was 23 years older than his wife and was marrying for the third time. By all accounts, he was a cold and stern man like many patriarchs of the age.

At school, the young Hitler showed little application and was fired with enthusiasm by one teacher only, a fervent German nationalist called Dr Leopold Potsch.

Hitler resolved to become an artist, apparently oblivious to his glaring lack of talent. His chosen career caused friction between himself and his father, who hoped the young Adolf would be a civil servant. It appears Hitler thought little of his father, who died in 1903, although he remained fond of his gentle mother. He even took steps to conceal the chequered background of Alois, who was born illegitmately of peasant stock.

Curiously, there is believed to have been Jewish blood in the family, which is perhaps why Hitler chose to hide his roots. For after he was twice turned down for the Academy of Fine Arts in Vienna he looked for something or someone to blame for his failure. He focused on the Jewish people.

When World War I broke out, Hitler joined the army and served with distinction in the trenches, winning two decorations for bravery. Yet he failed to rise above the rank of corporal despite his dedication to Germany. His brooding hatred of authority made superior officers uncomfortable.

Germany's failure to win the war and its political floundering following the conflict left Hitler with a profound desire to renew the badly battered national pride and make Germany great again.

He got the taste for politics when he attended regular meetings of the German Workers' Party in Munich from 1919 and discovered a talent for public speaking.

By 1921 membership had swelled, it had changed its name to the National Socialist German Workers' Party, or Nazi Party, and Hitler was its leader.

An attempted rebellion led by Hitler in 1923 against the Bavarian authorities landed him in jail. From his cell he wrote *Mein Kampf*, setting out the theories on which his thrust for power would be based. Central themes were the detested Treaty of Versailles, which ended World War I, and the reviled Jewish race.

Germany was still a democracy and Hitler's party failed to make much of a mark in the 1928 elections. Yet thanks to the support of an industrialist and newspaper owner, Hitler managed to spread his message effectively throughout the country.

This message was music to the ears of many of Germany's six million unemployed. His popularity grew until, in 1932, the Nazi party won more than a third of the votes cast in the election. The following year President Paul von Hindenburg was struggling to contain the burgeoning power of the Nazis and invited Hitler to become Chancellor in the hope it would satisfy his lust for power.

At last Hitler had the chance to seize total domination with a programme of intimidation and aggression. Then, a year later, on the death of President Hindenburg, Hitler assumed the post of Führer – leader. Fair and free elections were not held again in Germany in his lifetime. He set about making his dearest ambitions a reality. Communism and socialism were ruthlessly quashed, Jews were hounded and unemployment was slashed. Further, he sought to give the esteemed German race a new empire of which they could be proud.

armoured divisions and eight motorised divisions sweep across the country. The Polish air force is shot out of the sky. Poland appeals to France and Britain to intervene.
**Saturday 2:** Poland remains under

fire – with Luftwaffe jets raiding the capital, Warsaw, killing at least 21 people. The National Service Act is passed in Britain. Hitler remains confident the Western powers will not act against him.

A furnace in the grounds of the German Embassy in London is lit to incinerate and destroy scores of papers and documents.
**Sunday 3:** Britain issues Germany with a 9am ultimatum. Unless Hitler

*Left:* German soldiers march into the disputed city of Danzig (modern-day Gdansk) following aerial strikes by the Luftwaffe in its opening gambit of the war.

*Below:* British premier Neville Chamberlain was personally devastated when his peace bids came to naught.

gives firm assurances within two hours that he will withdraw troops from Poland, Britain will be at war with Germany. When the 11am deadline passes without word, Britain goes to war. Hot on her heels, Commonwealth countries including India, Australia and New Zealand, also declare war on Germany. Eire declares itself neutral.

Speaking from 10 Downing Street, Prime Minister Neville Chamberlain broadcasts the grim news. 'This country is now at war with Germany,' he tells the House of Commons when it meets at noon. His voice wavered as he added: 'For no one has it been a sadder day than for me. Everything I work for, everything I hoped for, everything I believed through my public life has crashed in ruins.

'I trust I may live to see the day when Hitlerism has been destroyed so as to restore the liberty of Europe.'

Soon afterwards Winston Churchill made a stirring contribu-

tion. 'Outside the storms of war may blow and the land may be lashed with the fury of its gale, but in our own hearts this Sunday morning there is peace. Our hands may be active but in our consciences are at rest. . . We are fighting to save the world from the pestilence of Nazi tyranny and in defence of all that is most sacred to man.'

France delivers a similar ultimatum to Germany due to expire the following day. But it fails to await the outcome of its message to Berlin. By 5pm France is at war with the Third Reich.

In a joint Anglo-French declaration, both governments stated they would avoid bombing civilians and added there was no intention of using poison gas or germ warfare. Japan assures Britain of her neutrality in the war.

King George VI makes a personal broadcast to the nation. 'The task will be hard. There may be dark days ahead, and the war can no longer be confined to the battlefield. But we

can only do the right as we see the right, and reverently commit our cause to God.

'If one and all we keep resolutely faithful to it, ready for whatever service or sacrifice it may demand, then, with God's help, we shall prevail.'

The Royal Air Force drops six million propaganda leaflets on northern Germany.

**Monday 4:** A War Cabinet is brought together with Winston Churchill as First Lord of the Admiralty and Anthony Eden as Dominions Secretary. Both men had been in the political wilderness, following outspoken attacks on the British policy of appeasement towards Hitler. Although Labour and Liberal politicians refuse to join the war team they pledge full support for Chamberlain's government.

British passenger ship SS Athenia, out of Glasgow, is sunk by a German U-boat. There are 112 fatalities, 28 of them American. It causes considerable anti-German feeling in the USA, causing the Germans to insist that the sinking was staged by Churchill in order to create tension between the two countries.

The RAF makes early strikes against ships at Wilhelmshaven in the North Sea entrance to the Kiel Canal, although with only limited success.

**Tuesday 5:** French troops fire their first shots of the campaign, engaging the Germans on the Western front and crossing into the Saarland. German troops continue to make

## Polish lancers on horse-back confront well-equipped German Panzers on the Bzura

huge gains in Poland, crossing the key Vistula river. The USA declares its neutrality, embargoing arms shipments to those countries at war.

**Wednesday 6:** General Jan Smuts persuades his South African cabinet to declare war on Germany.

The Polish government leaves Warsaw as the invaders threaten the city boundaries.

**Thursday 7:** German troops are sent in reply to French forays into Third Reich territory.

Identity cards are introduced into Britain through the National Registration Bill.

**Saturday 9:** Polish lancers on horse-

back confront well-equipped German Panzers on the Bzura river. German troops march on into Warsaw.

**Sunday 10:** Canada declares war on Germany.

**Tuesday 12:** The armed forces' entertainment organisation ENSA is formed.

An Anglo-French Supreme War Council convenes under Chamberlain and French premier Daladier. Convoys are planned for merchant shipping in an attempt to combat the threat from U-boats.

**Saturday 16:** Petrol rationing begins in Britain.

**Sunday 17:** Russia invades Poland from the east by prior arrangement with Germany.

**Monday 18:** Britain's aircraft carrier HMS Courageous is sunk by a U-boat torpedo. Although there are 687 survivors of the sinking, more than 500 sailors are lost.

**Tuesday 19:** Chamberlain declares that the war will not end until Hitlerism is defeated and destroyed. Privately, he believes that it will take three years to win.

The first war casualty list is published in Britain.

**Wednesday 20:** Chamberlain claims that at least six U-boats have been sunk by the Allies in the first few weeks of action.

**Friday 22:** Germany and Russia agree on the partition of Poland. The Soviets lay claim to 76,000 square miles in the east of the country, while Germany earmarks most of the west.

**Saturday 23:** Famous Austrian psychoanalyst Sigmund Freud dies.

**Wednesday 27:** Warsaw falls.

In a war budget, Chancellor Sir John Simon raises income tax to seven

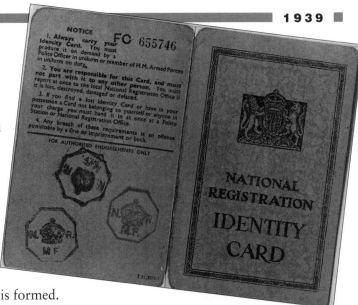

*Above:* **The identity card issued to all in a flurry of bureaucracy by the British government.**

shillings and six pence (thirty-seven and a half pence) in the pound, the highest rate ever levied.

**September 29:** Poland surrenders. An estimated 60,000 Poles were killed, 200,000 injured and a further 700,000 taken prisoner.

**September 30:** Polish government-in-exile bases itself in France.

## ◆ EYE WITNESS ◆

**E. Rickman was a schoolboy when the war broke out and served with the Home Guard as London was bombed.**

❝ I was a cyclist messenger for the Home Guard in Raynes Park, south west London, at the start of the war. When the air-raid sirens went it was my job to go around to arouse the members of the Home Guard and have them report for duty.

Just as I came back from doing that I reached off my brand-new £6 Raleigh bike to open the double gates of the detached house which was the Home Guard headquarters when a bomb dropped. I knew nothing more until I came around inside the building, lying on a settle in the hallway.

The sergeant told me a shell had landed in the road just three feet away from me. I was blown 35 feet onto the front steps. My bike was a write-off. I had not got a scratch or a bruise. ❞

*Above:* Actor Douglas Fairbanks was mourned by millions.

### ■ OCTOBER ■

**Sunday 1:** British men aged between 20 and 22 become eligible for conscription into the armed forces.

**Thursday 5:** Hitler enters the Polish capital, Warsaw, in triumph.

**Friday 6:** Hitler makes peace proposals to Britain and France. He assures neighbours Belgium and Holland of his friendship, too.

**Sunday 8:** RAF reconnaissance plane shoots down a German flying-boat in the North Sea.

**Monday 9:** The Prices of Food Bill is introduced to control profiteering. Chamberlain announces a committee of ministers to take charge of the British economy.

**Wednesday 11:** The British Expeditionary Force in France now numbers 158,000 men who, together with 25,000 vehicles, have been shipped across the Channel in just five weeks to help defend France.

**Saturday 14:** More than 800 men die when the battleship Royal Oak is torpedoed at her home base of Scapa Flow. Only 396 crew members survive the surprise attack. No one had believed a U-boat could penetrate the defences of the harbour or that a torpedo would pierce the outer defences of the ship.

**Monday 16:** German bombers attack the Firth of Forth and the naval base at Rosyth. Three British ships are damaged while four enemy bombers are brought down.

**Tuesday 17:** French troops pushed back in the Saar.

**Thursday 19:** The Turkish government signs a mutual assistance pact with France and Britain.

**Saturday 21:** The Luftwaffe attacks North Atlantic convoys.

**Saturday 28:** Nazis insist all Jews in the Third Reich should wear a yellow Star of David.

**Monday 30:** The British government produces a White Paper outlining the horrific treatment meted out to Jews in Nazi concentration camps. It declares: 'The treatment is reminiscent of the darkest ages in the history of man.'

### ■ NOVEMBER ■

**Monday 6:** First major air battle on the Western front takes place.

**Wednesday 8:** Hitler survives an assassination attempt in Munich, where he was celebrating the anniversary of his bid for power – the Munich Putsch – staged in 1923. Seven people are killed and more than 60 are injured when a bomb hidden near the platform from which the Führer was speaking exploded. Hitler himself had already finished his speech and left. The Nazi newspaper, the Volkischer Beobachter, claims British agents were responsible for the outrage.

**Monday 13:** First German bombs hit British soil when the Shetland Islands come under enemy fire.

Two German supply ships are scuttled after being cornered by the Royal Navy.

**Saturday 18:** Eighty people are killed when the Dutch ship Simon Bolivar hits a new type of magnetic mine laid in the North Sea. Other neutral ships are sunk by the same method. Minesweepers endeavour to clear the shipping routes of the hazards but their efforts are hampered by the mines running adrift.

Three IRA bombs explode in London's Piccadilly Circus.

**Wednesday 22:** German aircraft sow parachute-retarded mines in the Thames Estuary.

**Thursday 23:** RAF fighter aircraft shoot down seven German planes over France.

**Thursday 30:** The Soviet Union invades neighbouring Finland after the tiny independent country refused Stalin's demands to hand over some land. Heavy fighting is reported along Finland's defensive Mannerheim line.

### ■ DECEMBER ■

**Saturday 2:** South African Defence Force bombers force the German liner Watussi to be scuttled.

**Wednesday 6:** Britain pledges arms for Finland.

**Tuesday 12:** Hollywood film star Douglas Fairbanks dies in his sleep of a heart attack, aged 56.

**Wednesday 13:** The Battle of the River Plate. 'Pocket battleship' Admiral Graf Spee, which has been picking off merchant ships in the South Atlantic and Indian Ocean, is attacked by British cruisers Exeter, Ajax and Achilles. After a day-long battle, the Graf Spee limps into Montevideo harbour with 36 dead, 60 injured and widespread damage.

**Thursday 14:** The League of Nations expels Russia

*Above:* The life of Canadian soldiers in Britain appeared tranquil to those back home.

*Left:* Australian troops were the subject of curiosity when they marched through a British village.

for its hostile actions against Finland.

**Friday 15:** Uruguayan authorities order the Graf Spee out of the safety of its harbour before full repairs can be carried out.

**Sunday 17:** Hitler orders the Graf Spee be scuttled rather than fall into British hands. Captain Hans Langsdorff takes the 10,000-ton warship out of Montevideo harbour where she is blown up and sunk. Three days later Langsdorff kills himself.

**Tuesday 19:** First Canadian troops arrive on British soil.

**Friday 22:** Women working in munitions factories demand the same pay as men.

**Tuesday 26:** The first squadron of Australian airmen arrives in Britain.

**Sunday 31:** Determined Finns see off another Russian division.

# 1940

After the 'phoney' war ended, Britain was bombarded by Hitler's Luftwaffe, and city after city fell foul of the Blitz. Yet despite deprivation and desperation, the island stood firm while other European countries succumbed. Hitler's planned invasion was called off.

**Monday 1:** Conscription in Britain is extended to include all able-bodied men aged between 20 and 27.

**Friday 5:** Secretary of State for War Leslie Hore-Belisha resigns and is replaced by Oliver Stanley.

**Monday 8:** Butter, sugar and bacon rationed in Britain.

**Tuesday 9:** More than 150 people are feared dead after a Union Castle passenger liner hits a mine off the south east coast of Britain.

German bombers claim three merchant ships in the North Sea.

**Monday 15:** The British government comes under pressure to review its blackout policies after it is revealed that nearly twice as many people have been killed on the roads than by enemy action.

**Tuesday 16:** British submarines Seahorse, Undine and Starfish are sunk after operating in enemy waters.

**Wednesday 17:** A cold snap hits Europe with the River Thames freezing over in London for the first time in more than 50 years.

**Sunday 21:** War at sea intensifies as 81 crew are lost when the Grenville is sunk.

US golfer Jack Nicklaus is born.

**Monday 22:** British destroyer Exmouth is sunk by U-boat off Wick, Scotland, with the loss of all hands.

**Friday 26:** Nazi leaders warn Germans that listening to a foreign radio station is a serious offence, carrying the death penalty.

## FEBRUARY

**Thursday 1:** Frustrated by its lack of progress, the Red Army launches another offensive against the Finns in the disputed region of Karelia.

**Thursday 7:** Two convicted IRA men are hanged in Birmingham.

**Saturday 10:** In Czechoslovakia, Jews are ordered to shut down their shops and cease any business involvements.

## Hitler orders all German U-boat commanders to consider neutral shipping as fair game

**Tuesday 13:** Soviet Red Army troops make gains at last in their invasion of Finland.

**Friday 16:** The Royal Navy destroyer HMS Cossack sails into a Norwegian fjord and its sailors free 300 British prisoners from the German tanker Altmark. All the men had been taken when their ships were sunk by the Admiral Graf Spee. Britain protests to Norway about its apparent protection of the prison ship.

**Saturday 17:** Norway registers a protest with the British government about its flouting of neutrality.

**Monday 19:** Destroyer Daring is torpedoed, with 157 casualties.

**Tuesday 20:** Hitler orders all German U-boat commanders to consider neutral shipping as fair game. Norway, Sweden and Denmark register their anger at the ruling.

**Friday 23:** The crews of HMS Exeter and HMS Ajax are cheered through

*Above:* The passions depicted in the romantic melodrama *Gone with the Wind* still shine out 50 years later.
*Far left:* Vapour trails over St Paul's.

the streets of London when they return home after their successful battle against Admiral Graf Spee.

**Thursday 29:** Newcomer Vivien Leigh wins an Academy Award for her performance as Scarlett O'Hara in the hit film Gone with the Wind. The award for Best Actor goes to Robert Donat for his performance in Goodbye Mr Chips.

## MARCH

**Saturday 2:** British India liner Domala bombed in the English Channel with the loss of 100 lives.

**Thursday 7:** Prestige liner the Queen Elizabeth completes a secret dash from Britain across the Atlantic to wait out the war in the safety of American waters.

**Wednesday 13:** After a bloody conflict claiming hundreds of thousands of lives, the Russian war with Finland is concluded with a peace treaty. Russian troops were continually outmanoeuvred by their enemy. Only sheer force of numbers settled the war in Stalin's favour. The embarrassing rout has made Stalin look silly in the eyes of the world.

**Saturday 16:** A mission by American envoy Sumner Welles intended to prepare the ground for peace talks in Europe fails, with both Britain and Germany unequivocal in their refusals to negotiate.

Scapa Flow naval base is bombed by Luftwaffe. The action claims the life of the first British civilian killed in an air raid.

**Tuesday 19:** RAF seek revenge for the Scapa Flow raid by bombing a German air base.

**Wednesday 20:** Paul Daladier resigns as premier of France to be succeeded by Paul Reynaud.

**Monday 25:** The new two-seater Mosquito bomber aircraft makes its maiden flight.

**Wednesday 27:** Under the orders of SS chief Himmler, the foundations for the concentration camp at Auschwitz are laid.

*Below:* **Winston Churchill (centre) in 1940 with British and French senior military officers. From left to right, Ironside, Georges, Gamelin and Gort.**

# CHURCHILL

**Looking back, it seems Winston Churchill, Britain's best-remembered statesman, was born to be in politics.**

Churchill's father before him was a respected Conservative Member of Parliament and he was descended from an established and powerful family. Yet 'Winnie' had a sad childhood, in which he was noted only for his academic shortcomings. It appeared for much of his life that he would shine more at soldiering and writing than ever he could in the see-saw world of politics.

He was born in 1874, the son of Lord Randolph Churchill and New Yorker Jennie Jerome. He had little to do with his father, who despaired of his underachievement in the classroom. The young Churchill adored his beautiful mother but she in turn made her business elsewhere than the nursery. In her absence, there was a nanny, Mrs Everest, nicknamed 'Womany' by her charge, with whom she forged a deep and lasting bond.

He was rebellious and uncontrollable, and it wasn't until he discovered a love of English literature that Churchill put his mind to work at Harrow public school. He went on to the Royal Military College at Sandhurst, excelling in the subject of soldiering.

Flirting first with journalism, Churchill seized the opportunity to see some action on India's troubled North West Frontier in 1898. There followed a spell in the Sudan before he choose a life of politics. His first bid to enter Parliament was unsuccessful and he returned as a reporter to Africa to cover the Boer War.

Aged 26, Churchill won a seat in the House of Commons in 1901, representing Oldham for the Conservatives. Just three years later, frustrated by the confines of the Tory party, he became a Liberal. His change of colours happily coincided with a Liberal election victory. Now he was in the Cabinet, enjoying a taste of power until he unexpectedly lost his seat at the subsequent election.

While he was campaigning for a by-election he met Clementine Ogilvy Hozier, who was to become his loyal wife.

During World War I his reputation became stained with the debacle at Gallipoli. As First Lord of the Admiralty, Churchill was convinced the assault against the Turks would be a sparkling success. It turned into a bloody failure for which he carried the can. Churchill saw out the next few years as a soldier in France until he was recalled to the Cabinet in 1917.

Between the wars, Churchill fared best as a writer. He faded from the political scene after his brutish treatment of the workers during the 1926 General Strike. From the back benches he continually warned about the threat posed by Germany but few heeded his words.

Then, in 1939, as war was declared, Prime Minister Chamberlain capitalised on Churchill's experience and made him First Lord of the Admiralty once more.

Churchill's spirited commitment to Britain's role in the war won hearts and minds. By May 1940 he was head of a coalition government charged with bringing Britain through its darkest hour. And win through he did although his performance was by no means exemplary and his support was far from universal.

Many of the military disasters which plagued Britain during the opening years of the war could be laid at Churchill's door, notably the British rout in Norway in 1940 which cost Chamberlain his job.

Yet Churchill had one abiding point in his favour – he was committed beyond question to the defeat of Hitler. He refused to entertain ideas of a negotiated peace even when Britain appeared to be on the brink of defeat. His energy and enthusiasm for the obliteration of Nazism were inexhaustible. Such was his fervour he even overcame a loathing of Communism in general and Stalin in particular to bring about the downfall of Hitler.

Nevertheless, Labour was elected at his expense in the 1945 elections and he was compelled to lead the opposition until the Tory victory in 1951. Churchill stayed in politics until the end of his life. When he died on 24 January 1965, the nation recognised his colossal contribution with the honour of a state funeral.

**Thursday 28:** Dutch fliers shoot down a British bomber near Rotterdam in error, with the loss of one life.

### ■ APRIL ■

**Tuesday 2:** Scapa Flow comes under attack from Germans again, who also target North Sea convoys.

Mussolini orders a general mobilisation, involving all Italians aged 14 years plus.

Dutch troops placed on full alert along the German border.

**Wednesday 3:** In a Cabinet reshuffle, Churchill is given the task of directing the war effort.

**Friday 5:** RAF strikes at German ships in the Kiel Canal.

**Monday 8:** British submarines torpedo three German ships.

Germany invades Denmark and Norway. Denmark is overrun with only nominal resistance.

**Tuesday 9:** Germans take control of Norwegian capital, Oslo, with the arrival of airborne troops in order to ensure the Third Reich can maintain

> ## The German cruiser Blücher *is hit and sunk with loss of 1,000 crewmen*

vital supply lines from Scandinavia. Norwegian forces are driven back but still put up fierce resistance as they retreat. Major Vidkun Quisling, who gave his name to World War II traitors, sets up a national government in the occupied capital. He appeals for fighting to end, while Norway's King Haakon asks every Norwegian to take up arms.

**Wednesday 10:** Battle of Narvik.

**Thursday 11:** German cruiser Blücher is hit and sunk with the loss of 1,000 crewmen. Royal Navy

*Above:* **German soldiers feel the chill on their march into Norway.**

submarine Spearfish leaves the 'pocket battleship' Lützow with extensive damage.

**Saturday 13:** Second Battle of Narvik. The Allies emerge victorious, with the loss of eight German destroyers and a U-boat.

**Sunday 14:** Royal Navy submarine Tarpon falls victim to a minesweeper.

**Monday 15:** Allies land in Norway. Quisling's short-lived government resigns in favour of an 'Administrative Council'.

British unemployment figures fall to 973,000, the lowest jobless total since 1920.

**Tuesday 16:** British forces land in the Faeroe Islands.

**Wednesday 17:** Stavanger, the Norwegian port now in German hands, is raided for a second time by the RAF.

**Thursday 18:** British submarine Sterlet is sunk by German aircraft off the Norwegian coast.

**Friday 19:** The Swiss government orders a general mobilisation, in fear of an attack from Nazi Germany.

**Monday 22:** When the Allied Supreme War Council meets in Paris, Poland and Norway are represented.

**Wednesday 24:** British troops forced

to pull out of Trondheim after clashes with German forces.

**Thursday 25:** Allied forces driven out of Lillehammer, central Norway.

### ■ MAY ■

**Wednesday 1:** Trondheim is evacuated by the Allies. Norwegians surrender at Lillehammer.

German bomber carrying magnetic mines crashes in Clacton, Essex. Four Germans and two people on the ground are killed, and a further 156 are injured.

Women in Britain are given the green light to work in munitions factories by the Amalgamated Engineering Union.

Postage rates in Britain more than double, increasing from a penny to twopence halfpenny.

**Thursday 2:** Britain begins to evacuate its troops from Norway.

**Sunday 5:** Norwegian government-in-exile sets up in London.

**Monday 6:** American author John Steinbeck wins the Pulitzer Prize for his novel The Grapes of Wrath.

**Wednesday 8:** A Parliamentary

*Right:* Women at work on presses producing shells. It was in May 1940 that the Amalgamated Engineering Union gave the go-ahead for women in Britain to work in munitions factories.

motion rapping Chamberlain for the military failures in Norway fails by 81 votes. However, more than 40 government MPs join the opposition in condemning his leadership and a further 60 abstain.

**Thursday 9:** British upper age limit for conscription raised to 36.

**Friday 10:** Germany invades Holland, Belgium and Luxembourg with the by-now familiar tactics of 'Blitzkreig', or lightning war.

Chamberlain resigns. Churchill is prime minister, forming a coalition cabinet with Labour leader Clement Attlee as his deputy. 'I have nothing to offer but blood, toil, tears and sweat,' Churchill tells Parliament.

**Sunday 12:** The German armed forces continues their sweep through the Low Countries.

The Luftwaffe begins a bombing campaign in northern France.

In Britain, Germans are interned.

## Rommel wins a key tank battle in northern France, spreading fear among French forces

**Monday 13:** The Dutch royal family flees to London as Dutch troops pull back in the face of the German invasion of Holland.

**Tuesday 14:** German army units under Field-Marshal von Runstedt cross River Meuse and the rugged landscape of the Ardennes to enter northern France.

Germans capture key port of Rotterdam. Meanwhile, the Dutch

government arrives in London.

British boat owners are required to register with the government.

Local Defence Volunteers – soon to be known as the Home Guard – created to protect Britain in the event of parachute attack or seaborne invasion. In the space of a week, 250,000 men enlist.

**Wednesday 15:** Dutch surrender as the German forces roll into Belgium.

Rommel wins a key tank battle in northern France, spreading fear and confusion among French forces.

Britain's weekly butter ration per person is halved to four ounces.

**Thursday 16:** Belgian government quits Brussels for London.

**Friday 17:** Germany continues to make gains in Belgium and north eastern France.

General De Gaulle counter attacks at Montcornet.

The RAF strikes at Bremen and Hamburg, vital German fuel depots.

**Sunday 19:** General John Gort, commander in chief of the British Expeditionary Force in France, orders a withdrawal of his men to the English Channel.

**Monday 20:** Invading Germans force a wedge between retreating French and British troops.

**Tuesday 21:** Bombs fall on English Channel ports while the RAF hits refineries in occupied Rotterdam. Hard-pressed British troops in northern France mount a counter-attack at the town of Arras.

**Wednesday 22:** The Emergency Powers Act passed in Britain, bringing businesses under state control and bringing a new brand of authority over the working population.

**Thursday 23:** British troops in fierce fighting as they are backed up to the coast of northern France.

In Britain Sir Oswald Mosley, leader of the British fascists, and his cohorts are arrested.

**Saturday 25:** Survivors of the British Expeditionary Force are surrounded on the French coast. Advancing German units are just 20 miles behind them. The Royal Navy succeeds in snatching nearly 28,000 men to safety.

**Sunday 26:** Evacuation of British, French and Belgian troops – codenamed 'Operation Dynamo' – begins from Dunkirk. An official fleet is joined by a flotilla of small boats eager to aid the war effort and ready to brave enemy fire. Privately, officials estimate only 45,000 men will be saved. Within a week 338,226 men are taken back to Britain. There are 289 tanks, 64,000 vehicles and 2,500 guns left behind in France.

**Tuesday 28:** King Leopold III of Belgium surrenders.

**Wednesday 29:** Narvik, in Norway, is won from Germany.

**Thursday 30:** Italian dictator Mussolini makes his decision to enter the war known to Hitler.

---

## *The Luftwaffe bombs Paris, killing 45 people and injuring hundreds more*

---

### ■ JUNE ■

**Saturday 1:** British troops on the run again in Norway.

In case of invasion, British road signposts are taken down.

**Monday 3:** Last ships leave Dunkirk under cover of darkness.

The Luftwaffe bombs Paris, killing 45 people and injuring hundreds more.

A night curfew is placed on all aliens and stateless people living in the United Kingdom.

**Tuesday 4:** Germans seize Dunkirk, taking 40,000 French prisoners.

French planes bomb Munich and Frankfurt in the reply to the German sorties against Paris.

**Thursday 6:** Germans penetrate French defences along the River Somme, with the defenders suffering heavy losses.

*Right:* **Although thousands escaped, there were scores of Britons left dead in the ruins of Dunkirk.**

## ◆ EYE WITNESS ◆

**As a conscientious objector, Ron Tansley of Nottingham, England, refused to fight. After joining the Friends Ambulance Unit as a volunteer in 1940, at the age of 23, he nevertheless found himself in the thick of the action.**

❝ I was a pacifist but I realised that I couldn't just stand by. I had to do something if it was only humanitarian work. Some of my greatest friends were in the forces and I certainly had no animosity towards those who did join up.

The factory where I was working began making aeroplanes so I left.

I came before two government tribunals, both very sympathetic, which decided my reasons for not fighting were genuine. I then joined the Friends Ambulance Unit. I was in various hospitals up and down the country working on the wards, from operating theatres to casualty, treating Blitz victims in London and Liverpool.

After two years training I was sent to Birmingham to study German culture and language. In the autumn of 1944 I was sent to Ostend. About 40 of us went in sections of ten. Mostly our orders came from the Red Cross. From there we went to Antwerp, which was receiving 100 German rockets a day at the time.

We were attached to a fire station. Whenever there was an alarm, we followed the fire engines. Once we arrived at a bombed cinema where hundreds of British soldiers had been killed.

As the front line pushed forward to the Rhine, it was our job to bring people back from their homes to the safety of a large hospital so the tanks could go straight through. We kept putting more and more people inside this three-storey building and tried to feed and care for them as best we could. Then typhoid broke out. We had to wrap the dead bodies in paper or what linen we could find. There were no coffins. Several hundred people died.

While I was there a German lit a bonfire in the grounds. I was walking past with a German helper when suddenly there was an explosion from the bonfire. A piece of shrapnel just went straight through the middle of the man next to me and killed him.

Eventually, I was sent to Hamburg. On the way some Germans tried to give themselves up to us but we wouldn't accept prisoners. I have never seen anything like the sight of that city. There was utter destruction for miles and miles. I wondered why the women and children had to suffer so much.

Apart from medical work we also traced lost relatives and worked with refugees, including a German Quaker who was put in a concentration camp because he refused to fight. I helped put him in touch with a contact in England.

We got great admiration from the soldiers because we were there when we didn't have to be. I don't think I heard any adverse remarks except in the military hospital I worked at in England. ❞

*Right:* Adolf Hitler relished his victory over the French as a revenge for Germany's defeat in World War I.

**Friday 7:** Allied troops pushed back again. French aircraft bomb the German capital, Berlin.

**Saturday 8:** Norway falls.

**Monday 10:** Italy enters the war, declaring its opposition to Britain and France. The New York Times reports the move with derision. 'With the courage of a jackal at the heels of a bolder beast of prey, Mussolini has now left his ambush. His motives in taking Italy into the war are as clear as day. He wants to share in the spoils which he believes will fall to Hitler and he has chosen to enter the war when he thinks he can accomplish this at the least cost to himself.'

## *Italy enters the war, declaring its opposition to Britain and France*

**Tuesday 11:** Air raids begin on Malta while the RAF bomb the Italian city of Turin and petrol dumps in Italy's African colonies.

The RAF strikes German shipping in the Norwegian port of Trondheim.

**Wednesday 12:** Italian submarine sinks British cruiser Calypso off the island of Crete.

**Friday 14:** Victorious Germans enter Paris while Rommel captures the key northern port of Le Havre. The French government moves to Bordeaux in the south west.

*Right:* Germany's top brass, including von Ribbentrop and Rudolf Hess, joined Hitler in witnessing the humiliating peace deal made with France.

**Saturday 15:** The Soviet army occupies Lithuania.

**Sunday 16:** British submarine Grampus sunk by Italians off Sicily, the second British submarine loss in four days.

**Monday 17:** French leader Marshal Pétain orders his army to stop fighting as he seeks 'honourable' peace terms with Germany.

The liner Lancastria, carrying 3,000 British troops, is bombed at St Nazaire in northwestern France.

**Tuesday 18:** De Gaulle appeals to the French living in Britain to join him. 'Whatever happens, the flame of the French resistance must not go out and it will not go out.'

**Saturday 22:** French representatives sign an armistice at Compiègne, forced to use the same train carriage in which the Germans capitulated 1918. Hitler presided over the humiliation of France, half of which will now be occupied by Germany.

Italy bombs the British stronghold of Alexandria, Egypt.

**Sunday 23:** De Gaulle announces the launch of a French National Committee based in London which will continue to fight against Hitler.

---

### French representatives sign an armistice at Compiègne

---

**Monday 24:** France led by Marshal Pétain signs a peace accord with Italy near Rome.

**Tuesday 25:** A ceasefire in France takes effect from the early hours.

London hears air raid sirens in the early hours for the first time.

**Friday 28:** Churchill recognises Charles de Gaulle as the leader of the 'Free French', now forming into a volunteer legion.

## LINES OF DEFENCE

**During World War II, Europe was crossed with lines of defence, none of which would stand the test of a sustained offensive.**

**THE CURZON LINE:**
The line that divided Poland following its defeat by German and Russian forces in 1939. It had been drawn by Lord Curzon after World War I and allowed the Russians to claim they were only taking back what was rightfully theirs.

**THE MAGINOT LINE:**
French defensive line built between the wars which was easily overrun by Germany in 1940.

**THE SIEGFRIED LINE:**
Also known as the West Wall, Germany's border defensive line penetrated by Allied troops in 1944.

**THE MANNERHEIM LINE:**
The line between Lake Lagoda and the Gulf of Finland beyond the Russo-Finnish border; the main line of fortification for the Finns which was finally overwhelmed by superior numbers of Russians.

**THE GUSTAV LINE:**
Germany's line across Italy which ran through Cassino and encompassed some fearsome natural defensive positions. It held the Allied troops at bay for five months in 1944.

German aircraft bomb Jersey.

**Saturday 29:** Swiss artist Paul Klee dies. He had been a professor at Düsseldorf until expelled by the Nazis in 1933.

**Sunday 30:** Germans occupy the island of Guernsey.

### ■ JULY ■

**Monday 1:** Marshal Henri Pétain moves the French government to Vichy, where it operates as a satellite to the powerful Germans. The established Third Republic is dissolved and the familiar cries of 'Liberty, equality, fraternity' are to be replaced by the Germanic 'Work, family, fatherland'.

Jersey is occupied by the Germans. British forces had already pulled out after deciding that the defence of the Channel Islands would be too problematic. The British evacuated

many islanders, crops and cattle though some people chose to remain.

British milk increases to fourpence (two new pence) a pint.

*Right:* **Marshal Pétain, though leader of the new France, was a German puppet.**

*Right:* Leon Trotsky, born Lev Davidovitch Bronstein, and his wife in exile in Mexico shortly before Trotsky's death at the hands of a vicious Stalinist agent. Trotsky had been defeated by Stalin in the power struggle that followed Lenin's death.

The government asks women to conserve wood by wearing flat heels.

**Tuesday 2:** Hitler begins work on plans to invade Britain.

**Wednesday 3:** Royal Navy attacks a French naval squadron in Algeria to keep it out of German hands. It happens after a French commander ignores a British ultimatum to sail his ships to Britain or America. The bombardment from the British kills 1,000 French sailors.

**Friday 5:** Romania throws itself behind Hitler and the Axis powers.

Destroyer Whirlwind sunk by a U-boat off Land's End.

**Saturday 6:** British submarine Shark scuttled off Stavanger after sustaining damage in German attacks.

**Tuesday 9:** Royal Navy chases Italian ships back into port after skirmishes at Cape Spartivento.

RAF begins night bombing operations over Germany.

Tea rationing introduced in Britain. Everyone is allowed two ounces a week.

**Wednesday 10:** Battle of Britain gets underway with Luftwaffe attacks on English Channel convoys and a blitz on the Welsh docks. Luftwaffe chief Hermann Göring hopes to lure the RAF into dog-fights over the English Channel to deplete its waning strength still further.

In Britain the British Union of Fascists is barred.

**Saturday 13:** Italians launch an attack on the British from Ethiopia.

**Sunday 14:** Bastille Day in France is declared a 'day of meditation'. The Free French, led by de Gaulle, lay wreaths at the London Cenotaph.

**Tuesday 16:** Japanese government resigns under pressure from the powerful army.

**Wednesday 17:** Britain closes the Burma Road, a supply route for the Chinese army, following fierce demands from the Japanese.

**Friday 19:** Hitler, speaking at the Reichstag, appeals to the Allies to listen to reason and halt the war.

**Saturday 20:** British destroyer HMS Brazen is sunk off Dover.

## Battle of Britain gets underway with Luftwaffe attacks on English Channel convoys

Casualty list reveals 336 Britons were killed last month, 476 injured.

**Sunday 21:** Czechs join the host of exiled governments in London.

**Tuesday 23:** In a third War Budget, Chancellor Sir Kingsley Wood raises income tax to eight shillings and sixpence (forty-two and a half pence)

in the pound. A 33 per cent purchase tax on luxury items is also introduced to help cover the costs of war, estimated at £3,470,000 for the coming year.

**Wednesday 24:** Four hundred French sailors die when a neutral liner shipping them back to France is torpedoed by the Germans.

**Thursday 25:** In Germany the use of forced labour from occupied territories is announced.

British-held Gibraltar is evacuated of women and children.

**Monday 29:** Dover harbour attacked.

British Air Ministry accuses Germany of using Red Cross planes for reconnaissance.

### ■ AUGUST ■

**Thursday 1:** Russian foreign minister Molotov speaks out against Britain and America while declaring his country still neutral.

**Friday 2:** Italy gathers troops on the border of Libya, and Italian colony, and British-held Egypt.

A French military court condemns de Gaulle to death in his absence.

Meanwhile, the Vichy government continues to harry former leading lights of the Third Republic, including ex-prime minister Paul Daladier and former army commander General Maurice Gamelin, who have been arrested and charged with 'causing the defeat of France'.

**Sunday 4:** Italy invades British Somaliland from Ethiopia

**Monday 5:** Residents of the Third Reich will now need to carry an Ahnenpass, or Certificate of Ancestry, to prove they and their family have been kept racially pure during the past 150 years.

**Thursday 8:** Rates of pay for British servicemen increase by sixpence (two and a half pence) a day. The weekly rate for a private now stands at seventeen shillings and sixpence (eighty-seven and a half pence).

**Friday 9:** British government states its intention to withdraw its troops from Shanghai and north China.

*Below:* **Dulcie Street, Manchester, became one of hundreds of residential and commercial roads wrecked in the Blitz.**

# THE GEORGE CROSS

**World War II saw the institution of the George Cross. Its creation was announced by King George VI on 23 September 1940 with the words: 'Many and glorious are the deeds of gallantry done during these perilous but famous days. In order that they should be worthily and promptly recognised I have decided to create at once a new mark of honour for men and women of all walks of life.'**

The George Cross (left) is Britain's highest bravery award that may be received by a civilian. Among the first to receive one was Thomas Alderson, an Air Raid Precautions detachment leader on the home front, for bravery during enemy attacks on Bridlington in Yorkshire. Bomb disposal experts Squadron Leader John Dowland, Leonard Harrison and Major Cyril Martin also received awards. The George Medal (right) is the country's second-highest decoration for bravery awardable to civilians.

**Saturday 10:** HMS Transylvania is sunk off Northern Ireland after being hit by a torpedo.

**Sunday 11:** Britain's coastal ports come under bombardment from 400 Luftwaffe planes. British claim 65 hits for the loss of 26 RAF aircraft.

**Monday 12:** Wasting food is now against the law as Britain fears for future food supplies.

**Tuesday 13:** Christened 'Eagle Day' by the Germans, who believed they would have won dominance of the British skies by now, it has been

dominated by dog-fights across southern England. Once again, it seems British fliers inflict great losses on the attackers while sustaining far fewer casualties.

**Thursday 15:** Another day of bombardment this time from 1,000 Luftwaffe planes. Airfields and radio installations remain the prime targets of the German bombers.

**Friday 16:** Sixth day of aerial harassment of southern England by German air force.

**Saturday 17:** British warships attack ports in Italian-held Libya

The Duke of Windsor, the former King Edward VIII, who abdicated so he could marry American divorcée Wallis Simpson, is sworn in as governor of the Bahamas.

**Sunday 18:** Still more swoops by the Luftwaffe over southern England. The RAF suffers less than a quarter of the losses of the Luftwaffe.

**Monday 19:** Italian troops move into Berbera, the capital of British Somaliland. Evacuated troops head for Aden.

---

## 'Never in the field of human conflict was so much owed by so many to so few'

---

**Tuesday 20:** In Parliament, Churchill pays tribute to the courage of the men of the RAF. 'Never in the field of human conflict was so much owed by so many to so few.'

**Wednesday 21:** Exiled Bolshevik Leon Trotsky dies after assassin Ramon Mercader, a one-time confidant, plunges an ice-pick into his skull. Trotsky was working from his base in Mexico towards establishing international socialism. His killer was almost certainly working for

*Above:* German soldiers gather at a port in northern France in preparation for 'Operation Sealion', the invasion of Britain. Hitler was forced to postpone the operation, and in the end it never came.

Trotsky's old enemy, Stalin.

**Saturday 24:** London Blitz begins with an all-night bombing raid.

**Sunday 25:** RAF takes revenge for London strikes with a night raid on Berlin, dropping not only bombs but also propaganda leaflets. All aircraft involved were reported to have returned safely to base.

**Monday 26:** Luftwaffe planes shed bombs on County Wexford, killing three Irish girls. The Eire government makes a protest to Hitler.

**Tuesday 27:** Air raids continue over southern England, London, and now the Midlands. In total, 21 towns and cities are hit.

**Wednesday 28:** The Vichy government abandons laws in France which protect Jews.

**Thursday 29:** Germany says sorry to Eire over the Wexford bombing.

### ■ SEPTEMBER ■

**Sunday 1:** British destroyer Ivanhoe sinks off the Dutch coast after running into a mine.

**Tuesday 3:** Britain barters leases on two naval bases with the USA in exhange for 50 destroyers.

Hitler sets a date for 'Operation

Sealion', the invasion of Britain. It is to be 21 September.

**Wednesday 4:** A furious Hitler promises Britain will suffer for the air raids it carried out against Berlin.

**Thursday 5:** In the casualty figures for August, it is revealed 1,075 civilians were killed in enemy action, while 1,261 were seriously injured.

A Royal Navy submarine sinks the troop ship Marion, with the reported loss of 4,000 German fighting men.

**Saturday 7:** German air attacks on Britain are increased. Night raids on sites by the River Thames claim 306 lives but Britain declares it has suffered only about a third of the aircraft losses inflicted on Germany.

**Sunday 8:** More bombardments under cover of darkness, this time killing 286 civilians and injuring 1,400.

**Monday 9:** London under attack from 350 Luftwaffe planes causing devastation in the East End.

Italians bomb Tel Aviv, killing 111.

Tuesday 10: Buckingham Palace damaged in another night of heavy German bombing.

Wednesday 11: A daylight air raid on London kills more than 100 people while the Channel port of Dover comes in for heavy bombing.

Thursday 12: Germany claims the RAF are dropping destructive Colorado beetles over its potato crops.

## Buckingham Palace damaged in another night of heavy German bombing

Friday 13: Italy moves troops across the border from Libya into Egypt.

Sunday 15: Largest air raid to date launched against London. Meanwhile the RAF targets invasion forces gathering in French and Belgian ports. BBC assertions that 185 Luftwaffe planes were shot down over London in a day are later disproved. The actual figure was 56.

British units strike at advancing Italians in Egypt and claim to have inflicted severe losses.

Monday 16: London landmarks including Bond Street, Piccadilly and Park Lane, are struck in night raid.

Tuesday 17: With his attempt to cripple Britain through air raids apparently failing, Hitler postpones his invasions plans. 'Operation Sealion' is postponed short term.

In the Commons, Churchill announces that, in the first half of September, 2,000 civilians have died under enemy fire. The number of fatalities in the armed services in the same period is just 250.

Thursday 19: London and Brighton bombed. Minister of Labour Ernest Bevin announces that more than 51,000 have registered as conscientious objectors.

Sunday 22: The Japanese land in French Indochina.

Evacuee ship City of Benares, whose passengers include 99 children bound for Canada, is sunk by a U-boat torpedo. Only 46 survive while more than 300 are drowned.

◆ **EYE WITNESS** ◆

**Major John Voice joined the Indian Army shortly before war broke out. In January 1940 he joined the 3rd Battalion, 14th Punjab Regiment.**

❛ We went overseas to the Middle East in September 1940. In December we moved to the Sudan by troop ship. From there we were moved by rail and road to Eritrea. We found ourselves by the beginning of February in the operational area on Cameron Ridge in front of Keren. Apart from one or two skirmishes, this was our first major action.

We scaled Cameron Ridge on the night of 4 February. The terrain was mountainous, dusty and stony with rocks as big as a house. The best transport was mules, of which there were none. One company was used as a carrier force. During the day it was hot, at night it was cold.

I was in battalion headquarters on Cameron Ridge. The enemy had our range to a 'T'. Suddenly, I was knocked for six by enemy fire. I wasn't knocked out for long and after that I was quite conscious.

Captain Hugh Baker tried to put me on his back which was frightfully painful. The leg was shattered below the knee.

It was more comfortable for me to pull myself down the track. As I was pulling myself down this rough track on my hands and elbows I met the medical party coming up, led by Doc Smith of the Indian Medical Service. He gave me morphine and I was taken the rest of the way on a stretcher. I was evacuated in a Jeep ambulance. To the best of my recollection, the entire length of my right leg was put into plaster that evening.

It was more than six months before I started to walk again. Then it was with two sticks. By June 1943 I was sent back to India where I served for the rest of the war in my regimental depot. I became a company and then training battalion commander. My right leg was finally amputated mid-thigh more than 50 years later in August 1993 due to the injury and complications. ❜

*Left:* **It was a relief to the government when Buckingham Palace was bombed, showing war hit rich and poor alike.**

**Monday 23:** De Gaulle and a force of Free French are taken to Dakar, Senegal, by the Royal Navy.

**Tuesday 24:** London suffers 18th successive night raid. Southampton and Brighton also bombed.

The king introduces the George Cross and George Medal 'for valour and outstanding gallantry'.

## Civilian casualties during September amounted to nearly 7,000 dead and 10,000 injured

**Wednesday 25:** Norwegian King Haakon is deposed by the German invaders. Vidkun Quisling's government is installed.

**Friday 27:** Japan signs a ten-year pact with Germany and Italy cementing ties between the three. German foreign minister Ribbentrop declares: 'The pact is a military alliance between the three mightiest states of the world, comprising over 250 million people.'

More daylight raids on Britain.

**Monday 30:** British civilian casualties in September amounted to nearly 7,000 dead and 10,600 injured.

### ■ OCTOBER ■

**Tuesday 1:** A British island off China is occupied by the Japanese.

Finland signs a treaty of alliance with Germany.

**Thursday 3:** Chamberlain resigns Conservative Party leadership through ill-health.

**Friday 4:** Hitler and Mussolini meet at the picturesque Brenner Pass for a three-hour summit.

**Monday 7:** In further anti-semitic measures, Pétain repeals a long-standing law which gives Algerian Jews French citizenship.

German troops go into Romania on the pretext of helping maintain law and order.

**Tuesday 8:** Churchill tells Parliament the Burma Road is to be reopened.

**Wednesday 9:** The Conservative Party unanimously elects Winston Churchill as party leader.

The musician and future Beatle John Lennon is born.

Dutch puppet government declares that Jews and half-Jews can no longer work in the public domain.

**Saturday 12:** Hitler further postpones 'Operation Sealion', the planned German invasion of Britain, until spring 1941. Meanwhile, night raids continue over London.

**Tuesday 15:** Sixty-four people die when a bomb blasts through the roof of Balham tube station where scores of people take nightly shelter from the air raids.

Royal Navy submarine Rainbow is sunk by Italian submarine Toti.

**Monday 21:** Churchill, in a radio broadcast, makes an emotive appeal

*Below:* **Carnage after a bomb falls through Balham tube station, which was being used as a night shelter.**

to the wavering French. 'Frenchmen, rearm your spirits before it is too late.'

**Tuesday 22:** Sir Stafford Cripps, British Ambassador, tries to entice Russia back to the Allies with a tempting co-operation plan.

**Wednesday 23:** Hitler meets Francisco Franco, Spanish fascist dictator, to discuss Spain's possible entry into the war. Last year Hitler turned down Franco's overtures to join the Axis powers. Now he is keen to enlist Spanish help. Franco remains cool. Hitler also tries to persuade Pétain to join Germany against Britain but fails.

Football legend Pele is born in Brazil, with the name Edson Arantes do Nascimento.

### Britain's Fleet Air Arm bombs the Italian fleet at Taranto with spectacular success

**Saturday 26:** London suffers longest air raid yet, with widespread damage and many casualties.

**Monday 28:** Italians enter Greece from Albania. Churchill promises aid to the Greeks.

**Tuesday 29:** British troops bound for Crete to bolster Greek defences.

**Thursday 31:** British forces occupy a Cretan town while Italians make gains on the mainland.

Naples is bombed by the RAF for the first time.

British civilian casualty figures covering October reveal 6,334 dead and 8,695 injured.

### ◼ NOVEMBER ◼

**Friday 1:** Turkey announces its neturality in the conflict between Italy and its old enemy, Greece.

Britain mines the Bay of Biscay.

**Sunday 3:** Greeks score a significant victory against the Italian invaders.

**Tuesday 5:** Franklin D. Roosevelt is elected for the third time as American president. The Democrat, the first American to return to presidential office for a third time, triumphed over his Republican rival by a majority of five million votes.

**Saturday 9:** Neville Chamberlain, the former British prime minister, dies of cancer, aged 71.

*Above:* Franklin D. Roosevelt became a record breaker when he was returned to office for a third consecutive term.

Trades unions and employers organisations are made illegal in Vichy France.

**Monday 11:** Britain's Fleet Air Arm bombs the Italian fleet at Taranto with spectacular success. Three battleships, two cruisers and two other vessels are crippled. As a reprisal, Italy mounts its only air raid against Britain.

In America the Jeep is put through its paces by the army for the first time.

**Tuesday 12:** Soviet foreign minister Vyacheslav Molotov visits Berlin for talks with Hitler.

**Wednesday 13:** Fantasia, Walt Disney's cartoon set to classical music opens in New York.

**Thursday 14:** In Coventry, 554 civilians die in ten-hour bombing raid by the Luftwaffe, in which 400 tons of bombs rain down on the city.

**Friday 15:** In the Polish capital, Warsaw, 350,000 Jews are confined to a ghetto.

**Saturday 16:** The RAF makes its most devastating attack yet on Hamburg, dropping 2,000 bombs.

**Tuesday 19:** Greek rout of Italian invaders continues.

**Wednesday 20:** Hungary aligns itself with the Axis powers.

**Saturday 23:** Romania signs up with Germany and her allies, too.

**Wednesday 27:** Romanian extremists, known as the 'Iron Guard', begin a killing campaign, claiming more than 60 victims.

## STALIN

**The man who brought wholesale misery and death to his people set out in life hoping to be a priest. But he was expelled from theological college when his Marxist sympathies became known.**

Born in Georgia in 1879, Joseph Vissarionovich Dzhugashvili was a sickly child who survived the privations of a peasant upbringing to enter the theological college in Tblisi in 1894. But he had little time for the ritual of the Orthodox Church. Instead he was fired by the new socialist ideals brewing in Tsarist Russia. His growing involvement with this underground movement led to his expulsion from the college in 1899.

He became a Bolshevik in 1903 when the militant movement was led by Lenin. Before the 1917 Russian Revolution, he was repeatedly imprisoned and exiled for his radical views. In 1913 he was editor of the Bolshevik newspaper *Pravda* before another spell in Siberia.

There was little glory for Stalin, as he was now known, in the Russian Revolution or the years immediately following. Instead of fighting for the cause, he was battling on his own behalf, climbing up the rungs of power in the party. Then, as general secretary of the Communist Party, Stalin was waiting in the wings for absolute power on the death of Lenin in 1924. He strove to eliminate all his rivals and enemies, a pattern to which he was faithful throughout his leadership.

By 1929 he was undisputed leader of the Soviet Union. His simplistic way ahead was through five-year plans, which brutally enforced collectivised industry and agriculture on his people, making them poorer than ever before.

Peasants who objected were summarily shot or sent to labour camps where they would often perish in appalling conditions. An estimated ten million Russian peasants died while Stalin tried to modernise his country.

The terror he inflicted on his people knew no bounds. When he suspected a plot to oust him in the armed forces, he sought a terrible revenge, killing countless officers and men. And there were further purges, not only in the army but also among academics, teachers, politicians, judges and just about anyone who might conceivably disagree with him.

Privately, he was deeply unhappy. Two marriages failed and one of his sons committed suicide. His insecurities continued to fester, mirroring the liquidation of possible opposition.

Given this background, it is astonishing that Stalin managed to inspire such dedicated patriotism in his people after Hitler's attack. Yet still they rallied to his call. The mounting body count which had sparked the Russian Revolution during World War I failed to do anything other than unite the Soviet subjects.

Following the war Stalin's iron grip on the Soviet Union tightened still further. He orchestrated an empire and menaced non-Communist countries in the free world. Some say he became eaten up with suspicion to the point of being deranged. After his sudden death in 1953, his savage policies were denounced by his successors.

Royal Navy and Italian ships clash off Sardinian coast with both sides sustaining damage.
**Friday 29:** Initial plans for invasion of Russia are drawn up in Berlin.

**Saturday 30:** Civilian casualty figures reveal that 4,588 people were killed and more than 6,200 injured in the German attacks on Britain's major cities. Now Birmingham, Southampton, Sheffield, Manchester, Glasgow, Coventry, Dover, Liverpool and Brighton have all suffered appalling bomb damage as Luftwaffe chief Reichsmarschall Hermann Göring changes his tactics and aims to obliterate British industry.

### ■ DECEMBER ■

**Sunday 1:** Joseph Kennedy resigns as US ambassador to Britain. He is in opposition to what he believes is escalating American involvement in the conflict.

**Monday 2:** Franco is wooed away from Hitler with a British aid package. In return Franco declares he will stay neutral in the war.

**Tuesday 3:** Hungry Britons are promised extra rations of 4oz of sugar and 2oz of tea for Christmas.

**Wednesday 4:** Victorious Greeks begin to make headway in Albania against shamed Italians.

**Friday 6:** Italian chief of staff Marshal Pietro Badoglio is sacked following

*Below:* An early Jeep, the four-wheel drive 'general purpose' vehicle which revolutionised military transport during World War II.

the breaches of defences in Albania.
**Monday 9:** First British campaign in Africa gets underway when General Sir Archibald Wavell orders a surprise offensive against the Italians in the Western Desert. 'Operation Compass' is a success with 1,000 prisoners being taken.
**Thursday 12:** British troops capture 30,000 Italian prisoners in Egypt.
**Friday 13:** German forces move into Romania from neighbouring Hungary.
**Sunday 15:** Vice-Premier Laval is arrested when his plot to replace Pétain and align France more fully with Germany is revealed.
**Tuesday 17:** Hitler orders the release of Pierre Laval.

A German spy is hanged at Pentonville Prison, London, and a Winchester housewife is sentenced to death for working for the enemy.

**Saturday 21:** US novelist F. Scott Fitzgerald, author of The Great Gatsby, dies aged 44.

## 'Operation Compass' is a success with 1,000 prisoners being taken

An 18-year-old girl from Lancashire, who was kept in by her father who locked up her clothes was arrested in London after she escaped out of a bedroom window and caught a train to London without paying the fare. Elsie Fisher, who made her bid for freedom after finding some old clothes, refused to go home.
**Sunday 22:** Anthony Eden becomes Foreign Secretary and Lord Halifax is

appointed British ambassador to the United States.
**Sunday 29:** President Roosevelt tells Americans in a radio broadcast that the United States is 'the arsenal of democracy'. He proclaimed his intention was 'to keep you now, and your children later, out of a last-ditch war for the preservation of American independence'.
**Monday 30:** A request by miners for bigger beef rations turned down by Britain's Ministry of Food.
**Tuesday 31:** Civilian casualty figures for the month of December indicate 3,793 British people have been killed by enemy action, with 5,244 more being injured.

*Below:* **Hoses line the streets as firefighters go to work in London following a night bombing raid by aircraft of Hermann Göring's Luftwaffe.**

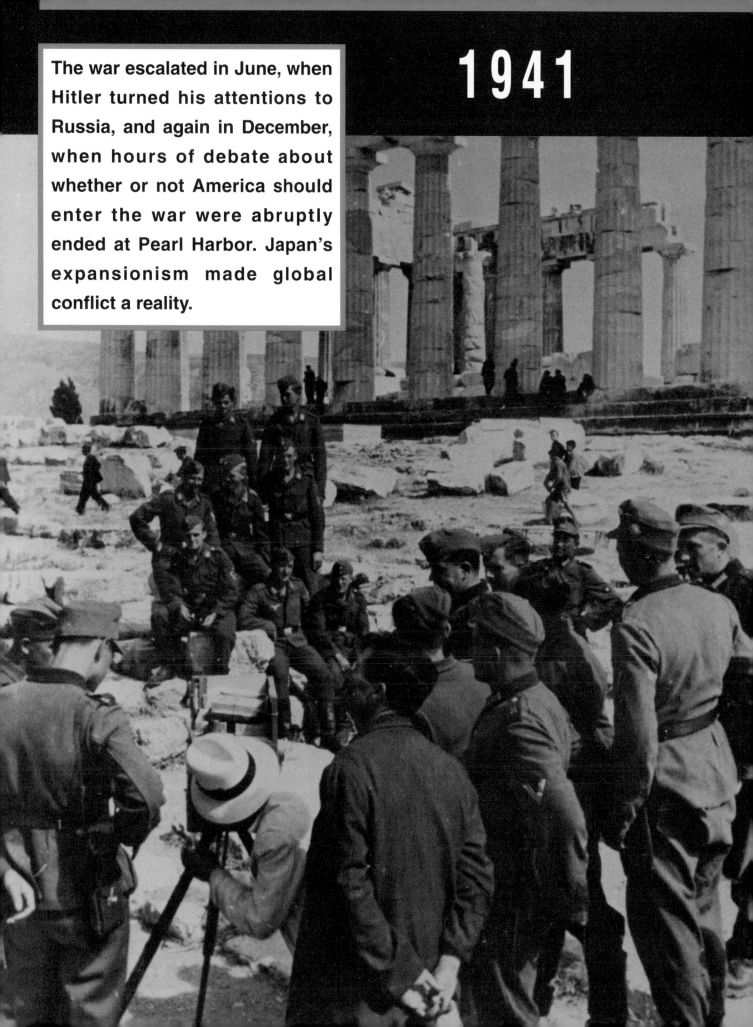

**1941**

The war escalated in June, when Hitler turned his attentions to Russia, and again in December, when hours of debate about whether or not America should enter the war were abruptly ended at Pearl Harbor. Japan's expansionism made global conflict a reality.

## ■ JANUARY ■

**Thursday 2:** Eire is hit by German bombs although no one is hurt.

**Friday 3:** Australian troops launch a major assault on an Italian stronghold in Libya, taking 5,000 prisoners.

**Saturday 4:** German actress Marlene Dietrich, the woman who turned down Hitler as a lover, turns her back on her native country and becomes a US citizen.

**Sunday 5:** The Libyan town of Bardia falls. The Allies capture 25,000 Italian prisoners.

**Monday 6:** British aviator Amy Johnson is killed, aged 38, when her aircraft plunges into the Thames. Her job had been to ferry newly built aircraft from factories to their bases around Britain.

**Wednesday 8:** Founder of the Boy Scout movement, Lord Robert Baden-Powell, dies aged 84.

British government suppresses the Communist newspaper, the Daily Worker, which continually snipes against the war effort. Only 11 left-wing MPs voted against the ban. Many have been angered at the stance of the newspaper, particularly its activities following air raids when leaflets were handed out to those who had been blitzed claiming the war was just a plot to make profits for capitalists.

**Friday 10:** Air attacks begin on Malta by combined German and Italian air forces.

**Saturday 11:** Cruiser HMS Southampton severely damaged by Luftwaffe as it fights Italian navy in the Sicilian channel.

---

### British and Australian forces capture Tobruk, in Libya, with the loss of just 500 men

---

**Monday 13:** Irish writer James Joyce dies in Zurich, Switzerland, aged 59, almost three decades after he last set foot in Ireland.

**Tuesday 14:** British government announces new controls on shopkeepers and food wholesalers in a bid to curtail the naked profiteering which has hit the market.

**Sunday 19:** British forces press on into Sudan and Italian-held Eritrea.

**Tuesday 21:** British and Australian forces capture Tobruk, in Libya, with the loss of just 500 men. The victory was marked by an Anzac hat being run up the flagpole in the absence of a Union Flag.

*Below:* Australian troops kick up dust on an exercise in the Western Desert.
*Inset:* The communist newspaper, the *Daily Worker*, barred by the government following its anti-war stance.
*Far left:* German troops in Athens.

capital of Italian Somaliland. Back-up troops include regiments from South Africa, the Gold Coast and the King's African Rifles.

**Wednesday 26:** Mussolini admits to the loss of 1,000 aircraft in addition to the 200,000 troops taken prisoner in the North African campaign. His only hope is the support of Germany.

**Friday 28:** British civilian casualties this month fall to 789 dead and 1,068 injured.

### ■ MARCH ■

**Saturday 1:** Italy pares the rations for its people by 50 per cent to allow food exports to ally Germany.

Bulgaria, already under German occupation, joins the Axis alliance.

**Sunday 2:** Turkey closes the Dardenelles, linking the Aegean with the Sea of Marmara, to all shipping without permits and Turkish pilots.

**Monday 3:** German troops proceed through Bulgaria towards Greece and are poised to move into Yugoslavia.

## An advance guard of the Afrika Korps arrives in Tripoli under the command of Rommel

**Tuesday 4:** Turkey, by now on full alert, refuses to join Germany's fight.

British troops mount a raid on Norway's Lofoten Island, sinking 11 German ships, destroying a munitions factory and a power station and setting fire to an oil depot. Aided by Norwegians, the British returned with 300 volunteers ready to fight against Germany.

**Monday 27:** British and Commonwealth troops make gains against the Italians in Eritrea.

**Wednesday 29:** South African troops invade Italian Somaliland.

**Friday 31:** RAF makes devastating strikes against key German ports.

### ■ FEBRUARY ■

**Wednesday 5:** Official estimates put the daily cost to Britain of the war at a staggering £11 million.

Italians flee the beleaguered town of Benghazi, only to run into a flank of British forces.

**Thursday 6:** Benghazi is captured by Australian forces.

**Saturday 8:** Englishman Percy William Olaf de Wet is sentenced to death in Berlin after being convicted of spying for France.

**Sunday 9:** After Laval turns down an opportunity to re-enter Pétain's cabinet governing Vichy France, Admiral Jean Francois Darlan becomes vice-president.

**Monday 10:** Iceland is bombed by the Luftwaffe.

The British government vows to close a loophole in call-up regulations which allows young men to avoid conscription by refusing a medical. The only penalty they face at the moment is a £5 fine.

**Wednesday 12:** First successful trial of penicillin is carried out in Oxford, on a policeman with septicaemia.

**Friday 14:** With the taking of Kurmak, the British claim the only Italians on Egyptian, Sudanese or Kenyan soil are those held prisoner.

An advance guard of the Afrika Korps lands in Tripoli, Libya, to aid the unsuccessful Italians. They are under the command of Lieutenant-General Erwin Rommel, who was a successful exponent of tank warfare in the West.

**Monday 17:** Bulgaria and Turkey sign a non-aggression pact.

**Saturday 22:** Rommel attacks British-held El Agheila.

**Sunday 23:** A unit of the Free French lands in Eritrea.

**Monday 24:** Hitler threatens to step up U-boat activities.

**Tuesday 25:** British Nigerian troops take control of Mogadishu, the

**Wednesday 5:** Britain breaks off diplomatic ties with Bulgaria.

**Monday 10:** Hitler invites Yugoslavia to join the Axis powers.

**Tuesday 11:** British diplomats arrive in Istanbul where a bomb in their luggage explodes, claiming two lives.

America agrees to allow Britain use of its military hardware without charge. The debt will be settled after the war. President Roosevelt likens it to lending a neighbour a hose to put out a fire. Churchill replies: 'Give us the tools and we'll finish the job.'

**Monday 17:** Minister of Labour Bevin calls for women to operate factories to free more male workers for military service. For many women, it is the first time they have worked outside the family home.

**Monday 24:** Rommel occupies El Agheila once more for the Germans.

**Tuesday 25:** Prince Paul of Yugoslavia signs an agreement with Nazi Germany.

## Italian navy defeated off Cape Matapan with loss of three cruisers

**Thursday 27:** A coup overturns the pro-Nazi government in Yugoslavia. Figurehead Prince Paul flees, leaving 17-year-old King Peter as sovereign. Street marches in favour of Britain and Russia and against Hitler are staged even though German troops are massing on the Bulgarian border.

**Friday 28:** Writer Virginia Woolf dies, aged 59, after apparently throwing herself in the River Ouse, Sussex.

Italian navy defeated off Cape Matapan with the loss of three cruisers. Britain loses two aircraft.

**Sunday 30:** Rommel mounts counter-offensive in North Africa.

**Monday 31:** Italy sinks HMS York and HMS Bonaventure off Crete.

British civilian casualties for the month rise again with continued raids on London, Portsmouth, Merseyside, Clydeside, Bristol and Plymouth. This time 4,259 people are killed and 5,557 injured.

*Below:* **The wreckage of the aircraft in which Rudolf Hess flew from Germany.**

## ■ APRIL ■

**Thursday 3:** Pro-German politician Rashid Ali stages a coup in Iraq to replace the government.

**Saturday 5:** Allied forces enter Addis Ababa, capital of Ethiopia.

**Sunday 6:** Germany invades Yugoslavia and Greece.

**Monday 7:** Germany makes early gains in Yugoslavia, forcing its army to the south. Britain promises aid.

The War budget increases income tax to a record 50 per cent.

**Wednesday 9:** Rommel retakes Bardia from the Allies.

**Thursday 10:** Pro-German Croatia is declared an independent state after Hitler's troops take Zagreb, its capital. Hungary joins the offensive against Yugoslavia.

Australian troops in North Africa pull back to Tobruk.

**Friday 25:** America extends its Atlantic patrols.

**Saturday 26:** With Tobruk under siege, Rommel's Afrika Korps makes headway in Egypt from Libya.

**Sunday 27:** German forces arrive in Athens and hoist the swastika over the Acropolis.

*Below:* **German paratroops receive fresh supplies in Crete.**

## ◆ EYE WITNESS ◆

**Frank Patten joined the Norwegian merchant navy in 1940, when he was aged just 14.**

❛ I joined a Norwegian ship at Liverpool. My first trip was on the *Heine* which set sail for America as part of a convoy. It was returning when it was torpedoed off the Irish coast on 10 February 1941. We thought we had made it when we were just blown up and sunk.

I was picked up by a destroyer. I just had what I stood up in – no shoes, just a vest and trousers. At Liverpool I received some compensation for the loss of my clothes.

Then I joined another Norwegian ship, called MT *Egda.* That was torpedoed by a U-boat in the Caribbean. I was midships when the torpedo struck. I was on the deck one minute, the next thing I knew I was in the water. That's when I saw angels so I reckon I must have nearly drowned.

I was picked up by an American ship and was kept in hospital in Baltimore for two months. Again, I only had what I was picked up in. They gave me suits, clothing, the lot – they were brilliant.

The next boat I joined was another Norwegian cargo ship, *Toronto,* which spent 92 days sailing from New York to Suez, then it ferried supplies around North Africa for the duration of the campaign before joining the Italian landings.

I finally got home to Liverpool in late 1943. I found my name was posted up outside Liverpool City Hall as dead. When the ship was torpedoed in the Caribbean everyone assumed I had drowned – and I never wrote home. When I walked into my house, my mum couldn't believe her eyes. ❜

**Saturday 12:** Belgrade surrenders. Allies pull back in Greece.

Tobruk surrounded.

**Sunday 13:** Moscow signs a neutrality pact with Japan.

**Monday 14:** Germans kept at bay in North Africa. In Greece they make further breakthroughs.

**Wednesday 16:** London suffers one of the heaviest night raids so far, with 500 planes dropping 100,000 bombs.

**Thursday 17:** Yugoslavian army surrenders. King Peter flown to safety by the RAF.

**Saturday 19:** Allied troops mount a campaign against Iraq.

**Monday 21:** Greek army capitulates. Within days the British withdrawal from Greece begins.

**Wednesday 30:** Civilian casualty figures continue to worsen. In April 6,065 people were killed on the home front and 6,926 injured.

## ■ MAY ■

**Friday 2:** British and Commonwealth troops complete their withdrawal from Greece, by the Royal Navy, with rearguard action by the Greek infantry protecting them from a German onslaught.

British and Iraqi troops skirmish for the first time.

**Sunday 4:** British troops occupy the airport and docks at Basra, Iraq.

**Monday 5:** Haile Selassie marches back into Addis Ababa, five years after being ousted by the Italians.

# MUSSOLINI

**Short, balding, blustering and tubby, Benito Mussolini was the most unlikely leader of the war. Yet here was Europe's first dictator, a man who held sway in his country for 20 years with tremendous success.**

His downfall only came when he aligned himself with Hitler, a stronger man with plentiful resources. The demands that the pair proceeded to place on little Italy stretched it to breaking point. The Italian people who for so long tolerated and even cheered Mussolini then bayed for his blood – and got it.

Mussolini was born in 1883 to a teacher mother and blacksmith father in the unprivileged surroundings of Predappio in Romagna. His father was a bar-room socialist and the young Benito soon picked up his ideas.

Uncontrollable at school, Mussolini still gained a diploma in teaching. To evade national service he skipped Italy for Switzerland in 1902.

Back in Italy by 1904, he became a radical socialist and climbed the echelons of the movement until 1915 when he went against party policy and supported national participation in World War I. Mussolini himself served in the Italian trenches and knew of the gruelling conditions experienced by soldiers.

Following the conflict he capitalised on the discontent of the homecoming troops and marshalled them into a fighting force nominally under his command. Italy itself was declining into anarchy. Mussolini timed his ascent to power perfectly, co-ordinating a march on Rome of his fascist supporters to sweep him into power.

In the face of such rampant support, King Victor Emmanuel III sacked the hard-pressed prime minister in October 1922, and asked Mussolini to lead the country instead. Now the fascist thugs who had caused mayhem on the streets were usefully employed keeping order. Mussolini was adored by the people when it seemed he had the power to restore authority where there was chaos.

His regime was shaken when leading socialist Giacomo Matteotti was murdered by fascists in June 1924. Nevertheless, Mussolini survived the scandal and went on to establish himself as dictator and Duce.

Internally, his placation of the Catholic Church and programme of public works worked wonders. Yet he yearned for an empire. So he invaded Ethiopia in 1935.

Mussolini observed with trepidation Hitler's rise to power. He knew that if he opposed his fellow fascist, the might of the German army would bear down through Italy while Britain and France could do little to help. So he joined forces with Germany, convincing himself that his undersized armed services would acquit themselves well if they had to.

Sidestepping the start of the war, Mussolini only became a German ally at the fall of France. His conviction that Britain would also collapse was a grave miscalculation. So was his involvement in East and North Africa and Greece where his troops suffered inglorious routs at the hands of the Allies and were saved from abject defeat only by the intervention of German forces.

Unwittingly, he offered Italy as a target for the Allies when they could do little to make an impression on the Third Reich. When Italy was invaded, it was clear Mussolini's days as dictator were numbered. He was ousted and arrested but saved from Italian justice in a daring rescue by German commandos.

Thereafter, he was propped up as a puppet dictator in northern Italy, unhappily realising the error of his judgements but unable to extricate himself from German authority.

It was when he tried to flee across the border from Italy to German territory in 1945 that he was finally brought to task by his countrymen. Partisans hauled him out of a German convoy and kept him prisoner until a communist leader decided he should be shot.

With him was his loyal mistress, Clara Petacci, who not only sacrificed a chance to save herself, but stood in front of the man she loved when the firing squad delivered the death sentence.

Their bodies were taken to Milan and strung up by the ankles, to be vilified by the angry mob. Mussolini's corpse was eventually retrieved by the Allies and buried quietly in a monastery.

*Above:* The twin fascist dictators of Europe: Mussolini of Italy and Hitler of Germany.

**Friday 9:** Liverpool suffers seventh consecutive night raid by Luftwaffe.
**Saturday 10:** Westminster Abbey, the House of Commons, the Tower of London and the Royal Mint are all hit in a mammoth raid on London, which kills 1,436 people. Hundreds are buried under rubble for hours until rescuers can reach them. For the first time, people are seen weeping on the streets. German High Command said it was a reprisal raid for the bombs which have fallen on the civilian quarters of Berlin.

Hitler's deputy, Rudolph Hess, parachutes into Scotland.
**Wednesday 14:** Singapore's defences are bolstered by the arrival of

sizeable Royal Navy and Royal Air Force contingents.

French police round up about 1,000 Jews in Paris and hand them over to the Germans.

**Thursday 15:** 'Operation Brevity', to relieve Tobruk, is launched.

Britain test-flies its first jet aircraft at RAF Cranwell. Frank Whittle is the engineer and designer.

**Friday 16:** Final batch of British reinforcements arrives in Crete.

RAF raids Cologne.

Italian forces surrender at Amba Alagi in Ethiopia.

**Sunday 18:** German vessels Bismarck and Prinz Eugen set sail in the Baltic.

**Monday 19:** Egyptian liner Zamzam is sunk by Germans in the South Atlantic. Among the casualties are 200 US passengers.

**Tuesday 20:** German paratroopers drop into Crete. Defending, the British, Anzac and Greek forces inflict heavy casualties on the airborne invaders.

*Below:* **Charismatic Luftwaffe chief Hermann Göring surveys a battle plan with his aides. The unique rank of Reichsmarschall was created for him by Hitler.**

**Wednesday 21:** America is asked to withdraw its representatives from Paris by the occupying Germans.

**Thursday 22:** Royal Air Force withdraws from Crete.

**Saturday 24:** The British battlecruiser HMS Hood is sunk off Greenland, with the loss of 1,300 lives. The Royal Navy vows to 'pursue and destroy' the 45,000-ton battleship Bismarck, responsible for the tragedy.

Crete is bombed by Germans, forcing King George II of Greece to flee to Cairo.

US cult singer Robert Zimmerman, better known as Bob Dylan, is born.

**Sunday 25:** Bismarck eludes its Royal Navy pursuers as it makes a dash from Greenland, aiming for the safety of a northern French port.

German navy chief Admiral Raeder warns US that its protective action of convoying British merchant ships would soon be considered an act of war by the Germans.

**Monday 26:** After Bismarck is spotted it is chased by every Royal Navy vessel in the region and is bombed by Swordfish planes from the Ark Royal, suffering severe

damage. The British continue attacking after dark. In the Mediterranean the Royal Navy aircraft carrier Formidable is bombed.

**Tuesday 27:** The Bismarck is finally sunk off the coast of France by torpedoes from the cruiser Dorsetshire.

**Wednesday 28:** Roosevelt announces that the American Neutrality Act is to be scrapped.

**Thursday 29:** More than 200 men are killed when the cruiser Orion comes under attack off Crete.

## *Pétain imposes new restrictions on Jews in Vichy France, barring them from public office*

**Friday 30:** Pro-Nazi Rashid Ali flees Iraq as his government collapses with the advance of British troops on the capital, Baghdad.

**May 31:** British evacuate to Egypt from Crete.

Australian women between the ages of 16 and 60 are banned from leaving the country, to conserve womanpower for nursing and associated services.

Peace is made in Iraq.

Civilian casualties for May amount to 5,394 dead and 5,181 injured.

### ■ JUNE ■

**Saturday 1:** Clothes rationing is introduced in Britain.

**Monday 2:** Manchester badly hit by an air raid. Reichsmarschall Göring tells the Luftwaffe: 'There is no unconquerable island.'

Industry of the Ruhr is bombed by Royal Air Force.

Pétain imposes new restrictions on Jews in Vichy France, barring them from public office.

**Wednesday 4:** Following a devastat-

## ◆ THE COMING OF THE DESERT FOX

In February 1941, Rommel arrived in North Africa in command of the Deutsches Afrika Korps. Germany's Italian allies were struggling in the desert, and Rommel had been dispatched to stiffen the Axis presence in the region.

He wasted little time in going on the offensive, striking at El Agheila in March, before launching a three-pronged attack across Cyrenaica at the start of April. The Australians in Benghazi retreated, and eventually pulled back into Tobruk, which was then isolated as the tide of Axis forces swept eastwards. On 25 April, the Afrika Korps crossed into Egypt. Yet the Allies were to recover and eventually succeeded in driving Rommel from Africa.

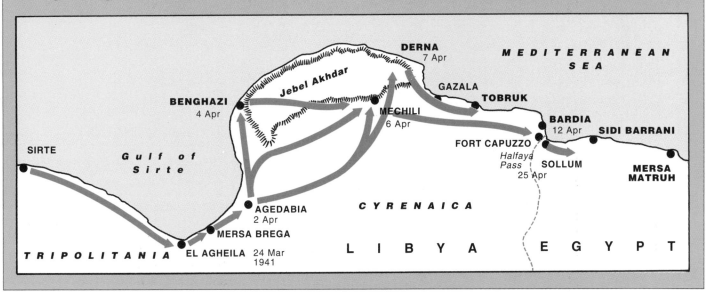

ing air raid on Alexandria the Egyptian cabinet resigns.

**Thursday 5:** At least 13,000 British prisoners were taken in Crete, the government admits.

**Saturday 7:** Launch of heavy night air raid on French Atlantic port of Brest by the RAF, in an attempt to destroy the German heavy cruiser, *Prinz Eugen*, which had operated with the battleship *Bismarck* during the latter's one and only cruise the previous month.

**Sunday 8:** Allied troops backed up by the Free French attack Syria. Colonial power Vichy France is outraged when Britain offers Syria its independence.

RAF launches largest air raid to date using 360 planes.

**Thursday 12:** RAF bombs Ruhr, Rhineland and a number of German ports in the start of a 20-night bombing campaign.

### Hitler tears up the agreement between Berlin and Moscow and launches invasion of Russia

**Sunday 15:** 'Operation Battleaxe', to relieve Tobruk, is launched.

**Monday 16:** British jobless figures at an all-time low with just 243,656 registered unemployed.

Last Italians fighting in Ethiopia surrender to the British in disarray.

**Tuesday 17:** 'Operation Battleaxe' fails, with British forces being beaten back by Rommel's forces.

**Thursday 19:** Germany and Italy expel American Embassy staff in retaliation for hostility to consuls representing Hitler and Mussolini.

**Saturday 21:** Empire troops take Damascus, with the defending Vichy

force fleeing in confusion.

**Sunday 22:** 'Operation Barbarossa' begins. Hitler tears up the non-aggression pact between Berlin and Moscow and launches invasion of Russia. Finnish and Romanian soldiers are with the German army along a 1,300-mile front. Churchill offers Stalin aid.

**Tuesday 24:** Axis troops advance through Russian territory, inflicting severe damage on the Red Army and Air Force with familiar Blitzkrieg tactics. Lithuania is overrun.

**Thursday 26:** Finland declares war on Russia.

**Sunday 29:** Luftwaffe chief Göring wins the internal power struggle in the Nazi hierarchy and is named as Hitler's successor.

■ **JULY** ■

**Tuesday 1:** Germans seize the Baltic port of Riga.

*Above:* **Retreating Russian troops practise a 'scorched earth' policy and destroy everything in their wake.**

**Thursday 3:** Stalin orders his retreating forces to destroy everything as they fall back.

**Friday 4:** British Communist Party declares it is no longer in opposition to the war and throws its weight behind the nation's efforts.

Coal rationing gets underway.

**Wednesday 9:** Russian soldiers are defeated at Minsk.

**Thursday 10:** Hitler encourages Japan to enter the war. He knows a new front to occupy Allied forces would significantly increase his chances of victory.

**Saturday 12:** A mutual assistance plan is signed by Britain and Russia in Moscow, restraining both from seeking a separate peace.

**Monday 14:** A Syrian peace agreement is signed.

**Tuesday 15:** Empire forces continue their march through the Middle East, entering Beirut.

**Saturday 19:** George Armstrong is hanged at Wandsworth prison, south-west London, for spying.

**Sunday 20:** Britain adopts a 'V-for-Victory' motif and urges all resistance groups in occupied countries to join the simple but effective campaign by chalking a 'V' on doors and walls at every opportunity.

**Tuesday 22:** First German air raid on Moscow. Meanwhile the land-based troops are halted by marshland.

**Wednesday 23:** A vital convoy breaks through the U-boat blockade and arrives in Malta.

## Japanese troops land in Indochina, occupying Saigon and stationing men in Phnom Penh

**Thursday 24:** All Britons are kicked out of Vichy France.

**Monday 28:** Japanese troops land in southern Indochina, occupying Saigon and stationing men in Cambodia's capital, Phnom Penh.

Unable to halt their actions, Marshal Pétain has given the blessing of Vichy, France, which controlled the region. The US reacts with total ban on trade with Japan.

**Wednesday 30:** US authorities seize 17 Japanese fishing boats suspected of spying around the waters of Hawaii.

Poland and Russia, finding themselves on the same side, sign an uneasy pact of friendship.

**Thursday 31:** With the let-up in raids on London and elsewhere, the civilian casualty figures fall, with 501 dead in July's air raids.

### ■ AUGUST ■

**Friday 1:** Roosevelt halts aviation fuel exports to Axis countries.

**Tuesday 5:** Romanian troops lay siege to the port of Odessa.

Wine drinking in Vichy France restricted to two litres per week.

**Thursday 7:** National Service is extended by 18 months in America.

Mussolini loses his second son, Bruno, in an air crash.

**Friday 8:** Russia's Red Air Force srikes at Berlin.

**Thursday 14:** Churchill and Roosevelt sign the Atlantic Charter, setting out the objectives of both nations during wartime and peace. While declaring that neither had territorial gains to make, it says that war-mongering nations had to be disarmed and that, following the conflict, 'all men shall be enabled to live in freedom from fear and want'.

**Saturday 16:** Britain and the Soviet Union sign an agreement that they will exchange resources.

**Wednesday 20:** In France 50,000 are held as the German occupiers try to root out railway saboteurs.

**Thursday 21:** In Paris, 5,000 Jews are rounded up and interned before being deported.

With Germans at the gates of Leningrad, Russian marshal Voroshilov tells the residents to defend the city to the last.

**Monday 25:** British and Russian troops march into Iran.

Stalin orders the destruction of the huge Lenin-Dnjeproges dam, completed only ten years ago to meet all the power needs of the Ukraine.

**Tuesday 26:** French Hitlerite Pierre Laval is shot and wounded by young Frenchman Paul Colette.

Canadian troops land on an Arctic island north of Norway in a bid to hamper coal supplies to Germany.

Germany admits to losses of 440,000 on the Russian front – more than in their offensives worldwide before 'Operation Barbarossa' got underway.

**Wednesday 27:** Iranian government negotiates a ceasefire.

British government commandeers domestic railways, paying compensation to the owners.

### ■ SEPTEMBER ■

**Tuesday 2:** Fighting between Germans and Russians reported within 30 miles of Leningrad.

**Wednesday 3:** Gas chamber at Auschwitz brought into use.

U-boat attacks US destroyer Greer off Iceland.

**Saturday 6:** All Jews in Germany are forced by law to wear a yellow Star of David when they appear in public. Further, they will require special permission from the police before leaving their neighbourhoods.

**Thursday 11:** King Leopold III of Belgium secretly marries Mary Lilian Baels, the 29-year-old granddaughter of a Flemish fisherman. As a 'commoner', she renounces claims to the title of queen and is to be known as Princess of Rethy.

**Friday 12:** Snow falls on the Russian front.

**Saturday 13:** Germans declare their intentions to allow fewer rations to Russian prisoners of war than to POWs of other nationalities.

**Monday 15:** German siege of Leningrad begins.

German troops come under fire on the Champs Elysees, the heart of German-occupied Paris.

## *Fighting between Germans and Russians reported within 30 miles of Leningrad*

**Tuesday 16:** Unpopular Shah of Iran abdicates in favour of his son, 21-year-old Mohammed Reza Pahlavi.

**Wednesday 17:** British and Russian units reach Iranian capital Teheran.

**Thursday 18:** Russians evacuate Kiev.

**Friday 19:** Kiev falls to Germany.

**Sunday 21:** Germans isolate the Crimean peninsula from the USSR.

**Wednesday 24:** Nine governments-in-exile put their names to the Atlantic Charter.

**Friday 26:** RAF flies in relief supplies to Leningrad.

**Monday 29:** Germans kill Jews left behind in Kiev.

**Tuesday 30:** Newcastle bombed for the second time. Civilian casualties from air raids in September amount to 217.

### ■ OCTOBER ■

**Wednesday 1:** An estimated 163,696 Jews are thought to be living within the borders of Germany.

**Thursday 2:** While Hitler sets his sights on Moscow, the Red Army presses German forces back around Leningrad.

**Friday 3:** The number of people killed on the road in Britain last year is up 65 per cent on pre-war figures.

**Tuesday 7:** Stalin allows religion once more in Russia in an effort to unite his beleaguered people.

**Thursday 16:** Soviet government pulls out of Moscow, although Stalin stays behind.

The Black Sea town of Odessa falls to the Romanians.

The Japanese government falls, to be replaced by hardline militarists.

**Friday 17:** German U-boat hits USS Kearny off Iceland.

**Saturday 18:** Germans within 70 miles of Moscow.

**Sunday 19:** A state of siege is declared in Moscow.

German papers reveal 673,000 Russian prisoners have been taken during October alone.

## American ambassador in Japan hears rumour of an approved plan to attack America

**Wednesday 22:** After a German military commander is killed by an assassin, 50 hostages are shot in Nantes, France.

**Thursday 23:** De Gaulle asks French resistance to bide their time after another 50 French people are killed in reprisal for the death of a German major. The Vichy government blames British agents for the killings.

**Thursday 30:** In the third U-boat attack on a US warship in a month, destroyer Reuben James is sunk off Iceland with the loss of 70 lives.

**Friday 31:** British civilian casualty figures for October are 262. Dover is the most severely hit target.

### ■ NOVEMBER ■

**Saturday 1:** Crimean capital Simferopol falls to the Germans.

**Monday 3:** American ambassador in Japan hears rumours of an approved plan to attack America and warns President Roosevelt.

**Thursday 6:** America gives Russia an interest-free loan amounting to $1,000 million.

German soldiers serving on the Eastern front begin to experience the pains of frostbite.

**Friday 7:** Churchill declares: 'Britain's resolve is unconquerable.'

**Monday 10:** Churchill warns that any act of war by Japan against America would be taken as an act of war against Britain.

**Thursday 13:** German troops in

*Below:* A tank struggles to stay moving as the bitterly cold Russian winter sets in on the Eastern front. Now frostbite claims more casualties than warfare does.

Russia are crippled as temperatures plunge minus 22 degrees Celsius.

HMS *Ark Royal* is hit by a German U-boat and sinks while being towed back into port.

**Tuesday 18:** British commandos mount a daring night raid on German headquarters in Libya. 'Operation Crusader', involving the British 8th Army, gets underway to liberate Libya.

**Wednesday 19:** German raider ship *Kormoran* attacks an Australian navy cruiser off Western Australia. Both are sunk.

An estimated 82,000 Poles have been shot or hanged since German occupation of Poland.

## *'Operation Crusader', involving the British 8th Army, gets underway to liberate Libya*

**Sunday 23:** A South African brigade is broken during an attack by Rommel near Tobruk.

New Zealand troops occupy Bardia, north east Libya.

**Tuesday 25:** 8th Army comes under attack from Rommel.

**Thursday 27:** American Pacific forces on alert.

**Sunday 30:** Japan's prime minister, General Hideki Tojo, warns he will 'purge' Anglo-American power bases in the Far East.

### ■ DECEMBER ■

**Monday 1:** Malaya and Hong Kong on alert in case of Japanese action.

**Tuesday 2:** The Royal Navy's *Prince of Wales* and *Repulse* sail to bolster defences of Singapore.

*Right:* Japanese prime minister Hideki Tojo, who was also minister of war.

 **◆ EYE WITNESS ◆**

New Zealander Peter Llewelyn, who served in North Africa, wrote about the plagues of flies which followed the troops there. His account appeared in the official history of New Zealand's involvement in World War II.

❝ ...And when you shut your eyes – and this is the plain truth – flies tried to open them, mad for the delectable fluid.

We couldn't always be killing them but we had to keep on brushing them away, otherwise even breathing would have been difficult. Our arms ached from the exercise but still they fastened on our food and accompanied it into our mouths and down our throats, scorning death when there was an advantage to be gained. They drowned themselves in our tea and in our soup. They attended us with awful relish on our most intimate occasions. ❞

German troops within five miles of the Kremlin.

**Friday 5:** Hitler abandons for the winter his goal of seizing Moscow.

**Saturday 6:** With the Japanese fleet already sailing south, Roosevelt makes a last-ditch appeal to Emperor Hirohito for peace.

Britain formally declares war on Finland, Romania and Hungary.

**Sunday 7:** Pearl Harbor comes under attack from 360 Japanese planes, with the loss of 2,729 lives. Malaya, China, the Philippines, Thailand and Hong Kong are also under attack by the Japanese.

**Monday 8:** Canada declares war on Japan.

**Tuesday 9:** Thai capital Bangkok is occupied by Japanese.

**Wednesday 10:** British Naval Force Z destroyed by Japanese. Prince of Wales and Repulse are sunk, the first major ships in history to be sunk by air power alone. British on the retreat in Malaya.

Siege of Tobruk is finally ended.

**Thursday 11:** Germany and Italy declare war on America.

**Friday 12:** Britain's army, navy and air force, aided by Free Norwegian troops, raid a German base in north Norway, sinking eight ships and killing or capturing an entire garrison.

Better equipped against the gruelling winter weather, Russian troops stage a series of attacks against the invading Germans.

**Saturday 13:** Widespread rumours that enemy parachutists had landed on the west coast of America were officially denied today. The US Army stated the reports had been thoroughly investigated and completely discredited.

**Monday 15:** Gun battles echo through Hong Kong.

**Wednesday 17:** Japanese land in North Borneo and are poised to win Malayan peninsula.

Rommel is forced to retreat in North Africa.

*Above:* **The pride of America's fleet lies shrouded in smoke following Japan's surprise attack on Pearl Harbor. Crucially, the US carriers were absent on exercise.** *Opposite:* **Victorious Australians march in Benghazi, Libya.**

**Friday 19:** Hong Kong is occupied by Japan.

Hitler, now in personal charge of his army, orders: 'No withdrawal'.

**Monday 22:** Philippine Islands invaded by Japanese.

**Tuesday 23:** Wake Island garrison surrenders to Japanese.

**Thursday 25:** Hong Kong garrison, just 6,000 strong, surrenders to Japanese when the supply of fresh water is in jeopardy.

Empire forces retake Benghazi.

More than 3,000 residents starve to death in Leningrad.

**Friday 26:** To cheers and riotous applause, British prime minister Winston Churchill addresses the American Congress.

## ◆ EYE WITNESS ◆

**Gordon Kendall, from Portsmouth, England, served with 4 Commando. In late 1941 he took part in the first British attack since Dunkirk, targeting the Norwegian islands of Lofoten and Vaagsö. Its success was a major morale booster for the dejected Allies.**

❝ Our job was to blow up fish oil tanks which the Germans were using to make nitroglycerine. There were 250 men involved from both 3 and 4 Commando and we made an amphibious assault at dawn on the landing ships *Beatrice* and *Emma*.

Lofoten wasn't so bad because there were only about 40 Germans on the island. We later called it the "coffee-break raid" because the place was full of Norwegians handing round cups of coffee.

Vaagsö was different altogether because there were 400 Germans there and we met some stiff resistance. But the mission was a complete success. We picked up some Quislings, who were pointed out to us by the Norwegian Resistance, and they were taken prisoner to be interrogated. We also took 120 islanders who wanted to fight with the Allies. They just dropped everything and jumped on our ships, even though they had no advance warning. I suppose their hatred of the Germans was so strong.

As a final touch just before leaving a naval demolition team detonated limpet mines on six German merchants.

We knew a lot was resting on this operation because it was the first time Britain had struck back since Dunkirk. In fact, the powers-that-be hadn't told us the whole truth. We were the sprat to catch the mackerel.

The Navy knew that two of the German fleet's biggest warships, *Tirpitz* and *Prinz Eugen*, were lurking in the fjords nearby. It was hoped our attack would lure them out to search for us. Had they followed us they would have found HMS *Rodney*, HMS *Nelson* and HMS *King George V* out there waiting for them. Unfortunately, they stayed put. ❞

# 1942

As Japan and Germany struggled to consolidate their gains, the Allies were preparing their fight back. Yet still the British, Americans and Australians were short on success stories. Could they turn the tide of war in their favour?

### ■ JANUARY ■

**Thursday 1:** Twenty-six countries sign a declaration of 'United Nations', stating that none will seek a separate peace with any Axis power.

A pit tragedy in Stoke on Trent claims the lives of 57 miners.

**Friday 2:** Japanese troops take Manila, in the Philippines.

**Saturday 3:** General Sir Archibald Wavell is made head of Allied forces in the south west Pacific.

**Tuesday 6:** US forces to be based in Britain, Roosevelt tells Congress.

**Sunday 11:** Japanese forces invade Dutch East Indies.

**Monday 12:** Kuala Lumpur, capital of Malaya, falls to the Japanese.

**Tuesday 13:** Allied conference pledges justice for war criminals at the end of the conflict.

**Thursday 15:** Japanese invasion of Burma begins.

**Saturday 17:** US world champion boxer Muhammad Ali is born.

Actress Carol Lombard dies when an airliner crashes in Las Vegas.

**Tuesday 20:** Nazi hardliner Reinhard Heydrich, nicknamed 'the hangman', announces a 'final solution' to the 'Jewish problem'.

Japanese daylight bombing raids begin on Singapore.

**Wednesday 21:** Field-Marshal Rommel launches another counter-attack in North Africa.

New Guinea, north of Australia, is bombed by the Japanese.

**Friday 23:** Australia demands extra reinforcements from Britain and US as Japanese forces edge closer.

**Monday 26:** US troops arrive in Northern Ireland.

**Wednesday 28:** Rommel takes control of Benghazi.

### ■ FEBRUARY ■

**Sunday 1:** Traitor Quisling forms a pro-German government in Norway.

**Monday 9:** Japanese forces land on Singapore Island.

**Friday 13:** Soviet Army presses back into White Russia, in the face of fierce German resistance.

**Saturday 14:** Fall of Sumatra in Dutch East Indies to Japanese

**Sunday 15:** Singapore falls with the loss of 9,000 lives. An estimated 80,000 Allied troops are taken prisoner by the Japanese.

**Tuesday 17:** Japanese invade Bali in Dutch East Indies.

*Left:* Carole Lombard, wife of Clark Gable, was killed in an air crash, returning from a US Bond-selling tour in the Midwest.
*Far left:* The Japanese take Bataan.

*Above:* Japanese soldiers capture Manila, the Philippine capital. It was defended by native soldiers and Americans.

**Wednesday 18:** In a bid to save precious resources, people are urged to bathe less and use no more than five inches of water. Shared baths are being encouraged.

**Thursday 19:** Japanese aircraft bomb Darwin, north Australia, killing 240 people and wounding 150 more.

## *Singapore falls with the loss of 9,000 lives. 80,000 Allied troops are taken prisoner*

**Friday 20:** Fall of the island of Bali to Japanese, cutting a vital air link between Australia and the Dutch East Indies.

**Sunday 22:** Air Marshal Sir Arthur T. ('Bomber') Harris appointed chief of Bomber Command.

**Monday 23:** Californian coast comes under fire from Japanese submarine.

**Friday 27:** Start of the three-day Battle of the Java Sea.

**Saturday 28:** Allied paras destroy a radar station in northern France.

# ROOSEVELT

Franklin Roosevelt was born in 1882 in New York, the product of an enlightened father and an all-consuming mother. When he was 18 he went to Harvard University and enjoyed the parties and competitive sports every bit as much as the studies.

His thoughts turned increasingly to politics when his fifth cousin, Theodore Roosevelt, won the presidency in 1901. That interest was compounded when he met and married Eleanor Roosevelt, niece of the president, who shared Franklin's passion for humanitarian causes. Not always a happy marriage, it remained a fruitful partnership to the end.

Anxious that his family links should not act as an automatic ticket, Franklin worked hard when he stood as the Democratic candidate in Duchess County, New York. It paid off and he was successful. And, as if to hammer the point home, he backed Woodrow Wilson above his cousin when it came to the 1912 presidential election.

In 1913, he became Assistant Secretary of the Navy in Wilson's administration, forming a life-long loyalty to the naval service.

Following the Republican victory in the 1920 presidential election, Franklin returned to his

**It was probably the most difficult job in history. When he was president, Franklin Delano Roosevelt had to steer his huge country out of the gruelling international depression.**

If that wasn't enough to contend with, along came a war in Europe which threatened to engulf the world. Roosevelt suspected it was an itch he would have to scratch. But at home there were keen isolationists who didn't want any more of America's youth sacrificed on the pyre of freedom and democracy overseas. An isolationist at heart himself, Roosevelt was also a realist.

The prospect of doing business with a triumphant Germany was not a happy one. Moreover, a Third Reich spread across western Europe and eastern Asia would surely soon turn its sights on the New World. Roosevelt took America as close to war with Germany as it could possibly get without committing troops. Then came the Japanese attack on Pearl Harbor and America, the victim, came into the conflict united and determined.

legal practice until, the following year, he was struck down by poliomyelitis. Now the active, enthusiastic campaigner was confined to a wheelchair and would remain so until he learned to walk again with the aid of a walking stick and leg braces.

It could have spelled the end of his career. But his wife Eleanor suddenly blossomed to work on behalf of her ailing husband until he could assume his duties once more.

By 1928, Roosevelt was governor of New York State and got a taste for reform. Four years on he won the presidential election. Domestic problems loomed, including large-scale unemployment and a delicate economy. His answer was the New Deal – legislation to aid banks, regulate currency, re-finance farmers and give strength to workers. The improvements were wholesale. His success at home and later as a war leader were sufficient to win him the presidential election a record four times in total.

Roosevelt died in 1945, shortly before his country's victories over Germany and Japan. His wife went on to be US delegate to the United Nations, a cause which her husband worked so hard to achieve, and also chair of the UN Commission on Human Rights.

Cruisers Perth and Houston attack Japanese vessels disembarking troops at Merak. Although both cruisers are lost, they sink a Japanese minesweeper and transport and damage three destroyers.

■ MARCH ■

**Sunday 1:** Fall of Java, in Dutch East Indies, to Japanese.
**Sunday 8:** Japanese forces land in New Guinea.

**Tuesday 10:** British expenditure on the war to date has already exceeded that spent in the entire duration of World War I.

*Cruisers Perth and Houston attack Japanese vessels disembarking troops at Merak*

**Saturday 14:** American troops arrive in Australia.
**Sunday 22:** Royal Navy successfully escorts a convoy to the beleaguered island of Malta despite an air and sea onslaught from the Axis powers. However, the supply ships are sunk while in the Maltese harbour.

A Polish newspaper editor is beheaded after being found listening to the BBC.

The BBC begins broadcasting

**Left:** Thousands of British and Australian troops were captured when Singapore fell to Japan.

George Cross from King George VI in recognition of its suffering and its stalwart resistance in the war.
**Sunday 19:** Japanese capture the Philippine island of Cebu.
**Friday 24:** Exeter is bombed in reprisal for the air raids on historic German towns.
**Sunday 26:** Hitler tells the Reichstag that the Russian winter has been the worst in 140 years but voices hope for success in a spring offensive.

US singer and actress Barbra Streisand is born.

messages in morse code to the French Resistance.
**Tuesday 24:** Despite public disquiet, the government refuses to hold an inquiry into the surprise and rapid loss of Singapore.
**Friday 27:** In a daring raid, the major Nazi U-boat base at St Nazaire in western France is wrecked by British commandos. Travelling aboard the destroyer Campbeltown, the commandos go into action after the ship has rammed open the dock gates. However, many are captured as they try to head off down river on speedy launches.

President and government of the Philippines flee to Australia.
**Saturday 28:** A large-scale RAF attack is launched against the Baltic port of Lübeck, a centre of industry as part of a round-the-clock strategy against key German-held sites.
**Tuesday 31:** In Belgium, the death penalty is brought in for those caught forging ration cards, as the food shortage becomes critical.

An Allied convoy defies German attacks and arrives at Murmansk in the USSR.

In the last four months, British civilian casualties have amounted to 189 killed and 149 injured.

**Right:** The war was brought home to Australians when the Japanese bombed Darwin, in the Northern Territory, setting fire to a US destroyer in the harbour.

## ■ APRIL ■

**Thursday 9:** Fall of Bataan peninsula, in the Philippines.
**Friday 10:** 'Death March' from Bataan to Camp O'Donnell starts. Of the 12,000 American and 64,000 Filipino captives who begin the

### In a daring raid, the U-boat base at St Nazaire is wrecked by British commandos

march, 2,330 Americans and 7,500 Filipinos die of exhaustion, dehydration and harsh treatment.
**Wednesday 15:** Malta receives

## ■ MAY ■

**Saturday 2:** HMS Edinburgh is sunk by a German submarine while escorting a Russian convoy.
**Monday 4:** British troops land in Madagascar, a province of Vichy France. The defending garrison surrenders with little resistance and the Allies gain a big naval and air base for their fight against the Japanese.
**Tuesday 5:** Naval battle of the Coral Sea commences.

*Left:* Bomb-weary Maltese residents and British soldiers were delighted to read about the island's medal honour.

**Saturday 9:** Malta is reinforced with 60 Spitfires from two aircraft carriers. Many are subsequently lost in the bitter air battles over the island.

**Monday 11:** Three destroyers, Lively, Jackal and Kipling, are sunk in attacks by German planes.

**Tuesday 12:** A U-boat steals into the entrance of the Mississippi and sinks a US merchant ship.

**Wednesday 20:** The US Navy recruits its first blacks.

**Tuesday 26:** Rommel signals the start

## Two Czech freedom fighters toss a bomb into the car of Reinhard Heydrich

of the third German counter-offensive in the Western Desert.

**Friday 29:** Two Czech freedom fighters toss a bomb into the car of Nazi chief of security, SS Obergruppenführer Reinhard Heydrich. He dies six days days later. In a revenge masterminded by SS chief Heinrich Himmler, 1,331 Czechs die and the village of Lidice is levelled. Its men are killed while women and children are interned.

Actor John Barrymore, a matinée idol and accomplished Shakespearean actor, dies aged 60 after a life hallmarked by outrageous drinking and womanising.

**Sunday 31:** Cologne is devastated by a thousand-bomber raid by the Royal Air Force. More than 2,000 tons of explosives were dropped on the city.

Sydney is raided by three Japanese midget submarines.

## ◆ EYE WITNESS ◆

**Eric Williams joined the Royal Corps of Signals as a boy soldier in 1935 and was serving in India when the war broke out. He was captured by the Italians in North Africa in 1942.**

❛ I was captured just outside Benghazi. As the driver for the General's reconnaissance, we were always sent in advance. Our lines of communications were so long we got cut off.

We were taken by cattle boat back to Italy, battened down in the hold. Then we were moved to Ancona on the east coast. In Italy there was a funeral a day. People just gave up. If they felt ill, they never fought it.

One morning we could hear the gunfire which sounded as though it was getting closer. The Colonel in command of the prisoners told us: "The British are coming." The next morning soldiers did turn up but they were in the wrong uniforms – it was the Germans. They put us in cattle trucks and took us to Freiburg in eastern Germany where we worked in a flax factory from 6am to 6pm. There was lots of forced labour there, including many girls from Poland.

If it hadn't been for Red Cross parcels containing tinned cheese, bacon and milk we would have starved. The food, particularly in Germany, was nothing but a slop. We did a sit-down strike on one occasion. The soldiers simply moved us along using their rifle butts. We stole food when we could and the Polish girls brought stuff in for us.

Eventually we were liberated by the Russians. Their treatment of the locals was appalling – but then the Russians had suffered a lot at the hands of the Germans. A friend and I commandeered a horse and cart and managed to get to American lines. I was finally flown to Aylesbury. But before I was allowed back in the country I was sprayed with DDT.

My mother lost three children and a son-in-law during the war. I was a prisoner of war missing for five months while my younger brother served in the Middle East. ❜

*Above:* Cologne cathedral stands defiantly among the debris following a thousand-bomber raid.

*Right:* Screen star John Barrymore died after a lifetime of dramatic achievement and living.

## ■ JUNE ■

**Monday 1:** Mexico declares war on Germany and Italy.

**Thursday 4:** Battle of Midway, between US and Japanese naval forces, commences in the Pacific. It is a turning point in the Pacific war.

**Saturday 6:** Mail from US servicemen serving overseas arrives in the US photographed on microfilm. It is then photostated and sent on to relatives.

**Monday 8:** Japanese forces bombard Sydney and Newcastle.

**Thursday 11:** A pit company deducts half a day's wages from the widow of a man killed in a midday mining accident to account for the time he wasn't at work, an outraged MP reports to Britain's House of Commons.

**Tuesday 16:** In the Mediterranean, one Italian cruiser and two destroyers are lost to the British in the battle of the convoys.

**Thursday 18:** Musician and future Beatle Paul McCartney is born.

**Sunday 21:** Tobruk falls after South African General Klopper surrenders to Rommel. British forces in North Africa fall back into Egypt.

**Monday 22:** In a national broadcast, Pierre Laval, deputy leader of Vichy, France, announces: 'I wish victory for Germany.'

**Thursday 25:** Cairo is in danger of falling into German hands after recent breakthroughs by Rommel.

**Sunday 28:** All Jews aged six and over in Vichy France are compelled to wear the Star of David.

## ■ JULY ■

**Wednesday 1:** Vichy France's Pierre Laval allows German soldiers to seek out Resistance hideaways in unoccupied France.

**Friday 3:** Sevastopol, the Black Sea port held under seige by 100,000 Soviet soldiers, falls to the Germans after almost a month of fierce fighting.

**Saturday 4:** First US Army Air Forces plane sees action in Europe, a Douglas A-20G Havoc.

**Monday 6:** The British 8th Army, under Auchinleck sends Rommel into retreat at El Alamein.

**Wednesday 8:** Hollywood movie actor Cary Grant marries Woolworth heiress Barbara Hutton.

**Friday 10:** The remnants of Convoy PQ17 from Britain to the USSR reach the safety of a Russian port. After instructions from the British Admiralty that the convoy was to scatter, U-boats and German aircraft picked off 29 merchant ships abandoned by their Royal Navy escorts.

**Saturday 11:** RAF Lancasters attack the Danzig docks, aiming to put U-boats out of commission.

**Monday 13:** Hitler orders General Paulus to capture Stalingrad.

**Tuesday 14:** In Yugoslavia the occupying Germans murder 700 people in retaliation for the killing of a Gestapo officer.

*Above:* **Born Archibald Leach, he was better known as Cary Grant. His marriage to Barbara Hutton lasted just three years.**

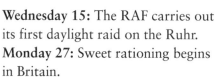

### ◆ EYE WITNESS ◆

**An anonymous American in training wrote these words in 1943.**

❛ We are scared easily. A blast on a whistle sends us running; the word "ten-Shun!" stops us from breathing; the sight of the Sergeant makes us tremble. The boys who were scared of dying, and those who weren't, see now that it will be a long time before they have an opportunity to do any dying; they are now scared of sergeants, commissioned officers, KP, and humiliation before their fellow men. ❜

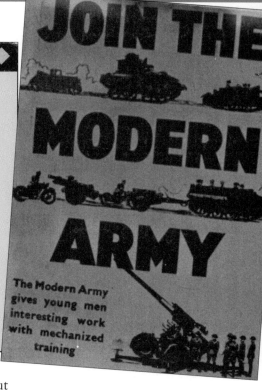

The Modern Army gives young men interesting work with mechanized training

**Wednesday 15:** The RAF carries out its first daylight raid on the Ruhr.

**Monday 27:** Sweet rationing begins in Britain.

**Thursday 30:** Conscription is introduced in Canada.

**Friday 31:** Leisure-motoring is banned in a British government move to conserve fuel.

Air Marshal Sir Arthur Harris, Bomber Command chief, announces in a radio broadcast to Germany that the RAF and USAAF will carry out daily and nightly air raids 'come rain, blow or snow'.

A group of concerned observers including a university professor aiming to aid refugees in Europe christen themselves the Oxford Committee for Famine Relief – or Oxfam for short.

### ■ AUGUST ■

**Monday 3:** Prime Minister Churchill arrives in Cairo to personally investigate the fall of Tobruk.

**Friday 7:** US Marines land on Guadalcanal, in the Solomons.

**Sunday 9:** Civil unrest spreads in India after the arrest of Mahatma Gandhi and other eminent leaders of the Indian Congress after they voted

to press colonial England to leave their country once and for all.

**Wednesday 12:** Monty arrives in North Africa to take command of the desert army.

**Wednesday 19:** The ill-fated commando raid by Canadian and British forces against German-held Dieppe, France, ends in disarray with large numbers of casualties and about 1,500 prisoners taken.

### *The ill-fated commando raid against German-held Dieppe ends in disarray*

**Thursday 20:** First US aircraft fly into Henderson's Field, Guadalcanal.

**Saturday 22:** Following the loss of elements of its merchant fleet to U-boats, Brazil declares war against Germany and Italy.

**Monday 24:** Sea battle off the Solomons commences.

The Duke of Kent, youngest brother of Britain's King George VI, is killed in a flying-boat crash on a trip to Iceland.

**Wednesday 26:** Japanese land at Milne Bay, Papua New Guinea.

Jewish residents of occupied France fall victim to the notorious Nazi round-ups for concentration or extermination camps.

**Monday 31:** Beginning of the Battle of Alam Halfa in North Africa.

---

## *Australians attack the Japanese along Papua New Guinea's treacherous Kokoda trail*

---

■ **SEPTEMBER** ■

**Friday 4:** The execution of a 19-year-old IRA member causes fury among Republicans in Northern Ireland, sparking clashes between police and protesters in Belfast.

**Saturday 5:** Australians drive Japanese from Milne Bay.

**Sunday 6:** Two police officers are shot dead by the IRA in Belfast.

**Thursday 10:** The RAF carries out a massive bombing raid against Düsseldorf, dropping 100,000 bombs in an hour.

**Friday 11:** Japanese forces halted on the Kokoda trail, Papua New Guinea.

**Saturday 12:** British transport ship Laconia is torpedoed and sunk by a U-boat, killing about 800 of the 1,800 Italian

prisoners of war aboard.

**Sunday 13:** 'Operation Daffodil' begins in North Africa, comprising commando raids on Benghazi, Barce and Tobruk.

RAF raids disrupt oil production in Ploesti, Romania, the site of a vital oil installation.

**Wednesday 16:** German 6th Army penetrates the suburbs of Stalingrad.

**Friday 18:** British troops seize a major port in Madagascar, threatening the capital, held by forces loyal to Vichy France.

**Sunday 20:** In Paris, 116 people are killed by German occupying forces in reprisal for a spate of attacks directed at German army officers.

**Wednesday 23:** Australians attack the Japanese along Papua New Guinea's treacherous Kokoda trail.

■ **OCTOBER** ■

**Saturday 3:** President Roosevelt freezes wages, rents and farm prices.

**Sunday 11:** Battle of Cape Esperance off Guadalacanal.

*Above:* **Street urchins like this Greek girl were the target of compassionate observers who founded Oxfam.**

*Right:* **Following sea battles off Guadalcanal, Solomon Islands, involving Japanese and US warships and warplanes, the US Marines were able to reinforce and re-stock the key island.**

*Right:* Boxer Joe Louis quits the ring and throws his weight behind the war effort.

US boxer Joe Louis retires from the ring.

**Wednesday 14:** Australian forces embroiled in fierce fighting with the Japanese high in the Owen Stanley mountains on Papua New Guinea.

Henderson Field, Guadalcanal, comes under fierce land, air and sea attack from the Japanese.

**Saturday 17:** Convoys assemble for 'Operation Torch', the Allied landings in Morocco.

**Friday 23:** Montgomery's 'Operation Lightfoot' begins in North Africa along the coast at El Alamein.

**Sunday 25:** The RAF causes havoc in northern Italy, carrying out 24-hour raids on the key centres of Milan, Genoa and Turin.

## 'Operation Torch' begins with Allied landings at Algiers, Oran and Casablanca

Wedding cakes made of cardboard decorated with chalk icing are the fashion in Britain after sugar-coated confectionery is banned.

**Monday 26:** Aircraft carrier USS Hornet is sunk by Japanese aircraft in the Battle of Santa Cruz.

Brutal street fighting continues in Stalingrad.

**Tuesday 27:** Monty regroups his troops of the 8th Army for a second offensive at El Alamein.

**Friday 30:** Afrika Korps trapped by advancing Australians near Alamein.

*Right :* Many Americans got their first taste of action in the 'Torch' landings in North Africa which finally settled the desert war.

Pvt. Joe Louis says—

"We're going to do our part ...and we'll win because we're on God's side"

■ NOVEMBER ■

**Monday 2:** 'Operation Supercharge', the second El Alamein offensive, gets underway in the desert, forcing Rommel to retreat.

**Friday 6:** Heavy rain hampers the whirlwind advance made by Montgomery at Mersa Matruh.

Women are finally permitted to enter church in England without wearing hats.

**Sunday 8:** 'Operation Torch' begins with Allied landings at Algiers, Oran and Casablanca.

Pierre Laval cuts diplomatic relations with the US.

**Monday 9:** Field-Marshal Rommel recieves long-awaited reinforcements in Tunisia.

**Tuesday 10:** Resistance to the Allies in Algeria comes to an end following an order to lay down arms from Admiral Jean François Darlan, the military commander representing Vichy France.

**Wednesday 11:** German troops move into Vichy France in 'Operation Anton'. The last vestiges of French independence are removed.

**Thursday 12:** First naval battle at Guadalcanal.

**Friday 13:** Libyan port of Tobruk back in Allied hands.

**Saturday 14:** The US triumphs in the second sea battle of Guadalcanal.

Australian troops find fresh success in Papua New Guinea.

**Sunday 15:** Monty triumphs in the second Battle of El Alamein.

Japanese convoy destroyed by US off Guadalcanal.

**Thusday 19:** Red Army opens its winter offensive with counter-attack on the German flanks at Stalingrad.

**Friday 20:** Turin suffers the worst bombing raid inflicted on Italy during the war.

Monty reaches Benghazi.

**Monday 23:** German 6th Army and four Panzer divisions, under General Paulus, encircled and trapped at Stalingrad, as Russians launch 'Operation Uranus'.

French West Africa switches sides and joins the Allies.

**Friday 27:** French fleet scuttled as Germans enter Toulon, Vichy France.

**Sunday 29:** Coffee rationing gets underway in the US.

## German 16th Army and four Panzer divisions encircled and trapped at Stalingrad

### ■ DECEMBER ■

**Tuesday 1:** Australians capture Gona, New Guinea.

Petrol rationing starts in US.

Britain's blueprint for the welfare state is unveiled. The plan, drawn up by Sir William Beveridge, is backed by the unions but opposed in some sectors of commerce.

**Tuesday 8:** Rommel's hard-pressed forces withdraw to Tunis.

**Sunday 13:** Britain's Jewish population marks the suffering and killings among their counterparts in Europe with a day of mourning.

**Monday 21:** British and Indian troops embark on the first Arakan offensive in Burma.

**Tuesday 22:** Four children aged between two and 15 are killed in an explosion at their home in Margate, Kent. It is thought to have been caused by an unexploded mortar bomb found and brought home by the eldest of the children.

**Wednesday 23:** Britain has ordered from Canada powdered eggs equivalent to 63,000,000 shell eggs, it is announced in Ottawa.

A mother of two from Bedford,

England, is killed when a plane crashes in flames on to her house following a mid-air collision. The woman's children were rescued from the wreckage.

**Thursday 24:** Admiral Darlan, military chief in Algeria, pays the ultimate price for switching his allegiances from Vichy France to the Allies. He is shot by an assailant and dies before he reaching hospital. His assassin was a Frenchman loyal to Marshal Pétain, presently held captive by the Germans.

**Friday 25:** British 8th Army reaches Libyan coastal town of Sirte but finds toughening resistance from Afrika Korps units ensconced in hilltop defensive positions.

**Thursday 31:** Battle of Barents Sea.

*Above:* **French warships lie crippled at their moorings after being scuttled following Nazi moves on the port of Toulon, southern France.**

# 1943

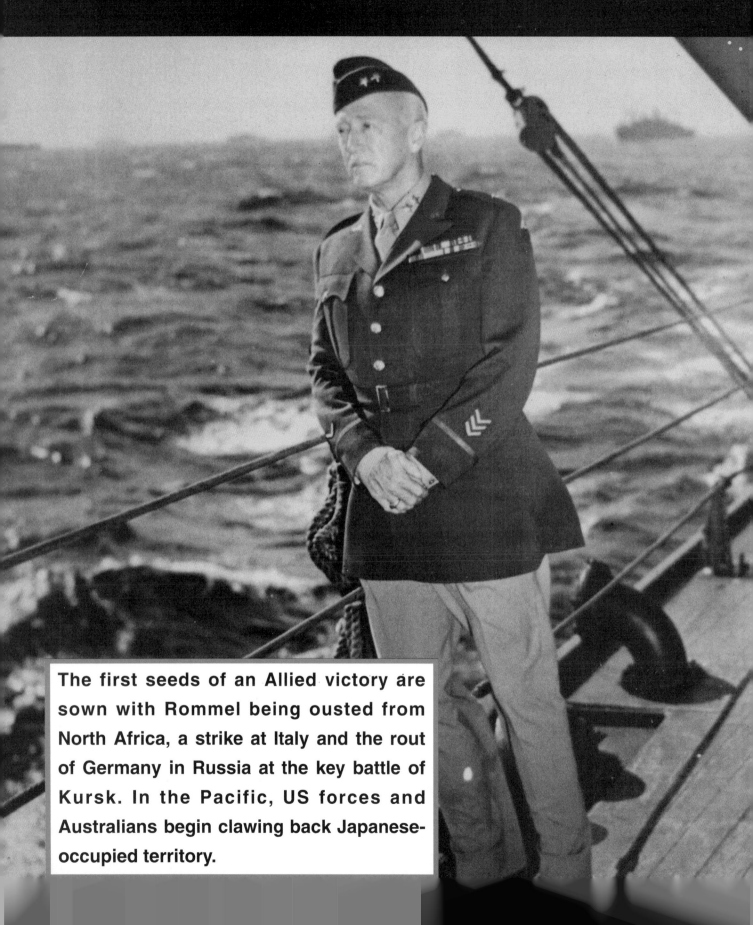

The first seeds of an Allied victory are sown with Rommel being ousted from North Africa, a strike at Italy and the rout of Germany in Russia at the key battle of Kursk. In the Pacific, US forces and Australians begin clawing back Japanese-occupied territory.

## ■ JANUARY ■

**Monday 4:** Japan begins evacuation of Guadalcanal.

**Tuesday 5:** Lieutenant-General Mark Clark appointed commander of the US 5th Army.

**Thursday 14:** Churchill and Roosevelt attend Casablanca Conference with de Gaulle.

**Monday 18:** Tiger tanks used for the first time by the Germans in Tunisia.

**Saturday 23:** Britain's 8th Army moves into Tripoli.

End of Casablanca Conference – Roosevelt demands 'unconditional surrender' of the Axis powers.

**Tuesday 26:** Russians capture Voronezh on the River Do, taking 52,000 German prisoners.

**Wednesday 27:** US 8th Air Force undertakes first bombing raid on Germany, targeting Wilhelmshaven and Emden.

**Sunday 31:** Paulus surrenders at Stalingrad. It is the first field defeat experienced by Germany.

The RAF makes two daylight raids on Berlin, disrupting speeches by Nazi bigwigs to mark ten years of fascism in Germany.

## ■ FEBRUARY ■

**Thursday 4:** 8th Army units enter Tunisia, to meet a volley of German counter-attacks in the coming weeks.

**Friday 5:** Mussolini sacks his son-in-law Count Ciano and assumes the post of foreign minister himself.

**Saturday 6:** Matinée idol Errol Flynn is acquitted on three rape charges.

*Above:* Lieutenant-General Mark Clark, soon to command the invasion of Sicily.

Two women claimed the star had molested them. Flynn, 33, denied the allegations. It took a jury 13 hours to come to its decision.

**Monday 8:** Russians liberate the city of Kursk in central USSR.

**Wednesday 10:** Gandhi begins a 21-day fast in protest at his incarceration in Poona jail.

**Sunday 14:** Chindits cross the River Chindwin in Burma.

*Above:* The Casablanca Conference.
*Left:* Major-General George Patton.

*Right:* Heart-throb Hollywood star Errol Flynn is cleared of rape.

*Surrender at Stalingrad. It is the first field defeat experienced by Germany*

*Above:* Stuttgart is a city in ruins after giant new bombs rain down on its industrial heart. The weapons used were the 8,000lb 'Blockbuster' and the 4,000lb 'Factory-smasher'.

**Tuesday 16:** SS chief Himmler launches plans to eliminate the Jewish ghetto in Warsaw.

**Thursday 18:** Labour MPs cause uproar in the House of Commons when the coalition government refuses to name the day for the introduction of the welfare state.

### ■ MARCH ■

**Monday 1:** Weak from lack of food, Mahatma Gandhi brings his protest fast to an end.

**Tuesday 2:** Battle of the Bismarck Sea commences.

Berlin is the target for an explosive 900-ton air raid by the RAF.

**Saturday 6:** Rommel leaves Africa.

**Sunday 14:** Strategic foothold of Kharkov in Russia is recoccupied by the Germans.

**Wednesday 24:** Cabinet Secretary Lord Maurice Hankey brands the measures taken to combat the U-boat menace 'our greatest failure'.

**Friday 26:** All Britons in Vichy France are put under arrest by a jittery German army. They fear an Allied invasion is imminent.

---

### First Arakan offensive ends in retreat for the British and Indian forces

---

**Saturday 27:** German resistance workers explode bridges on the River Oder in Frankfurt.

**Sunday 28:** Russian-born composer Sergei Rachmaninov dies at his home in Beverly Hills, aged 69.

**Tuesday 30:** First Arakan offensive ends in retreat for the British and Indian forces.

### ■ APRIL ■

**Monday 5:** The Vichy regime hands Daladier, Blum, Reynaud and Mandel, all prominent politicians before the war who have resisted Nazism, to the Germans.

**Monday 12:** Another stringent budget puts a 100 per cent tax on luxury goods.

**Wednesday 14:** Rommel evacuates his troops from Tunis.

**Thursday 15:** A mighty 8,000lb bomb called a 'Blockbuster' is dropped on Stuttgart along with 4,000lb 'Factory-smasher' bombs.

**Sunday 18:** Admiral Yamamoto killed over Bougainville when his plane is shot down by American fighter aircraft.

**Tuesday 20:** In Britain, church bells, banned except to indicate the launch of a German invasion, are being permitted to ring again by a government convinced that the risk of German occupation is past.

**Monday 26:** A row between Stalin

## RAF Lancasters from 617 Squadron carry out the famous 'Dambusters' raid on the Ruhr

and the Allies blows up over German claims that Russian secret police officers murdered 4,000 Polish army officers. The Germans uncovered a mass grave at Katyn near the Russian city of Smolensk. They claim the

officers were taken prisoner by Russia after the fall of Poland in 1939. The Polish government-in-exile is anxiously seeking clarification while Stalin is allegedly furious over the issue.

**Thursday 29:** The RAF embarks on its biggest mine-laying exercise of the war in the busy Baltic Sea.

### ■ MAY ■

**Saturday 1:** American miners announce a strike in protest at a pay freeze.

**Sunday 2:** As Roosevelt is poised to seize the mines to prevent the stoppages, miners, unions in America call off the dispute.

**Monday 3:** The British government makes part-time war work compulsory for women between the ages of 18 and 45.

*Above:* **Actor Leslie Howard perished in a plane crash en route from Spain.**

**Tuesday 4:** The rift between Poland and Russia is patched up with General Sikorski, the Polish leader, instructing Poles to ally with Russia. Soon afterwards, Stalin announces his plans for a strong and free Poland at the end of the war.

**Friday 7:** Tunis falls to Allies. The North African campaign is over.

Second Washington Conference of Allied leaders gets underway.

**Sunday 9:** Martial law is declared in Holland by Germans convinced that an Allied invasion is coming.

**Friday 14:** A hospital ship is torpedoed off Australia by a Japanese submarine, killing up to 300 people.

**Monday 17:** RAF Lancasters from 617 Squadron carry out the famous 'Dambusters' raid on the Mohne and Eder dams, bringing flooding and severe disruption to the Ruhr.

**Thursday 20:** More than 100 aircraft are destroyed when Allied planes attack Italian airfields.

**Sunday 30:** Churchill and de Gaulle arrive in triumph at Algiers.

**Monday 31:** A French 'provisional government' is established by General de Gaulle and General Giraud in Algiers.

### ◆ EYE WITNESS ◆

**Olive Boddill was working in a factory before she joined the Land Army in 1943.**

❝I was 18 when I volunteered for the Land Army. I left my home in Leeds, Yorkshire, to work on farms in Grantham, Lincs.

There I lived in a hostel with 39 other Land Army girls. We were posted out to different farms, potato-picking or other work, including driving. I had never driven before and I didn't do it very well, either.

We wanted to get away from parental control and enjoy ourselves. I didn't think too deeply about the reasons behind volunteering.

We worked alongside Italian prisoners of war. They were glad to be in England. They admitted they didn't like fighting which is why they surrendered very quickly. We used to trade our cigarettes for their cake.

One day when I forgot my packed lunch a farmer invited me in for something to eat. All my friends were jealous, thinking I was going to have a slap-up meal. Instead, he showed me the orchard out the back and told me to eat all the rotten apples on the ground.

We had to make our own entertainment at first until troops including the US air force were stationed near us. Then there was plenty to do.

The village "pub" was run by Stan Laurel's sister Olga, a former music hall artiste, in her living room.

The Americans had lots of money and they were very generous when our boys couldn't afford to be. We got a lot of cigarettes, sweets and goodies. Every birthday they threw a party and sent down a truck for us. Many were there one minute and gone the next. We were very hard about these things. We just accepted it.

We saw a lot of planes crash – damaged planes trying to make their way home. People were immune to death during the war.

One day I saw two planes collide in mid-air. That weekend I was hitch-hiking home to Leeds. A bloke jumped on the same lorry. He was going to Leeds too, to inform the parents of one of the men in those planes that their son was dead. It was upsetting but you got very blasé about these things in wartime.❞

### ■ JUNE ■

**Thursday 1:** British actor Leslie Howard dies when the airliner he is travelling on is shot down in the Bay of Biscay. Howard, best remembered as Ashley Wilkes in Gone with the Wind had been visiting Spain, in an effort to persuade cinemas there to screen British-made movies.

**Monday 7:** Italian troops begin to pull out of Albania.

**Friday 11:** The Mediterranean island of Pantelleria surrenders to the Allies

## Epic tank and air battle for Kursk begins between Germans and Russians

after 13 days of continuous air bombardment. The island – a halfway point between Tunis, now in Allied hands, and Sicily – was battered into submission by waves of attack aircraft and fell before a seaborne invasion was necessary.

**Friday 16:** Japanese lose 100 aircraft over Guadalcanal.

**Sunday 18:** Field-Marshal Wavell, once sacked from North Africa, is appointed Viceroy of India.

**Monday 19:** In Berlin, Goebbels triumphantly reports the city is 'free of Jews'.

**Wednesday 21:** French Resistance leader Jean Moulin is arrested after a meeting of undercover agents was betrayed to the Gestapo.

**Sunday 25:** Sicily comes under fire from Allies.

**Friday 30:** Amphibious offensive against Japanese in the Solomon Islands begins.

*Right:* **The invasion of Sicily was a vital blow at Hitler's Europe. Despite its success, many Germans escaped.**

### ■ JULY ■

**Sunday 4:** General Wladyslaw Sikorski, leader of the Free Polish government and army, is killed in an air crash. The Liberator plane ran into trouble soon after leaving Gibraltar and crashed into the sea.

**Monday 5:** Epic tank and air battle for Kursk begins between Germans and Russians.

**Thursday 8:** President of the National Resistance Council Jean Moulin is dead after lengthy torture by the Gestapo. The 44-year-old was also known as 'Max'.

**Saturday 10:** The invasion of Sicily by Allied Forces, 'Operation Husky', gets underway.

**Tuesday 13:** The tank battle at Kursk ends in defeat for Germany.

**Sunday 18:** A German U-boat shoots down a US airship off Florida Keys, the only airship lost by America during the war.

**Monday 19:** A bombing raid by US planes over Rome causes hundreds of casualties. Yet despite the immense tonnage of explosives dropped by the aircraft, the architectural treasures of the city remain intact.

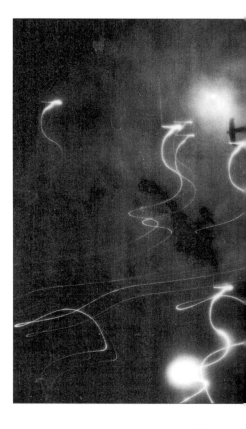

**Thursday 22:** US 7th Army, led by General Patton, seizes Palermo, Sicily, and heads for Messina. Meanwhile Monty's 8th Army is held up by retreating Kesselring.

**Sunday 25:** Mussolini resigns and is arrested. In his place as Prime Minister comes Marshal Badoglio.

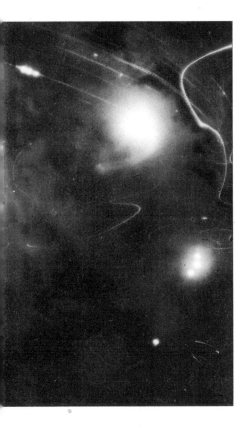

*Above:* Flares light up the path of a Lancaster bomber over Hamburg.

**Tuesday 27:** A firestorm rages in the German city of Hanover after an incendiary raid by the Royal Air Force. It followed three days of continuous raids on the city.

◼ **AUGUST** ◼

**Monday 2:** A further raid by the RAF on Hamburg brings the death toll there to 40,000, with 37,000 seriously injured.

**Friday 6:** Naval battle of Vella Gulf in the Solomon Islands.

**Saturday 14:** Rome declared an 'open city'.

**Sunday 15:** Marshal Badoglio, now heading a new Italian government, sends a peace emissary to Spain.

**Tuesday 17:** German soldiers in Sicily are finally either captured or escape to the mainland.

**Tuesday 24:** Quadrant Conference in Quebec between Churchill, Roosevelt and Canadian prime minister Mackenzie King ends after eight

# ◆ THE BATTLE OF KURSK

The high point of the German push east was reached in November 1942. The Soviets then launched a winter offensive that formed a bulge, or salient, in the invaders' line around the city of Kursk. In summer 1943, the Germans attacked Kursk, with the 9th Army, under General Kluge, striking from the north and the 4th Panzer Army, under Field-Marshal Manstein, attacking from the south in a pincer movement. Unfortunately for the Germans, the Russians had forewarning of the operation, cancelling the element of surprise and enabling them to assemble a formidable defence. In the ensuing battle 6,000 tanks were involved, along with two million men and 4,000 aircraft. The battle was an epic, but when it was over, it was the Germans who were in retreat.

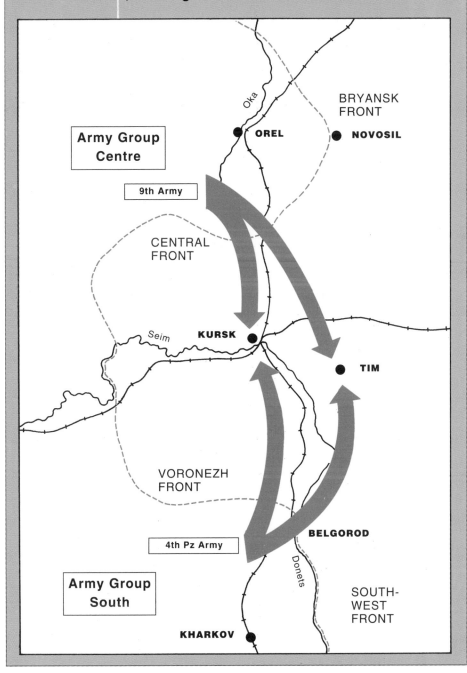

*Above:* **Popular pianist Fats Waller was just 39 when he died in 1943.**

days, with all leaders confident that victory is within their grasp.

**Wednesday 25:** Admiral Mountbatten is appointed Supreme Allied Commander in South East Asia.

**Thursday 26:** Russian forces begin a five-pronged assault on the German-held Ukraine.

**Saturday 28:** Bulgaria's King Boris dies after being shot by an assassin.

### ■ SEPTEMBER ■

**Friday 3:** Invasion of Italy begins. A ceasefire between Italy and the Allies is agreed but kept under wraps for five days.

**Thursday 9:** Allies land at Salerno in 'Operation Avalanche' in the face of fierce defensive fire from defending German forces.

**Friday 10:** German troops under von Vietinghoff seize Rome.

**Sunday 12:** Mussolini is sprung from prison in a plan approved by Hitler.

**Monday 13:** Germans stage a counter-attack at Salerno.

**Friday 17:** British and American forces join up in Italy to push back the Germans.

**Monday 20:** British Chancellor, Sir Kingsley Wood, dies suddenly, and is replaced by Sir John Anderson.

**Wednesday 22:** The introduction of Pay As You Earn (PAYE) is announced to British tax-payers. For the first time everyone will get a tax code number and their revenue dues will be deducted at source instead of demanded subsequently.

**Wednesday 29:** Polish trades union leader turned president Lech Walesa is born.

### ■ OCTOBER ■

**Friday 1:** US 5th Army reaches Naples, a key Italian port.

**Monday 4:** The island of Corsica is taken by the French Resistance, their first victory in their struggle to oust the Germans from their homeland.

**Tuesday 5:** US starts shelling Wake Island in the Pacific.

**Monday 11:** British midget submarines attempt to sink *Tirpitz*,

### ◆ EYE WITNESS ◆

**Derek Brooks, from Porchester, England, served on board HMS *Ramillies* and saw action at D-Day as the battleship gave supporting fire to paratroops storming Pegasus Bridge.**

❛ During a lull in the gunfire I managed to snatch a few moments' fitful sleep while sitting at the anti-aircraft artillery. Something woke me up and I peered my head over the side of the placement to see what it was. At that very moment both the 15-inch gun turrets engaged simultaneously. The shock waves blew me straight out of my seat.

They don't make alarm clocks like that any more. ❜

the mighty German battleship.

**Wednesday 13:** Italy declares war on Germany.

**Tuesday 19:** In the first exchange of its kind, 4,200 British prisoners of war are swapped for a similar number of Germans on neutral Swedish territory.

Italian partisans join forces with Tito's Yugoslav resistance movement to fight the Germans.

**Thursday 21:** A daring exploit by the French Resistance in Lyon springs 14 of their colleagues from jail.

## *Allied troops encounter stiff resistance from Germans holed up around Monte Cassino*

**Friday 29:** Troops stand in for striking dockers in London.

**Sunday 31:** Allied troops encounter stiff resistance from Germans holed up around Monte Cassino.

### ■ NOVEMBER ■

**Monday 1:** US Marines land at Bougainville in the Solomons.

**Saturday 6:** Red Army enters Kiev, in German hands since the first thrust of 'Barbarossa'.

**Thursday 11:** The Lebanese government is arrested and held for ten days by irate French troops after making a declaration of independence.

**Tuesday 16:** German forces defeat the defending British and Italian garrison of Leros in the Dodecanese.

**Thursday 18:** Massive bombing raid by RAF on Berlin with 350 4,000lb bombs falling on the Reich's capital.

**Saturday 20:** Sir Oswald Mosley, leader of the British Union of Fascists, is released from jail on the grounds of ill-health. He will remain under house arrest.

**Monday 22:** Churchill and Roosevelt meet with China's Chiang Kai-shek in North Africa in an historic conference on the war against Japan.

**Tuesday 23:** Tarawa, in the Gilbert Islands, is captured by the US Marines with just 17 of the defending Japanese force of more than 4,500 left alive. More than 1,000 Marines died in 'Operation Galvanic', one of the most arduous amphibious landings experienced by the Americans during the war.

**Sunday 28:** Teheran Conference begins, with the big three, Churchill, Roosevelt and Stalin, meeting to discuss the war efforts.

■ **DECEMBER** ■

**Thursday 2:** Ernest Bevin, the Minister of Labour, announces that one in ten men called up between the ages of 18 and 25 will be sent to work at the coal face. The government is concerned about the shortage of miners after an exodus of young men to join the forces. The 'Bevin Boys', as they have been tagged, will be selected by ballot.

**Saturday 4:** Churchill and Roosevelt meet Turkish president Ismet Inonu in a bid to forge closer links between the three countries.

## Eisenhower is named as supreme commander for the Allied invasion of western Europe

**Sunday 5:** Tito forms a provisional government of Yugoslavia.

**Friday 10:** Roosevelt visits Malta to witness for himself the effects of months of siege laid by the Germans and Italians.

**Sunday 12:** Rommel appointed commander in chief of German defences along the Atlantic Wall.

**Wednesday 15:** US jazz pianist and composer Thomas 'Fats' Waller dies, aged 39.

**Sunday 19:** A war crimes trial held in Kharkov, Russia, finds three Germans guilty. All are hanged.

**Wednesday 22:** British children's author and illustrator Beatrix Potter dies, aged 77.

According to government figures, there will be enough turkeys for only one in ten families this Christmas.

**Friday 24:** US General Dwight D. Eisenhower is named as supreme commander for the Allied invasion of western Europe.

**Saturday 25:** US Marines land on New Britain.

**Sunday 26:** Battle of the North Cape. German surface raider, the battle-cruiser *Scharnhorst*, is sunk by the Home Fleet, spearheaded by HMS *Duke of York*.

*Below:* General Dwight D. Eisenhower launched plans for D-Day months before it took place.

# 1944

Halfway through the year, the Allies played a trump card. The invasion of Normandy was a sparkling success, even though there were still months of grinding battle to endure before an overall triumph was secured.

## ■ JANUARY ■

**Sunday 2:** Russian armies are within 20 miles of Poland.

**Tuesday 4:** Hitler presses all children over the age of ten into the war effort.

**Thursday 6:** Russian forces move into Poland.

**Tuesday 11:** Mussolini has his son-in-law Count Ciano executed on a charge of treason.

**Saturday 15:** Germans dig in around Monte Cassino.

---

### The abbey atop Monte Cassino is destroyed by air and artillery attacks, but resistance continues

---

**Sunday 16:** Eisenhower appointed Supreme Commander of the Allied Expeditionary Force.

**Saturday 22:** Allies land at Anzio. However, a plan to cut through the German flank is doomed.

*Above:* A German shell smashes into one of the landing vehicles at Anzio, Italy.
*Right:* Inspired by Gauguin and van Gogh, Edvard Munch was best known for his painting *The Scream*.
*Far left:* The US 7th Army at Saarbrucken.

**Sunday 23:** Norwegian artist Edvard Munch dies, aged 81. His work became a major influence on 20th century impressionism.

**Thursday 27:** Leningrad is relieved after a siege lasting 900 days.

**Monday 31:** After first pounding it from the air and the sea, US forces land on Kwajalein in the Marshall Islands. A week-long battle leaves 16,300 Japanese dead with just 264 taken prisoner.

## ■ FEBRUARY ■

**Wednesday 2:** All French men aged between 16 and 60 are forced to work in Germany.

**Sunday 6:** Second Arakan offensive ends in failure for Britain.

**Tuesday 8:** 'Operation Overlord', the

invasion of Europe, is given the green light in Whitehall. Now begins months of detailed planning in time for the massive amphibious landing to take place in Normandy in June.

**Sunday 13:** Weapons for the French Resistance are dropped by the Allies in Haute-Savoie, south east France.

**Tuesday 15:** The abbey atop Monte Cassino is destroyed by air and artillery attacks but resistance by the Germans continues. Governments on both sides of the Atlantic are forced to defend the decision to bomb the Christian cultural treasure.

**Wednesday 16:** Allies at Anzio under pressure from German counter-attack.

**Thursday 17:** Plans for a national health service at the end of the war are announced in Britain.

**Friday 18:** Truk, in the Central Pacific, comes under US fire with its airfield and harbour being destroyed.

Luftwaffe commences another blitz of London.

Eisenhower receives Russia's highest military honour, the Order of Suvorov First Class.

**Tuesday 29:** US troops landed on the Admiralty Islands, in the South West Pacific, in 'Operation Brewer'.

### ■ MARCH ■

**Wednesday 1:** Chindits enter Burma once again, this time by glider.

**Saturday 4:** It is announced that tests in Bath, Britain, prove that children conceived in the winter are more intelligent.

**Wednesday 8:** Japanese launch 'Operation U-Go' against British troops in Burma.

The engine of Britain's Spitfire aircraft is is to be enlarged.

---

## *Japanese forces drive a wedge between British forces at Kohima and Imphal in Burma*

---

**Thursday 9:** Japanese take action against Bougainville.

**Sunday 12:** Travel between England and all parts of Ireland is banned to prevent word of the invasion plan reaching Germany.

**Wednesday 15:** Further attacks

*Above:* **A plane crash claimed the life of Major-General Charles Orde Wingate.**

against the German-held strongpoint of Monte Cassino carried out by Allied forces.

**Thursday 16:** Japanese forces drive a wedge between British forces at Kohima and Imphal in Burma.

**Friday 17:** New Zealand forces reach the railway station at Monte Cassino.

**Saturday 18:** Imphal is reinforced by an Indian division from Arakan.

Germans begin an occupation of Hungary.

**Friday 24:** Major-General Orde Wingate, creator and commander of the Chindits, dies in a plane crash.

**Tuesday 28:** MPs vote to give women and men teachers equal pay.

**Wednesday 29:** Allied forces under siege at Imphal by Japanese troops under Lieutenant-General Mutaguchi.

### ■ APRIL ■

**Saturday 1:** Fifty people die when US bombs neutral Switzerland in error.

**Sunday 2:** Russians enter Romania.

**Wednesday 5:** Kohima is under seige.

Germany begins rounding up and deporting Jews from Hungary.

**Sunday 9:** General Charles de Gaulle is created commander in chief of the Free French forces.

**Monday 10:** Odessa is freed by the advancing Red Army.

**Sunday 16:** Stalin orders his troops not to allow any retreating Germans to escape as Russian forces surge through the Crimea.

**Tuesday 18:** Kohima is reinforced.

**Thursday 20:** Troops drive London's buses following a strike.

The Royal Air Force drops 4,500 tons of bombs on occupied Europe.

**Saturday 22:** US troops land in Hollandia, New Guinea.

**Thursday 27:** The British government bans foreign travel in a bid to keep the invasion plans quiet. Visitors are already barred from approaching within ten miles of the British coast.

**Sunday 30:** Britain's first pre-fabricated homes go on show in London. After the war, the steel-framed single-

storey homes will alleviate the housing shortage after the war brought about by enemy bombing.

### ■ MAY ■

**Wednesday 3:** British and Indian troops notch up a triumph at Arakan by taking a vital link road.

**Tuesday 9:** Sevastopol is liberated by the Red Army.

**Friday 12:** Final German forces are evacuated from the Crimea.

**Monday 15:** Rommel clamps down in Vichy France, cancelling all passenger train services and raiding the diplomatic bags for foreign powers held at the Vichy war ministry. His aim is to stop the Resistance sending and receiving messages.

**Tuesday 16:** Gustav line in Italy finally penetrated by Allied forces.

**Wednesday 17:** German forces withdraw from Cassino.

**Thursday 18:** Monte Cassino falls to Polish troops. The Gustav line of defences is ruptured.

## The 'Great Escape' from Stalag Luft III ends in disaster when 47 recaptured airmen are shot

**Tuesday 23:** Allied troops held down in Anzio finally break out.

**Thursday 25:** Chindits forced to

*Above:* **Londoners were riding high while the troops operated the bus services, offering free transport on selected routes.**

withdraw under heavy counter-attack from Japanese.

Tito flees to a hilltop hideaway as Germans seize Bosnia.

**Sunday 28:** The 'Great Escape' by officers from Stalag Luft III in Silesia. It ended in disaster when 47 recaptured airmen were shot by Gestapo.

**Wednesday 31:** For the first time in months, Britain suffers no civilian casualties during May.

### ■ JUNE ■

**Saturday 3:** Battle of Kohima ends in Allied victory.

## ◆ EYE WITNESS ◆

**Melvin Marr Middleton was with the Third Brigade of the 7th Canadian Infantry Division. He joined up at the end of 1940 when he was 26.**

'After six months training in Canada I arrived over here with nothing but my grey coat and some spare socks in my pocket. I was issued with a Bren gun which I carried through the war. But I never had a single round of ammunition. They just didn't give me any. It did seem ridiculous to me but at the same time I just had to get on with it. If we ever ran into action, I hoped they would give me some ammunition.

I was in a mobile workshop repairing optical equipment like binoculars, dial sights and range-finders. I landed in France on D-Day-plus-four and was based five miles outside Caen. Still nobody in the workshop had ammunition. Perhaps they were afraid we would shoot ourselves.

We followed the infantry up to service their instruments. Because we were in a truck we became a target. The soldiers used to bring up their instruments in the middle of the night, put them outside the door and disappear. They would come the next night to collect them.

While I was in Europe I travelled in a Jeep when the Germans started shelling. The driver hit a shell crater and I bounced up in the air, landing with my back across the seat. At the time the medics told me it was bad bruising. Only when I left the forces in 1963 was I told that I had caused permanent damage to my back which puts me in a wheelchair today.'

This man is your FRIEND

Canadian

He fights for FREEDOM

★ ★ ★

other remain 'the outstanding problem of Allied diplomacy'. Disagreements between the two sides arose after America refused to acknowledge de Gaulle's left-of-centre French Committee as the provisional government of France.
**Tuesday 13:** First V1 flying bomb lands in England.

In the Battle of Villers-Bocage, British tanks take a hammering and are forced to withdraw.

### D-Day begins. British take Bayeux. American forces capture Ste Mère Eglise

**Thursday 15:** US Marines land on Saipan in the Marianas.
**Friday 16:** Sustained attacks by V1 bombs over southern England.

King George VI visits Normandy invasion forces behind the front line.
**Sunday 18:** Assisi in Italy is taken by the 8th Army.
**Monday 19:** Battle of the Philippine Sea in which 250 Japanese aircraft are brought down in the 'Great Marianas Turkey Shoot'.

**Sunday 4:** Rome falls to Allies.
**Monday 5 June:** Twelve British minesweepers clear the waters in preparation for the Normandy landings. Airborne forces are dropped behind enemy lines.

King Victor Emmanuel III of Italy abdicates in favour of Crown Prince Umberto.
**Tuesday 6:** D-Day begins.
**Wednesday 7:** British take Bayeux.
**Thursday 8:** American forces capture Ste Mère Eglise.
**Friday 9:** Invading allied armies meet up in Normandy.
**Saturday 10:** An England XI beats the West Indies by 166 runs at Lords in a benefit match for the Colonial Comforts Fund.

*Right:* A triumphant British newspaper announces the arrival of troops in Rome.

**Sunday 11:** London newspaper The Observer reports that relations between the British and Americans on one side and Free French leader General Charles de Gaulle on the

Gales wreck the giant Mulberry harbours ferried to Normandy to provide unloading facilities for the invading Allies.

**Wednesday 21:** A thousand-bomber raid on Berlin is staged by the US Army Air Forces.

**Thursday 22:** Imphal is relieved.

Allies seize V1 rocket site at Cherbourg, northern France.

**Monday 26:** 'Operation Epsom' to take Caen in Normandy is mounted by British and Canadian troops.

**Thursday 29:** Cherbourg is liberated by US forces.

**Friday 30:** Civilian casualties in Britain during June amounted to 1,935 dead and more than 5,900 injured, due to the V1 bombs.

'Epsom' ends with five-mile gain, but Caen is still in German hands.

### ∎ JULY ∎

**Monday 3:** Russians recapture town of Minsk.

London children face evacuation again due to the danger of V1 'doodlebug' flying bombs.

**Thursday 6:** Appalled at the progress of the Allies in France, Hitler sacks von Runstedt as supreme commander of his western forces.

**Friday 7:** Caen is comprehensively bombed by the Royal Air Force.

**Sunday 9:** Caen is finally taken by British forces.

**Wednesday 12:** US 5th Army, under Lieutenant-General Mark Clark, pushes through Tuscany, northern Italy.

**Thursday 13:** Red Army seizes Vilna, the capital of Lithuania.

**Monday 17:** 8th Army under General Leese crosses the River Arno and is poised to take Florence.

US forces capture the town of St Lô in Normandy.

Rommel is badly injured in an aircraft attack.

**Tuesday 18:** 'Operation Goodwood' on the outskirts of Caen, designed to wipe out lingering German resistance, gets underway.

**Wednesday 19:** Russian troops enter Latvia on the Baltic.

**Thursday 20:** Roosevelt wins the

*Above:* An LST is crammed full on its way to the beaches of Normandy and the liberation of France.

nomination to run for a fourth term of office. Harry S. Truman is his running-mate.

High-ranking German officers Colonel Count von Stauffenberg and Lieutenant-General Olbricht make an unsuccessful attempt on the life of

Like the D-Day forces, US troops in the Pacific faced tough and dangerous landings, such as this one on Saipan.

the Führer. Three German officers are killed when a bomb concealed in a suitcase went off under a conference table in an East Prussian headquarters. Hitler, who was shaken but unharmed, broadcast to Germany afterwards. 'A very small clique of ambitious, unscrupulous and, at the same time, criminally stupid officers laid a plot to remove me.'

**Friday 21:** US Marines land on Guam in the Marianas.
**Monday 24:** 'Operation Cobra'

*Below:* **British infantrymen march out of the shadow of the Duomo, the grand cathedral of Florence.**

pulled off by the US forces shatters the stalemate in Normandy.
**Tuesday 25:** Canadians force their way south of Caen.
**Wednesday 26:** Japanese counter-attack on Guam.
**Thursday 27:** Guam is captured by the Americans.
**Friday 28:** Red Army captures Brest-Litovsk on the River Bug.

---

## High-ranking German officers make an unsuccessful attempt on the life of the Führer

---

### ■ AUGUST ■

**Tuesday 1:** Warsaw up rising begins as the Polish Home Army takes on the German occupying forces.
**Thursday 3:** German occupying forces leave the Channel Islands.
**Saturday 5:** Japanese prisoners of war held at Cowra Camp, New South Wales, Australia, stage a mass break-out. In the early hours, 1,100 storm the barbed wire, overcome a machine-gun post and kill its crew. A fire begun in the camp huts kills 12 of them; 31 committed suicide, 200 were killed by guards and 108 were wounded. The rest were recaptured.

**Tuesday 8:** Canadians head towards Falaise in Normandy, soon to be joined by the US 3rd Army after it completes its clearance of St Malo and Le Mans.

One field-marshal, four generals and three other officers are sentenced to death for their part in the July bomb plot to assassinate Hitler. They are to be hanged by piano wire from meat hooks.
**Thursday 10:** Japanese resistance on Guam virtually eliminated – although the last Japanese soldier to surrender fails to emerge from the jungle there until 1972.
**Saturday 12:** The 'Pluto' pipeline from the Isle of Wight to Cherbourg begins operations to supply the Allies with adequate fuel for their operations in France.
**Tuesday 15:** 'Operation Anvil', the

invasion through southern France, gets underway.

**Wednesday 16:** Canadian forces take Falaise in Normandy.

**Saturday 19:** Field-Marshal von Kluge, a senior German officer aligned to the July bomb plot to assassinate Hitler, commits suicide.

Marshal Pétain is arrested by the Germans and taken to Belfort.

**Sunday 20:** French troops liberate Toulon on the south coast of France.

Russians follow the Danube south.

**Monday 21:** Falaise gap is finally closed to fleeing German troops.

**Tuesday 22:** German battleship Tirpitz, sister ship to Bismarck, comes under attack from Allied aircraft.

**Wednesday 23:** Romania concedes

defeat to the Soviet Red Army.

**Friday 25:** Paris is liberated by Free French troops led by General Leclerc. German commander von Choltitz defies Hitler's orders by refusing to burn the city.

Romania declares war on Germany.

**Saturday 26:** US and British forces head east of the River Seine.

Bulgaria withdraws from war.

**Sunday 27:** Chindits evacuated to India from Burma.

**Monday 28:** Marseilles is freed by invading forces.

**Thursday 31:** Monty is promoted to the rank of field-marshal.

### ■ SEPTEMBER ■

**Friday 1:** Canadian troops take Dieppe and Rouen. The US 5th Army takes Pisa.

**Sunday 3:** The British Guards Armoured Division liberates Brussels.

The Allies wreck 900 German motorised vehicles and 750 horse-drawn vehicles on the Mons to Brussels road.

**Wednesday 6:** The Red Army reaches Yugoslavia.

**Friday 8:** First V2 attack on London.

The Belgian government returns to its homeland from exile in London.

The Red Army takes Bulgaria.

---

## *Paris is liberated by the Free French troops, led by General Leclerc*

---

**Sunday 10:** Prague falls to Russian The Red Army takes Bulgaria, while Finland signs a peace accord with Stalin.

US troops enter Luxembourg.

**Tuesday 12:** US 1st Army in Germany near Aachen.

Remaining German pocket at Le Havre surrenders.

*Below:* **A bomber lies upturned on the beaches at Guam in the Marianas, where US Marines are landing.**

*Above:* **Allied troops parade at the Arc de Triomphe following the recapture of Paris. The city was liberated by the Free French.**

**Friday 15:** Siegfried line is broken by the US 1st Army.

US forces land in the Palau Islands.

**Sunday 17:** 'Operation Market Garden', in which Allied troops

---

### British 2nd Army, under General Dempsey, reaches the Rhine

---

parachute into Nijmegen and Arnhem, begins.

**Tuesday 19:** British paratroopers of 1st Airborne Division isolated at Arnhem when bad weather prevents the arrival of reinforcements.

Finland signs a ceasefire with the Soviet Union.

**Sunday 24:** British 2nd Army, under

*Right:* **Paratroopers salvage what they can from a crashed glider after descending into Arnhem.**

Lieutenant-General Dempsey, reaches the Rhine.

**Monday 25:** Chinese commander Chiang Kai-shek requests that US General 'Vinegar' Joe Stilwell, mastermind of Chinese defences against Japan, be sacked.

**Tuesday 26:** Remnants of the British airborne force that dropped at Arnhem are withdrawn.

**Wednesday 27:** German forces counter-attack at Nijmegen.

■ OCTOBER ■

**Monday 2:** The Greek capital, Athens, is evacuated by Germans.

British troops land on Crete.

**Monday 9:** Churchill visits Moscow for talks with Stalin.

**Wednesday 11:** US aircraft attack Luzon in the Philippines.

**Saturday 14:** Rommel, another senior German incriminated in the July bomb plot to kill Hitler, commits suicide rather than risk public

**Thursday 19:** Germans pull out of Belgrade, the Yugoslav capital.
**Friday 20:** US forces land on Leyte in the Philippines.

Aachen, the first German town to fall into the hands of the Allies, capitulates to the US 1st Army.
**Monday 23:** The three-day naval Battle of Leyte Gulf begins.
**Friday 27:** Kamikaze attacks launched on American ships operating in the Philippines.
**Saturday 28:** De Gaulle orders French Resistance fighters to lay down their arms.
**Monday 30:** Organised mass exterminations come to an end at Auschwitz concentration camp.

### ■ NOVEMBER ■

**Thursday 2:** Germans pull out of Greece altogether.
**Friday 3:** Flushing in Holland is taken by the British and Canadians.
**Friday 10:** The Allies acknowledge the government of Albania headed by

condemnation as a traitor. The world is told he died after his car crashed during an aircraft attack in July.

British forces enter Athens.
**Monday 16:** Hungary withdraws its request for peace with the Allies when its head of state's son is kidnapped by crack German commando officer Otto Skorzeny.
**Wednesday 18:** A people's guard, or Volksturm, is created by Hitler for the defence of the Fatherland.

## ◆ EYE WITNESS ◆

**Shell Lawr, from Ontario, enlisted in 1941 and arrived in Normandy three weeks after D-Day as a truck driver.**

❝ I was lucky that I didn't see too much action. I'm glad I did join up but I would never do it again. Myself and two brothers went into Normandy and we are all still alive which might be a record. But I was as scared as hell.

Yet I recall one incident which kept me laughing for days. We were just by the Rhine river at dawn. I saw a horse and buggy coming towards me with three men in it. They were dressed in top hats and tails. All three were Canadians – and they were all loaded, or drunk. They told us they were heading off to see what the boys in the front line were doing. What a sight – talk about as drunk as a lord. Some American sailors were with us. They went AWOL from their ship for a couple of days because they hadn't seen any action. ❞

*Left:* US Marines plunge through the surf, determined to chase the Japanese out of the Philippines.

# ◆ THE ALLIES BOMB GERMANY

By 1944, systematic bombing of Germany by RAF and USAAF aircraft was well underway. In general terms the RAF's Bomber Command, under Air Marshal Sir Arthur Harris, concentrated on high-volume area bombing by night, whereas the UK-based US 8th Air Force favoured precision attacks against specific targets by day. In the early days of the offensive, the latter course was very costly in terms of men and machines, since Allied fighter escorts were limited in range and once they had turned for home the bombers were at the mercy of Luftwaffe interceptors. In time however, fighter-escort range increased, until by 1944 bombers could be protected right across Germany.

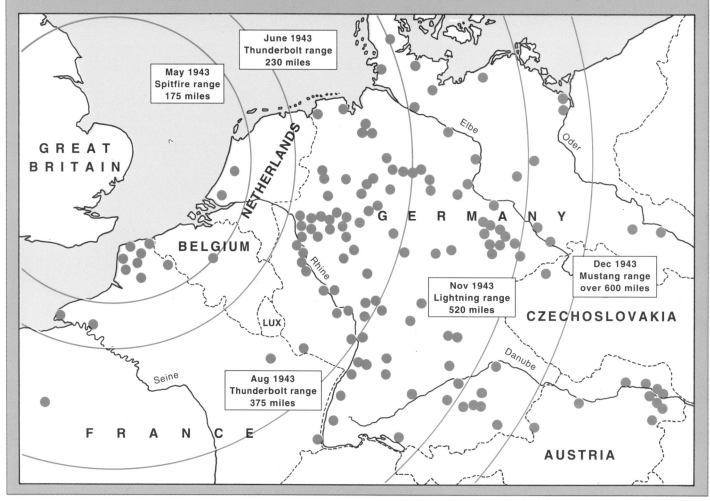

partisan Enver Hoxha.

**Saturday 11:** Britain's Home Guard dissolved today after four and a half years domestic defence.

**Sunday 12:** Tirpitz, the giant German battleship, comes under attack once more in Norway by the RAF. The units involved include 617 Squadron (Dambusters). This time the vessel sinks under the onslaught of 12,000lb 'Tallboy' bombs.

**Saturday 18:** US 3rd Army enters Germany in force.

**Friday 24:** Allies breach the Saar, putting the industrial arm of Germany under threat.

**Sunday 26:** Antwerp is open for merchant ships to supply the Allies, at last providing a fresh supply source for the front-line British and American forces.

**Monday 27:** American B-29 planes bomb Tokyo.

In Britain, 70 people are killed by a massive explosion at an RAF bomb dump near Burton on Trent.

**Thursday 30:** Churchill celebrates his 70th birthday.

### ■ DECEMBER ■

**Friday 1:** Germans pull out of the hotly contended Suda Bay, Crete.

**Sunday 10:** De Gaulle signs a treaty of alliance with Stalin.

**Wednesay 13:** The development of 'new towns', to be created for Londoners miles away from the capital, is unveiled today in a blueprint for the future drawn up by

*Top:* **Incendiaries shower down on Tokyo, causing mammoth damage.**

*Above:* **Bandleader Glenn Miller disappeared on a flight to France.**

**Major Chester 'Chet' Hansen was aide to Lieutenant-General Omar Bradley, commander of the American ground forces in Europe.**

❝ One of the sticking points came in the matter of Antwerp in the British sector. Had Monty cleared the resistance there quickly we would have been able to bring supplies in through Antwerp. We didn't get supplies through the port until November. We lost the whole month of October and that was critical. Bradley thought it was the most outrageous mistake of the war.

Had we been able to use Antwerp and bring in supplies we might have been able to avoid the dreadful winter. We all got bogged down and took terrible casualties. The advance was pretty well stopped.

The Battle of the Bulge made relations worse between the US and the British. It came as a terrible surprise. No one ever expected the Germans to mount a counter-offensive in that force. Many people thought the war was coming to a close. Back in the Pentagon they were already planning the movement of troops to the Pacific.

We felt Monty delayed too long in attacking the German flank. The British still had memories of Dunkirk when Hitler had cut off the BEF in the same way. But we thought the British panicked.

When the Bulge was reduced Monty had a little press conference. He made it appear he had come like St George to save to US forces from disaster. It infuriated us. He admitted afterwards it was a dumb thing to do. ❞

Professor Patrick Abercrombie. Other suggestions include ring-roads around London and the development of Heathrow airport, at this time little more than an airstrip with huts.
**Saturday 16:** Battle of the Bulge, also known as the Battle of the Ardennes, the surprise German counter-attack, gets underway in the Ardennes. A total of 24 German divisions, including ten armoured divisions, combine for the push, which aims to capture the Belgian port of Antwerp. In fact, only one is up to full strength. Still, the Germans force a wedge between the two Allied prongs of attack and race towards their target.

Bandleader Glenn Miller goes missing on a flight to France. The man who was turned down for active service so he could entertain the troops with his distinctive sound was 40 years old.
**Monday 18:** British troops in Greece act to quell a left-wing rebellion aiming to seize control of the country.
**Friday 22:** German Panzers are driven back from the Meuse.

Japanese resistance on the Philippine island of Leyte is ended.

# 1945

At last the evil regime of Hitler was ended and peace returned to Europe. It took a further four months to halt the fighting in the east. Japan refused to bow to the inevitable Allied victory until two atomic bombs killed thousands of its people.

*Left:* Brave Polish fighters took on German troops in the Warsaw uprising, only to be cruelly defeated.

## The Battle of the Bulge ends, with 120,000 Germans dead, injured or taken captive

### ■ FEBRUARY ■

**Thursday 1:** US 6th Army pushes towards Manila in the Philippines.

**Saturday 3:** Berlin is raided by 1,000 B-17 bombers, flying with a 900-strong fighter plane escort.

**Sunday 4:** The Allied conference gets underway at Yalta in the Crimea.

**Tuesday 6:** SS commander Himmler reports that German commanders in Poland have been shot for 'cowardice and dereliction'.

**Wednesday 7:** German engineers sabotage the Schwammanuel Dam in the face of advancing US troops.

**Sunday 11:** German resistance in Budapest is eliminated.

**Monday 12:** Yalta Conference ends with major players Churchill, Roosevelt and Stalin working out a

### ■ JANUARY ■

**Monday 1:** The final attempt by the Luftwaffe to halt the Allied invasion, code-named 'Operation Bodenplatte', gets underway with widespread bombing of French, Belgian and Dutch airfields.

**Wednesday 10:** US 6th Army lands on Luzon, Philippines, running into fierce Japanese opposition.

**Wednesday 17:** Warsaw liberated by Polish troops.

**Thursday 18:** Germans mount a push to break through Russian lines and reach the Danube.

**Monday 22:** Vital supplies route, the Burma Road, is reopened, providing a crucial boost to China's war effort.

**Tuesday 23:** St Vith, the last remaining German stronghold in the Bulge, is overwhelmed by American troops.

**Thursday 25:** Germans begin evacuating troops from Prussia and Pomerania across the Baltic to sidestep a Russian pincer action.

*Left:* Eisenhower and Tedder after the German surrender at Rheims.

*Right:* Allied troops were taken by surprise by the German winter counterattack that led to the Battle of the Bulge.

**Saturday 27:** Auschwitz concentration camp, in southern Poland, is liberated by the Red Army.

**Sunday 28:** The Battle of the Bulge ends with 120,000 Germans dead, injured or captive. Americans lose 8,600 troops with a further 47,100 wounded and more than 21,000 posted missing.

**Tuesday:** Hungry Berliners riot as they try to seize extra food. Several women are killed when they upturn a potato truck.

*Left:* US B-17s were in the forefront of the battle against the Third Reich.

*Left:* US B-17s were in the forefront of the battle against the Third Reich.

◆ **EYE WITNESS** ◆

**John Strachan joined the US army in 1941 when he was 17 and was in the first wave of soldiers to hit Utah beach. Subsequently, he fought through Normandy and in the Battle of the Bulge.**

❝ I was cautious and scared. I guess that is why I lasted as long as I did. Morale was very high. Here was a group of men ready to fight. We were so geared up, young boys who became men overnight. We did some street fighting in Cherbourg. Then we went all the way to Paris. The reception from the French people was unreal. It meant freedom for them. The wine flowed and there was dancing in the streets. They really celebrated – and we joined in, too.

Getting injured during the Battle of the Bulge was the worst part of the war. I was hurt by a German 88 in both legs and my right arm. It felt like someone had driven a freight train into me. My nerves were severed. I never realised something could hurt as much as that did. They shot me with morphine before I was flown home. Afterwards, I was in hospital for two years. ❞

final plan to defeat Hitler and Japan. Also, the zones of influence around Europe and the world for each country have been drawn up.

**Tuesday 13:** RAF sparks firestorm in Dresden in a night raid involving 800 Lancaster bombers, causing as many as 250,000 deaths. American B-17s

---

## The US Marines capture Mount Suribachi, the highest point on Iwo Jima

---

continued the attack in daylight. Condemnation of the destruction is immediately voiced in London.

**Wednesday 14:** Russian troops make important gains in Silesia, one of the manufacturing centres of the Reich.

**Friday 16:** US Navy pounds the island of Iwo Jima.

**Monday 19:** US Marines land on Iwo Jima for a bloody battle.

**Thursday 22:** 'Operation Clarion', in

which the Allies hope to paralyse German communications by destroying road and rail networks, gets underway.

**Friday 23:** After four days of bitter conflict, the US Marines capture Mount Suribachi, the highest point on Iwo Jima, and raise the US flag.

**Saturday 24:** Premier Ahmed Maher Pasha is shot dead after declaring Egypt to be at war with the Axis powers. His killer, 28-year-old lawyer

*Right:* US Marines nose down in the sands of Iwo Jima.

Mahmoud Essawy, who was pro-Hitler and anti-British colonialists, was later hanged.

**Tuesday 27:** The Allies enter the German town of Mönchengladbach.

**Wednesday 28:** A lend-lease agreement is signed between the US and France.

### ■ MARCH ■

**Friday 2:** Japanese resistance on Corregidor is ended.

**Sunday 4:** Meiktila in Burma is seized for the Allies.

**Monday 5:** The city of Cologne falls to the Allies.

## A bridgehead is established east of the Rhine

**Wednesday 7:** A bridgehead is established east of the Rhine when the US 1st Army crosses the broad river at Remagen Bridge. When a sergeant spotted the bridge intact, he raced to it with his men, forcing the Germans nearby to flee. Booby traps placed on the bridge exploded but were too small to cause any serious damage.

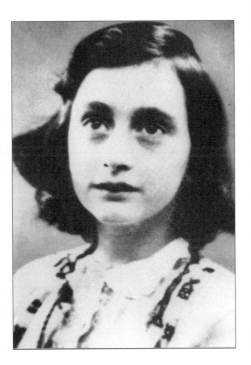

*Left:* **Anne Frank recorded the moving and mundane in her daily diary.**

**Thursday 8:** American troops move into Bonn.

**Saturday 10:** A fire raid by Boeing B-29 Superfortresses devastates Tokyo, leaving thousands dead.

Tran Kim declares that Vietnam is now independent.

**Sunday 11:** Cambodia, following the example of neighbouring Vietnam, declares itself independent.

**Monday 12:** Dutch Jewish girl Anne Frank dies in Belsen. The 15-year-old kept a diary about her harrowing months in hiding in her native Amsterdam before being rounded up by the Nazis and taken to the concentration camp with her family.

**Thursday 15:** The Duke of Windsor resigns as governor of the Bahamas.

**Sunday 18:** In Japan, anyone over the age of six is ordered to assist in the war effort.

*Above:* **Ambulances wait for the injured after the collapse of the Remagen Bridge.**

### ◆ EYE WITNESS ◆

**Peter Strachan was in the 147th Brigade of the Royal Army Signals Corps and joined the invasion of Normandy.**

❛ Unknown to me, the Germans had pushed us back. I was driving along according to a map reference I had been given. It was pitch dark amongst some trees. I saw some trenches about 50 yards long. They looked nice and safe so I stopped the truck and hopped in one to get some kip. I saw shadows further up, about 30 yards away. They didn't talk and I didn't talk. I dozed off. As day broke these shadows moved off. Some men in the British infantry later came up and asked what I was doing. "You shouldn't be here," they told me and went on to explain the area – and the trench itself – had been in the hands of the Germans overnight. I slept with the enemy without even realising it. ❜

### ■ APRIL ■

**Sunday 1:** US 10th Army, under General Buckner, lands on Okinawa.
**Friday 6:** Numerous kamikaze attacks on the US fleet off Okinawa.
**Saturday 7:** Russian troops reach the gates of Vienna.

Giant Japanese battleship Yamato is sunk by US naval air action.

## President Franklin Delano Roosevelt, four times elected to office, dies, aged 63

**Monday 9:** Fifty-nine-day seige at Königsberg, East Prussia, ends when Russians storm the fortress there.
**Thursday 12:** US president Franklin Delano Roosevelt, four times elected to office, dies, aged 63. Harry S. Truman takes over as president.
**Friday 13:** Allies liberate Belsen and Buchenwald concentration camps.

**Monday 19:** The Burmese city of Mandalay is cleared of Japanese forces and subsequently falls to Slim's 14th Army.
**Sunday 25:** Mayor of Aachen Karl Oppenhoff is assassinated by fanatical German youths called the 'Werewolves' who objected to his co-operation with American forces.

*Below:* Harry S. Truman is sworn in as president, following Roosevelt's death.

**Monday 26:** Final Japanese counter-attack on Iwo Jima, where just 216 Japanese prisoners are taken out of a force numbering 21,000. American casualties are high, almost 20,000 dead or wounded.

David Lloyd George, Britain's leader in World War I, dies, aged 82.
**Tuesday 27:** Battles rage for control of Danzig and Gdynia, on Polish territory, between German and Russian forces.

**Friday 20:** US 7th Army, under General Patch, reaches Nuremberg.

Hitler celebrates his 56th birthday.

**Monday 23:** US 8th Army captures Cebu in the Philippines.

Blackout restrictions are lifted in London.

Hitler orders the arrest of Göring after the Luftwaffe supremo attempts to take command of Germany.

**Wednesday 25:** US troops meet their Red Army counterparts on the banks of the Elbe at Torgau.

Delegates meet at the San Fransisco Opera House to structure the United Nations.

**Thursday 26:** Brutal fighting continues on Okinawa.

Marshal Pétain, leader of Vichy France, is arrested as he tries to flee across the Swiss border.

**Saturday 28:** Mussolini is captured and killed by Italian communist partisans. His body is hung by the ankles alongside that of his mistress Clara Petacci outside a petrol station in the Piazza Loretta, Milan. Mussolini, wearing a German cap, had been hiding under a pile of coats in a convoy of cars stopped and searched by the partisans. Commu-

## ◆ EYE WITNESS ◆

**George Greenaway, of New Westminster Bridge, British Colombia, served with 85 Canadian Bridge Company of the Royal Canadian Army Service Corps. He was attached to the British 21st Army Group following the D-Day invasion.**

❛ There was a great deal of work for us, especially once the advance reached Belgium and Holland. There was just so much water about.

We were equipped with bridges like the Kapok, for foot soldiers, or the Bailey, for vehicles. These would be prepared downstream, away from enemy action, and then towed or steered up on their own motors to the spot where they were needed. Very often, we had to move fast to a location at extremely short notice.

This sometimes backfired on us. I remember when we arrived in Brussels it was decided the men wouldn't be confined to barracks. After the hard battles of Normandy it was felt they could relax a little.

Of course it didn't take the guys long to disappear into the backstreets of Brussels. Almost as soon as they had gone, however, we got an order to move out immediately. It got our CO rather overexcited. He ended up firing his pistol into the air at random in an attempt to recall all his men!

One thing struck me during our advance through Normandy and that was the way the French had stored away a few little luxuries, even though they had lived through some horrendous hardships. In the towns and villages there would always be people lining the streets and holding out bottles of liquor for us. Some of it was Calvados and it laid out some of our people stiff like boards. ❜

nist partisan leader Cino Moscatelli held a short trial before he was condemned to death and shot with a machine gun.

**Sunday 29:** Hitler weds Eva Braun and appoints navy chief Grand Admiral Karl Dönitz to succeed him as Führer.

**Monday 30:** Hitler shoots himself in his Berlin bunker. His new wife dies by his side having taken poison.

Kamikaze attacks sink 20 ships off Okinawa.

US troops liberate the concentration camp at Dachau, near Munich.

*Left:* **Another Japanese-held island, this time Cebu, is taken by US forces.**

### ■ MAY ■

**Tuesday 1:** British airborne troops drop south of Rangoon.

**Wednesday 2:** Berlin is occupied by the Red Army.

German forces in Italy surrender to Field-Marshal Harold Alexander, Supreme Allied Commander in the Mediterranean.

> ## Germany's General Alfred Jodl signs the instrument of surrender of all German forces

**Thursday 3:** British take Rangoon.

**Friday 4:** Surrender of German troops in Holland, Denmark and north west Germany is made to Field-Marshal Montgomery.

**Saturday 5:** Kamikaze attackers claim another 17 ships off Okinawa.

Germans in Norway surrender.

**Monday 7:** Germany's General Alfred Jodl, army chief of staff, signs the instrument of surrender of all German forces in the Allied HQ at Rheims. Afterwards, he said: 'With this signature the German people and the German armed forces are, for better or worse, delivered into the victors' hands.' For the Allies, General Bedell Smith, Eisenhower's chief of staff, signed the document.

**Tuesday 8:** VE Day.

**Wednesday 9:** Germany's surrender is ratified in Berlin.

Prague is occupied by the Red Army to the cheers of its residents.

**Thursday 10:** Japanese forces west of the Irrawaddy river are isolated.

**Saturday 12:** German forces on the island of Crete surrender.

**Monday 14:** An incendiary bombing raid on the city of Nagoya aims to knock out vital Japanese industrial bases, the first in a series of annihilating aerial attacks.

**Saturday 19:** Japanese resistance on Luzon is mopped up.

**Monday:** Belsen concentration camp is razed.

**Wednesday 23:** SS commander Heinrich Himmler commits suicide while in British custody.

**Friday 25:** Invasion of the Japanese home islands is planned.

**Monday 28:** More than 100 Japanese aircraft shot down over Okinawa.

**Tuesday 29:** William Joyce, the traitor 'Lord Haw-Haw', is arrested after being shot in the thigh by two British officers on the Danish border.

### ■ JUNE ■

**Friday 1:** Japanese forces in retreat on Okinawa.

**Tuesday 5:** Division of Germany into four zones of occupation drafted.

**Wednesday 6:** Hitler's remains are discovered under the Chancellery.

**Thursday 7:** Papua New Guinea's Wawek Harbour welcomes its first Allied cargo ship for three years.

**Saturday 9:** The Royal Air Force introduces its latest plane, the Vampire jet fighter.

**Sunday 10:** Australian forces invade Borneo.

*Left:* **President Truman is just one of the dignitaries signing the UN Charter.**

**Above:** The war is over in Europe but not in the east, as phosphorous shells explode over Japanese lines on Okinawa.

◆ EYE WITNESS ◆

Isaac Banks, from Edinburgh, was called up on his 28th birthday and became a machine-gunner in the Middlesex Regiment. Of Russian-Jewish descent, he spent months driving trainees for the Special Operations Executive before requesting to go back to his battalion. He landed in Normandy two weeks after D-Day.

"In Holland I was driving a lorry which was used as an ambulance. I saw my mate Tommy White standing in the doorway of a house. As I looked at him he was killed by an explosion, just like that. It was so quick. I had known him since 1940 as we joined up together. I had to take his body to the burial ground in the truck.

I saw plenty of anti-Jewish signs. In the Dutch parks I tore down signs reading "Juden Verboten" (Jews Forbidden). I met a young lady in Holland and asked her if there were any Jewish people about. She directed me to a friend who had spent the war in hiding. I used to bring bread and other bits of food to the family."

**Tuesday 12:** General Dwight D. Eisenhower is awarded the freedom of the City of London and the Order of Merit.

**Friday 15:** German foreign minister Ribbentrop is captured by the British in Hamburg.

**Monday 18:** Lieutenant-General Simon Bolivar Buckner, commander of the US 10th Army, is killed by shrapnel on Okinawa.

Britain begins demobilisation.

**Wednesday 20:** Japanese forces begin surrender on Okinawa.

**Monday 25:** World Charter of Security is presented at the San Francisco Conference, signed by delegates of 50 countries, laying the foundations of the United Nations.

### ■ JULY ■

**Friday 6:** Allied troops hold a victory parade in Berlin.

**Saturday 14:** The ban on Allied troops fraternising with German women is lifted.

**Sunday 15:** London's West End lit up once more, along with the nation's street lamps, after years of blackout.

**Monday 16:** First atomic explosion takes place at Los Alamos in the New Mexico desert.

## *Japan is told by Allied heads to surrender or face 'prompt and utter destruction'*

**Tuesday 17:** Potsdam Conference opens. Subjects to be covered include postwar division of Germany.

A massive air raid involving 1,500 American and British bombers attacks Tokyo. Meanwhile, Honshu is bombarded from the sea.

**Monday 23:** Marshal Pétain goes on trial for treason in Paris.

**Thursday 26:** Labour Party achieves sweeping triumph in the British general election, winning 393 seats to the Tories 213. Clement Attlee become prime minister.

Japan is told to surrender by the Allied heads at Potsdam or face 'prompt and utter destruction'.

**Saturday 28:** Carrier aircraft numbering 2,000 attack targets on the Japanese home islands.

An American B-25 bomber hits the Empire State Building when it is shrouded in fog, killing 13 people and injuring 26.

**Tuesday 31:** The Potsdam Conference ends in discord as the Allied leaders fall out over the face of post-war Europe. The sticking points are the new German and Polish boundaries and the insistence by Britain and America on free elections in Eastern Europe.

## *First atomic bomb is dropped on Hiroshima, killing about 80,000*

### ■ AUGUST ■

**Wednesday 1:** Pierre Laval, the pro-Nazi former deputy leader of Vichy France, is put on trial for treason after being handed over to the French by the Americans.

**Thursday 2:** Boeing Superfortresses drop 6,600 tons of incendiaries on five Japanese cities.

**Monday 6:** First atomic bomb is dropped on Hiroshima, killing about 80,000 people and injuring 80,000.

**Tuesday 7:** Marshal Tito bars King Peter II from returning to Yugoslavia.

**Wednesday 8:** Russia declares war on Japan and invades Manchukuo.

**Thursday 9:** A second A-bomb is dropped, this time on Nagasaki. The death toll is about 40,000 with 60,000 injured.

**Friday 10:** Japan indicates its willingness to surrender.

**Monday 13:** In the absence of an

*Above:* Attlee sweeps into power after the British general election.

unconditional surrender from Japan, carrier aircraft launch a propaganda attack on Tokyo.

**Tuesday 14:** Japan agrees to an unconditional surrender.

**Wednesday 15:** VJ Day.

Pétain, 89, is sentenced to death for treason but reprieved by de Gaulle on account of his age.

**Thursday 16:** Japan's Emperor Hirohito appeals to all Japanese troops to lay down their arms.

**Friday 17:** The government plans to demobilise servicemen at a rate of 171,000 a month.

**Sunday 19:** Japanese surrender in Manila and Java.

**Monday 20:** Vidkun Quisling, the Norwegian traitor who supported the Nazis, goes on trial.

**Tuesday 28:** Japanese forces surrender in Rangoon.

**Wednesday 29:** Allied occupation of Japan begins.

**Thursday 30:** The world's largest submarines, built by Japan, surrender to the Allies after just one voyage.

*Left:* The destructive power of the atomic bomb is illustrated at Hiroshima.

## ■ SEPTEMBER ■

**Sunday 2:** Formal surrender document signed by Japan aboard the USS Missouri in Tokyo Bay.

**Wednesday 5:** The British return to Singapore.

**Friday 7:** Shanghai is surrendered by the Japanese, two days before hostilities cease throughout China.

**Saturday 8:** General Hideki Tojo attempts suicide by shooting himself in the heart. However, American medics arrived in time to save his life.

'Tokyo Rose', the US-born Iva Togori, who broadcast Japanese propaganda messages to US troops is arrested. She was later sentenced to ten years' imprisonment and fined $10,000. In 1977, she received a pardon from President Gerald Ford.

**Monday 10:** Quisling is found guilty of treason and sentenced to death.

**Wednesday 12:** Admiral Mountbatten receives surrender of all Japanese forces in South East Asia.

*Below:* **Thousands flocked to the White House to mark Japan's surrender.**

## ◆ EYE WITNESS ◆

**Peggy Morris Riley was a WAAF based at Portreath in Cornwall. She worked in the operations room, plotting aircraft positions. She met and married an American sailor and left Britain in 1946 to live in the US.**

" In the ops room, we had four different watches. I was in D watch. We worked for six days then we had 56 hours' leave. The two girls I worked with – who were later my bridesmaids – and I would hitch-hike down to Falmouth which was where the action was. There were probably eight men to one woman. I danced with everyone, from the Free French to Poles and even Russians. That is where I met my husband in July 1944, after he had been involved in the D-Day landings. We were engaged in December 1944 and got married in May 1945.

I arrived in New York on 3 March 1946. I was 21 years old. It was an adventure for me. I loved my husband. And although I missed my parents and two brothers at first, they came out to join us in 1948.

At first I couldn't understand a word my mother-in-law said. I could understand anything the men said but the women seemed to be talking a different language.

I didn't know anything about domesticity – I didn't even know how to cook an egg. One day we went out to lunch in a restaurant. I had never seen a hamburger before in my life. This one was about four inches thick. After rationing at home, it looked enormous to me. The others tucked in but there was no way could I get my mouth around it. I came to the conclusion then and there that you had to have a big mouth to be in the USA. "

**Thursday 13:** Japanese forces surrender in Burma.

**Sunday 16:** Japanese forces surrender in Hong Kong.

**Monday 17:** The commandant of Belsen and guards from Belsen and Auschwitz go on trial at Lüneberg.

William Joyce is tried for treason in London.

**Wednesday 19:** Prime Minister Clement Attlee announces that it is the British government's intention to allow India its independence 'at the earliest possible date'.

### ■ OCTOBER ■

**Tuesday 2:** Peace is negotiated between warring Vietnamese fighters and French troops.

**Thursday 4:** In Britain 17,000 dockers go on strike for more pay.

**Friday 5:** Japan's new premier is to be Baron Kijuro Shidehara.

**Sunday 7:** The first prisoners of war to return home from the Far East arrive in Southampton. Their emaciated figures and tales of appalling treatment shock the waiting relatives.

**Tuesday 9:** Laval is sentenced to death for treason.

**Wednesday 10:** Joseph Darnand, head of the pro-Nazi French Militia, which helped round up Jews in France, is executed.

*Above:* Peace returns to the world with the official international ceremony.
*Right:* The Japanese surrender papers.

**Monday 15:** Pierre Laval is executed by firing squad.

**Wednesday 17:** A military coup fails when Colonel Juan Peron is returned to power in Argentina by popular demand.

**Tuesday 23:** Communists emerge as the biggest party in the French elections after clinching 142 seats to the Socialists' 140.

**Wednesday 24:** Quisling is executed in Norway by firing squad.

## *Nazis, including Hess, Göring, Ribbentrop and Dönitz, go on trial at Nuremberg*

**Wednesday 31:** Allied troops on alert after a British brigadier is killed trying to negotiate a peace between the Dutch government and rebels on the islands of the Dutch East Indies.

### ■ NOVEMBER ■

**Saturday 3:** Britain's dockers end a seven-week unofficial strike over pay.

**Monday 12:** Tito wins a landslide victory in the Yugoslav elections.

**Tuesday 13:** General Charles de Gaulle is elected president of France.

**Friday 16:** The United Nations Educational, Scientific and Cultural Organisation (UNESCO) is founded.

**Saturday 17:** Josef Kramer, otherwise known as 'the butcher of Belsen', is sentenced to death.

**Tuesday 20:** Nazis, including Hess, Göring, Ribbentrop and Dönitz, go on trial at Nuremberg.

### ■ DECEMBER ■

**Thursday 6:** An Anglo-US loan agreement is signed, amounting to £1,100 million for British coffers.

**Monday 10:** The minimum daily wage for British workers is fixed at ten shillings. In America the figure is 75 cents.

**Friday 21:** US general George Smith Patton dies in a German hospital from injuries he received in a car crash. The 60-year-old general won plenty of enemies among the Allies thanks to his blunt speaking and apparent lust for action.

**Saturday 22:** Britain and the US recognise Marshal Tito's government in Yugoslavia.

**Thursday 27:** An International Monetary Fund (IMF) and a world-wide bank to boost world economy are launched.

*Above:* General de Gaulle, war hero, wins the presidency of France.